COLONIAL MASSACHUSETTS

A HISTORY

A HISTORY OF THE AMERICAN COLONIES
IN THIRTEEN VOLUMES

GENERAL EDITORS:
MILTON M. KLEIN & JACOB E. COOKE

BENJAMIN W. LABAREE

COLONIAL MASSACHUSETTS

A HISTORY

kto press

A U.S. DIVISION OF KRAUS-THOMSON ORGANIZATION LTD.
MILLWOOD, NEW YORK

First printing 1979

Printed in the United States of America

Library of Congress Cataloging in Publication Data

Labaree, Benjamin Woods.
    Colonial Massachusetts: a history.

    (A History of the American Colonies)
    Bibliography: p.
    Includes index.
    1. Massachusetts—History—Colonial periods,
ca. 1600-1775. I. Title. II. Series.
F67.L34   974.4'02   79-33
ISBN 0-527-18714-3

FOR L. W. L.
A Creative Scholar
An Inspiring Teacher
An Affectionate Father

CONTENTS

ILLUSTRATIONS

EDITORS' INTRODUCTION

The American colonies have not lacked their Boswells. Almost from the time of their founding, the English settlements in the New World became the subjects of historical narratives by promoters, politicians, and clergymen. Some, like John Smith's *General History of Virginia*, sought to stir interest in New World colonization. Others, such as Cotton Mather's *Magnalia Christi Americana*, used New England's past as an object lesson to guide its next generation. And others still, like William Smith's *History of the Province of New-York*, aimed at enhancing the colony's reputation in England by explaining its failures and emphasizing its accomplishments. All of these early chroniclers had their shortcomings but no more so than every generation of historians which essayed the same task thereafter. For it is both the strength and the challenge of the historical guild that in each age its practitioners should readdress themselves to the same subjects of inquiry as their predecessors. If the past is prologue, it must be constantly reenacted. The human drama is unchanging, but the audience is always new: its expectations of the past are different, its mood uniquely its own.

The tercentenary of John Smith's history is almost coterminous with the bicentenary of the end of the American colonial era. It is more than appropriate that the two occasions should be observed by a fresh retelling of the story of the colonization of English America not, as in the case of the earliest histories, in self-justification, national exaltation, or moral purgation but as a plain effort to reexamine the past through the lenses of the present.

Apart from the national observance of the bicentennial of American independence, there is ample justification in the era of the 1970s for a modern history of each of the original thirteen colonies. For many of them, there exists no single-volume narrative published in the present century and, for some, none written since those undertaken by contemporaries in the eighteenth century. The standard multivolume histories of the colonial period—those of Herbert L. Osgood, Charles M. Andrews, and Lawrence H. Gipson—are too comprehensive to provide adequate treatment of individual colonies, too political and institutional in emphasis to deal adequately with social, economic, and cultural developments, and too intercolonial and Anglo-American in focus to permit intensive examination of a single colony's distinctive evolution. The most recent of these comprehensive accounts, that of Gipson, was begun as far back as 1936; since then a considerable body of new scholarship has been produced.

The present series, *A History of the American Colonies*, of which *Colonial Massachusetts* is part, seeks to synthesize the new research, to treat social, economic, and cultural as well as political developments, and to delineate the broad outlines of each colony's history during the years before independence. No uniformity of organization has been imposed on the authors, although each volume attempts to give some attention to every aspect of the colony's historical development. Each author is a specialist in his own field and has shaped his material to the configuration of the colony about which he writes. While the Revolutionary Era is the terminal point of each volume, the authors have not read the history of the colony backward, as mere preludes to the inevitable movement toward independence and statehood.

Despite their local orientation, the individual volumes, taken together, will provide a collective account that should help us understand the broad foundation on which the future history of the colonies in the new nation was to rest and, at the same time, help clarify that still not completely explained melodrama of 1776 which saw, in John Adams's words, thirteen clocks somewhat amazingly strike as one. In larger perspective, *A History of the American Colonies* seeks to remind today's generation of Americans of its earliest heritage as a contribution to an understanding of its contemporary purpose. The link between past and present is as certain as it is at times indiscernible, for as Michael Kammen has so aptly observed: "The historian is the memory of civilization. A civilization without history ceases to be civilized. A civilization without history ceases to have identity. Without identity there is no purpose; without purpose civilization will wither."*

With Virginia, Massachusetts dominates the history of the American colonies. In the settlement, development, and rebellion of these oldest of Britain's North American mainland possessions, historians have traditionally observed, in microcosm, the progress of all the colonies from dependencies of the Crown to independent states. The history of the Bay Colony particularly appeared to offer singular evidence of characteristics that later generations would ascribe to Americans as a whole: the stout desire for freedom which motivated those making the hazardous westward voyage, the stubborn courage which enabled the first settlers to conquer the wilderness and its natives, the skill which permitted Englishmen to establish and nurture institutions of self-government in the New World, the civilizing strain which led to the early creation of schools and printing presses, and the spirit of independence demonstrated by a persistent refusal to accept outside control. Not surprisingly, it was the dramatic events in Boston Harbor, on Lexington Green, and at Concord Bridge which later Americans commemorated as symbols of national, not merely parochial, expressions of the right to independent political status. In our own day, historians interested in demography, family structure, social stratification, the evolution of legal institutions, and the process of community building have similarly found their models in the towns and villages of Massachusetts. Studies of colonial Andover, Boston, Concord, Dedham, Hingham, and Plymouth have become prototypes of research in what is called the "new social history."

Despite all this attention, colonial Massachusetts has not been the subject of a full-scale treatment since Thomas Hutchinson's three-volume history, the first of which appeared as early as 1764 and the last no later than 1828, long after its author had died. An eighteenth-century chronicle, penned by a staunch loyalist and ultimately a refugee from the Bay Colony, scarcely seems an appropriate memorial to early Massachusetts' contributions to our national history. Among its limitations, Hutchinson's account suffered from its author's confessed incapacity for "painting or describing characters." Believing that the facts could best speak for themselves, Hutchinson produced a canvas without portraiture

---

* Michael Kammen, *People of Paradox* (New York, 1972), 13.

and a drama without *personae*. The present volume by Benjamin Labaree not only synthesizes a century and a half of fresh scholarship but compensates for Hutchinson's deficiency by presenting a gallery of historical figures through which he skillfully illustrates the changing contours of the Bay Colony's development. Some are familiar—Massasoit, John Winthrop, Jonathan Edwards, Sam and John Adams; others, less so— Edmund Rice of Sudbury, William Pynchon of Springfield, Ebenezer Mackintosh of Boston, and James Parker of Lexington. Symbolically, they reveal the colony's progression from its beginnings as a fishing settlement through a brief interlude as a Puritan New Zion to its emergence in the eighteenth century as a prosperous commercial center, if not a jewel in Britain's imperial crown.

What differentiated Massachusetts from its sister provinces, Labaree discerns, was a persistent, if aberrant, conviction that it was as much a commonwealth as a colony. In 1780 it institutionalized that conviction in a constitution which confirmed legally what John Winthrop had expressed surreptitiously 150 years earlier when he took the charter of the Bay Company with him upon his departure from England. When Massachusetts moved into statehood, it did so not only with an assurance, born of experience, that it could govern itself, but also a deep-seated consciousness—part of its Puritan past—that moral corrosion, if unchecked, could undermine the most exuberant of commonwealths. This dual legacy of the colonial past was not only to trouble the leaders of the new Bay State but also those of the larger American republic as they moved from rebellion to independence. The colonial history of Massachusetts, viewed in conjunction with the history of the other twelve colonies, may thus help clarify the meaning of a revolution whose inception, however fortuitous, produced consequences so momentous that they live with us still.

Milton M. Klein
Jacob E. Cooke

PREFACE

The history of colonial Massachusetts is so well known that one might well ask why the present work has been undertaken, aside from its obvious place in a series on the thirteen original colonies. Although the Bay Colony plays a prominent role in all general histories of early America and monographic studies concerning Massachusetts and its communities have proliferated, there has been no modern history of the colony from its beginnings through to the adoption of the state constitution in 1780. A new volume on colonial Massachusetts is therefore needed to bring together the results of more recent scholarship along with earlier views that have stood the test of time. This book has also given me the opportunity to express many interpretations of early Massachusetts developed over twenty-five years of my own research, writing, and teaching.

The history of colonial Massachusetts falls naturally into three parts. The seventeenth century was dominated by the task of establishing permanent settlements in both the Plymouth and Massachusetts Bay colonies. This process, spread over several generations, inexorably bound the colonists to the territory they had occupied, possessed by that which they possessed, to paraphrase Robert Frost. Before the close of the century, however, most of the Old World values brought by the immigrant generation were altered beyond recognition. Standards for church membership were slackened so that a converting experience was no longer required. In town-meeting acrimonious debate replaced consensus. Surplus produce from farm and shop now began to flood the market-place and provide exports for a rising merchant class. Crown-appointed officials wielded authority under a new royal charter, drastically altering a once-easy relationship with the mother country.

Plymouth colony disappeared altogether. The consequences of these and other changes shook Massachusetts Bay for over a decade at century's end.

Through the first half of the eighteenth century the Bay Colony expanded rapidly. Settlers pushed far into the interior and founded scores of new towns. The economy expanded as well, with increasingly complex relationships between farmer, artisan, storekeeper, and merchant gradually replacing a simpler exchange of goods. Seacoast towns doubled and redoubled in population, gaining a myriad of new social problems along with economic opportunity. The political system also grew more complex with royal officials and their supporters vying for power against an increasingly ambitious General Court representing the towns. The habit of looking to the mother country in cultural matters continued but was challenged by an awakening self-awareness by the colonists. A sweeping revival of old religious principles clashed with more modern views. By 1760 the Bay colony was a prosperous, confident, and vibrant society of independent farmers, workers, merchants, and professionals. In contrast to their seventeenth-century forebears, the inhabitants of this middle period became a part of the British empire, politically through royal government, economically by their expanding maritime trade, and militarily by their involvement in the numerous wars between the mother country and France.

It was the dispute over its relationship with Great Britain that gave definition to the culminating period in the history of colonial Massachusetts. New imperial policies designed to raise a revenue through taxation seemed to challenge the colonists' idea of local self-government. Measures adopted by Great Britain to enforce both the old Navigation Acts and Parliament's new legislation appeared to threaten the well-being of the Bay Colony inhabitants. Within a decade what had begun as a debate became a war. When forced to choose between allegiance to their nation and possession of their country most men of Massachusetts chose to defend the lands which they and their forebears had occupied for a century and a half. Their act of defiance became an act of independence; it only remained for them to form a new state government to complete a process of possession that had begun in 1620–1630.

All history involves an intriguing juxtaposition between individuals and groups of people. Earlier generations of Massachusetts Bay historians singled out in their writings particular leaders as indispensible "builders of the Bay Colony." More recent scholars have turned their attention to communities and other groups of anonymous inhabitants. Each approach has its strengths and weaknesses. In many earlier histories the work of ordinary people has been overshadowed by the accomplishments of their leaders, while in modern studies the significance of individuals has often been obscure. In the present study I have attempted to combine the advantages of both approaches by introducing each chapter with a particular person. All men are unique; none is "typical." Each of the men I have chosen was respected by groups of their contemporaries as leaders. Some of them have been recognized by historians as well, while others were unknown beyond their local communities and have remained obscure ever since. Yet each of them illustrates the subject matter of the chapter which he introduces without dominating it and represents, however imperfectly, those of his fellows in similar circumstances or with similar interests. It is my hope that by this method the integrity of both individual and group has been preserved.

In writing this book I have had the help of the many scholars whose works are acknowledged in the bibliography. Throughout the project its editors, Milton M. Klein and Jacob E. Cooke, have shown both patience and encouragement. At a particularly perilous time their unstinting effort kept the series alive and brought this volume into being. I would also like to acknowledge my gratitude to the staff members of the Essex Institute, the Massachusetts Historical Society, and the American Antiquarian Society, who have over the years assisted me in my various research projects into the history of Massachusetts Bay. The two institutions with which I have been affiliated during the preparation of this work, Williams College and Mystic Seaport, have generously allowed me ample time for its completion. Rosemary Lane at Williams typed the basic manuscript, and Margaret Grisham at Mystic not only typed the bibliography and helped with the index but handled much of the related correspondence as well.

Through several summers my wife and children have respected my need for many hours of solitude in my barn-study for research and writing while they patiently postponed their own proposals for family projects. Over the years my greatest single debt as a professional historian has been for the model set before me by the man for whom this volume is dedicated.

Benjamin W. Labaree
Vinalhaven, Maine
August 1978

COLONIAL MASSACHUSETTS

A HISTORY

1

THE LAND

From his home atop Mount Hope at the edge of Narragansett Bay the young Wampanoag chief Massasoit enjoyed an uninterrupted view of the lands for miles around him. The territory of his own people ranged eastward for about forty miles to the Atlantic Ocean and another forty miles south to the shores of Buzzards Bay. Beyond the Wampanoags, along the sandy stretches of Cape Cod, the Nausets lived, and to the north around the shores of Boston Bay the Massachusets made their home. North of them were the Pennacooks and still farther to the north and east, beyond the river Piscataqua, were the warlike Tarratines, also known as the Abnakis. West of the Massachusets, in turn, lay the lands of the Nipmucks, and beyond them, in the great valley of the Connecticut River, was the home of the Pocumtucks. Still farther west the Mahicans roamed through the Berkshire hills. These then were the principal tribes occupying the land that would some day take from one of them its name—Massachusetts.

Massasoit knew that these tribes and their neighbors had not always lived in constant harmony, but they were all members of the great Algonkin nation. Massasoit believed that these lands had always belonged to Algonkins and would always remain theirs. But on both counts the Wampanoag chief was wrong.

* * *

For most of its existence, of course, the land that became Massachusetts belonged to no man, for it was uninhabitable. Beneath the soil where Massasoit lived lay a hard bed of granite, its upper strata eroded and washed away after millions of years to expose in places the bare rock itself. Then, about six hundred thousand years ago at the beginning of the Pleistocene Age, the climate turned so cold that winter snows no longer entirely melted during the following summers. Immense ice sheets gradually accumulated and spread down across the land only to recede northward during the next warming trend. Four times in all, short periods of intense cold disrupted longer stretches of warm weather. The last advance of ice, the so-called Wisconsin stage, gave final shape to the surface of the land Massasoit looked out on. For as it surged forward, like a giant bulldozer the glacier scraped the sedimentary rock beneath it to a depth of ten or fifteen feet. Boulders were broken to rock as they were shoved along, then into stones. Many of those that had traveled farthest were ground into pebbles and sand. Wherever the land proved least resistant the glacier followed, carving the deep valleys and U-shaped dales found throughout the New England landscape. Harder rock formations sometimes resisted the onslaught to survive as monadnocks like Wachusett Mountain rising majestically above the neighboring plains. At its greatest extent this last ice sheet covered even the highest peaks of the White Mountains. The crust of the earth groaned under the immense weight, and then gave way, sinking as much as seventeen hundred feet beneath its original level.

About twelve thousand years ago the climate again turned warmer, and the glacier no longer advanced. Slowly at first, then quite rapidly, more ice began to melt each year than had fallen in snow the previous winter. As the glacier retreated, it left behind the results of its work. Much of the debris scraped from the lands to the north now formed the ridges or terminal moraines that marked the glacier's furthest advance. Smaller, recessional moraines took shape wherever the glacier paused in its retreat. Meltwater rushing down from the face of the retreating ice sheet etched deep channels into the land and spread the glacial till over broad outwash plains. These water courses would ultimately become the major rivers of New England.

For a time after the warming trend began, the New England coastline lay far beyond Cape Cod. Then the accumulated mass of meltwater running off the glaciers all over the northern hemisphere raised the level of the world's oceans. At the same time the land mass slowly lifted again as the weight of the ice sheet lessened, but nowhere did it reach its previous level. Instead, the seas gradually flowed inland, drowning the low-lying coastal plains and reaching far into the land mass itself. First to disappear beneath the seas were the most distant glacial deposits—Georges Bank and Nantucket Shoals. For many centuries the depressions now called Massachusetts Bay, Nantucket Sound, and Buzzards Bay remained dry land, but then the seas broke through to inundate them as well. Soon only the morainal ridges forming the backbones of Cape Cod, Nantucket, Martha's Vineyard, and the Elizabeth Islands stood like "fragile outposts" against the onrushing sea, and even here the waters still work against the land, shaping and reshaping the coastline in a never-ending battle. In Boston Bay the glacier left behind hundreds of little hillocks called drumlins, and some of these, too, escaped total submersion to become harbor islands and peninsulas such as Gallups, Nahant, and Bunker Hill. To the north the bedrock face of Cape Ann and the Maine coast have met the raging ocean with more resistance, but even there the sea has inexorably worn away the land's edge. The sea is still slowly rising along the coast of New England—perhaps as much as six feet in the three centuries since Massasoit last gazed out over Massachusetts Bay.

Except for the morainal ridge running along the spine of Cape Cod, the land of the Nausets was virtually flat, dotted here and there with ponds and low-lying bogs. The Cape itself and the eastern half of the Wampanoags' territory to the west was in fact the northern tip of a coastal plain that stretched southward along the entire Atlantic seaboard. From Boston Bay on the north around Cape Cod and into Buzzards Bay scores of narrow estuaries and broader bays cut into the soft shoreline. Across the coast plain the last glacier had spread a thin, sandy soil, the final product of its centuries of toil. To this base was added, over time, the decayed remains of early plant life, along with still more sand blown in from nearby beaches. While ample rain fell each year, much of it immediately percolated through the porous surface soil or was quickly evaporated by the warm sun and steady winds. Only around the low-lying bogs and ponds was the soil moist enough to support the profuse organic life necessary to develop a thick layer of humus.

A few miles into the interior the coastal plain gave way to a gently rising landscape interspersed with small hills and many ponds. This hilly belt began far to the north and east of Boston, along the edge of the Maine coast, where the distant Penobscot tribe lived in uneasy proximity to the fierce Abnakis. Through the lands of the Pennacooks, the Massachusets, the Nipmucks, and through the western part of Massasoit's own territory the hills reached their way into Connecticut and Rhode Island. Fast-flowing rivers swept down from the interior highlands north of Boston. The Penobscot and Kennebec in Maine, and the Piscataqua and Merrimack farther south, cut narrow valleys into the land en route to the Atlantic, while smaller rivers drained into Boston and Narragansett bays. Only the domed prominence of the Blue Hills south of Boston Bay and the flat Narragansett Basin farther to the south disrupted the eye's scan as it swept across this belt of low-lying hills in eastern Massachusetts. Here the soil was somewhat richer than along the coastal plain and encouraged a denser vegetation which in dying added to the accumulating humus underfoot. Throughout the hilly region, however, large rocks left by the retreating glacier permeated the soil to great depths.

As one passed through Nipmuck country to the west the land gradually rose to an elevation of one thousand feet in places before sliding off into the valley of the mighty Connecticut River, home of the Pocumtuck tribe. For ten miles on either side of the river's winding course was a broad floodplain, abruptly transected by the several ridges of the Holyoke range. To the west the land rose more steeply into the foothills of the Berkshires, where Mohawks occasionally sent hunting and raiding parties down the Housatonic and Deerfield river valleys in defiance of Mahican claims to the territory. In marked contrast to regions farther east, the central Connecticut valley had rich soil. Two large ice-front lakes had once covered the valley, and their bottoms accumulated deep deposits of clay. After the lakes drained away, the river that followed their beds spread tons of silt out over its broad floodplain each spring. Mixed with the clays already there the valley soil became the most fertile in all Massachusetts. To the west of the valley in the Berkshire hills the soil was thin and subject to constant erosion because of the precipitous slope of the land. Only in the narrow valleys of the Deerfield, Housatonic, and Hoosac rivers could one find an adequate cover of humus.

The climate throughout the various regions that have become Massachusetts has many common characteristics and several significant local differences. Rainfall, for instance, averages about forty inches a year falling in about equal amounts each month in all sections. But in the Connecticut valley and the Berkshires, where the winters are noticeably colder than farther east, a much greater portion falls as snow. Two factors account for the difference in temperature ranges. First is the higher elevation of the interior. More important, the coastal regions experience somewhat milder winters because of the moderating influence of the Atlantic Ocean. Although the coast enjoys longer autumns, for the same reason, spring also comes as reluctantly here as in the western regions. The prevailing southwest wind, especially along the coastal plain, keeps the summer temperature reasonably cool. Overall, the area of Massachusetts endures cold winters, slow springs, warm summers, and lingering autumns with ample rainfall through all seasons of the year.

Because of climate and altitude differences the forest that covered most of New England in Massasoit's time included a wide range of vegetation. The area later defined as Massachusetts was comprised of four or five distinct forest zones. In the sandy coastal areas of the Nausets and Wampanoags pitch pine and scrub oak predominated, especially where vegetation lay exposed to salt spray and beach sand. Among the dunes beech plum and rose hips prospered. In the more fertile pockets around ponds, under the stands of red and white oak, a rich variety of berries, fruit trees, and flowering shrubs flourished, while in the bogs cranberries grew.

Two transitional zones extended along the hilly belt, embracing the lands of the Abnakis in Maine and the Pennacooks north of Boston, extending across the territory of the Massachusets around Boston and a part of the Wampanoags' land farther south, and reaching all the way into the interior regions occupied by the Nipmucks and Pocumtucks. Here were a great variety of hardwoods—black, red, and white oak, chestnut, maple, ash, and shagbark hickory. Throughout the area, but particularly in the northern and central parts, the major stands of softwoods were hemlock, tamarack, and white pine, the latter reaching to majestic proportions. In open areas where the soil was acid, blueberries could be found, while raspberries and bunchberries seemed to flourish everywhere, along with dogwood, sumac, and black cherry. On the higher slopes of the Berkshire hills, the white oak and hickory gave way to beech, sugar maple, and yellow birch, with white pine and hemlock predominating among the softwoods. At the highest elevations of the Berkshires, and throughout the interior parts of Maine, was a zone dominated by the red spruce, balsam fir, and occasional stands of white pine.

In Massasoit's day the waters off the Massachusetts shore abounded in a wide variety of fish. On the further shoals fat cod and haddock swirled about in pursuit of schools of herring. Closer to shore were giant tuna and swordfish, while along the sandy bottom halibut and flounder thrived. In the spring, shad struggled up the brackish rivers to lay their eggs, a journey that the Atlantic salmon also made. Interior lakes and streams were home for trout and pickerel. Along the rocky shores of Cape Ann and the Maine coast, lobsters flourished in prodigious numbers. Throughout the coast waters there were clams and quahogs, and in the warmer bays of Cape Cod, scallops and occasional oysters could be found as well.

Along the waterways of Massachusetts lived a number of animals— otter, mink, and beaver. In the nearby fields and woods the most common inhabitants were probably squirrels, chipmunks, woodchucks, raccoons, and rabbits. Deeper into the forest dwelt the white-tailed deer, while the bobcat, black bear, and wolf preferred a still more remote habitat. Only in the northern woods of Maine was the moose in evidence. In the spring and fall a wide variety of ducks and geese passed by on their migratory flights. Eagles, ospreys, and hawks were also seasonal inhabitants of Massachusetts. In the forests were turkey, pheasant, grouse, and woodcock. Twice each year enormous flights of passenger pigeons flew overhead.

Not so many centuries after the last glacier retreated from New England, say around 10,000 B.C., the Fluted Blade Hunters made man's first appearance in Massachusetts. Massasoit would have been disappointed to know that they were not Algonkin. As their name suggests, these people hunted game with a specially shaped point, a number of which have been found at Bull Brook in Ipswich. How long the Fluted Blade Hunters flourished in Massachusetts is uncertain, but apparently a gap of several thousand years separates them from the next inhabitants, whose sites have been traced to the Archaic period dating from about 3000 B.C. A weir uncovered in Boston during excavations sixty years ago indicates that men were fishing there around 2500 B.C. At Wapanucket, in southeastern Massachusetts, are the remains of a small village which flourished two hundred years later. Here the outlines of a half dozen circular houses stand amid a myriad of tools, utensils, and weapons. Other settlements apparently dating from about the same period include those of the Red-Paint people and the Oyster Shell tribes who lived along the coast.

The relationship, if any, between these early people and the later inhabitants known as Algonkins remains unclear. Some specialists believe that the Indians might have begun their occupation of New England as early as the Archaic period; others suggest far later dates. The Algonkins had probably come in from the southwest, perhaps in search of fresh hunting grounds in response to some environmental change. Most authorities are agreed, however, that they had occupied the northeastern seaboard for many centuries before the European colonization of America. If such a lengthy occupation gives man title to land, then in the days of Massasoit this land truly belonged to the various Algonkin tribes who dwelt there.

The Algonkin Indian was of sturdy form, strongly muscled and well coordinated, with a coppery red skin, black hair, and dark, deep-set eyes. In the summers the women often wore only a simple deerskin wraparound skirt, the men a breech cloth, and the children nothing at all. Weather rather than modesty required somewhat more clothing in cooler seasons. Then the women added a jacket and the men leggings and shirts also fashioned from animal skins. For outdoor work both sexes wore tough hide moccasins. The Algonkins took great pride in their appearance, particularly on ceremonial occasions. They trimmed their clothing with bits of fur or animal hair. The women wore their hair long, dressing it with bear fat, and they liked to decorate their faces with bright red or black pigments. The men were even more expressive in their use of facial paints. They shaved or plucked out the hair on the sides of their heads to leave only a narrow scalplock, which they treated with a mixture of soot and animal fat. They also tied bits of shell, bristles, or other objects into their hair for further decoration. Both men and women generally wore an embroidered headband which held a number of bright feathers. The most prized of all decorative materials was wampum—beads fashioned from the white shell of the conch or whelk and the purple segment of the quahog shell. Strings and belts of wampum served many other purposes: as gifts, as a means of remembering a ritual, or as confirmation of public agreements, but only rarely as actual payment for goods and services.

Algonkins lived in the domelike structures they called wigwams, made of birchbark or woven grass mats over a framework of bent saplings. A hole in the center of the roof carried off most of the smoke from the fire beneath. Packed earth served as the floor, while low platforms around the perimeter provided sitting and sleeping space. Most Algonkin tribes also built conical tipis, especially as temporary shelters while on the move. Large panels of birchbark were sewn to long poles, which were bound together at the apex with an opening to permit the smoke to escape. The women fashioned baskets from reeds, made pottery from gaily colored clay, and a range of other utensils from bark and wood. The Algonkins devised ingenious ways to make twine by twisting fibers taken from the inner bark of various trees. Thongs were also fashioned from the hides and sinews of animals. Of course, their tools were shaped from stone or occasionally from animal bones.

Among the Algonkins' larger pieces of equipment were the canoes, snowshoes, and sleds used for transportation. They needed a boat strong enough to withstand the choppy waters of large lakes and bays yet light enough to be portaged around falls. The canoe answered the need exactly. Its frame consisted of cedar, to which large strips of birchbark stitched together were sewn, the seams made watertight with generous daubs of pitch. Like the snowshoe, the birchbark canoe exemplified the Indians' remarkable ability to fashion equipment from the materials readily at hand in adapting to their natural environment.

The Algonkins subsisted primarily as hunters and gatherers. Each family group usually hunted in its own clearly defined territory, using bow and arrow for the larger game which they attempted to lure into range by various calls. Snares and traps were set for smaller quarry. Hunting was best during the late fall and winter months, when the lack of foliage deprived game of natural cover and the snow made tracking easier. Then, too, fur-bearing animals carried their thickest pelts. The favorite game of Algonkin hunting parties was probably the white-tailed deer. Not only was its flesh delicious but its skin also provided the basic material for clothing. Northern tribes considered themselves fortunate to bag an occasional moose or black bear, but all hunters willingly settled for the lowly rabbit or squirrel when faced with starvation. In the fall and spring, migrating flocks of waterfowl supplemented the turkey and grouse, which were welcome targets whenever discovered. In the late summer and fall the Indians gathered nuts and berries from the forests, and in the early spring they tapped the sugar maple tree for its sweet sap.

In April the Algonkin families moved out of their winter quarters to the coastal regions, where the men had cleared fields by the slash-and-burn method. Now the women became farmers for the season, planting maize in hills fertilized with alewives and other spawning fish from the nearby streams. Among the corn hills were planted squashes, beans, and several varieties of grain. While the men fished and hunted, the women cultivated the fields. In September all joined in harvesting the crops before moving back into the interior valleys for the winter.

Coastal tribes such as the Penobscots and Nausets became skilled fishermen. In the spring they set weirs in the rivers to trap shad and alewives as they moved upstream, and in the summer they moved to the bays and even out to the offshore islands, where they caught herring, mackerel, and other schooling species. Along the shores the Algonkins gathered shellfish both for eating and for the decorative use of the shell. In the autumn the rivers offered salmon and sturgeon, much of which was then dried and stored away for the winter.

The precise terms of land tenure among the Algonkins remains unclear. Some authorities suggest that each family group enjoyed exclusive hunting privileges in a particular area and that use by others required special permission. Families seemed to hold planting rights in certain fields as well. In both cases, furthermore, these rights apparently passed down from one generation to the next, the hunting grounds along the male line and the planting rights generally through the female. Despite this evidence, however, most historians have concluded that while Algonkin family groups may have held rights to the use of land, they had no concept of private ownership such as the English colonists would bring to the New World. After several years of planting or hunting in the same area, the village moved on to other locations as crops, game, and firewood became scarce. The Algonkins also regularly burned the underbrush in their favorite regions to deprive game of cover. One side effect was to provide fresh browse for deer in the burned-over areas; another was to prevent many parts of the forest from reaching a climax equilibrium. Planned or not, the policy proved in most cases to be good land management.

Hunting was inexorably woven into the customs and rituals of the Algonkins. They believed that animals had once inhabited the earth in human form and therefore they felt a strong kinship with them. The spirits of animals slain by hunters could wreak terrible vengeance unless treated with respect. Killing more game than was required to feed the family or throwing the remains to the dogs were taboos in most tribes. The novice hunter usually gave away his first trophy as an act of humility. Algonkins often took their individual and family band names from birds or animals, and each hunter had a guardian spirit from the animal world to accompany him on long trips. The tribal cultural hero, such as the Penobscots' Gluskabe, occasionally took on the appearance of an animal to work his mysterious ways. Certain members of the community, the so-called medicine men and women, seemed to possess particular powers of communication with this spiritual world. In times of famine, disease, or other danger their services were in high demand.

Hunting as a way of life also influenced the social structure of the Algonkins. In the winter when food was scarce and conditions harsh, Indian society was often reduced to its smallest unit—the nuclear family. Here the father was the unquestioned authority. Women performed a wide variety of household and agricultural chores without effective complaint. Family bands of brothers and perhaps even first cousins lived close to one another, and sometimes two or three shared a single large wigwam, particularly when the men were off on hunting or war parties. In the summer the Algonkins lived together in much larger communities, often consisting of as many as one hundred wigwams. A sachem or sagamore and his council of elders provided what little government was necessary, settling arguments, giving advice where needed, and representing the village in tribal councils.

Major decisions often required a meeting of all the villagers, called by some tribes a powwow. Such meetings sometimes went on for days before a satisfactory solution was reached. Each community was a part of a particular tribe—the Penobscot, the Massachuset, or the Nipmuck. And each tribe had its own grand sachem, like Massasoit of the Wampanoags, whose duty it was to mediate disputes among the villages and, with the council of sachems, weigh such serious considerations as peace or war with neighboring tribes. Although each sagamore inherited the position from his father, his effectiveness as a leader depended on his skills of persuasion, for Indians regarded all unnecessary authority with healthy skepticism. Few sachems ruled by bombast, and in fact several of the most respected were women.

Relationships among the various tribes of the northeast were not always friendly. When parleys among the sachems failed to settle territorial disputes, warfare began. Sometimes several villages banded together to fight a common enemy, and occasionally two or three tribes might form a temporary alliance or a more permanent confederacy. The aggressors first worked up the necessary courage and enthusiasm through war dances that sometimes lasted a day or more. Then small parties of warriors set out to raid the enemy's villages. The attackers crept as close to their quarry as possible; then with whoops and cries designed to terrify the fainthearted among the foe while bolstering their own spirits, they swooped down on their victims. An Indian battle rarely followed any discernible tactical plan. Rather, it quickly devolved into a free-for-all, each participant bent on downing a foe while avoiding a similar fate himself. Weapons included the bow and arrow, a tomahawk, some sort of spear, and a knife. As the skirmish progressed, victorious warriors cut the scalplock from the heads of their victims as trophies of their bravery. The enemy camp was then plundered and destroyed, and prisoners taken back home. There the hapless among them were subjected to the most excruciating tortures as a test of their mettle before being put to death. The more fortunate captives were adopted into the victorious tribe to replace its own fallen warriors.

* * *

Young Massasoit looked out from his home atop Mount Hope. In the reckoning used by some people the day was called the twenty-fifth of May, 1602. The Wampanoag sachem had reason to wonder about the future. To the west across the bay lived the troublesome Narragansets, who might at any time break the peace that now existed between their peoples. His own tribe, whose name meant Eastern People, had long dominated the small tribes in their area. How much help could he expect from the Nausets and Sakonnets in the event of war? Massasoit was a peaceful man, content to let his braves hunt and fish rather than make war against their neighbors, but he had to be prepared to defend his tribe's territory against all trespassers, and the Narragansets had always been a serious threat. Massasoit could not know that invasion by a far more dangerous enemy had already begun, for on that spring morning of May 25, 1602, Bartholomew Gosnold and his party of Englishmen landed scarcely thirty miles away, on one of the islands in the chain named for their Queen Elizabeth, probably Cuttyhunk.

2

ENGLISH ROOTS

Sometime before John Winthrop reached the age of thirty in 1618 his father gave him the responsibility of managing all the affairs of the family manor in Groton, County of Suffolk, England. Although comfortably well off and widely respected by his neighbors, John began to feel a vague discontent stir within him. "We might rejoice greatly in our own private good," he wrote his brother-in-law in 1622, "if the sense of the present evil times and the fear of worse did not give occasion of sorrow."

Winthrop was not alone in his anxiety. In the early years of the seventeenth century, a mood of uncertainty slowly spread across the English countryside. In the hamlets of East Anglia, in West Country villages, in the towns of Wiltshire and Hampshire, young men sensed that the settled world their fathers had known was changing. The land that had sustained parents and grandparents promised meager support for the enlarged numbers of their own generation. New uses for old fields—particularly the pasturing of sheep and the cultivation of grains—increased the demand for extensive tracts. Only families like the Winthrops with sizable holdings or with money to buy more land could be certain of economic survival. But even they were affected by the spiritual changes that swept through the English middle classes, converting to Puritanism many of the same anxious people whose economic world appeared reasonably secure. The Stuart successors to Elizabeth I seemed to offer tyranny in place of tolerance. The England of the early seventeenth century was truly a vexed and troubled land.

* * *

Recent historians have concluded that the population of sixteenth- and seventeenth-century England was affected by far more radical changes than earlier observers believed. A steady influx of Irish, French, Dutch, and Walloons and a constant movement by Englishmen themselves within the island kept both town and country populations astir. A high death rate remained another source of disturbance. Infant mortality and the dangers of childbirth, of course, have until very recently afflicted the human race everywhere. Added to that was a high incidence of accidental death among adult males working on farms, in the cities, and at sea. Diseases of epidemic proportions—smallpox, tuberculosis, and most notably the plague—took a heavy toll among that half of the population which lived at or below the poverty level. Perhaps it was typhus, more probably bubonic plague, but whatever its nature the malady struck heavily in the year 1603, with effects lasting in some communities for a half dozen years or more. In 1625 another epidemic broke out, first in the West Country but then rapidly spreading eastward into more populous areas. Twice again in the years before 1640 the disease returned to take a devastating toll among the folk of countryside and town alike. Despite these hazards, however, the population of England increased rapidly during the first decades of the seventeenth century, until by 1640 there were more than an additional one million inhabitants struggling for survival than at the turn of the century.

Obviously both countryside and town could and eventually would absorb increasing numbers of people, but the process was slow and, for some, painful. Making matters particularly difficult during this period in English history was the revolution taking place in patterns of land use. Well before the end of the sixteenth century, landowners throughout England, but particularly in the West Country and in East Anglia, had begun to turn away from the traditional open-field system of agriculture in favor of enclosing the lands. Sheep, cattle, and wheat for market all required large-scale operations for efficient production. But what was efficient for the landowner was disastrous for the peasant, who thereby lost the security of his place in the old manorial system. Many displaced countrymen obtained jobs as agricultural workers, but most of these laborers could find only seasonal employment, and during particularly hard times, there were no jobs at all. Some landless laborers roamed about the countryside while others drifted into the towns and cities, all in search of a means to support themselves and their dependents.

John Winthrop (1588–1649). Artist Unknown. Courtesy of the Massachusetts Historical Society.

Flight to the cities resulted in a rapid increase of urban populations throughout England, but particularly in such major cities as London and Bristol. London's population increased by 50 percent during the first forty years of the seventeenth century. Most of the newcomers succeeded in finding at least intermittent employment in new business and industrial enterprises, but the rapid influx greatly aggravated the already serious problems of urban life such as sanitation, fire protection, and public health. Men who lived in the seaport communities ran the additional hazard of impressment into the navy or the army during the Thirty Years' War, which began in 1618. The chances were slim of returning from one of the various English military expeditions to the continent. The many refugees from the countryside who did not succeed in one community were forced to continue the search elsewhere, remaining a part of the rootless, restless element of English society, victims of the social and economic changes all around them. In rural areas and towns alike the first four decades of the seventeenth century seemed to offer only depression, disease, and disarray. For that half of the population at or below the poverty level, the future held little promise.

During the same period another group of Englishmen, most of whom had every reason to be economically and socially secure, also joined the ranks of the restless malcontents. These were the Puritans, men and women who had become dissatisfied with various aspects of the established Church of England. The catalogue of complaints the Puritans leveled against the church had reached impressive proportions by the end of the sixteenth century. They objected to the number of unregenerate sinners who belonged to the church. The presence of such people had always been a problem to Christians despite occasional efforts at reform. Now the Puritans proposed to expel or exclude unrepentant sinners from their midst altogether. They found the leadership of the Anglican Church equally unsatisfactory. Many clergymen were ineffectual as preachers, but worse still were those whose corrupt lives utterly disqualified them from positions of spiritual leadership. The Puritans condemned such clergymen as one Mr. Levit, parson of Leden Roding, who was "a notorious swearer, a dicer, a carder, a hawker, and hunter" and who had fathered a bastard child. Even more disturbing to the devout Puritans were the numerous vestiges of Romanism still found in the Anglican Church. They complained about particular liturgies, rituals, and restrictions but especially about the structure of the church with its archbishops, bishops, and other hierarchical officers.

Most Puritans agreed on the kind of organization they wanted: one in which individual churches could control their own membership and be controlled by it. That is, they urged that the power of excommunication and other means of discipline rest in the hands of local pastors and other leaders, all of whom were to be elected by the members and not subject to a higher structure of officials. Whatever overarching government might be necessary could be provided by occasional meetings of the pastors themselves. The central principle was that the church itself was to consist only of true believers who set themselves apart from the unregenerate and who covenanted together in the never-ending struggle to strengthen their faith.

Most English Puritans believed that the best way to achieve their reforms was to gain control of the government and thus the church itself. But a smaller group of dissidents had another idea. These were the Separatists, Puritans who could not wait for the uncertainty of political triumph to test their beliefs. Separatists suffered constant harassment from the Anglican establishment, and some of their leaders paid with their lives. Others took the hint and left for the Netherlands. One such group, under the leadership of John Robinson, settled first in Amsterdam in 1607, then moved to Leyden, before crossing the Atlantic to Plymouth in 1620. But to the vast majority of Puritans, who considered all Christians duty-bound to support their church in spite of its failings, separatism remained a serious deviation, for once a group accepted the principle of separation, its members would themselves be threatened by internal divisions forever after.

One such orthodox Puritan was John Winthrop of Groton Manor. Along with others who had caught the "fever," for Winthrop Puritanism became an intensely personal matter. He struggled with an inner tension—how to live a good life in a world that was evil. The answer lay not in escape through abstinence, removing such sources of temptation as sex or drink, but rather in disciplining oneself to live in moderation. Beyond this personal challenge to lead a godly life, Puritans like Winthrop incurred the further obligation to join in the struggle against the evils that permeated society. His experience as an attorney in the King's Court of Wards in London exposed him to one of the corrupt governmental practices of the day, the exploitation of underage heirs of deceased landowners by their court-appointed guardians and by the Crown itself. To a Puritan like Winthrop such corruption exposed his country to the wrathful punishment of a vengeful God.

Puritans took their cause to the people during the first decades of the seventeenth century. They wrote pamphlets, gave lectures, and delivered sermons throughout the land to persuade fellow churchgoers to support their efforts at reform. They turned also to Parliament as a means of correcting the ills of the realm. Under James I, who succeeded Elizabeth in 1603, reformers made modest headway. But when Charles I became king in 1625, the situation rapidly deteriorated. Parliament refused to rubber-stamp policies it considered unwise and failed to provide the king with the funds he needed. In retribution Charles dissolved the Parliament and attempted to raise money on his own authority in the guise of a loan. Several Puritans went to jail for opposing the new levy, and matters stood at an impasse. Meanwhile these political evils were matched by the spread of a religious idea which Puritans considered a heretical vestige of Catholicism. Arminianism, the belief that man could gain faith by his own will alone, became a particularly serious threat. Charles's wife was Catholic, for one thing, and for another he appointed an Arminian, William Laud, first Bishop of London and later Archbishop of Canterbury. Under Charles's sponsorship Arminians rose to positions of great influence throughout the church. Parliament supported the Puritans in their struggle against both political tyranny and religious heresy as best it could. But in 1629 Charles dissolved Parliament with the clear intent of ruling thereafter without it. Unwilling either to foment political revolution or to follow the Separatists out of the church, Puritans like John Winthrop seemed at their wits' end by 1629.

* * *

The expansion of English society had reached new proportions by the end of the sixteenth century. The same economic impulses that prompted the gentry to enclose their lands led also to a broadening of English interests beyond the shores of the homeland. More than three generations had elapsed since John and Sebastian Cabot had carried the Tudor flag far to the west and established an English claim to North America, though William Hawkins did explore the African coast in 1540. Finally, from 1562–1569 his son John undertook a series of voyages in which he purchased slaves along the Guinea coast and sold them to Spanish colonists in the West Indies, an incursion not welcomed by Spanish officials when they learned about it. One of Hawkins's captains was Francis Drake, the pride of Plymouth and soon destined to become a national hero for his exploits against the Spanish Armada. While Drake and his fellow sea-dogs fought the Spaniards for supremacy of the sea, other Englishmen searched for a practical water route to the Far East, then considered the ultimate source of overseas wealth. Merchants in Bristol and other ports pooled their resources in joint-stock companies to underwrite these early voyages, and at the beginning of the seventeenth century associations such as the East India Company were chartered on a permanent basis.

Meanwhile navigators sailing for other European nations had begun to search along the North American coast for a passage to the Pacific. Their voyages took them into the waters of what later would be called New England. Under the French flag, Giovanni da Verrazzano spent the summer of 1524 exploring the coastline from North Carolina to Maine; his charts and descriptions greatly aided those who followed. The next year a Portuguese shipmaster in Spanish service, Esteban Gómez, made his landfall near the present island of Mount Desert. During the summer months he explored and charted the entire coast of later-day Massachusetts Bay all the way to Cape Cod.

For those who sought to discover a convenient sea route to the East the American continent was an obstacle to be circumvented, but for other maritime adventurers America itself became the land of promise. Because Spanish power remained strong in the Caribbean and South American areas, Englishmen turned their attention to the vast northern continent to which, through the Cabots' discovery, they had a valid claim. Sir Humphrey Gilbert proposed in 1576 the establishment of a permanent trading post in America primarily as a way station to Asia but also as a home for some of England's needy and troublesome people. Meanwhile, rumors of a fabled land of gold and silver—Norumbega it was called—gave further incentive for explorations along the northeastern section of the coast. During the next decade the Richard Hakluyts, father and son, urged their countrymen toward a more aggressive overseas policy. The father emphasized the economic gains of maritime commerce and the colonization of unwanted Englishmen abroad, while the son valued more highly the strategic advantages to be gained against Spain and Portugal. Together they were a persuasive pair. In a private tract called *A Discourse Concerning Western Planting* written for Queen Elizabeth in 1584, the younger Hakluyt urged his sovereign to support overseas expansion as a national policy. The Virgin Queen refused direct assistance, but she did lend strong moral support to those of her subjects engaged in such enterprises.

Although the queen's favorite, Walter Raleigh, failed in his attempts to establish a permanent colony in North America, others continued the effort. English and European fishermen had for years summered along the coasts of Newfoundland and Nova Scotia so that they could dry their catch before heading for home in the autumn. In August 1583 Sir Humphrey Gilbert had sailed into St. Johns harbor and repossessed it in the name of the queen, with the intent of establishing a permanent settlement somewhere along the northeastern coast. He was unable to find a suitable location, however, and after losing one of his vessels, headed back to England to organize another expedition. But Gilbert himself was lost in a mid-Atlantic gale, and colonization in New England would have to wait for others to pick up the initiative.

In 1602 English shipmaster Bartholomew Gosnold set sail from Falmouth harbor for New England with a party of thirty-two men, twenty of whom intended to become permanent settlers. After a tedious passage of seven weeks Gosnold made land some place along the coast of Maine. From there he sailed southward along the coast in search of the bay discovered by Verrazzano in 1524 and now called Narragansett. Somehow Gosnold successfully worked his way through the shoals that lay off an immense sandy spit, which he promptly named Cape Cod for the abundance of fish he discovered in the bay. His vessel entered Nantucket Sound from the south, and after further exploration, Gosnold finally chose a small island for his settlement, probably Cuttyhunk, westernmost of the Elizabeth Islands, which separate Buzzards Bay from Vineyard Sound. Gosnold had picked a strategic location. Not only did the island command two important bodies of water, but it also embraced a large pond with an island in the middle, an ideal site for a fort. Within a few days, however, the band discovered that their food supply would last only six weeks, and eight of the twenty intended colonists decided to return with the vessel to England. After gathering a meager cargo of cedar logs and sassafras, Gosnold and his men set sail for home, bringing to an inglorious end the first attempt by Englishmen to establish a permanent settlement in the territory later to become Massachusetts Bay Colony.

During the next few years several mariners further explored the New England coast. Martin Pring led a two-vessel expedition to the coast in 1603 for sassafras, which he found in plentitude around the present-day harbor of Plymouth. One of the great explorers of all time, Samuel de Champlain, accompanied a French expedition headed by Sieur de Monts to establish a settlement near the mouth of the St. Croix River, now the boundary between Maine and New Brunswick. While a member of this group, Champlain spent most of the next two years carefully charting and studying the New England coast as far south as Nantucket Sound in search of a better site for a settlement. But two winters on the coast had taken a dreadful toll in lives, and besides, political enemies at home succeeded in undermining de Monts' standing at court. He was forced to abandon his efforts in 1607 and return to France. Just as English hopes to colonize this part of America had flickered by the failure of Gosnold, so now did French ambitions fall short of fulfillment.

As each explorer returned from the North American coast, either he or an associate generally wrote a report of his findings which Richard Hakluyt or others gladly published. Two writers, for instance, wrote narratives of the Gosnold expedition in glowing phrases. John Brereton reported the fishing around Cape Cod to be as good as off Newfoundland and the banks closer to shore and not so deep. He spoke of sowing wheat and barley which in just fourteen days grew to nine inches in the "fat and lustie" soil. Brereton waxed enthusiastic about the great variety of trees: "high timbred Oakes . . . , Cedars, strait and tall . . ., Walnut trees in aboundance, the fruit as bigge as ours." On the mainland shore, Brereton reported, "we stood like men ravished at the beautie and delicacie of this sweet soile." "Meadows very large and full of greene grass and diverse cleere Lakes of fresh water" held him spellbound. The other chronicler of Gosnold's voyage, Gabriel Archer, kept to a more literal description of what he saw, but even he proclaimed the land to be "the goodliest continent that ever we saw, promising more by farre than we any way did expect."*

One of the most influential accounts was that written by James Rosier about the voyage led in 1605 by George Waymouth to the Muscongus Bay region of Maine. His very title must have attracted considerable attention: *A True Relation of the Most Prosperous Voyage. . . .* Among the specific natural resources of the land which Rosier considered of value were the fir trees which produced turpentine and pitch; timber; fish, especially in the rivers; and everywhere the rich, black soil. Again and again Rosier commented about how suitable the region was for coloniza-

---

* Henry S. Burrage, ed., *Early English and French Voyages . . . 1534–1608* (New York, 1906), 335; Collections of the Massachusetts Historical Society, 3rd series, VIII: 72–81.

tion. "Every day we did more and more discover the pleasant fruitful-
nesse," he wrote, "insomuch as many of our Companie wished themselves settled here, not expecting any further hopes or better discovery to
be made." Indeed Rosier constantly compared what he saw with his
homeland, and Maine came out on top. The strawberries were bigger,
the harbors more secure, the climate more healthful. (They had arrived
in May and left in July!)

Rosier's account of the Waymouth expedition greatly impressed two
wealthy Englishmen, Sir Ferdinando Gorges and Sir John Popham, chief
justice of the realm. In company with Richard Hakluyt and others they
persuaded James I to charter the Virginia Company in 1606, to consist of
two branches. The Plymouth Company, with Gorges, Popham, and several other West Country merchants and gentlemen as members, was
granted the right to colonize the region lying between the 38th and 45th
parallels. The London Company received jurisdiction over the area from
the 34th to the 41st parallel, while both companies had equal rights to
settle the overlapping territory so long as they kept one hundred miles
apart. In the spring of 1607, the Plymouth Company outfitted an expedition to establish a colony in the region described so enthusiastically by
Rosier. In command were Raleigh Gilbert, Humphrey's son, and George
Popham, a nephew of the sponsor. The expedition was in trouble from
the outset, for it did not arrive on the Maine coast until early August, too
late to plant crops around its chosen settlement at the mouth of the
Kennebec. Most of the company did manage to survive the winter, however, except for Popham, but in the spring Gilbert had to return to
England because of his brother's death. Deprived of their leaders, the rest
of the settlers lost heart and returned home too. Meanwhile, the London
Company had sent its own expedition to the Chesapeake Bay region,
where it established a colony at Jamestown in the spring of 1607. Although brought several times to the brink of extinction, the little settlement survived. Not for thirteen more years would an English community take root in the region farther north.

The Virginia Colony made several contributions to the ultimate success of settlement in Massachusetts Bay. One came in the form of Captain
John Smith, a veteran of two winters at Jamestown, who in 1614
explored the shores of what he now named New England. His account of
the voyage, published two years later, and its accompanying map, added
still further to knowledge of and interest in the northeastern part of the

continent. But New England required more than a name to succeed. It
needed a group of colonists sufficiently motivated to stay no matter what
the discouragements. Jamestown had had troubles enough in its early
years. Only the fortuitous arrival of a relief fleet in 1610 kept the settlement going. The sterner winters and thinner soil of New England demanded still more from its potential settlers.

Such a group, known to us as the Pilgrims, had its beginnings in the
village of Scrooby in Nottinghamshire. Here in the first years of the
seventeenth century a small band of Puritans under the secular leadership
of William Brewster decided to form a separate church for the proper
worship of God. Within a few years, however, the Scrooby Separatists
began to pay for their heresy with fines and imprisonment. Already a
neighboring group had emigrated to Holland to escape such persecu-
tion, and in 1608 the Scrooby group followed suit. Upon arriving in
Amsterdam, they discovered numerous other Separatist churches, and
among them all minor bickerings soon broke out. With John Robinson
taking over as minister they moved to Leyden in 1609, where they remained in peace and harmony for another dozen years. Some found a
comfortable livelihood in the cloth industry; others acquired new skills
as artisans. And the Dutch remained hospitable enough.

As the years passed, however, the Separatists grew increasingly concerned about the dilemma confronting them. To remain in Holland
meant either forsaking their English heritage and becoming Dutchmen
or reconciling themselves to lives as permanent aliens in a foreign country. Neither alternative seemed particularly attractive. And the problem
became still more serious when the older generation contemplated their
children's future. By the summer of 1617 the leaders were giving serious
consideration to still another removal, this time across the seas to the
country vaguely known to them as Virginia. They recognized the advantages of settling near the established colony at Jamestown, but not too
near, for as they put it "they should be in as great danger to be troubled or
persecuted for the cause of religion as if they lived in England; and it
might be worse." Thus the leaders weighed the various risks and concluded that removal to an unsettled part of the Virginia Company's lands
in America offered the most promising future. Therefore they sent two
representatives to London to discuss arrangements with company officials. There they found Sir Edwin Sandys, an influential member of the
company, sympathetic to their proposals. More difficult was obtain-

ing the assent of James I and finding the necessary capital to underwrite the venture. By the end of 1619 these problems had been solved, the latter through the assistance of Thomas Weston, ironmonger, who headed a group of London merchants looking for promising fields for investment. At the last minute Dutch interests offered to stake the emigrants to a settlement in New Amsterdam, but the Separatists decided in favor of colonizing under English jurisdiction.

The tentative agreement with Weston's group established a joint-stock association. Its shares were valued at £10 each, the approximate cost of transporting one colonist to America, and could be purchased either with cash (making one an adventurer) or by agreeing to emigrate to the proposed new settlement (thus becoming a planter). Each colonist over the age of sixteen counted as one share if transported by the company and as two shares if he paid his own way. Thus a family emigrating at its own expense might acquire as many as ten or twelve shares, two each for the parents and children over sixteen, and one for each minor child. The colonists were obliged to work for the company for seven years, at the end of which time the assets of the enterprise were to be divided between planters and adventurers according to the number of shares held. The Pilgrims insisted that they be permitted to work for themselves two days a week and that their houses and other improvements not be subject to division at the end of the seven-year period. The adventurers refused to grant these more generous terms, however, and the Pilgrims finally capitulated. In the summer of 1620 those of the Leyden group who had finally decided to emigrate purchased a leaky old vessel, the *Speedwell,* to take them to Southampton, where they were to meet with other planters who would join them for the passage to America on board the chartered ship *Mayflower*. Upon arrival, however, the Leyden group refused to sign the new agreement, and the important business was left unresolved. Temporarily without financial support from Weston, they had to sell some of their provisions to raise the money necessary for port clearance. More troubles ensued when the *Speedwell* proved incapable of an Altantic crossing. With as many colonists on board as possible, 102 in all—many of them not even Puritans—the *Mayflower* finally set sail from Plymouth, England, on September 6, 1620, bound west toward an unknown future.

At about the time that the Pilgrims were negotiating with Thomas Weston, the Plymouth branch of the Virginia Company went out of existence and was succeeded by a group known as the Council for New England, with a royal grant of all the land lying between 40° and 48° north latitude. The council in turn lavishly issued grants to various others intending to establish settlements in New England. Thomas Weston dropped out of the group supporting the Pilgrims at Plymouth in 1622 to organize a settlement of his own at Wessagusset in Boston harbor. In the following year the Dorchester Adventurers, a group of English merchants interested in the fisheries, recognized that a permanent settlement in America could support both the economic and spiritual needs of the fisherman during their long season on the New England coast. First they tried Gloucester harbor on Cape Ann (ironically to become America's premier fishing port in the nineteenth century) and then moved to Naumkeag (later Salem) but with no greater success. Agriculture and fishing simply did not mix. By 1628 many of the settlers had abandoned the outpost, some going to Monhegan, others returning to England. But out of this humble beginning would come the founding of the Massachusetts Bay Colony.

In the spring of 1628 a group of six men, including John Endicott of Devon, received a grant from the Council for New England for all the land lying between lines three miles north of the Merrimack River and three miles south of the Charles. Now in fact a part of this territory lay within an area already granted by the council to one of its own members, Sir Ferdinando Gorges, who happened to be absent when the grant was made. It also encompassed the remnants of the old Dorchester Adventurers' settlement at Salem, now presided over by Roger Conant. The new group took the title: The New England Company for a Plantation in Massachusetts-Bay. The stated objective of the venture was the development of trade in such commodities as fish, timber, sassafras, and furs, which they hoped could be obtained in profitable quantities. In order to raise the capital necessary for such an undertaking, however, the original group had to appeal for help to merchants in London. Among more than a dozen newcomers were Matthew Craddock, Sir Richard Saltonstall, John Venn, and a number of Puritan merchants from East Anglia. In June 1628 John Endicott led a group of fifty settlers to New England, where they landed at Salem and took over the struggling community there.

Infusion of Puritan money did more than put the group on a sound financial footing, however. It paved the way for a revolutionary transformation of the company's entire purpose and mode of operation. In order to secure the patent against the counterclaims of Gorges and others, the investors obtained a royal charter in March 1629 confirming their title to the lands in New England and incorporating their organization as The Governor and Company of the Massachusetts Bay in New England. Most such charters authorized some sort of governing body chosen from among the members to manage the affairs of the company and also required this group to meet at stated times and at a stated place during the year. But the Puritan lawyer who helped draft the charter for the Massachusetts Bay Company omitted any reference to the place of residence for the company. Just what the intention of such an omission was is difficult to determine, but the result was of great significance: the company was not required to hold its meetings in England. The directors could if they wished move the company's headquarters to Massachusetts Bay itself. In 1630 that is precisely what happened.

The Massachusetts Bay Company had by 1629 a Crown title to a large stretch of territory, a royal charter constituting its authority to govern its affairs, and a score of wealthy merchants willing to invest money in its operations. It lacked only settlers to make a successful undertaking. Charles I and Bishop Laud saw to it that there would be a goodly supply of potential colonists, for shortly after signing the Massachusetts Bay Company charter, the king dissolved Parliament and announced his determination to rule without calling another. For numerous Englishmen, but particularly for Puritans like John Winthrop, the doors at home seemed to be closing all around them. Singly and in small groups men began seriously to discuss the possibility of emigration. In fact, as we have seen, the tide had already begun to flow in 1620. Many would follow in the wake of the *Mayflower* to the shores of Massachusetts, some to live at Plymouth itself, others to begin new communities. The vast majority of Puritans remained behind, of course, supporting the revolutions of 1640 and 1688 and gaining a more secure position in England. Altogether, however, in the period 1620–42, nearly eighty thousand Englishmen left their homeland. A small segment moved to the continent, as had the Scrooby Separatists before them, but most of the emigrants, perhaps as many as sixty thousand, chose America. In addition to the settlements in Virginia and Massachusetts there were others in Newfoundland, Bermuda, the West Indies, and Guiana on the coast of South America. Before the first flood came to an end in 1642, many of the intervening regions became settled as well.

Like most migrations the movement of large numbers of Englishmen resulted from factors pushing them out of their homeland as well as from other factors pulling them toward the New World. We have already noted how tumultuous life had become for thousands of Englishmen. Those in the countryside faced eviction from their small holdings as landlords turned to enclosure as a means of improved yields. Townsmen enjoyed new opportunities on the wave of increasing consumer demands, but the competition was greater still, from a rising population and the influx of country people into urban communities. In the southern parts of England, from Devon in the West Country to East Anglia, everything seemed more crowded, more chaotic, less easy to comprehend. And those who professed their opposition to the established church faced more than disruption. By 1630 they had become the specific objects of governmental harassment. At the same time the news from America was encouraging. After weathering a serious crisis in 1621–22 Jamestown seemed to have secured a sound footing; and reports from Plymouth reiterated the enthusiasm expressed in earlier descriptions of that part of America. One pamphlet in particular—Edward Winslow's *Good Newes from New England,* published in 1624—gave encouraging information to those who might wish to follow the Pilgrims. Private correspondence from friends and relatives lent further testimony to their well-being in America.

It is difficult to determine precisely what characteristics of New England most appealed to the many different people who ultimately decided to migrate, just as the major reasons for leaving England varied from person to person. Perhaps the best way to understand why so many Englishmen came to America is to consider a specific example. The most important participant in the Puritan migration was, of course, John Winthrop. Winthrop was not an original member of the Massachusetts Bay Company, but in the late spring of 1629 he began to discuss the company's prospects with some of its London backers. He became convinced of their sincerity in supporting a new settlement in America, although he probably also recognized that they expected a profit. In contrast he noted the hardship that surrounded him in Suffolk—the unemployment, the high cost of land, the necessity to practice deceit in business and the professions in order to stay ahead. In higher social circles this corruption took the form of extravagant living. Winthrop's own son Henry was among the offenders.

Along with other Puritans, Winthrop was convinced that God would soon punish England for its wicked ways. Was it not possible, they wondered, that He made the New World available to the faithful as a place of refuge. The fact that America was unsettled (at least from the white Europeans' point of view), that it seemed from all reports to be a land of milk and honey, and that it was separated by a wide body of water from the Old World all contributed to its appeal as a place of refuge. To a people for whom all things answered to some divine purpose, the fact that numerous Puritan ministers seemed to favor a migration to America was further evidence. Winthrop himself reasoned that "when God intends a man to work he sets a Bias on his heart so as though he be tumbled this way and that yet his Bias still draws him to that side, and there he rests at last." For many of the Puritans, then, removal to America fulfilled a divine plan. But a major obstacle of conscience still had to be overcome. Were not men of ability like Winthrop more needed at home to help lead the good fight against the sin and tyranny that was abroad in the land? Was not migration to America in fact a disguised form of the separatism abhorred by conservative Puritans? Only after much debate could Winthrop satisfy himself that he could more effectively serve God by preserving a purified part of the church in the New World than by vainly struggling against corruption in the Old. He hoped the purified new church would become the nucleus for saving its parent.

For Winthrop the decision to emigrate involved a still greater commitment. Neither the governor of the company, Matthew Craddock, nor any of its directors intended to become settlers in America; their unanimous choice for leader was John Winthrop. Winthrop recognized that if the undertaking had any value at all, it would need strong leadership to succeed, and so after months of deliberation he decided to accept the company's offer, but not without some strings attached. In August 1629 Winthrop met at Cambridge with about a dozen leading Puritans and agreed to sail to New England the following spring provided that the company charter "be first by an order of court legally transferred and established to remain with us and others which shall inhabit upon the said plantation." By accepting the terms of the so-called Cambridge Agreement the English directors of the company voluntarily renounced their control of the company in favor of those who were willing and able to invest their lives as well as their fortunes in the New World. This transfer of authority symbolized the fact that the Massachusetts Bay Colony would from the outset manage its own affairs.

In the spring of 1629 the Massachusetts Bay Company sent out five vessels to Naumkeag with two or three hundred passengers and ample provisions. Then in March 1630 the company gathered together the most impressive fleet yet to sail for British America. On board the flagship *Arbella* was John Winthrop and the company charter; trailing behind were ten more vessels carrying altogether seven hundred passengers, along with forty cows, sixty horses, and tons of additional cargo. Six more vessels arrived later that summer to bring the total number of passengers for the two seasons 1629–30 to over twelve hundred. In *Arbella*'s wake would come to Massachusetts Bay another two hundred vessels with twenty thousand settlers before the great Puritan migration ended in 1643. No English overseas colony before or since began on such a scale.

3

AMERICAN PLANTATIONS

Few Americans of the late twentieth century have experienced the trauma of leaving their homeland to begin life anew in a distant and unknown country. When they do travel abroad, modern transportation permits an easy return to their place of origin. This was not so with the first New Englanders. The break with their homeland for Pilgrims and Puritans was almost irreversible, and the long passage across the Atlantic left a profound and lasting impression upon them.

For William Bradford the move to New England was only the last of several—from his birthplace in Austerfield, Yorkshire, to Amsterdam, to Leyden, like the peregrinations of so many others whose restlessness would take them from Scotland to Ireland, or from France to Canada, or from Ireland to England before they made the ultimate move to America. To leave familiar surroundings behind was not the major problem for most of these immigrants; it was the abandonment of the friends and relatives who make one's native land home. For most of the immigrants coming to New England the shock of breaking these human ties was somewhat lessened by the fact that so many acquaintances joined them in the new enterprise. They could more easily face together the frightening prospect of an ocean crossing and the unknown dangers of the New World. Most of the men and women who came to Plymouth and Massachusetts Bay, then, came as part of a group, and this fact made a significant difference to them personally and to the outcome of their endeavors.

The ocean separating America from England was a formidable barrier. The English Channel was challenge enough; once past the Cornish coast and into the Atlantic itself the mariner faced even more hazardous conditions. Prevailing winds over the North Atlantic are southwesterly, making headwinds almost all the way across for any vessel sailing to the New World. Furthermore the North Atlantic current is also adverse. In the eastern part of the ocean this current flows at little more than half a knot, but as one approaches the American shore the Gulf Stream reaches a velocity of nearly two knots. These conditions make the North Atlantic a difficult stretch of ocean at any time, but each season of the year has its particular weather hazards. Winter gales are succeeded by icebergs and fog lasting well into summer. A few months of fair weather soon give way to the late summer and autumn hurricane season, a number of these tropical storms reaching well into the North Atlantic.

The navigator planning a westward crossing was thus faced with a number of compromises. A more southerly route, via the Azores or, occasionally, the Canary Islands, gave the mariner favorable winds and avoided the adverse currents but exposed him to tropical storms for a longer period of time and of course resulted in a greater distance to be sailed. A route at the far north, on the other hand, while avoiding the North Atlantic current, did not offer a favorable wind until mid-ocean and had the additional hazard of ice and fog through the first half of the year. Under almost any circumstances, therefore, crossing the Atlantic was a navigational challenge of considerable proportions. With a little luck such a passage could be made in about six weeks, rarely in less than five, and would more likely take eight or ten if one encountered storms or consistently adverse winds.

The vessels available for such an undertaking were of sturdy enough construction; most seagoing vessels can take a more severe pounding in the open water than can their passengers and crew. Disease and starvation carried off from 10 to 15 percent of those who made the passage. The greatest danger lay in approaching the coast, especially a lee shore such as New England from Cape Cod northward during easterly storms. Seventeenth-century vessels, being square-rigged with the principal sails carried on yards, were ill suited for windward work. The *Mayflower*, for instance, carried square sails on both fore and main masts, the mizzen and head sails only of fore-and-aft design. She was a fairly large vessel for her day, measuring 180 tons burden, with a hull length of about ninety feet. Her high aftercastle, a remnant of an earlier time, was twenty-seven feet above the waterline and must have made her difficult to handle in a stiff breeze. A crew of thirty was quartered forward, the captain and mates sharing the spacious aftercabin. A large three-decked hold for cargo and provisions occupied the space amidships. A small number of passengers could generally find bunks in the tween decks or, if fortunate, in the aftercabin itself. But when over one hundred people sought passage on board, as in the case of the Pilgrims, every available space became home for someone among the group.

Brief as it is, William Bradford's account of the *Mayflower*'s crossing relates to us some of the major hazards and minor irritations common to such passages. An arrogant crew member constantly mocked the Pilgrims' seasickness and other discomforts (he was carried off by a "grievous disease" in mid-ocean); a fierce storm cracked a deck beam amidships (but the crew succeeded in making repairs with the aid of a jack post the Pilgrims had brought along from Holland); their landfall on a strange and poorly charted coast soon put them "amongst dangerous shoals and roaring breakers" (they worked their way out of the foul water and into a safe harbor). Remarkably, only one of the Pilgrims' company died during the passage. Another was miraculously rescued after being swept overboard in a storm. For the thousands of immigrants who would follow the *Mayflower* to Massachusetts Bay in the next two decades the conditions of the crossing were much the same. Some would experience more severe storms, others would suffer through devastating shipboard epidemics, and a few would perish in shipwrecks at the very end of their journey. But when the hazards of the North Atlantic and the small size of seventeenth-century vessels are considered, one can only marvel that so many people did survive the crossing.

Both Pilgrims and Puritans found broad religious significance in the crossing of the Atlantic. The sea became their Sinai desert, its transit a challenge and a test; beyond lay Canaan, the promised land. For Puritans safe passage proved that they were God's chosen people. Once across, the ocean would protect them, symbolically at least and practically as well, from future harassment by their old enemies. Pilgrims and Puritans were fleeing from an old society as much as they were searching for a new opportunity. But by the same token, that vast sea was now, in the words of Bradford, as "a main bar and gulf to separate them from all the civil parts of the world." True, the ships that brought them could take them back again, but once those vessels cleared for home, the settlers were plunged into a degree of isolation that few could have imagined. For centuries the Atlantic had prevented Europeans from establishing permanent settlements in North America, had preserved it from the ravages of war, disease, and the white man's exploitation of earth's natural endowment. It was, in short, the tempestuous Atlantic that made America a "new" Canaan for the generation of William Bradford and John Winthrop.

The *Mayflower*'s landfall at Cape Cod on November 9, 1620, marked the end of a nine-week passage across the Atlantic. As their ultimate destination the group's leaders seem to have had in mind the mouth of the Hudson River, barely within the limits of the Virginia Company's charter grant. Knowing what we do now about the site, no one could seriously doubt their shrewdness. But in the attempt to double Cape Cod en route to the Hudson the *Mayflower* fell in among the dangerous shoals of Pollock Rip, and Captain Christopher Jones wisely put back. Thus did the infamous waters of the New England coast determine the course of Massachusetts history. After putting around, the vessel worked its way north into the snug anchorage at the tip of Cape Cod now known as Provincetown. There she remained for several weeks, until an alternative place for permanent settlement could be found. Some of the company went off on an overland expedition as others assembled the small boat, called a shallop, which they had brought along for exploration by water. Meanwhile, the other passengers continued to live on board the *Mayflower*, although four of them died during the period, including William Bradford's wife. The group exploring by land encountered a small party of Indians, who promptly disappeared into the woods. The expedition soon came across some cleared fields and the remains of a small settlement. Buried in the sandy soil were found caches of Indian corn which were brought back to the ship. A few days later the group exploring in the shallop were attacked by another band of Indians, whom they drove off with musket fire and shouts. As the crew coasted along the shores of Cape Cod the weather turned foul, but they pushed on, in search of the harbor they had earlier learned about, which they would call Plymouth. They found it on December 21. The harbor provided a safe anchorage for good-sized vessels; there was a hill which could be fortified; ample supplies of fresh water flowed through the land; and nearby lay fields already cleared by the Indians, who seemed fortuitously to have abandoned the site altogether. The shallop promptly returned to Provincetown with this good news, and in the next few days the *Mayflower* cautiously made its way to Plymouth, where it dropped anchor on the 26th.

When dissidents on board the *Mayflower* learned that they would not be settling within the boundaries of "Virginia," they threatened to go their own way once ashore. But the Pilgrim leaders took advantage of the fact that the company had authorized the planters to establish their own local government in America pending further directions from home. They drew up a covenant providing for a "civil body politic for our better ordering and preservation" which bound all its signatories to "all due submission and obedience" to the laws and ordinances which "shall be thought most meet and convenient for the general good of the Colony." All of the adult males in good health signed the Mayflower Compact before going ashore. The simple yet eloquent language of the document put into political terms the basic principle of the Pilgrims' religious organization—the covenant. The fact that the government was originally *formed* by the consent of those who bound themselves to abide by its laws, however, did not necessarily mean that they would *operate* that government. Bradford was not inclined to share the political power of his office with the general populace, and in practice, Plymouth was for many years ruled by the governor and several assistants, who were annually elected by the freemen—all of the adult males except servants. But the document remains as a monument to the idea that just government *originates* in the consent of those it is to govern.

For the remainder of that first winter the colony struggled to survive. Captain Jones decided not to return to England until spring, and the company continued to live aboard the *Mayflower* until shelters were built on shore. The long journey and subsequent winter season began taking its toll, however. By spring nearly half of the original company had perished. At one time, Bradford reported, only six or seven persons were strong enough to care for the others. Among those men were William Brewster, the colony's minister, and Miles Standish, the militia captain.

The coming of spring brought the first sustained contact between Indians and whites in New England, after initial brushes with a few Nausets on the Cape. The Pilgrims had settled within Wampanoag territory, on the site of a village of the Patuxets, a tribe that had been wiped out by a mysterious plague a few years before. As befit his position as host, therefore, the Wampanoag chief Massasoit came to visit Plymouth one March day, having been preceded by Samoset and Squanto, two other Algonkins who had learned English some years before. On behalf of the Wampanoags, Massasoit signed a treaty with the Pilgrims in which each party pledged peaceful relations and agreed to support the other if attacked by an aggressor. Later in the spring the Pilgrims returned Massasoit's visit to his headquarters at Sowams. With the exception of occasional squabbles of minor importance Wampanoags and Pilgrims lived at peace for over half a century because each needed something from the other. The Pilgrims, of course, wished to occupy the Wampanoags' land, while Massasoit wanted support in case the Narragansets attacked him. In the following year, in fact, the Narragansets sent a challenge directly to the Pilgrims, but Bradford parried the threat with a show of strength. Squanto remained with the Pilgrims as interpreter, showing them how to plant corn and where to catch fish. In the fall he led a group of colonists to what would soon be known as Boston harbor, where they traded with Indians of the Massachusets tribe for beaver and otter skins.

As their first year in America came to a close the Pilgrims had good reason to rejoice. In the fall they put up their bounty of corn and beans, stored away their catch of fish, waterfowl, and venison, and celebrated their good harvest with a feast of thanksgiving. At the end of November a small vessel called the *Fortune* arrived at Plymouth with thirty-five newcomers, including the wives and children of several of the pioneer settlers. They were welcome, of course, although the fact that they landed with no provisions put a strain on the Pilgrims' recent harvest. Immediately the *Fortune* was laden with a return cargo of clapboards and skins, worth altogether nearly £500. The *Fortune* had brought a petulant letter from Thomas Weston, who scolded the planters for their failure to send back any produce with the *Mayflower*. In his reply Bradford patiently introduced Weston to the facts of New World life, explaining the difficulties experienced by the infant colony and defending his group from Weston's unreasonable charges of "weakness of judgment." The *Fortune* also brought a new patent for the settlement issued by the Council for New England. The Pilgrims were greatly relieved by this document, because they had of necessity established their settlement outside the jurisdiction of the Virginia Company, and its legality was therefore open to question. Now the polity they founded on the Mayflower Compact was beyond challenge. The new patent granted one-hundred-acre tracts to planters who paid their own way to the settlement and suggested that they might be given greater control over their own affairs after the first seven years. With these encouraging indications for the future, the Pilgrims cheerfully accepted the necessity of half rations through the balance of the winter. For several years thereafter the Pilgrims continued to depend on outside sources—Indians, fishermen, and other colonies—to supplement their own food production.

While the Pilgrims struggled through their first few years, several other settlements met with discouraging failure within the boundaries of present-day Massachusetts. In the summer of 1622 a letter from Thomas Weston announced that he had sold his interest in the Plymouth adventure and was sending out sixty men to establish his own settlement, probably without authorization from the Council for New England. When the motley group arrived, Bradford took pity and allowed the men to remain at Plymouth for several months to recuperate. In September those who could removed to Boston Bay, where they established a settlement at Wessagusset (present-day Weymouth). This group seemed devoid of strong leadership, its rude members treating the neighboring Massachusets Indians so abusively as to threaten the delicate peace that the Pilgrims had established. Learning from their friend Massasoit that the Massachusets were plotting revenge against both Wessagusset and Plymouth, the Pilgrims reluctantly decided to attack the tribe's leaders as the only means of preventing a major war. The strategy succeeded, but the Wessagusset settlement could not survive the crisis. Most of its members headed for the coast of Maine, where they could more easily find passage on a fishing vessel bound home.

Meanwhile Ferdinando Gorges laid grandiose plans for a fishing and trading plantation in New England, and in the summer of 1623 his son Robert settled at the now abandoned site at Wessagusset. But young Gorges and his companions barely survived the winter. With the coming of spring the group broke up, some of them heading back to England with Gorges, others scattering along the coast. A clergyman named Braxton settled in the shadow of Beacon Hill; another young man, Samuel Maverick, ensconced himself on Noddles Island in Boston Bay. Throughout the decade refugees from this and other unsuccessful plantations scattered along the coast from Boston Bay to the coast of Maine. And at Natascot (present-day Hull) could be found Roger Conant, John Lyford, John Oldham, and others who had left Plymouth, willingly or otherwise. Most of these isolated pioneers would be either swept aside or taken in by the Puritan flood that would shortly overflow the Massachusetts Bay area.

In the summer of 1625 still another group, this one under a Captain Wollaston, tried to establish an independent settlement in Massachusetts near the former site of Wessagusset. The following year an English lawyer named Thomas Morton seized control of the settlement after Wollaston left for Virginia, and renamed it Merrymount. Morton had fled from an adverse legal judgment in England, with a company of indentured servants, to establish his own plantation in America. He led his settlement "into licentiousness and into all profaneness" according to Bradford. They drank to excess, set up a maypole, and invited Indian women to make sport with them. Partly out of disgust with Merrymount's immorality, partly out of jealousy over its successful competition in the Indian trade, but mainly because Morton and his men were selling firearms to the natives, the Pilgrims could not tolerate the new-comers as neighbors any longer. In 1628 Miles Standish with a small band of militia succeeded in breaking up the offensive community and sending its leader back to England.

By far the most significant of these tiny outposts was the one on Cape Ann. In 1623 the Dorchester Adventurers sent out their first fishing expedition to New England, leaving a handful of men at Cape Ann over the winter to establish a permanent plantation which would in time, it was hoped, raise the produce necessary to support the company's fishing fleet. The first two seasons failed to produce profitable returns, and the Adventurers strengthened the operation by hiring Conant, Oldham, Lyford, and others, who had settled at Natascot. The Plymouth people claimed title to the site of the Cape Ann settlement, but the dispute was soon compromised. No matter how hard they tried, however, the new leaders could not successfully combine farming and fishing. They found the granite face of Cape Ann as unpromising for crops as the fishermen were inept at farming. In 1626 the Dorchester Adventurers admitted bankruptcy, and the enterprise folded, like so many others before it. Conant stayed on in New England, however, and with a few others moved to Naumkeag (present-day Salem), where he reported to John White, one of the former Adventurers, that conditions were somewhat better for a permanent settlement. White had long dreamed of establishing a religious colony in New England. As mentioned earlier some of the Dorchester associates now combined with Londoners and others to get the new enterprise underway. The result was the founding of the New England Company in 1628, which would soon be rechartered the following year as the Massachusetts Bay Company. On the rock which Roger Conant precariously occupied would be built one of the most successful colonies ever established under the English flag.

As a first step, in June 1628 the new company sent out John Endicott with forty men, fresh provisions, and orders to take over the settlement at Naumkeag from Conant, initially as leader and later as governor of the settlement. Endicott was by all accounts a tough man, well suited to the task of paving the way for the larger enterprise to follow, though a difficult man for whom to work. One of his first acts was to dismantle a large house built by the Dorchester planters at Cape Ann and have it reconstructed at Naumkeag for his own use. He also invested the site of Merrymount, scattering the handful of stragglers remaining from Morton's settlement and hewing down the offensive maypole. Endicott staked out a claim at Mishawum (now Charlestown) as well, where his men began the construction of a second village in anticipation of the additional settlers soon expected. The leaders of New England Company realized that in absorbing the old Dorchester grant they were in fact treading on ground claimed since 1623 by Robert Gorges. They were therefore careful to see to it that the new charter of 1629 creating the Massachusetts Bay Company settled the boundary problem in their favor—a fully legal if somewhat unethical way to circumvent the Gorges interest. When the first fleet sent out by the new company arrived at Naumkeag in June 1629, Endicott put the men to work building more houses, clearing fields, and planting crops.

In June 1630 the vanguard of the Winthrop fleet arrived, but its leaders did not find Naumkeag to their liking and therefore sent an expedition to look for a more suitable site as their principal settlement. Some of the newcomers were satisfied with Mishawum, while others chose the Shawmut peninsula (Boston), Mystic (Medford), or Watertown. Despite the scale on which the colony began, Massachusetts Bay did not altogether escape the difficulties that all American settlements suffered during their first years. About two hundred died, mostly from hunger and resultant illnesses. Only the timely arrival of the ship *Lyon* in February 1631 with a cargo of provisions saved others from a similar fate. When the *Lyon*'s master was ready to leave for England, however, almost one hundred settlers who had seen all they wanted of the Puritans' land of Canaan clambered aboard to return with him. Some of the company's backers, learning of these initial hardships, despaired of the colony's survival and withdrew their promised support. During these critical months the firm leadership of John Winthrop spelled the difference between success and failure. He gave generously of his own resources to the common good and dispatched men to buy corn from Indians and other settlers wherever possible; but most important he led by example, putting his servants to work establishing a productive farm up the Mystic River. By the time his wife, Margaret, arrived to join him in the autumn of 1631 the inhabitants had attained sufficient prosperity to shower their governor and his wife with gifts of hogs, poultry, venison, and other wild game.

Winthrop and his fellow Puritans fully realized the necessity for economic survival in the New World, but even in these early years they never lost sight of the primary purpose of their coming to America—the establishment of a community dedicated to the fulfillment of God's will. In mid-ocean Winthrop delivered to his fellow passengers a sermon explaining the exact nature of the undertaking. He believed that God had chosen the Puritans as a special people to save the Christian church and to be themselves saved. "Thus stands the cause between God and us; we are entered into Covenant with him for this work; we have taken out a commission. . . ." Winthrop looked upon the company's safe arrival in America as a sign of God's "ratification" of the agreement. Thereafter it was the Puritans' responsibility to uphold their end of the pact by forming a covenant among themselves to "do justly, to love mercy, and to walk humbly with our God." This second covenant, the one formed among the Puritans themselves, became the very basis for both church and community in Massachusetts Bay. "We must be knit together as one man in this work," Winthrop continued. "We must entertaine each other in brotherly Affection, . . . abridge ourselves of our superfluities for the supply of others' necessities, . . . rejoice together, mourne together, labor and suffer together, always having before our eyes our Commission and Community in the worke."

Puritans were to strive toward the goal of an ideal Christian community not only as an end in itself but also as a model for other plantations to follow. "We shall be as a city upon a hill, the eyes of all people are upon us," Winthrop wrote. If the Puritans succeeded, the founders of any future settlement would pray that God make it "like that of New England." But if the Puritans should fail in their mission, Winthrop warned, "we shall open the mouths of enemies to speak evil of the ways of God . . . and shame the faces of any of God's worthy servants and cause their prayers to be turned into curses." Thus the challenge was clearly laid down even before the Puritans set foot on the shores of Massachusetts Bay. They must succeed in establishing a community according to God's holy will or risk discrediting themselves and their Lord forever.

Although Winthrop had a fairly good idea of the goal while still on board the *Arbella,* he could not very well know the best means for achieving it until he had become familiar with the land whither his company was bound. Once arrived in America the leaders were almost immediately forced to make some changes in the form of government for the colony. The charter called for all the members or freemen of the Massachusetts Bay Company to meet four times a year as the General Court in order to make necessary laws for governing both company and colony. At one such meeting each year these freemen were to elect a governor, deputy governor, and eighteen assistants, who were to meet monthly as an executive council to administer the government. But since only a dozen or so company members had actually come to Massachusetts in the first years of the colony, political power rested in the hands of very few men. As Englishmen the ordinary colonists in Massachusetts Bay would have had no notion of government by the people, and surely John Winthrop had no reason to believe in popular rule. But at the first General Court, held in October 1630, a number of men showed up and expressed their views on various issues by a show of hands. The leaders took the hint and invited all adult males of the colony who wished to do so to become freemen. One hundred sixteen, virtually all of the men then in Massachusetts Bay, accepted the offer. They gained less political power than this would indicate, however, for at the same time the General Court ruled that freemen could elect only the assistants, who would in turn choose a governor and deputy governor from among themselves. Furthermore, the right to enact legislation was henceforth to rest with the governor and assistants rather than with the whole body of freemen as the charter provided. Finally, in the spring of 1631 the annual meeting of the General Court ruled that only church members could be admitted to freemanship in the colony. They were then to acknowledge their submission to the government by an oath of loyalty, in a sense an owning of a secular covenant not unlike that of the Mayflower Compact. Within a few months Winthrop had begun to transform the government of a trading company into a structure suitable for running the religious community that he and his fellow Puritans had had in mind from the beginning. But Winthrop fully intended to retain as much control over this community as he could.

Another problem arose from the fact that the population was already slowly spreading over a widening geographical area around the Boston Bay region. In 1632 the Court of Assistants provoked a serious dispute by levying a tax on the various towns to defray the cost of erecting a palisade around one of them (Cambridge). The people of Watertown believed that the assistants had no such authority, but Winthrop countered with the claim that the Court of Assistants had the same taxing powers enjoyed by Parliament, inasmuch as the members of both bodies were chosen by the freemen. This quarrel led eventually to a number of significant changes, the first of which were adopted by the General Court in May 1632. Thenceforward the governor and deputy governor were to be chosen by the freemen at the annual General Court (although still only from among the assistants) instead of by the assistants themselves. The court also authorized each town to appoint two men to consult with the Court of Assistants in matters of taxation. But the major changes came in May 1634 when this advisory group demanded to see the charter. There it was discovered that full legislative power lay in the hands of the freemen. The General Court meeting in May 1634 thereupon ordered that it alone had the right to levy taxes, grant lands, and make laws. But at the same time its leaders realized that the whole body of freemen would be too unwieldy for such functions. Thereafter towns were authorized to send deputies to all the General Court sessions except the annual spring election meeting, at which all freemen were to cast their ballots in person.

Freemanship remained limited to a small number of inhabitants within the colony, and John Winthrop had opposed even this extension of political power, yet within five years after the arrival of the *Arbella,* the locus of political power in Massachusetts had moved from a self-perpetuating group of one dozen company assistants to the whole body of freemen, whose local interests were represented by deputies with full legislative authority. The Commonwealth of Massachusetts Bay was born.

*   *   *

The establishment of plantations in New England brought men and women conditioned by centuries of European civilization face to face with a strange new environment which they could view at first only as an uninhabitable wilderness. The rocky coast of Maine, the extensive tidal marshes of the shores north and south of Boston, and the trackless forests of the interior might be appreciated for their beauty by later generations of Americans, but for the first settlers New England was a hostile land,

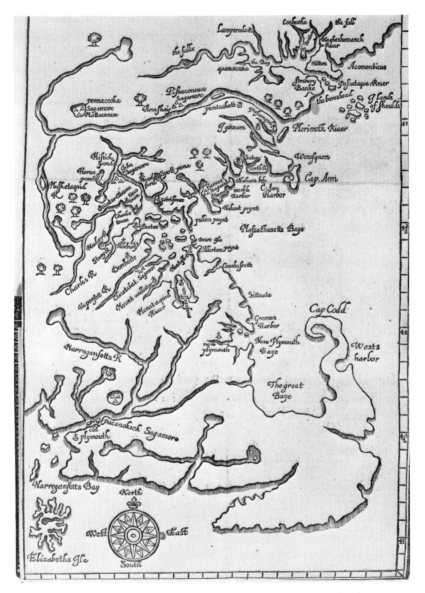

South Part of New England, 1634. From William Wood, *New England Prospect*.
Courtesy of the Essex Institute, Salem, Mass.

inhabited if at all by wild beasts and savages, neither of whom had known the beneficent love of God. According to the Book of Exodus the Lord had kept the Jews wandering through the wilderness for forty years as a test of their faith before finally showing them the way to the promised land. Puritans were not sure whether the New England wilderness was a similar testing ground or the promised land itself. Their instinctive first reaction was to erect a barrier between themselves and the threatening darkness around them. Beyond the edge of settlement, expansion was prohibited. The wilderness threatened in spiritual as well as physical ways, for the Puritans believed that as God ruled the civilized regions so Satan held sway in the wilderness through all sorts of natural and supernatural weapons in the eternal struggle for men's souls. All the more reason for Puritans to fear the wilderness and to defend themselves against whatever dwelt beyond the edge of settlement.

Yet this essentially negative attitude toward the New World could not long satisfy a people who, after all, sought more than mere survival in this new environment. To make a more comfortable living for themselves and, if possible, a profit for their English backers, the Puritans would have to adopt a more aggressive attitude toward their surroundings. They had little difficulty finding ample justification for such a view in the Scriptures. Had not God ordered in Genesis 1:28 that man should "be fruitful and multiply, and replenish the earth and subdue it . . ."? As Christians they believed that God had created all the earth for the use of mankind and that He had placed man in dominion over the land and all its creatures. As Puritans, furthermore, they believed that God had given them the New World as their particular refuge from a sinful Old World. Obviously, however, they would have to conquer the New World's wilderness in order to bring its promise to full flower. The Puritan occupation of New England thereafter became a war of conquest. In this battle the new arrivals exploited those resources they found most useful and ignored or destroyed the rest. The fact that they destroyed so little in the first century is testimony to the tenacity of the wilderness rather than to the forbearance of the settlers. Nevertheless, more fragile resources, such as the Indians and their culture, fell before the onslaught.

The Puritans' choice of sites for initial settlement had been made with survival primarily in mind. Because their only link with the Old World was by sea, these settlements naturally nestled beside good natural harbors—Plymouth, Rockport, Salem, Boston. These locations also gave ready access to the fishing grounds offshore, where a plentiful catch could be hauled throughout much of the year. At first timber for the construction of homes and vessels lay close at hand everywhere along the coast, but in time the choice of river valleys for settlement—the Mystic, the Charles, the Merrimack—was dictated by the need to bring out timber from the interior forests. Rivers also provided an easy means of transporting people and supplies to and from the hinterland, and they supplied fresh-water fishing—the Atlantic salmon, sturgeon, and shad. As we have already noted, the soil along river beds tends everywhere to be more fertile, and eastern Massachusetts was no exception. Here could be found the broad meadows—champion land in the language of Englishmen—some of which had been cleared by the Indians and much of which was naturally free of forestation. In the marshes behind the beach-dune barriers grew salt hay, the most desirable of all fodder for an Englishman's cattle. And so from their first settlements along the edge of the sea the Pilgrims and Puritans established their beachheads in the hostile New World and then began their invasion inland.

Whatever optimism appeared in the first reports from New England was designed to recruit increasing numbers of immigrants and encourage greater financial support from England to help in subduing the virgin wilderness. Those who, like the Puritans, arrived in June of the year had some cause for optimism. But Massachusetts in December was a rather different place from its summer aspect, more formidable, too, than any part of the English homeland in winter. All but the boldest promoter recognized that New England was no instant paradise in which the inhabitants needed only to pluck ripe fruit from the overhanging boughs. Hard work alone would convert this wilderness into a productive land. But gradually over the first years of exploration New Englanders formed a more detailed and far more accurate picture of their natural surroundings. As they came to know the land they were to make their home, they grew cautiously more optimistic about the future. They were, in fact, coming to terms with their new homeland, measuring its strengths and weaknesses, considering it neither a paradise nor an unconquerable wilderness, but a land in which God's commandment to subdue it could in time be realized.

Early settlers in New England saw in the native American Indian human evidence that Satan possessed the wilderness. Here were men totally ignorant of God's presence in the world. As human beings who did not know God they could only be possessed by Satan. Their way of life—ignorant as they were of "civilized" ways—appeared to support such an explanation. Indians seemed to be worshipping Satan in their wild dances and other pagan rites. The threatening hostility of some Indians, particularly the Pequots and Narragansets in southern New England and the Abnakis to the east, simply confirmed the Devil theory among Puritans. Just as they believed that God encouraged them to subdue the wilderness so, too, the Puritans viewed the inhabitants of that wilderness as fair game for conquest. In fact the conversion of Indians to Christianity had been for many years the goal of European Protestants and Catholics alike. As a tactical move in the endless war against Satan, of course, redeeming native Americans was a legitimate goal. Those Indians who resisted Christian advances deserved to be treated as troops of the Devil.

With the exception of a few individuals, the first generation of settlers deeply distrusted the Indians around them. Uncertain of their numbers, whereabouts, or intentions, the Europeans were all too willing to suspect the worst. At bottom this anxiety bespoke the normal human fear of the unknown. To the Englishman the Indian, like his wilderness habitat, was wild, irrational, unpredictable—in a word, savage. As often happens, such fears ultimately became the basis of self-fulfilling prophecy, but in Massachusetts Bay that did not occur until much later in the century. In the meantime, settlers took every precaution to protect themselves from the danger that lurked beyond the pale. Selling guns and ammunition to Indians was strictly prohibited; trade was carefully regulated; natives were discouraged from moving in and out of white settlements. In short, day-to-day relationships between the two races were kept to a minimum. Under such circumstances it should not be surprising that most settlers remained fearful of the unknown native. When efforts to Christianize the heathen seemed to lag, pessimists cited the failure as evidence of Satan's continuing mastery over them. The resisting Indian was fair game for destruction, for his very resistance revealed his true allegiance to Satan. To expect Puritans to live in peaceful coexistence with such neighbors demanded too much. Like the wilderness itself, savagism would have to give way to civilization. Otherwise, only one unthinkable outcome could result—the triumph of savagism over civilization.

4

COMMUNITY LIFE

Edmund Rice, lately of Berkhamsted, Hertfordshire, knew that to survive in the wilderness, to reform the church, and to secure a decent subsistence, he and his fellow immigrants had to preserve their unity. The keynote that John Winthrop had sounded on board the *Arbella* in 1630—that "we must be knit together as one man in this work"—must have rung in Rice's ears as he crossed the Atlantic a few years later with his wife and nine children to settle at Watertown. Unity meant well-organized towns and congregations and families, but unity also required that individuals subordinate their own interests and values to those of the whole. Failure to do so would result in a weakening of church and society, perhaps even its total disintegration. But for men like Edmund Rice the opportunities offered by migration occasionally overweighed the obligation to remain a part of an established community. Twice again after coming to America, Edmund Rice would move, each time to towns he himself helped to found—to Sudbury in 1638, to Marlborough in 1660. Through a "budding" process familiar to horticulturists, one community produced others, until by the end of the seventeenth century scores of towns encompassing hundreds of square miles would compose the colony of Massachusetts Bay. How could the principle of unity survive in the face of the seemingly superior principle of growth?

When Edmund Rice landed in Watertown around 1637, he discovered that the community already considered itself full, or nearly so; recent comers like himself had arrived too late to receive a freehold grant from the town's founders. They were faced with the disagreeable alternative of either purchasing an estate or remaining landless. Few men were so committed to the principle of unity as to accept such a choice, especially when they saw vacant land stretching so far into the horizon around them. Land was the key to all that was necessary and worthwhile in life. A man needed his own for the support of his family and to give him standing in his community and a voice in its affairs. The proposition that an individual not only could but should possess a part of the earth's surface and all the natural life on it was the very basis of the society that was growing up around Massachusetts Bay. So it had been in the Old World as well, but there the limited amount of available land prohibited most men from realizing the goal of ownership. In the New World a man could dare to dream of possessing his own estate.

Beyond the practical fruits of possession lay other considerations. Ownership implied control; and mastery over even a small part of the natural world enhanced man's self-esteem and appeared to fulfill the Biblical commandment to "subdue the earth." Furthermore, such possession more sharply identified the owner as a resident of a particular community, or of a singular part of that community. Thus a resident of the "Clapboard Trees" section of Dedham, for instance, acquired the image of being somewhat different from those who lived, say, in the village. Stereotypes, to be sure, but stereotypes generate their own dimensions of reality. And so the quest for land in the New World would give to Edmund Rice and thousands like him far more than security and position. It would help him to fulfill his role as a Christian and in the process add new definition to his very being.

The process of establishing a town varied somewhat in detail, for no official guide existed to instruct would-be founders along the proper path, but within a decade after 1630 a general pattern had begun to emerge as a model for the future. First a group of settlers, usually numbering thirty or forty adult males who were discontented with some aspect of their previous residence, petitioned the General Court for a grant of land for the purpose of founding a new community. In making such a grant, the court generally gave leaders of the group considerable latitude in selecting the site, so long as it was not too distant from existing communities. Defense against Indians, social cohesiveness, and religious conformity all argued in favor of a cautious plan of expansion. An exploratory committee for the new group looked for an unoccupied region well endowed with natural meadowland, ample water, good woodland, and accessibility to the more settled parts of the colony. Such a tract might include about forty square miles, although the founders of Dedham received a grant five times as large.

Any Indian claims to the area had next to be extinguished, generally through a treaty negotiated by the General Court. Much has been written of the heavy-handedness by which English settlers dealt with Indian claims. Unquestionably the white man was determined to possess these lands with or without the consent of the natives, but the evidence is strong that, in New England at least, newcomers legalized the transaction by purchasing the land, usually with such trade goods as the metal tools the Indians badly wanted. At the time the natives seemed to consider such an exchange of scarce metalware for a part of their own vast holdings a fair trade, especially as they were customarily permitted to continue hunting and fishing in the unoccupied parts of their former territory. Puritans of the seventeenth century would have strenuously denied any conscious intention of cheating the natives. The fact that the Indians' growing dependence on European goods directly contributed to the ultimate breakdown of their society was a result that neither whites nor Indians could anticipate. Nor could it have been prevented short of wholesale withdrawal of whites back to the Old World.

With a clear title to their grant, leaders of the proposed town next drew up a covenant setting out the principles upon which their new community was to be founded. Dedham's covenant was perhaps typical for the period. First came a commitment to Christian love as the governing principle of the intended inhabitants' daily lives. Secondly, the covenanters agreed to "receive only such unto us as may be probably of one heart with us" in their determination to lead godly lives. There would be no room in Dedham for dissenters or malcontents. In the realization that differences would inevitably arise even among loving men and women, the next section of the covenant provided for the mediation of disputes by impartial third parties. On a still more practical level, the fourth part of the covenant pledged the property owners in the town to pay their share of the public costs and to obey all laws and ordinances adopted to further the peace and orderly progress of the community. Men received into the town at its founding were to sign the document not only for themselves but for their successors forever. The principles upon which Dedham was founded were therefore intended to continue in perpetuity.

With the covenant prepared, the founders of the new town turned to the difficult task of selecting men to join them in the undertaking. Those applicants residing in the old town or nearby might be known well enough, but what of the young man from Salem or the older one freshly

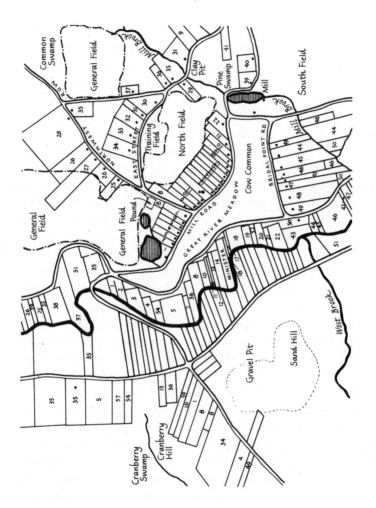

Sudbury, Mass., during the 1640s. From Sumner C. Powell, *Puritan Village* . . . (1963). Courtesy of the Wesleyan University Press.

arrived from England? Did he agree with the proposed method of distributing land? Was he a man of some substance in his previous community? Why had he left? Was he a church member? Answers to these and other searching questions could best be discovered by personal interview. As each man was accepted into the group, he owned the covenant and earned the right to examine subsequent candidates. It was not entirely a buyer's market, for every town needed certain individuals and was prepared to offer extra land to an inspiring minister, an experienced miller, and perhaps a skilled blacksmith. Gradually the numbers increased until at last the limit was reached, a number determined perhaps by the house lots available or by an estimate of how many families the land might initially support.

Meanwhile began the difficult task of "ordering" the town, the process by which inhabitants acquired their land. Once again precedents were scarce, alternatives were plentiful, and critical decisions had to be made by imperfect men. A land committee had already made a more precise survey of the town's grant. Its members chose a suitable location for the village center, if possible on a site that could be easily defended, perhaps alongside a river as in the case of Newbury, or on the top of a gentle rise, as in Deerfield. An adequate water supply was another requirement. The basic choice of land system between "open field" and "enclosed," or some combination of the two, had probably been made by the original petitioners in favor of the system they had been accustomed to in the old country. Each plan had its own particular advantages. Open fields meant that scarce equipment could be shared, labor pooled, and the cohesiveness of the community preserved because some of the land was set aside for all to cultivate cooperatively. But it often demanded a greater spirit of cooperation than many men were capable of sustaining. Except for his house lot, a man's holdings were scattered about in several areas around the perimeter of the village. An enclosed system, on the other hand, by granting individual plots of one hundred or more acres, quickly led to the dispersal of population as men moved out from their village houses to take up residence on their tillable acreage.

Finally came the actual division of the land according to the system agreed upon. The committee which had examined applicants for admission assigned each successful candidate a specific place within the group. In Sudbury, for instance, the minister Edmund Brown was ranked number one, a wealthy investor came second, the miller third. Edmund

Rice held eighth position, perhaps on the strength of his position in his former village of Berkhamsted. These rankings usually determined the size and location of one's lands within the town, leading citizens receiving the more favorable grants. Thus Edmund Rice received a fine four-acre house lot fronting the central Commons on Mill Road, thirty-three acres of river meadow, and fifty-four acres of upland across the river. He also received strips of the open fields, and since only a small proportion of the town's grants was initially distributed, Rice could look forward to shares of future divisions. By right of being an original settler Rice became one of the town's proprietors, who exercised exclusive control over all common lands. Later arrivals to the town might qualify to vote in town meeting, but they could become proprietors only by invitation or by the purchase of a proprietor's share. Now a vacant tract of wilderness was about to become a new town within the colony of Massachusetts Bay.

With the initial distribution of the land completed, the first inhabitants could at last move out to their new grants. Here they raised crude houses on the lots around the central commons, began the long process of clearing common fields and their own upland plots for cultivation, and started to fence in the pasture lands to restrain their livestock. In the succeeding months the residents would also establish a church and a town government.

*   *   *

As in the ordering of the town, the gathering of a church followed no hard and fast rules. Dedham's experience is probably representative of the procedure followed in many of the earliest communities. Most of the first inhabitants were from different parts of the old country and strangers to each other. Those desiring to form a church—initially a group of about eight or ten in Dedham, for instance—began with a series of informal meetings held at each of their houses, in turn, to become better acquainted and to exchange ideas. Here they formulated a number of questions and propositions by which they could examine themselves and others in more particular detail. A statement of the "duties of Christian love" headed the list. Because of man's spiritual weakness they recognized the need for external support that only an established church could provide. This church was to consist of "visible saints and believers agreeing to live together in spiritual communion." A profession of faith and "the fruit of it" constituted visible evidence of the inner grace a man needed to qualify for church membership. These men were then to bind themselves to God by a covenant which each would own. The list of propositions ended as it had begun, with another commitment to the principle of brotherly love.

A cynic might assume that all the members of the original group, having devised the rules of the game, would surely make the starting team. But in Dedham only six of the first ten initially qualified for church membership, though one of the others was soon after admitted along with a newcomer to town. The founding members then offered themselves to the whole town for examination. Those who met this further test appointed a day "to make our public profession and enter into solemn covenant with the Lord and one another" in the presence of ministers and elders from other communities. Once again questions were invited but no challenge was raised. With the covenant accepted, therefore, the new church was born, and its eight members could get on with the tasks of calling a minister, electing officers, examining additional saints for membership, and constructing a meetinghouse. In the succeeding months forty-eight people were admitted as members, almost equally divided among men and women, including four servants and representing well over half of the town's thirty-five families. And by the end of the church's first decade three-fourths of the families of the town had at least one church member.

In what would become known as the congregational form of church government, the religious society thus formed in Dedham had only the most informal ties with similar churches in other communities. The attendance of pastors from neighboring towns and perhaps one or two magistrates at the owning of the covenant and ordination of the pastor conveyed the only approval necessary for the proceedings. Authority to call, ordain, and dismiss pastors rested with the church members themselves, led by their regularly elected deacons and other officers. These principles were spelled out in the so-called Cambridge Platform drawn up by Richard Mather and others in 1648 to guide future church founders.

The establishment of town government was authorized by the General Court in 1635, and numerous towns took advantage of this opportunity to regularize their local political affairs. Like so many other institutions in Massachusetts, the "town meeting" began as a meeting of the townspeople and became institutionalized after the fact. The procedure rarely followed a set pattern, but a common structure soon emerged nevertheless, although marked by local differences. Scores of historians have attempted to trace the New England town to one or another root source, but the founders probably drew upon a rich variety of sources— their experience in English village government, the requirements of a wilderness environment, and their own particular vision of the future. Underlying the whole undertaking was an abiding sense of the need for unity, cooperation, and order. The task was not an easy one, as seen in Dorchester. Like many communities in Massachusetts Bay, Dorchester's local government had functioned since its establishment in 1630 through regular meetings of most of the town's adult males. By 1645, however, disorderly town meetings necessitated the establishment of specific bylaws.

Dorchester's "platform of government," as it was called, combined a set of traditional practices with new expectations. The bylaws provided first for an annual town meeting in April to elect seven selectmen and other officials needed to manage the town's affairs. At this meeting grievances were aired, alterations made in the bylaws if necessary, and other matters concerning the town's liberty and power discussed. The bylaws gave the selectmen broad powers to execute local ordinances. They had authority to settle disputes among inhabitants, supervise the work of lesser officials, keep the town's financial accounts, and maintain orderly procedures at town meetings. The selectmen were to meet at least eight times a year (monthly except during April, July, August, and October) to hear complaints and to conduct their regular business. Any inhabitant who dared to slight either the officers or their orders was subject to a stiff penalty, a provision clearly reflecting previous difficulty in this respect.

In adopting these bylaws Dorchester's town meeting delegated considerable authority to the selectmen. For the remainder of the seventeenth century, in fact, the greater share of political power in many towns rested in the hands of these chosen leaders. Within a few months after adoption of the bylaws in Dorchester the selectmen prepared a set of rules to assure the orderly conduct of all town meetings. Any freeman who failed to attend such a meeting without good excuse was fined sixpence. There was to be no speaking out of turn, nor any private janglings on the side, nor any other confusion. One of the selectmen serving as moderator would see to that. Nor could any freeman leave the meeting without the selectmen's approval, nor would any other inattention to the business at hand be brooked. Furthermore, no motions or other proposals could be made from the floor without the prior knowledge of the selectmen.

In most communities the selectmen held the initiative in political affairs, conducting more business and meeting more often than at the town meetings. The latter body served primarily as a check on the selectmen, choosing them each year and usually approving their actions. Yet even here the role was passive, for most incumbents easily gained reelection almost at will. In the period from 1636 to 1689, 43 percent of Dedham's selectmen had served more than seven years. In Sudbury, Edmund Rice was among five men who sat on the board of selectmen for at least eleven of the town's first eighteen years. Such experienced men enhanced still further the respect accorded the office. A small group of men likewise dominated the influential minor offices of the town. The same five men in Sudbury, for instance, held a total of sixty-four other posts, which along with the selectmen's seats meant that each of the five occupied an average of 1.4 posts per year throughout the period 1638–1655. It must be recognized, on the other hand, that during the same period 52 percent of the eligible adult males served as selectmen for at least one year, and an even greater percentage held other offices. At the very outset frequent meetings of the town as a whole settled most of the major issues. Then, as men turned increasingly to their own efforts to break land, build homes, and fence fields, they left community decisions in the hands of trusted leaders. This pattern continued in most Massachusetts towns for several decades, until the first generation of settlers had passed and internal differences brought unaccustomed tensions to the communities of the commonwealth.

Much of the time the inhabitants of individual towns must have felt that the struggle they waged for survival depended solely on their own efforts. In fact, however, few communities stood entirely isolated from the rest of the colony. Most were contiguous with other towns and upon incorporation sent deputies to the General Court. It was the court, too, that delegated the major share of political power to the local level, so that the inhabitants drew up their own bylaws, organized their own church, raised their own taxes, and made most of their own political decisions free from outside interference. As a new town gained in strength, still more rights and duties devolved upon it from the General Court. Colony taxes were to be assessed and collected, militia officers chosen, and a trainband organized. Each of these functions implied that the town was after all part of a larger commonwealth. Nothing emphasized this interdependence in the new communities more than did the threat of Indian attack. When total war did come in 1675 each town depended upon the alertness and courage of its neighbors, and the old adage about the strength of a chain took on special significance. Unity meant more than local solidarity; it required an awareness of the community beyond. And survival sometimes depended upon it.

*   *   *

The myth that the first English inhabitants in America lived in log cabins died hard at the hands of Harold R. Shurtleff many years ago, but aside from architectural specialists only those Americans who have visited Plimoth Plantation, Salem's Pioneer Village, and similar restorations have had a clear idea of what early colonial housing was actually like. The fact that early settlers lived in dugouts, wigwams, and daub-and-wattle cabins has been difficult for succeeding generations of romantic Americans to accept. The more substantial cottages with their clapboard siding, timbered chimneys, and thatched or planked roofs, which began to dominate the scene after the first decade or two of settlement, seem more in keeping with popular views of the past, although the dirt floors and tiny chambers remain hard to envision.

Architectural historians apparently now agree that there was no typical seventeenth-century house in Massachusetts Bay; but most surviving examples seem to have evolved from a common beginning—the one-room dwelling with massive stone chimney at one end, a small entranceway or "porch," and a stairway leading to the sleeping loft above. The entire floor plan might encompass a space twenty to twenty-five feet long and perhaps sixteen or eighteen feet wide. A more affluent family could build a two-room house, with a parlor added at the other side of what then became a central chimney with two fireplaces. Occasionally one-room houses were later expanded in this fashion, but the task was difficult. As his family grew in size or affluence the settler might well add to the back of his two-room house a lean-to which accommodated a large kitchen behind the center chimney (a bake oven and fireplace having

John Ward House, Salem, 1685. Courtesy of the Essex Institute, Salem, Mass.

been added) and two chambers at either end of the addition. The lean-to also provided increased sleeping space upstairs under the eaves. This construction lengthened the back roof of the original building and has been popularly known as the "saltbox" style. By the end of the seventeenth century numerous new houses were built with the lean-to an integral part of the original structure, but there were many families still so poor that they could afford no more than the simple one- and two-room dwellings of the earlier generations.

Enough seventeenth-century frame houses have survived in Massachusetts to make the details of their construction readily observable. Siting the house on the lot came first: on a slight knoll to assure good drainage and a dry cellar; close to the road for accessibility; front facing south if possible for maximum warmth in winter and to put the sloping rear roof toward the north wind. Building a two-story house required the cooperation of a number of men. First the cellar hole was dug and fieldstone walls laid up on the dirt floor. Next came the heavy oak sills, squared like the other timbers by broad axe and adze to the desired size. Front and rear walls were assembled flat on the ground, then raised into place by as many men as necessary. Corner posts had already been mortised to receive the tenoned end girts, which were locked into place with treenails to hold the front and back walls erect. Floor joists, chimney girts, and summer beams gave further strength to the frame, to which was finally added roof rafters, studs, and other light pieces.

For siding most builders in Massachusetts used clapboards—long narrow boards rived out of cedar or pine logs and fastened directly onto the studs with an inch or so of overlap. By the end of the century, however, shingles nailed to board sheathing became more common and a few houses in less exposed locations had only rough plaster walls. Thatched roofs of earlier houses gradually gave way to shingles, too. The massive center chimney took up considerable space in the cellar and ground floor, before tapering into a narrower stack as it emerged through the roof. The scarcity of good lime in Massachusetts forced most masons to bind the fieldstones with a clay mortar. Expensive brick was reserved for the exposed chimney top. In addition to the large kitchen fireplace and bake oven each downstairs room and at least one upstairs chamber had its own fireplace as well. A smoke hole for curing meats was often added to the chimney where it passed through the garret.

As prosperity increased throughout Massachusetts Bay in the last quarter of the seventeenth century, home builders could afford numerous refinements unobtainable to earlier generations. The cost of glass had kept windows to a minimum in both size and number, but now they became more common. Plain wainscot and primitive plaster walls gave way to fancy woodwork, boxed timbers, and fine lime plaster walls. Decorative touches were added too: fine molding and in some cases paneling; a carved handrail with turned newel post and balusters for the front staircase. Furniture, too, was at first expensive and therefore simple, much of it heavy and solid and rarely upholstered. Toward the end of the century chairs and tables became somewhat more decorative, and one might find an occasional piece imported from England in some of the finer homes. Candles and simple grease lamps provided woefully inadequate lighting, and the only source of heat was the fire that glowed in the several hearths. The free-standing stove and oil lamp would not be introduced until later in the next century.

In the ordering of most Massachusetts towns, the founders selected the site for the first habitation with considerable care. In some cases house lots were laid out around a central green or common. But sometimes terrain or other considerations required that the town be planned along a single central street, one end of which might lead into an open market square. Complementing the dwellings constructed in the heart of the village were several other buildings of importance—the meetinghouse, the parsonage, a school, tavern, several shops, and perhaps one or two garrison houses for defense against Indian attacks. The green itself was usually left as open space on which to muster the local militia, graze livestock, or simply enhance the village prospect. In many towns construction had to conform to certain regulations. Some enforced a minimum setback rule; others regulated the size of dwellings or the materials used. No one seemed to argue with the necessity for such rules. Most towns prescribed the pattern of streets as well as their width and other characteristics. Only a few villages developed helter-skelter without any plan at all, but the topography of a town like Boston, say, surely gives credence to the popular myth that cows rather than people laid out most of the original streets.

The essence of seventeenth-century Massachusetts life lay not so much in the village center as in the land around it. Whatever else we should know about these men and women in their scores of little villages, we must come to sense their closeness to the soil: each day determined not by the whims of man but by the requirements of nature; each year given to the planting, cultivation, and harvesting of the fields according to a schedule not of man's making but of the seasons; a lifetime devoted to the gradual acquisition and clearing of land whose worth reached far beyond a lifetime into the future. Each day's labor was an integral part of the year's endeavors, and each year became a part of a lifetime goal. As a man worked for his own survival, so, too, he worked for his children and for their children. At the end of a lifetime of toil he might have little in the way of worldly goods to pass along, but he did leave his land to mark the essential achievement of his being. The home lot itself, with house and barn, garden and orchard; pastures carefully fenced by stone or rail; the upland cleared of stumps and under cultivation; the forest beyond waiting its turn to be subdued.

Such as we were we gave ourselves outright
. . .
To the land vaguely realizing westward.*

The center of family life was the farm. At first scattered about in several parcels, the typical seventeenth-century farmer forsook his village home as soon as practicable and settled anew on some larger lot of land closer to his major holdings. A kitchen garden under the watchful care of the wife yielded beans, cabbage, and other fresh vegetables in season and a variety of produce for winter keeping in the root cellar. Nearby the farmer might have planted a number of fruit trees. Now apples, pears, cherries, and plums could be enjoyed in the summer and early fall, with enough left over for preserves as well as sweet and hard cider. Outbuildings with various yards and pens for livestock and poultry completed the usual home-lot arrangements.

The fortunate farmer possessed among his grants several acres of natural meadow of abandoned Indian fields. If so, he could graze his livestock and put in an initial crop of corn or grain without much preparation. But most of his land was likely to have been heavily forested. Here, of course, was a plentiful supply of wood for his fireplace, for fencing, and for the construction of his dwelling place and outbuildings. But as families increased or as old fields lost their meager fertility, it

---

* Robert Frost, "The Gift Outright."

became necessary to clear new lands. Large trees had best be girdled first, then felled. Timber not needed or unsuitable for other purposes was burned along with the underbrush to enrich the soil. Next came one of the most difficult tasks—removing the stumps. Grubbing around the roots helped to loosen the soil, but sometimes several teams of oxen were required to haul out the remains. Then came another onerous task of digging out the rocks and large stones which seemed to grow like weeds in New England. Even so the first ploughing was no easy matter. Oxen had to work a heavy plow through the tough topsoil, entangled roots, and deep stump holes before the farmer could plant his first field crops. A hard-working landowner with a good yoke might be able to clear one or two acres each year without neglecting his other duties. A man could not help but become part of the land that he himself brought from wilderness to cultivation.

Once cleared, the fields were ready for their first crops. Indian corn, wheat, and rye were the most common, although peas and beans, oats, barley, and other grains were also raised in considerable quantity. Calculations based on Plymouth records show that in the 1640s an acre of land could produce eighteen bushels of corn worth £2 3s. When sown to wheat, however, an acre of typical Massachusetts soil yielded only eight bushels, and other grains fared no better. The inventory of a Plymouth farmer who died in 1650 discloses total holdings of about 30 acres, of which 5½ were planted to corn, 2½ to wheat, 2½ to rye, and 1 to peas. The balance of his land supplied his timber and served as pasture for his livestock. This ratio of one acre cultivated in every three owned was typical for a mid-seventeenth-century farm, but during the next two generations the ratio increased to two acres under the plow in every three.

Various breeds of English and European cattle provided milk and beef for the family. Oxen were a necessity, as we have already seen, and so was the family horse. Sheep and goats provided wool, mutton, and milk, and pigs were a common source of meat because they could fend for themselves and reproduced at a prodigious rate. Chickens, ducks, and geese provided meat and eggs for the table with little trouble. For much of the year the farmer could let his livestock run free in pasture, but pigs had a bad habit of breaking loose and raising havoc in the garden areas. During the winter most of the farm animals were kept close by in the yard and were fed whatever oats, hay, and other grains the farmer had stored for the purpose. Autumn was the usual season for slaughtering, the meats being hung, smoked, or salted down for winter consumption.

To work his farm the owner required three basic tools—a plow, a harrow, and some sort of cart. Most seventeenth-century plows found in Massachusetts were simple wooden implements with an iron coulter to cut the soil ahead of the plowshare. The harrow consisted of several heavy timbers in the form of a rectangle or triangle mounting a number of iron spikes to break up the soil. Most carts were simple two-wheeled vehicles which could carry various cargoes both material and human. Without a sturdy cart no farmer could manure his fields or harvest his crop. In addition to these major items were a wide variety of rakes, shovels, hoes, scythes, and other hand tools which the farmer could make himself.

In Plymouth Colony the fields were often dry by the middle of March so that the husbandman could get his plowing done and first plantings in by the middle of May. In interior regions, however, the farmers had to contend with a prolonged mud season, which often delayed plowing until late April or beyond. During the summer months the yeoman concentrated on getting in a good hay crop, and in a long summer he might well make two hayings. By the end of August it was time to begin harvesting the wheat and other grains. Corn, pumpkins, and winter squash were left till last. Through the darkening autumn weeks the family husked the corn, threshed the wheat, and put up preserves for the winter. The yield was disappointing by English standards, only eight or ten bushels of wheat per acre, and eighteen bushels of corn. The soil was thin, and the early settlers had neither the time nor the incentive to experiment with new techniques to increase productivity. There was plenty of land, after all. No need to devote scarce time and labor to intensify the yield from a few acres. The American way to greater production was to cultivate more land.

Despite their inefficient methods, the farmers of Massachusetts soon produced more foodstuffs than their families could consume. And as succeeding generations grew to adulthood and put more acreage under the plow, the aggregate surplus grew still larger each year. At first the steady stream of newcomers into the province depended upon these foodstuffs for survival, but emigration fell off sharply after 1640 and new markets had to be found. By mid-century Boston was becoming an entrepôt for a number of neighboring communities as far away as Ipswich, Concord, and Dedham. Farmers found a growing market for a variety of country produce, particularly beef and pork, wheat, firewood, shingles, and staves. Even a farmer as far inland as William Pynchon at Springfield sent 1,500 bushels of grain to Boston in 1652. The merchants then exported much of this produce overseas to the West Indies, the Azores, and other Atlantic islands, and to Spain. Taking their profits in sugar, wines, or bills of exchange, the shipmasters then called at London or Bristol to purchase return cargoes of woolens and other manufactures. By the second half of the century, then, the average farmer of Massachusetts Bay was acquiring the means to purchase some of the goods that could raise his standard of living beyond the level of bare subsistence.

* * *

Men living close together at the edge of the wilderness were bound to disagree and occasionally quarrel about numerous matters large and small. The towns of Massachusetts Bay were no exception. Community leaders exerted their best efforts to reconcile differences and to maintain a consensus within the town. This goal was sought not for the sake of some abstract principle like democracy but rather for the practical purpose of maintaining unity. For disunity, dissension, disorder were but different names for what Puritans feared most—the disintegration and ultimate collapse of their endeavor to establish a New Zion in the wilderness. Thus it was that wherever men gathered to discuss their common affairs—in private homes, on the streets of the village, in the taverns— the men of the community strove to hammer out differences and find a consensus upon which all could agree. In town meetings, the historian Michael Zuckerman has written, "they legitimized those agreements, so that subsequent deviation . . . became socially illegitimate and personally immoral as well, meaning as it did the violation of a covenant or the breaking of a promise."*

For a while it worked. After all, the founders of the town had examined each applicant before accepting him into the group. He had to own the covenant by which he agreed to the community's basic principles. This was a process that worked both ways, for it gave the prospective inhabitant an opportunity to size up the new town as well; no one

---

* Michael Zuckerman, *Peaceable Kingdoms: New England Towns in the Eighteenth Century* (New York, 1970), 94.

would wish to move into a community with potentially incompatible neighbors. If a miscalculation had been made despite these precautions, the individual was free to move on to another town, or he could be warned out by the selectmen. Control over church membership offered another way to protect the community from dissidents. Antisocial behavior met with immediate chastisement from the elders; persistent wrongdoing resulted in the spiritual and social ostracism of excommunication. Not many men had the strength of will to continue marching to a different drum under such circumstances—at least not many men of the first generation.

But in the long run consensus politics were doomed to failure, for they could not cope successfully with the dynamics of growth and expansion. What happened in Edmund Rice's town of Sudbury in the middle decades of the seventeenth century illustrates the kind of problems most communities had to face sooner or later. First came a relatively minor squabble over the need for a new meetinghouse to accommodate the increased numbers of inhabitants eager to participate in town affairs. Next was a major showdown on a long-postponed task of dividing a two-mile grant of land given the town by the General Court in 1649. Conservatives led by most of the selectmen proposed a division based on the assessment of estates and the size of families then resident in the town. Such a procedure would have favored the established leaders at the expense of more recent arrivals and younger people. The plan was roundly defeated. A countersuggestion that the new land be distributed in equal portions "to every man" was overwhelmingly adopted the next day. But the conservative selectmen held a few cards of their own. They refused to carry out the new plan and struck back at the dissident group by ordering that thereafter the number of livestock each inhabitant could graze on the commons land be proportionate to his original meadow grant. Those with small holdings or none at all would thereby find themselves seriously handicapped. "If you oppresse the poore, they will cry out," one of the victims complained as the town met to consider whether to approve this action. "If you persecute us in one city, we must fly to another." Now it was out in the open; the sacred principle of community was threatened as never before. Each voter then signified his position in favor or against by standing at one end or the other of the meetinghouse, physically demonstrating the end of consensus politics in Sudbury. A tie vote led immediately to bitter wrangling over technicalities of the procedure itself, and another vote could not take place. But at the next election only one of the conservative selectmen retained his seat. In a few months the new board set aside the offending order regarding the commons and proceeded to divide the new grant into equal lots according to the will of the majority.

But victory for the liberals came at the cost of the community itself. The fact that the pastor, Edmund Brown, actively supported the conservatives and refused to accept the verdict of the electorate led eventually to a boycott by many of the liberals of church lectures and services. When Brown called upon neighboring pastors to investigate the dispute, townspeople became still further provoked. They did everything they could to hamper the proceedings, but to no avail. The council of visitors leveled ten specific charges against John Ruddock, the liberals' leader, and judged the cancellation of the previous selectmen's order concerning the Commons to be "A GREAT SIN." Another investigating group, this one from the General Court itself, made further findings in favor of the conservatives. The stalemate seemed more hopeless than ever.

Throughout the dispute Edmund Rice tried to steer a middle course. He abstained from several of the polarizing votes, perhaps in hope of establishing some basis for consensus, but in vain. When John Ruddock invited him to join in a petition to the General Court for land on which to establish a new town, Rice agreed. In 1656 the court obliged with a grant of about thirty-six square miles to the west of Sudbury. Ruddock, Rice, and thirteen others thereupon began once again the long process of establishing a new community in the wilderness, which in 1660 became the town of Marlborough. The land was indeed, in Frost's words, "vaguely realizing westward."

5

ZION IN THE WILDERNESS

The Reverend Richard Mather, of Toxteth Park, Lancashire, found himself, like so many other English Puritan ministers, in deep trouble. For refusing to conform to the doctrines and procedures of the Church of England, he was suspended from his parish in 1633 and again the following year. Like so many of his fellow Puritans Mather finally concluded that only in New England could he do the Lord's work according to his conscience. In the spring of 1635, therefore, he sailed on board the *James* for Massachusetts Bay. A gale of wind nearly wrecked the vessel on the Isles of Shoals, but by God's "overruling providence" they sailed out of danger and reached Boston in mid-August. Mather was not the first Puritan to regard his salvation from a storm at sea as a sign that God wanted him to reach New England safely in order to do His work.

The following spring Richard Mather became the minister of the parish of Dorchester. He shared in the struggle to gather a church of regenerate members out of the worldly settlers in the town and served the parish for thirty-three years, until his death in 1669. Mather and his wife, Katherine, served the Lord in another way as well, for the couple had six sons, including Increase Mather, born in Dorchester in 1639, who in turn became the father of Cotton Mather (1663–1728). Altogether these three generations of Mathers provided nearly a century of firm leadership to the people of Massachusetts Bay. Only the Winthrop and Adams families could match their extraordinary contributions.

*   *   *

That part of the new world to which Mather and other English Puritans immigrated in the first half of the seventeenth century has been labeled

by academic and popular historians alike as "Puritan New England."
The paired implications that only Puritans settled there and that they
settled nowhere else in America are equally misleading. Puritans could
be found in most of the other colonies, and many New Englanders made
no claim to being Puritan in their religious beliefs. Part of the historian's
problem is one of definition. Indeed, Americans have always had difficulty defining Puritanism. For a people who have separated religion
from their own daily lives as completely as have most present-day Americans, Puritans naturally seem uniquely obsessed by religious conviction.
Yet for most Europeans of the seventeenth century, whether Catholics,
Lutherans, or Jews, religious faith provided a central core for their existence; in this respect Puritans merely expressed the religious commitment of their own time. They have been criticized as a people who could
not or would not enjoy themselves and consequently tried to prevent
everyone else from having any fun. And yet the most superficial study of
Puritan communities has revealed the inappropriateness of this interpretation. Perhaps most inaccurate is the view that Puritans spent all of
their time spinning fine theological arguments in preference to con-
templating more worldly issues.

Many paths lead to an understanding of Puritanism in seventeenth-
century Massachusetts, and no one explanation can possibly account for
all of the variations in doctrine and practice which different Puritans
emphasized at different times throughout the period. To begin with the
major religious concern of the Christian era—the question of personal
salvation—Puritans accepted the Biblical evidence of man's fall from
grace. Firsthand observation of their own society permitted them no
illusions that they had succeeded in driving sin out of Massachusetts Bay,
and any one of them with a pinch of candor recognized that despite all
effort his own life left a continuing trail of sinful actions and attitudes.
No doubt some men led more exemplary lives than others, but neither
good deeds nor devout stances could offset an individual's burden of sin.

Like almost all formal religious beliefs, Puritanism embodied an explanation of life after death which gave the sect a distinct flavor. Although no man deserved salvation, Puritans maintained, God had nevertheless before the beginning of time selected some to be saved as a manifestation of his mercy. God called these men out of their natural state of
sin and death to eternal life, "enlightening their minds spiritually and
savingly to understand the things of God, taking away their

heart of stone . . . , renewing their wills . . . , and determining them to that which is good. . . ." Man was helpless to predict this call or in any way to bring it about, but "being quickened and renewed by the Holy Spirit,"* he was able to respond to the call. The sins of the elect were pardoned, and they became "justified" as righteous persons, not because of their own conduct but because Christ by His sacrifice on the Cross has endured their punishment for them. Thereafter, with God's help, they were given the strength to struggle more successfully than others against sin both within themselves and in those around them. Although the elect could never fall from this state of sanctification, failure to lead godly lives brought God's displeasure upon them, and they became deprived of His holy light until they confessed their sins and renewed their faith.

Even if man had no power to earn his way to salvation, devout Puritans like Richard Mather and his son Increase firmly believed that man should nevertheless prepare himself to receive God's grace no matter how great the odds against his being among the elect. This doctrine of preparation, as it was called, required that men give careful study to the Bible, attend divine services and lectures, constantly resist the incursion of sin into their own lives and communities, and pray for forgiveness. By undergoing a prolonged period of humiliation the individual thus prepared himself for God's grace in case he had been chosen to receive it. This period of preparation has been aptly compared in its psychological aspects to the training undertaken by athletes. Most will never become champions no matter how hard they train because they simply do not possess the innate skills required. Maddeningly enough to ordinary people, a few highly talented individuals set records without any training whatever. But despite these obviously discouraging aspects, most aspiring athletes train anyway, perhaps only because it is difficult for the ambitious man to assume a totally passive existence. And the Puritan was nothing if not ambitious in his religious life. But the doctrine of preparation opened seventeenth-century Puritans both at the time and ever after to the charge that preparation was but a thinly disguised doctrine of works. Increase Mather's own son Cotton was a strong opponent of preparation, maintaining that it encouraged the heresy known

---

* "Savoy Declaration," printed in Alden T. Vaughan, ed., *The Puritan Tradition in America, 1620–1730* (New York, 1972), 121–28.

as Arminianism—that man could earn salvation by his own efforts.

All three generations of Mathers (and other Puritans) could agree, however, that the most important step in the individual's religious progress was his conversion, or regeneration, as it was often called. Theologically speaking, conversion was the bestowal upon a person by God of those special powers which assisted him thereafter in his struggle to live a righteous life. From the individual's standpoint regeneration was his awareness of this gift, a conviction that in fact he was among the elect. Sometimes, as in the classic case of St. Paul, conversion came all of a sudden, usually in conjunction with some personal experience of traumatic dimensions. More often, especially for those who accepted the doctrine of preparation, regeneration came more slowly, as a gradual sense of one's own election, a process accompanied by periods of doubt and even despair, but invariably followed by ever-growing assurance. For Increase Mather it began with an illness he suffered at the age of fifteen and was intensified by his mother's death soon after. In the sanctified state that followed regeneration one had to continue striving for perfection despite the knowledge that only in afterlife could that goal be reached. One had to take care not to become so assured of election as to believe, as did Anne Hutchinson, that one could actually enter into direct communication with God. This was the heresy of Antinomianism (in some ways the opposite extreme to Arminianism) and like the Quaker doctrine of the "inner light" was roundly condemned by all good Puritans.

Fortunately, the believers did not have to pursue their quest alone, for although Puritanism emphasized individual salvation, it also called for a church instituted among the faithful. The essence of the Puritan church was the fact that it consisted of "visible saints," the regenerate of the community, who gave witness of their conversion to a committee of church elders. The importance of the church lay in its several functions. For one thing, it provided fellowship among like-minded individuals, strengthening their separate resolves to lead holy lives. The covenant of the church of Woburn, first owned in 1642, expressed this factor in clear language: "We that do assemble ourselves . . . from the bottom of our hearts agree together through His grace to give up ourselves, first unto the Lord Jesus . . . and therewith one unto another, as in a church body, to walk together in all the ordinances of the Gospel, and in all such mutual love and offices thereof, as toward one another in the Lord."

The institution of the church also provided the strong leadership which almost all religious sects of the seventeenth century deemed necessary. In calling Thomas Carter to be their pastor, the church members of Woburn chose a young man who would assist them in their religious lives by becoming a teacher and friend to them. Although they sought the advice and approval of other ministers in the area, the choice was finally their own; it was they alone who would support Carter, and they alone who could remove him from office if he proved unsatisfactory. The position of pastor and of other church officers was more clearly defined in the Cambridge Platform of 1648, principally drawn up by Richard Mather as a guide to church organization and government. The pastor's especial duty was "to attend to exhortation and therein to administer a word of wisdom." A separate teacher, "to attend to doctrine and therein to administer a word of knowledge," was also authorized but only the larger parishes could at first afford to support both positions. Distinct from the pastor and teacher were the elders, whose particular responsibility was the governance of the church. They ordained the officers, admitted (or excluded) members, kept a watchful eye on the lives of their fellow saints, and gave day-to-day direction to church affairs as required. Church deacons had special charge of financial matters including the minister's support, all of these officers to be freely elected by the church members. "Although churches be distinct . . . and therefore have not dominion one over another," the platform explained, "yet all the churches ought to preserve church communion one with another." Herein lay the essence of Congregationalism. The platform spelled out numerous ways in which this communion might be carried out while emphasizing the independence of each parish. Only a duly assembled synod, a meeting of elders and other delegates from the churches, could settle disputes between churches and establish common doctrine, as in the case of the Cambridge Synod itself, and even here the authority was advisory only. The power to correct any church that broke off from other churches or followed "any corrupt way of their own" lay with the governor.*

The absence of rigid ecclesiastical authority did not preclude a similar pattern of religious practices in the various local churches. Like-minded people tend to act alike, at least in those matters in which they agree. Each community constructed a meetinghouse as soon as it could,

---

* "Cambridge Platform," in Vaughan, *Puritan Tradition*, 98–114.

large enough to seat all of the members in family pews, or boxes, assigned at first in order of social rank. On Sundays two services were held, each begun with a prayer from the pastor and a chapter of Scripture from the teacher, followed by a psalm or two lined out by one of the elders. In the morning service the pastor then delivered a lengthy sermon on some theme found in whatever Biblical passage he selected as his text. In the afternoon the teacher, if there was one in the church, delivered the sermon; otherwise the pastor performed once more. Each service closed with another prayer. Most sermons followed the particular logical structure attributed to the French Huguenot martyr Petrus Ramus, consisting of a series of questions to which the preacher provided alternative answers and then pointed out why one of them was the preferred response. By such a construction the pastor could lead his listeners toward an ultimate conclusion which, it was hoped, they could agree rested on a series of examined truths and was therefore itself impeccable. The procedure appealed more to the intellectual than to the emotional aspect of the religious experience. Church services were not altogether devoid of ritual, however. Once a month the sacrament of the Lord's Supper was celebrated, as was the sacrament of baptism whenever the occasion arose. Special days of fasting and thanksgiving marked particular occurrences, such as a bountiful harvest or deliverance from some affliction like an epidemic or an Indian war. But as one commentator has pointed out, Puritanism was more preaching than praying.*

The church also gave its members a sense of direction and purpose beyond the problem of their own individual salvation. For the devout covenanted not only with each other, but together they covenanted with God to serve Him by establishing and maintaining His true church. Some historians, like Perry Miller, have emphasized the idea that Puritans believed they had been sent by God to the New World to erect a model community which Europeans could then imitate. John Winthrop seemed to have such a goal in mind when he said on board the *Arbella* that "we shall be as a city upon a hill, the eyes of all people are upon us," and that if successful, "men shall say of succeeding plantations, the Lord make it like that of New England." Other historians, among them Robert Middlekauff, have pointed out that Puritans like Richard Mather denied any special status for those who went to New England. "We do

---

* Vaughan, *Puritan Tradition*, 82–83.

not think ourselves to be the only prophets," Mather wrote to his old parish in England in 1645, "nor that we only are able to give a word of counsel or comfort to our countrymen: . . . such arrogant apprehensions are far from us." In part the difference lay in the obvious fact that not all Puritans agreed on every particular; then, too, the situation in England had changed between 1630 when Winthrop wrote and 1645, by which time revolution had broken out in the mother country. But Winthrop more than Mather sensed a greater separation between New and Old England. When Puritans in the mother country went their own way after 1642, ignoring and even criticizing the achievements of the emigrés, many New Englanders lost their sense of purpose along with their audience, but by the 1650s the founding generation was dying out, and the second generation was coming to maturity. For younger Puritans the mission would take on a more parochial dimension: they accepted the fact that New England had thereafter to stand alone, apart from the mother country both in purpose and in function.

*   *   *

If Puritanism embraced only concepts dealing with salvation and worship, few of its advocates would have left England for another land. Most English Puritans indeed did remain in the mother country, where they continued to worship much as they pleased with relatively little interference, by seventeenth-century standards at least. But to those who emigrated to Massachusetts Bay particularly, Puritanism had a larger meaning, one that proposed a model for society as a whole, not just for the religious institutions within society. The band of Puritans then coming to the New World had covenanted together to support each other in all reasonable ways. But beyond this covenant lay another, which the group collectively made with God to establish its new society under His laws in return for divine protection.

The essence of this new society lay in the word order. Once again John Winthrop's "Model of Christian Charity" clearly stated the heart of the idea. First, God created man in various orders, "some rich, some poor, some high and eminent in power and dignity, others mean and in subjection." The purpose for such an arrangement, Winthrop speculated, was the enhancement of mutual dependence, one upon another, that "they might all be knit more nearly together in the bond of brotherly affection." Differences among individuals came about, then, for the glory of God and the common good. This ordering of society in ranks led logically enough to the requirement that society remain orderly. It was in part the disorder of early seventeenth-century English society that prompted so many Puritans to emigrate elsewhere. Not only must each individual maintain firm control over his own life but so must the entire group remain orderly. And because weak individuals exposed the whole community either to incursions of the Devil or the angry chastisements of the Lord, how individuals behaved was the business of the community as a whole.

To maintain social order the community relied on three institutions: the church, the state, and the family. By "church," it should be emphasized, was meant a group of devout Puritans who voluntarily gathered together on the local level. Unlike most other states in the Western world of the seventeenth century Massachusetts Bay had no established church in the sense of a centralized institution enforcing an orthodox religious or social creed through a hierarchical structure. Throughout the colony there were churches aplenty, but no Church. The authority exercised by Puritan leaders depended entirely upon the consent of the localities in which they were located. Discipline was the business of the elders, not the minister, and in the end all leaders were held accountable to those they led. Furthermore, the scope of church authority extended only to the individual's relationship to the church, with excommunication the ultimate sanction. For those habitual offenders to whom such a punishment bore little stigma, the authority of the local church was obviously minimal. Church censure could not in fact deprive one of any civil office or power he might hold.

Many historians have argued, however, that the way in which the "Puritan Church" exercised authority over society was through its alleged control of the state. To make such a case one must ignore the overwhelming evidence not only that there was no such "Church" but also the fact that religious leaders were strictly prohibited from exercising political authority of any sort. Ministers could not hold seats in the General Court, for instance, nor could they effectually intervene in local affairs against the will of the inhabitants. When the Reverend Edmund Brown attempted to do so in Sudbury, as we have seen, he was firmly told to mind his own business. Civil authorities in practice exercised far greater influence in religious affairs than did religious leaders in matters of state. The governor, for instance, could and occasionally did chastise individual churches which seemed to wander from accepted doctrine.

Broadly defined, the state enjoyed sweeping powers of control over society as a whole. Each town could exclude from residence anyone it wished and could warn out those whose behavior was deemed offensive. Puritans did not undergo the hazards of an ocean crossing to share their new Zion with those they considered heretics. As Nathaniel Ward put it in his *Simple Cobler of Aggawam* (1647), "All Familists, Antinomians, Anabaptists, and other Enthusiasts, shall have free liberty to keep away from us, and such as will come to be gone as fast as they can, the sooner the better."* Such a fate befell Anne Hutchinson for denying the doctrine of preparation and asserting that God placed Himself directly within a saint (like herself) and thereafter guided his or her every action. When Mrs. Hutchinson testified that God had spoken directly to her, she was denounced as an Antinomian and was banished forthwith to Rhode Island. Other dissenters, particularly Baptists and Quakers, were sent packing for their beliefs by action of the civil magistrates. By the 1650s attitudes had so hardened that Sir Richard Saltonstall, who had been one of the first settlers in Massachusetts Bay but who had since returned to England, sharply criticized his former colonists for their religious intolerance.

In the first decades of the colony several efforts were made to bring under one head the various laws then governing the province. One such effort, *The Body of Liberties,* written by Nathaniel Ward in final form in 1641, resembled a bill of rights for both institutions and individuals rather than a code of laws. Then in 1647 the General Court appointed several committees composed of both civil and ecclesiastical leaders to draw up a set of laws for the commonwealth. The labors of these groups resulted in *The Laws and Liberties of 1648,* the first modern code of laws in the Western world. Fully one-third of the statutes were formulated by the committee members themselves, and another third had been enacted by the General Court while the committees were at their work, so that the result was largely innovative. The principle of an orderly society appeared throughout *The Laws and Liberties* but perhaps nowhere so clearly as in the preface or epistle addressed to the populace:

* Nathaniel Ward, *Simple Cobler of Aggawam in America* (1647), quoted in Vaughan, *Puritan Tradition,* 199.

> If any of you meet with some law that seems not to tend to your particular benefit, you must consider that laws are made with respect to the whole people and not to each particular person . . . as thou yieldest obedience to the law for common good, but to thy disadvantage, so another must observe some other law for thy good, though to his own damage.

And to deny a distinction between the laws of God and the laws of men the preface closed with the assertion that "there is no human law that tendeth to common good . . . but the same is mediately a law of God, and that in way of an ordinance which all are to submit unto and that for conscience sake."*

Most inhabitants of Massachusetts Bay first experienced the constrictions of authority within their own families. For Puritan society depended even more on this institution than on either the church or the state to maintain order within it. It was in the nature of things that within the family husband was superior to wife, parents to children, and masters to servants. A married woman was duty-bound to obey her husband in every respect, although she was in no way a servant to him. He could not administer corporal punishment nor order her to act in disobedience to acknowledged divine law. And in matters pertaining to their children and servants, if any, husband and wife shared equal authority. Many modern observers might well conclude that under such circumstances marriage in seventeenth-century Massachusetts depended more on command than affection for its durability. But despite the belief prevalent among succeeding generations of the young that they were the first to discover love and sex, evidence abounds that these feelings were widely expressed in Puritan Massachusetts. While Anne Bradstreet might not be admired today either as a poet or as a liberated woman, no one has seriously charged her with hypocrisy when she wrote of her husband, Simon:

> If ever two were one, then surely we.
> If ever man were lov'd by wife, then thee;
> If ever wife was happy in a man,
> Compare with me ye women if you can.
> I prize thy love more than Mines of gold.

---

* *The Laws and Liberties of 1648,* in Vaughan, *Puritan Tradition,* 163–66.

Or all the riches that the East doth hold.
My love is such that Rivers cannot quench,
Nor ought but love from thee, give recompence.
Thy love is such I can no way repay,
The heavens reward thee manifold I pray.
Then while we live, in love lets so persever,
That when we live no more, we may live ever.*

Children under the age of sixteen were in an even more subordinate position to their parents than were wives to husbands. In this respect, of course, the Puritan child stood no differently from children in other seventeenth-century families. All youngsters owed strict obedience to their elders. In some ways, however, children of Massachusetts were somewhat better off, for in the Bay colony at least parental authority implied responsibility as well. Parents were required by law to provide proper care and upbringing for their children; failure led to severe penalties. This responsibility included—beyond the obvious requirements of housing, feeding, and clothing—guidance toward the youngster's ultimate occupation. The choice of a calling, whether husbandry, a craft, or a trade for the boys, or housewifery for the girls, was usually made before the age of fourteen, so that the seven-year period of apprenticeship might be completed by the age of twenty-one. The word "calling" implied for the Puritan youngster that his choice of occupation fulfilled the will of God. The difficulty lay in discerning what occupation God had best fitted one for, and here the child needed all the help he could get from his elders. The wrong decision at this stage could lead to a lifetime of unhappiness. Apprenticeship served another purpose as well: it removed children from the direct control of the family at just that time when the effectiveness of parental authority began to wear a little thin. Indeed, civil authorities sometimes ordered difficult sons above the age of sixteen remanded to the care of foster parents rather than enforce the death penalty for such "stubborn and rebellious" sons, as called for in The Laws and Liberties of 1648.

Upon apprenticeship the young Puritan became subject to another authority—that of his master. By this move the child joined with

---

* "To my Dear and loving Husband," in Kenneth Silverman, ed., Literature in America: The Founding of a Nation (New York, 1971), 72.

thousands of other seventeenth-century men and women in the rank of servants. As in other relationships, both law and tradition spelled out the mutual duties and responsibilities of each party. All servants owed obedience, faithfulness, and reverence to their masters; failure to behave accordingly subjected the offender to chastisement, first by the master, but if that proved ineffectual, then by the courts. But as in the relationship between husband and wife, no master could command his servant to wrongdoing, nor was physical abuse permitted, although many a bruised servant (or wife) must have balked at testifying against the head of the house. In return for their labors servants were entitled to room, board, and clothing from their masters, and for all voluntary servants some sort of freedom dues at the expiration of their terms. The apprentice of course gained the training and experience necessary to fulfill his own calling.

For the devout Puritan the significance of the family went far beyond its role in maintaining order in society, as important as that function was. The head of the family was expected, in addition, to look after the spiritual welfare of both the children and the servants in his charge. The family was in fact the very basis of organized society. Most church covenants, for instance, called upon their members to maintain family prayers and to instruct their children in Christian doctrine. A conscientious father, such as Cotton Mather, shared much of his own spiritual life with his children. By example as well as by teaching, then, the Puritan child might find his own way toward spiritual health, according to Puritan lights.

* * *

The Puritans of Massachusetts Bay shared with other Calvinists the belief that only through knowledge of the Scriptures could one learn of God's divine plan for himself and all mankind. While one might gain such understanding by attendance at sermons and religious lectures, these exercises were designed as a complement to rather than a substitute for the individual's own acquaintance with the Scriptures. Since all men were born ignorant, learning to read became a necessary part of every child's education. In requiring the establishment of reading schools in each of the towns in 1647 the General Court stressed this religious motive by asserting that it was "one chief project of that old deluder, Satan, to keep men from the knowledge of the Scriptures." But Puritans respected humane learning for its own sake as well, and as a means of improving society. The legislature therefore required that every town of at least fifty households appoint a teacher to instruct in reading and writing all the pupils sent him. It should be noted that the law did not require attendance on the part of the community's children, but many parents must have welcomed this means of providing the rudiments of an education for their youngsters. Charges for schooling might be borne in whole or in part by the parents, although fees were usually waived for children of poor families, and some costs were defrayed out of public funds. In the early years after passage of this law numerous towns failed to comply, for the financial burdens of establishing a school were considerable, but gradually through the century most communities in the Bay colony set up at least one elementary school.

Several of the older towns had in fact already established schools long before the statute of 1647. One such community was Dorchester, which in 1642 adopted a detailed set of rules and regulations for its elementary school. Administrative matters came under the charge of three elected wardens or overseers. These officials selected the schoolmaster, subject to the town's general approval, and provided him with a salary out of tuition or other revenues. The wardens saw to the general condition of the schoolhouse itself and to the supply of firewood and other necessaries. Most important, of course, was their responsibility in seeing that the schoolmaster did his job, as defined in subsequent provisions of the town bylaws. In general, the master was to instruct all his pupils, whatever the status of their families, "both in human learning and good literature, and likewise in point of good manners and dutiful behavior towards all, especially their superiors." From March to October school began at seven in the morning and ran until five in the afternoon, with two hours out at midday. For the balance of the year the day was shortened one hour at each end. Once each week the master was to determine by public examination what if anything his scholars had learned on the preceding Sabbath and to note any misdeeds they might have committed. And one afternoon each week was set aside for instruction in whatever Christian catechism the wardens of the town had provided. Finally, the schoolmaster had explicit authorization to administer appropriate chastisement to his scholars whenever in his judgment such measures were justified.

The earliest known catechism used in Massachusetts Bay was John Cotton's *Milk for Babes, Drawn out of the Breasts of both Testaments Chiefly* . . . first printed in London in 1646 and reprinted in Cambridge a decade later. Primers, or first readers, included such religious material as the Lord's Prayer, the Ten Commandments, and the titles of the books of the Bible in order. *The New England Primer,* which first appeared in Boston toward the end of the seventeenth century, contained the famous alphabetical rhyme which began "In *Adam*'s fall/We sinned all." Other moral lessons encountered by the young scholar as he learned his ABCs included "The Idle *Fool*/Is whipped at school," "*Peter* denies/His Lord and cries," and "*Time* cuts down all/Both great and small." Under the heading "The Dutiful Child's Promises" were found "I will fear God, and honor the King," "I will honor my father and mother," and "I will submit to my elders." Among the "Lessons for Youth," another alphabetized list, the scholar learned that "Foolishness is bound up in the heart of a child, but the rod of correction shall drive it far from him," and "It is good for me to draw near unto God." From these examples it is clear that while religion permeated the instructional material of the day, of equal importance were the familial precepts drummed into the children by these primers. The schools thus joined the church, the state, and the family as instruments of establishing and sustaining social order.

Once a town reached one hundred families, according to the law of 1647, it was to establish a grammar school to prepare those students who wished to continue on to the university. As interpreted in the seventeenth century the law did not require towns to maintain a separate grammar school and master if the elementary school teacher were a college graduate himself, able and willing to instruct the grammar scholars. The full course of most grammar schools ran for seven years, students beginning at the age of eight or nine. Judged from the curriculum of the Boston Latin School at the turn of the century, these institutions offered an extensive classical education in which religious and moral lessons had little place. After acquiring the basics of Latin grammar during the first three years, the scholars studied the works of Aesop, Ovid, Cicero, and Virgil in turn. In the last two years they took up classical history and began the study of Greek. Although the purpose of the curriculum was preparation for the university, at least half the students throughout the seventeenth century failed to continue on for various reasons.

Those young men of Massachusetts Bay who, at the age of sixteen or

so, were determined to acquire a university education had only two practical alternatives: matriculation at the college in Cambridge named for
its first benefactor, John Harvard, or attendance at one of the English
universities. Although a number of young scholars chose the latter
course, the dangers and costs were considered prohibitive to most ambitious scholars and their families. The founding of Harvard in 1636 (and
its continuous operation thereafter) was a remarkable achievement for a
frontier society, especially considering the fact that no other English
colony undertook such an ambitious project at a comparative stage in its
development. In the history of Western colonization only the universities in Mexico and Peru could match it, and they had full support from
Spain and the Catholic Church. It should be noted, however, that the
inhabitants of Connecticut, New Haven, and New Hampshire also gave
generously in support of the college.

After a shaky start the college found stability under its second president, Henry Dunster. Although training for the ministry was the primary reason the General Court founded Harvard, fewer than half of its
465 graduates during the seventeenth century took pulpits. Modeled on
that of Emmanuel College, Cambridge, the curriculum offered a broadly
liberal education in "good literature, arts and sciences," and "all other
necessary provisions that may conduce to the education of the English
and Indian youth of this Country in knowledge and godliness." Most of
the books and all of the instruction were in Latin, for mastery of that
language was essential for admission. The program emphasized logical
thought, especially the writings of Petrus Ramus, languages (Hebrew
and Greek particularly), arithmetic, astronomy, and Biblical studies.
The private libraries and commonplace books of young Harvard scholars
reveal still wider interests: English essays and poetry, Spanish literature,
medicine, and a smattering of other scientific topics. The future ministers and grammar school teachers of Massachusetts Bay, as well as those
youths headed for other callings who graduated from the college at Cambridge, began their adult lives with a fine grasp of their Western
humanist heritage.

One can measure the effectiveness of education in seventeenth-century
Massachusetts in several ways. The literacy rate among adult males signing deeds and other legal documents stood consistently over 90 percent,
while for women the rate averaged around 50 percent. By comparison,
Virginia, with no compulsory school system, showed rates of 60 and 25

percent, respectively. How many more inhabitants of Massachusetts could read, but not write, has not been ascertained. Perhaps a more satisfactory indicator can be found in the widespread possession and publication of books and pamphlets within the colony. Stephen Day established a press in Cambridge in 1638, printing his first works the following year. In 1640 he produced the famous volume now known as the *Bay Psalm Book.* By 1700 Boston ranked behind London as the empire's second largest publishing center. In addition to works printed in Massachusetts Bay, the booksellers of Boston and Salem imported a wide range of titles from the mother country for their customers. More than one-half were books on religious subjects, with school texts and practical guides (on farming, medicine, seamanship) following behind. Works of law, literature, and history were also popular items. Of course, many of the first settlers brought with them as many of their own books as they could, or had their libraries sent over later, and these volumes became the nucleus of private collections handed down through the family for generations. About half of the estates probated in Essex and Middlesex counties during the seventeenth century contained at least some books beyond a Bible, but few could boast of the collection of Cotton Mather, which by 1700 had surpassed two thousand, close to the number possessed by Harvard College itself at the time.

One might well argue that reading, collecting, and even printing books are comparatively passive indicators of a society's intellectual accomplishments. Perhaps the true test of a culture lies in the works written by those men and women educated in Massachusetts Bay during the seventeenth century. Of unpublished materials other than a few letters, verse, and legal documents, little has survived; inhabitants of small communities had no reason to carry on a wide correspondence; few seemed to have either the time or inclination to keep diaries; and most of what they may have written has long since been discarded. No wonder that our best source for evaluating the intellectual achievement of the period is found in the published works of a small handful of writers, many of them ministers. Because Puritans viewed their progress in settling a wilderness as a sign of God's approval, they did not hesitate to publish histories of their accomplishments for others to read. The earliest historians, William Bradford and John Winthrop, were of course educated in England, and therefore credit for the first native history of the region goes to Nathaniel Morton, of Plymouth, whose *New England's*

Memorial was published at Cambridge in 1669. Thereafter came a number of more skillful endeavors, including William Hubbard's *History of New England* (finished in 1680 but not published for over a century) and Increase Mather's *Brief History of the War with the Indians* (1676). Cotton Mather's magisterial history, *Magnalia Christi Americana,* appeared just after the end of our period, in 1702.

Of other literary genres, poetry was by far the most common. By the standards of modern-day critics, few seventeenth-century poets would probably merit the title at all, and if they all wrote dreary religious works like Michael Wigglesworth's *The Day of Doom* (1662), the point would not be worth arguing. But a few other writers showed both sensitivity and skill in commenting on their New World experiences. Anne Bradstreet's lyrical expression of marital bliss is matched by her other verse, particularly her nature poetry, in which she seems to prefigure New England transcendentalists two centuries later in writing of the divine presence within the natural world and her own relationship to it. Benjamin Thompson produced a narrative poem, *New England's Crisis* (1676), on that traumatic episode, King Philip's War, and numerous other historical verses appeared in the various almanacs of the day. Perhaps the most accomplished poet of the period was Edward Taylor, minister of Westfield, whose verse remained unpublished (and undiscovered) until this century. Like most other Puritan poetry, religious themes dominate Taylor's work, but it was written with a fervor that tells us how keenly he could feel as well as think.

Yet another measure of a society's intellectual mettle lies in its ability to explore new fields, best illustrated in the case of the Puritans by their interest in the natural world. Would-be scientists of seventeenth-century Massachusetts suffered the same handicaps as their counterparts in the mother country: the discipline commanded little attention in the universities at first, and the works available reflected the hopelessly outdated views of Aristotle and Ptolemy. But from the 1650s on, Harvard scholars fully accepted the views of Copernicus, Galileo, and Kepler in preparing the almanacs published annually at Cambridge. No Massachusetts inhabitant could match the attainments of John Winthrop, Jr., who had settled in Connecticut, but Thomas Brattle, Increase Mather, and his two sons Cotton and Nathaniel all showed great interest in the several comets that appeared in the latter decades of the century, and they published useful essays on their observations. While by no means great accomplishments, they demonstrate a flexibility of mind that helped set the stage for the intensive scientific inquiry that would come in the eighteenth century. Judged by the works of Nathaniel Morton, William Hubbard, the Mathers, Anne Bradstreet, and Edward Taylor, among others, the educational milieu of seventeenth-century Massachusetts did indeed, as the charter of Harvard College called for in 1636, "advance learning and perpetuate it to posterity."

Were we to take only the Puritans' own word for it, their Zion in the wilderness was a dismal failure. By the 1660s, as we shall later see, increasing numbers of second-generation Puritans decried the imperfect society they found themselves a part of in the wilderness. Their self-criticism stemmed in part from attributing more to the intentions and accomplishments of their fathers than was perhaps merited. (There was a little of the "good old days" romanticism even in Puritans!) In part it came from underestimating the strengths of their own generation. Yet another source of their disquiet lay in the traditional role played by Puritan ministers of reminding their flock that sin was rampant among them all and that the Devil stood ready to profit from their every weakness. But historians do not have to judge a people by their own standards alone, either for good or for ill; to do so is to renounce the advantages of hindsight and perspective. The Puritans of Massachusetts Bay and their Pilgrim cousins of Plymouth Colony, though in less spectacular fashion, had both succeeded by the second half of the seventeenth century in transmitting to the New World many of the highest values of the world they left behind. They recognized the importance of a disciplined society, while lamenting the fact that no structure of authority would exist without dissenters. In the congregational form of their churches, they left full control of spiritual affairs in the hands of the worshippers themselves; and in the establishment of a system of public education, they provided for the future growth of succeeding generations. Perhaps the most significant contemporary testimony to the promise of Massachusetts Bay is found not in the writings of any Puritan but in the actions of one of them. In 1657 Increase Mather sailed to England, apparently determined to remain there as a minister. But in March 1661, discouraged by the prospects of a life in Restoration England, he returned to his native Massachusetts. Increase Mather had come home to stay.

6

EXPANSION

At about the same time that John Winthrop became an assistant of the newly chartered Massachusetts Bay Company in the spring of 1629, another country gentleman who had embraced Puritanism also joined the board. In the year following, William Pynchon sold his estates in Essex and left for Massachusetts Bay, where he settled at Roxbury. There he established himself in the fur trade, and within two years dominated the Bay colony's share of that profitable business. In 1636 Pynchon moved closer to the source of his supply, founding the town of Agawam (later Springfield) far up the Connecticut River beyond the Dutch and Plymouth posts. There he carved out a personal empire, marketing several thousand pounds of furs each year, along with produce raised by the farmers who flocked to the rich bottom lands along the river. Such enterprise ran counter to the ideas of more conservative Puritans, and in 1652 Pynchon decided to return to England. He left his river domain to his son John, who diversified the operations where possible in the face of declining revenue from the fur trade. When the outbreak of King Philip's War threatened these settlements in 1675, John Pynchon led his neighbors in defense of their homes.

The Pynchons represented a different kind of Puritan from John Winthrop and Richard Mather. Devout they were, but the business of getting on in this new world seemed more important to them than preparation for the next. The conservatives may have succeeded in driving out the elder Pynchon, but they could not stem the expansion of Massachusetts Bay not only across the *territory* encompassed by its charter but more significantly across the full range of economic activities which that charter granted. Under the leadership of men like William and John

Pynchon, Massachusetts Bay would truly become a commonwealth in its own right by the end of the 1670s.

*   *   *

Expansion had been a part of the pattern of settlement in both Plymouth and Massachusetts Bay almost from their founding. By 1640 Plymouth had added seven new towns to its colony, while Massachusetts in half the time could boast twice as many. In addition, settlers from both colonies had begun to move into other areas of New England, where they came under the jurisdiction of Connecticut, New Haven, Rhode Island, and New Hampshire. Several factors generated pressures for growth: the continuing immigration of newcomers, particularly into Massachusetts Bay; the high birth rate; and the never-ending quest for economic opportunity which had brought many of the early settlers to the New World in the first place.

In the decade after the Winthrop fleet reached Boston at least ten thousand Englishmen followed its wake to Massachusetts. Men, women, and children arrived with whatever household goods they could bring, ready to pick up their lives as families where they had left off in the mother country a few months before. Many of these groups went either directly to settlements on the frontiers of the Bay colony or did so after a winter in an established town. Others founded Weymouth and Hingham on the southern shore of Boston Bay, and still others pushed inland along the Charles River to Watertown and Dedham, or farther into the interior, to Concord and Sudbury. The quest for farmland was the major but by no means the only economic reason for this continuing movement. Cattle-raising brought the first settlers to Newbury, and the promise of fur trading led to the founding of Concord, Chelmsford, and Lancaster. In 1633 the adventurer John Oldham blazed an overland route to the Connecticut valley, where both New Netherland and Plymouth colonies had already established fur-trading posts. Puritans from Cambridge, restless in the shadow of Boston, were led by the Reverend Thomas Hooker in 1635 to settle the town of Hartford. Other malcontents from Dorchester and Watertown soon joined them, founding Wethersfield and Windsor in 1636. By 1640 at least one thousand settlers inhabited these distant communities, which by then had become a part of the new colony of Connecticut. Other groups of exiles followed

1636 (handwritten, right margin)

John Wheelwright north to New Hampshire and Roger Williams south into Rhode Island.

Once established, most of these towns grew rapidly, not only from the influx of later arrivals but also from a high birth rate combined with a relatively low death rate. A study of Andover tells the story for the first generation. The thirty-odd families that settled the town in 1646 produced an average of 8.3 children, of whom 7.2 survived at least to the age of twenty-one. The family heads of this generation lived to an average age of 71.8 years, their wives just one year less. During the 1650s the town recorded only one death for every nine births, and in the following decade, one for every five. Studies of Hingham, Dedham, and of Plymouth Colony seem to suggest a similar pattern in those communities as well. No wonder, then, that the population of Massachusetts continued its rapid rise even after immigration fell off sharply during the Cromwellian years in England.

It was not long before the continuing spread of settlements from the towns of Massachusetts Bay and Plymouth Colony collided with the territorial claims of other colonies as well as with each other. From about 1640 to 1675 considerable friction developed among various colonizing interests in the New England area, resulting almost always in the extension of Massachusetts. The Bay colony's interest in the Connecticut valley, for instance, conflicted with Dutch claims out of New Amsterdam and with the ambitions of the English colonies of Connecticut and New Haven. To the north and east, the expanding Puritans of Massachusetts challenged and eventually overran counterclaims to the territories familiar as New Hampshire and Maine. Before the end of the seventeenth century, the Bay colony had absorbed all of these regions as well as Plymouth and the offshore islands of Martha's Vineyard and Nantucket, formerly claimed by New York.

Efforts to colonize the coast of Maine had been made intermittently from the first years of the seventeenth century, but with little success, except for seasonal outposts of fishermen from Europe. Then in 1622 the Council for New England granted to Sir Ferdinando Gorges and Captain John Mason all of the land between the Merrimack and Kennebec rivers, an area to be called the Province of Maine. The grant to the Massachusetts Bay Company in 1629, with its boundary three miles north of the Merrimack, conflicted with several other claims to this territory, but none of the disputes seemed to impede its gradual settlement. By 1630

Plymouth Colony had founded a trading post on the Kennebec at the present site of Augusta and would establish another at the head of Penobscot Bay at Castine. Several hundred settlers were living at Saco, Kittery, York, and farther along the coast at Pemaquid, at Sheepscot, and on the St. George's River near present-day Thomaston. Meanwhile, other overlapping grants and a parting of the ways between Gorges and Mason left to the latter the nucleus of what would ultimately become the colony of New Hampshire. Soon the small community at Strawberry Bank (later Portsmouth) the mouth of the Piscataqua River was joined by other settlements along the shores of Great Bay, including John Wheelwright's group of exiles from Massachusetts at Exeter.

Massachusetts could not easily disguise its interest in what became known as the "eastern lands." By 1643 the General Court had succeeded in annexing all of the communities around the Piscataqua River and Great Bay. They would remain under the jurisdiction of Massachusetts until 1678. Maine was next. In 1652 the General Court reinterpreted the language of its charter to claim much of the disputed area from the Piscataqua to the Kennebec. Although the change was disapproved by the Privy Council, representatives of Maine's settlements accepted the jurisdiction of the Bay colony anyway. The province of Maine remained a part of Massachusetts for the balance of the colonial period, finally gaining statehood in its own right in 1820. The Bay colony's neighbors to the south had more success in maintaining independence. The exiles who fled to Rhode Island with Anne Hutchinson and Roger Williams acquired their own charter as a separate colony in 1663, although boundary disputes continued to mark their relationship with Massachusetts until well into the next century. Plymouth Colony held its own with its more powerful neighbor for a surprisingly long period, considering the numerous points at which their interests and ambitions came into conflict. In the early years Massachusetts depended on Plymouth's agricultural surplus, and trade between the two colonies formed a bond of mutual interest. Numerous inhabitants from each colony moved across the vague boundary lines to settle in the adjoining province. Each government found cooperation with its English-speaking neighbor especially helpful in the face of threats from Dutch, French, and particularly Indian attack.

In 1643 the need for cooperation gave birth to the United Colonies of New England, a loose confederation that bound together the four Puritan commonwealths of Massachusetts Bay, Plymouth, Connecticut, and New Haven. Each colony elected two commissioners who met annually with their six colleagues to manage relations among the members and with Indians and foreign powers. Because contributions of money and soldiers were proportioned to the population of each colony, Massachusetts bore the heaviest burden. But since the commissioners met at Boston twice as frequently as in the other capitals, the Bay colony wielded considerable influence over the proceedings, though at first most decisions seem to have been reached by unanimous agreement.

The continuing threat of Indian troubles in the wake of the Pequot War in 1637 had encouraged formation of the confederation in the first place, and much of its subsequent work attempted to maintain the peace. An equally serious danger came from the Dutch, whose claim to territory as far east as the Connecticut River was ultimately resolved only by the conquest of New Netherland by the Duke of York in 1664. At the same time the commissioners were establishing new areas of cooperation. Agreements for the mutual return of fugitives, for the support of Harvard College, for common legal procedures, and for the construction of roads all served to bring these four New England colonies closer together. In economic affairs the confederation established regulations to protect the mackerel fishery and tried to introduce a degree of uniformity into currencies and measures. But in 1646 a bitter controversy arose over Connecticut's right to levy an impost on goods coming down its river, for the maintenance of the fort at Saybrook. William Pynchon, in charge of the trading post at Springfield, refused to comply, and the Massachusetts General Court adopted discriminatory duties at Boston to force Connecticut to back down despite its support from the other two colonies. Massachusetts further undermined the confederation in 1653 by withholding its quota of soldiers from a joint attack against an Indian band on Long Island which had threatened the interests of Connecticut and New Haven there. From then on the effectiveness of the United Colonies steadily declined and with it whatever hope there might have been for a voluntary union of New England's Puritan colonies. In 1686 England would provide its own version of unification.

*   *   *

The growth of Massachusetts Bay in the middle decades of the seventeenth century was not merely a one-dimensional physical expansion.

Equally significant was the development of the commonwealth's economy beyond the simple pursuits of its farmers. To be sure, over 90 percent of its inhabitants lived off the land, most of them as subsistence farmers who produced little or no surplus for market. And yet the dynamic element in the colony's life was already taking shape during these early decades. Three natural resources—fish, fur, and timber—would give to seventeenth-century Massachusetts Bay a diversity which no other colony would achieve for another hundred years. The significance of these activities has usually been counted in terms of pounds sterling, but of equal importance, then and now, was the fact that fishing, fur trading, and lumbering offered the men of Massachusetts an alternative way of life from that of farming, alternatives that would enrich the society and culture of Massachusetts with new skills and customs. These diverse activities, then, would bring a qualitative expansion to the Bay colony which mere numbers could never measure.

No other part of the North American continent gave better access to the sea than the coast of Massachusetts Bay and the province of Maine. Boston spread across a hilly peninsula jutting into a spacious harbor, blessed with a score of offshore islands and two sandy spits protecting its outer approaches. By mid-century Boston shared the bay with half a dozen other communities from Hull to Winthrop. North of Boston the rockbound peninsula of Cape Ann sheltered the ports of Marblehead, Salem, Gloucester, and Rockport. Beyond Cape Ann the towns of Ipswich and Newbury nestled among the salt marshes behind the protective dunes of Plum Island, and the mouth of the Merrimack harbored Newbury's "waterside" community. Most of the early settlements in Maine clung precariously to the edge of the land along craggy peninsulas and broad inlets. To the south of Boston Bay the shore of Plymouth Colony was dotted with natural harbors from Scituate to Cape Cod's Yarmouth and Eastham. Both of Boston's rivers, the Mystic and the Charles, rose from headwaters close to the sea, but the Connecticut, the Merrimack, and the Kennebec offered routes that reached far into the great woods of northern New England. Their numerous tributaries led in turn to the home of the beaver and other fur-bearing mammals. Forest and sea beckoned to the adventurous men of Massachusetts and Plymouth.

The bounty of fish on the banks off the coast of New England had attracted English, French, and other Europeans to those waters as early as the sixteenth century, in the years after the Cabots' discoveries. A major impetus to the establishment of permanent settlements in New England came from fishing interests. Despite the proximity of Jeffreys', Still-wagen, and other banks, the people of Plymouth showed little interest in fishing, except for the seining of alewives in the salt rivers along the coast to provide fertilizer for the thin soil of the region. By default, offshore fishing became the special province of Massachusetts, whose charter specifically granted the company fishing rights in coastal waters and adjoining seas and the resources needed to construct and maintain a fishing fleet. The hanging of a carved codfish in the State House memorialized, as the resolution of 1784 put it, "the importance of the cod-fishing to the welfare of the commonwealth as had been usual formerly."

The Puritans came well prepared for this undertaking with several shipwrights and quantities of naval stores and other materials needed for the construction of fishing vessels. A number of early settlers had been fishermen in the old country; those who founded Marblehead, for instance, had come from Cornwall and the Channel Islands. And, of course, sooner or later the Bay colony absorbed the fishing communities that had already been established on Cape Ann and along the coast of Maine. At first these men confined themselves to in-shore fisheries, mackerel, hake, haddock, and pollack, reaching the grounds in small shallops, averaging thirty or forty feet, with a small shelter forward and two or three fish holds. A crew of three manned the vessel and a fourth remained ashore to cure the catch. As the industry expanded in mid-century the smaller shallop slowly gave way to the larger and sturdier ketch necessary to reach the offshore banks.

Until the 1640s New England fishermen shared these offshore grounds with their former countrymen from Devon and Cornwall. In fact these English fishermen sold some of their wares directly to the New England settlements. Then in 1640 the outbreak of revolution in the mother country sharply curtailed the ability of English fishermen to send out their vessels to the waters of the New World. From then on the fishing activities of Massachusetts Bay expanded rapidly. In 1641 three hundred thousand cod were brought in; later in the decade the single village of Marblehead reported earnings of £4,000 from its fishery. Much of this catch was undoubtedly marketed at home, but gradually the lines of commerce would reach out to more distant markets—the Chesapeake colonies, the Caribbean, southern Europe, and England itself. In 1635 the Reverend Hugh Peter, of Salem, urged the inhabitants of the coastal towns to go fishing. The General Court cooperated by establishing a commission to manage the infant industry and by offering tax exemptions on vessels and equipment for seven years.

The men who made all of this possible were fishermen as roughhewn as the rocky ledges of their home waters. Among the residents of Marblehead in 1644 not a single church member could be found. Seventy-five years later a newly arrived minister complained that Marblehead's fishermen were as "rude, swearing, drunken, and fighting a crew as they were poor." Early inhabitants of Cape Ann's fishing towns, whose settlement predated that of the Bay colony itself, refused to defer to the Puritan newcomers, and it was many years before the authority of Massachusetts was firmly established over the communities farther east in Maine. Of the fishermen of this region a visitor cautioned that "if a man of quality chance to come where they are roystering and gulling in *Wine* with a dear felicity he must be sociable and *Roly-poly* with them . . . or else be gone."* Distance made such control difficult, of course, but more significant was the independent way of life that fishing seems always to have generated whether in England's West Country or the coast of Maine. At a time when most farmers of Massachusetts still lived in tightly knit communities dominated by the settled institutions of church and town, the fishermen of the colony went their own way. No wonder some of the wealthier inhabitants of the area welcomed the Bay colony's extension of jurisdiction when it came in the 1650s.

Along with the fisheries, the fur trade provided another potential foundation for the commercial development of Massachusetts. Even before the first permanent settlements a few of the itinerant fishermen and adventurers along the coast also traded with the Indians for peltry which they then sold upon their return to England. In its first two decades Plymouth Colony had high hopes of developing the fur trade into a major source of income. Through its posts on the Penobscot, Kennebec, and Connecticut rivers the Pilgrims had, as John Winthrop lamented in 1634, "engrossed all of the Cheif places of trade in New England." But within a few years Winthrop's colleagues had forced their neighbors from Plymouth out of several of their trading posts and had established bases in new areas; in the Merrimack River watershed, farther up the Connect-

---

* Bernard Bailyn, *The New England Merchants in the Seventeenth Century* (Cambridge, Mass., 1955), 14.

icut River, and ultimately into the interior of New Hampshire. Neither colony could sustain a profitable business in furs for more than a decade or two, however. The rivers they controlled led into the interior, to be sure, but for the most part these regions were only thinly populated by Indians able to carry out the actual trapping. Unlike the Dutch in New Amsterdam or the French in Canada, the English colonists could not tap the vast waterways of the interior. By mid-century, the fur trade of Massachusetts had dwindled away almost entirely and only the few giants of the trade, such as William Pynchon, had anything to show for it.

Timber proved to be a far more reliable base for the Bay colony's expanding commercial activities. The supply did not depend on contact with Indians, nor was permanent settlement of the logging area necessary. Merchants looking for long-term investments eagerly acquired title to vast stretches of virgin forest in western Massachusetts, New Hampshire, and Maine. Agents hired lumberjacks, built sawmills, and supervised the production of clapboards, staves, shingles, and other wood products. The Hutchinsons of Boston owned no less than nineteen sawmills in New Hampshire alone to provide a steady source of lumber particularly for their West Indies trade. By far the most valuable product of the northern forest was the majestic white pine suitable for masts. First Cromwell's expeditions of the 1650s and then in the following decade the naval wars that Charles II waged against the Dutch drastically depleted the Admiralty's reserves of masts. Bostonians saw their opportunity along with the merchants of Portsmouth and soon a steady supply of mast trees, each worth well over £100, reached the mother country. "A blessing," Samuel Pepys called the arrival of one shipment in the midst of war in 1666, "without which, if for nothing else, we must have failed the next year." By the end of the century New Hampshire gained firm control of its own hinterland, and the merchants of Boston looked to Maine and the interior of Massachusetts for timber to feed their rapidly expanding markets in the Caribbean.

The fishermen, woodsmen, and trappers of Massachusetts Bay could not do their work alone. In the earliest years they had depended upon English merchants for the capital with which to acquire the basic tools of their trade. Equally important, Englishmen purchased the fruits of their labor for market. But as settlement expanded, Boston and Salem men began to take over these commercial activities, and by the middle of the seventeenth century an enterprising group of merchants was established in the Bay colony. The rise of these entrepreneurs depended in almost every instance on their ability to call upon London-based relatives for capital, stock, and marketing arrangements. The Hutchinson family, for instance, made its commercial start in Boston by selling English goods sent on by the London merchant Richard Hutchinson. Henry Shrimpton, who came to Boston a brazier in 1639, borrowed heavily from his brother in London to launch his own mercantile career. He was worth about £12,000 at his death in 1666. Many of these businessmen had family connections in other colonies as well. The Hutchinsons relied on their cousin Peleg Sanford of Rhode Island to conduct their trade with the West Indies. These family connections led to another source of income after the outbreak of revolution in England by supplying Cromwell's West Indian expeditions with naval stores and provisions.

In one of the first voyages sponsored by colonial interests the Boston-built *Trial* carried fish to Bilbao and Malaga and returned in 1643 with wine, olive oil, fruits, and linen. Other vessels exchanged fish at Fayal and Madeira for wine and sugar. The Canaries became another port of call, and pipestaves were added to fish as an export.

Bay colony mariners opened an even more significant trade route in the mid-1640s. Information about the West Indies, recently settled by English, Dutch, and French colonists, suggested that a promising commercial connection might be made with Barbados, Nevis, Antigua, Guadaloupe, and other Caribbean islands. In 1645 a Boston vessel sailed via Madeira to Africa, picking up a cargo of blacks to be sold as slaves in Barbados, where colonists concentrated all their capital and labor on the establishment of sugar plantations. Boston merchants quickly read the development of the West Indies to mean a fine market for New England fish and provisions, lumber, barrel staves, shingles, and other wood products. Horses were needed there to work the sugar mills and blacks from Africa in seemingly unending numbers for field hands. By mid-century the merchants of Massachusetts Bay had also extended their lines of trade to the tobacco colonies of the Chesapeake and to the fishing settlements in Newfoundland. The lucrative business of sending giant mast trees to England for the naval yards also dates from this period, and the shipwrights of the Bay colony began to discover an English market for colonial-built vessels.

It was inevitable that such far-flung commercial interests would eventually bring Massachusetts face to face with the fact that it was, after all, a part of the English empire and not an independent nation. Cromwell's Parliament had enacted a broad-reaching statement on mercantile regulations in 1651, but political turmoil at home and lax enforcement overseas rendered the law a virtual dead letter in the Bay colony. With the restoration of Charles II in 1660, however, came a series of acts that within a decade firmly established a policy of mercantilism and carefully spelled out the place of the American colonies within such a plan. The goal of this new system was to establish the English empire as self-sufficient, particularly at the expense of French, Spanish, and Dutch interests. The several Navigation Acts of the 1660s restricted the commercial intercourse of the empire to vessels built, owned, and predominantly manned by English or colonial inhabitants. Articles of foreign manufacture (except for salt and certain wines) could be imported into the colonies only through England, where they became subject to a prohibitive duty to protect similar English articles. Likewise, certain plantation produce such as tobacco, naval stores, and sugar could be exported solely to the mother country. These laws in effect guaranteed an active role for the shipbuilders, merchants, and mariners of the Bay colony within the commercial structure of the empire and under the protection of the English navy.

The way in which the merchants of Massachusetts operated within the confines of this system, however, became a major issue in the 1670s. To some extent the problem stemmed from uncertain language in the Navigation Acts. The legitimacy of importing wines from the Canaries, for instance, depended upon whether one considered those islands a part of Europe or of Africa. There could be no doubt that the exportation of tobacco and other enumerated commodities to France and Spain was illegal, and yet Boston merchants needed these returns for the purchase of foreign manufactured goods (which was illegal as well). With other American merchants Bostonians made use of the "broken voyage," temporarily entering enumerated articles into their own colony to fulfill the letter of the law before shipping them out to foreign markets. Nor did the law permit direct trade with Scotland, Ireland, or the Channel Islands, but the New Englanders found these routes highly profitable. By 1672, one group of Englishmen complained, Massachusetts was employing two or three hundred vessels each year in various kinds of illicit trade. The result was passage of the Navigation Act of 1673, which imposed a plantation duty on enumerated commodities and required a bond that they be delivered to an English or colonial port. The customs commissioners appointed officials in each major port to enforce the law. When in 1676 Edward Randolph arrived as agent in Boston, the end of an era was close at hand.

Stimulated by its burgeoning commerce, Boston became during the middle decades of the century the "metropolis of New England," as Samuel Maverick put it. Its population reached three thousand by 1660. Wharves reached into the harbor, warehouses stretched along the waterfront, a jumble of shops and markets lined the streets. At the center of commercial activity stood the townhouse, built through the generosity of one of Boston's leading merchants, Robert Keayne. The ground floor was left open to provide space for farmers and others to display their produce. On the main floor above were courtrooms, chambers for town officials, and an armory.

Almost every seacoast community in the colony was affected by this burst of mercantile activity in one way or another: a rising demand for fish from Marblehead and Cape Ann; for vessels built along the salt rivers; for timber that came down the Merrimack and Kennebec. By 1666 the colony reportedly had a fleet numbering thirty vessels of over one hundred tons and seven hundred of smaller measurement. Scores of other colony-built vessels were sold to English merchants who took advantage of the lower cost of timber in American shipyards. Inland communities felt the impact of this commercial revolution in less direct ways. The seaports were no longer self-sustaining; they depended increasingly on the hinterland as a market for their imports and as a source of foodstuffs both for local consumption and for export to the Caribbean. But as the inhabitants of inland communities gained markets for their surplus produce and the ability to purchase the English goods they desired, they lost much of the independence they had known in the early years. Complaints against the Boston merchants for high prices, hard credit, and other unfair practices began to mount. The gulf between town and country widened in these middle decades, as Boston, Salem, Charlestown, and a few other coastal towns became different sorts of communities altogether.

Not content with their role in the commerce of the empire, the merchants of Massachusetts explored the feasibility of establishing their own manufacturing operations as well. John Winthrop, Jr., persuaded a number of English Puritans to form the Company of Undertakers for the

Iron Works in New England in 1642. The General Court cooperated by issuing a generous charter granting the group extensive lands, exemption from taxes, and a monopoly for twenty-one years. Initially located in Braintree but with its main works subsequently established in Saugus, the company began operations in 1646 under the direction of foundrymen brought from England. Within two years the works were producing a ton of iron each day for the manufacture of pots and other hardware. But Winthrop proved an inefficient manager, as did several of his successors, and the English investors finally refused to raise further capital to meet operating deficits. Years of litigation followed, ending with the complete failure of the company in 1676. Efforts to establish furnaces in other localities met a similar fate. Entrepreneurs also attempted the manufacture of cloth goods with equally disappointing results. A fulling mill at Rowley employing cloth workers from Yorkshire ran for a time, but it could not successfully compete against homespun in cheapness or English cloth in quality. The shortage of capital, skilled labor, and prosperous customers doomed to failure these early efforts to establish profitable manufacturing despite initial assistance from English investors and a sympathetic legislature. The way to wealth in Massachusetts would continue for the remainder of the colonial period to be the exchange of New World raw materials for the manufactures of the Old.

*   *   *

The first Indians of New England to resist the pressure of expanding Massachusetts were themselves newcomers to the region. A band of Mahicans had come from the upper reaches of the Hudson valley at the end of the previous century and forced their way into what became southeastern Connecticut, then the territory of the Niantics, where their ferocity earned them a new name, Pequot, meaning *destroyer*. For a short time there was the possibility that the Pequots and English settlers might establish peaceful lines of trade. All such hopes were shattered in 1636, however, with the brutal slaying of John Oldham, well-known fur trader and adventurer. Massachusetts authorities suspected allies of the Pequots from Block Island and assembled a retaliatory expedition under John Endicott. After destroying the Indian settlements on the island, Endicott moved on to Pequot Harbor, at the mouth of the Thames, which his men vandalized for two days. After Endicott's return to Massachusetts the Pequots took their revenge against their white neighbors along the Connecticut River, committing the most brutal atrocities against those unfortunate enough to fall into their hands. The cause of peace would surely have been better served if another commander than Endicott had led the expedition of 1636; still, the Pequots had impressed neither Indians nor whites with their willingness to remain good neighbors. Massachusetts and Connecticut had little choice but to declare war, which they did in the spring of 1637.

The Pequot War set the pattern for the hostilities between Indian and European that followed thereafter. Unrelieved brutality by each side; little sense of common cause on the part of the Indians; superior cooperation among the whites only by comparison; and unconditional surrender. Connecticut bore the brunt of the early fighting, but forces from Massachusetts arrived in plenty of time for the kill. And kill they did. In a surprise attack on the main fort at Pequot Harbor all but seven of about five hundred Pequot braves, squaws, and children fell before the English muskets and the arrows of their Indian allies or perished in the flames that engulfed the village. The colonists exulted in their easy victory. John Underhill, head of the Massachusetts men present, compared the slaughter to David's war against the Philistines. "We had sufficient light from the word of God for our proceedings," he concluded matter-of-factly. Massachusetts soldiers under Israel Stoughton conducted the mopping-up operations in the weeks that followed, with considerable assistance from natives who had lived under the Pequot heel for years. Remnants of the dreaded tribe were hunted down and killed without quarter. One band met their end in a swamp near present-day New Haven, where they were slaughtered like fish in a barrel. At the end of hostilities the Pequot tribe was expunged from the records altogether and its few survivors parceled out to other tribes. The Indians of New England would thereafter know the price of rejecting *pax Massachusetts*.

The Narragansets had already made formal alliance with Massachusetts (in 1636) and after supporting the English cause in the Pequot War, Chief Uncas of the Mohegans signed a treaty with Governor Winthrop. But the need for friendly relations with whites was about all the two tribes could agree upon. A dispute between them came to a head in 1643 and resulted in the death of the Narragansets' chief Miantonomo at the hands of Uncas. The episode drove a wedge between the Narragansets and the United Colonies that could never quite be mended. For three decades thereafter New Englanders waited for the other shoe to fall, expecting that eventually they would have to put the Narragansets "in their place," as they had the Pequots.

In Massachusetts the steady advance of white settlement had by mid-century left numerous Indian villages behind the frontier. Several of these tribes, such as the Pennacooks and Massachusets, submitted en masse to the jurisdiction of the surrounding Bay colony. In addition natives living within the colony as individuals fell under similar white control. Despite the intention of most authorities to deal justly with these native residents, the differences in language, law, and custom put the Indian at a serious disadvantage. Added to these handicaps was the inescapable fact that most Puritans looked down on Indians as inferior heathens. The natives' low status in Massachusetts encouraged behavior characteristic of the oppressed in every society—loitering, drunkenness, petty theft, and minor assault—which authorities invariably prosecuted with righteous vigor as though they were serious crimes. The resulting public record confirms the prejudices which in large measure brought about the misconduct in the first place.

A few Puritans took seriously the professed missionary goal of the colony to convert Indians to their brand of Christianity. To do so was no easy task; conversion for Indians required the same awareness of grace as for whites and that experience usually came only after years of "preparation" through Biblical study and concentrated soul-searching in and out of church. Despite these obstacles several ministers devoted their careers to bringing Christianity to the Indians of Massachusetts. By far the most dedicated of these men was the Reverend John Eliot of Roxbury. He learned Algonkin and in 1646 conducted his first service in that language, in the Indian village of Nonantum. The reports of his work over the next several years helped persuade Cromwell's Parliament to establish in 1649 the Society for Propagation of the Gospel in New England, which provided funds for missionary work. Eliot had already concluded that Indians intent on serving God needed the same kinds of reinforcement as did whites—community, church, school. In 1651 he founded Natick, the first town for praying Indians. There the natives built a meeting-house and fort, laid out several streets, and established a town government. Convening a true church proved more difficult because of the Puritans' rigorous standards. Not until 1660 did the ministers and elders of neighboring parishes give their approval to the neophyte Christians of Natick. By then another praying town had been established at Pun-

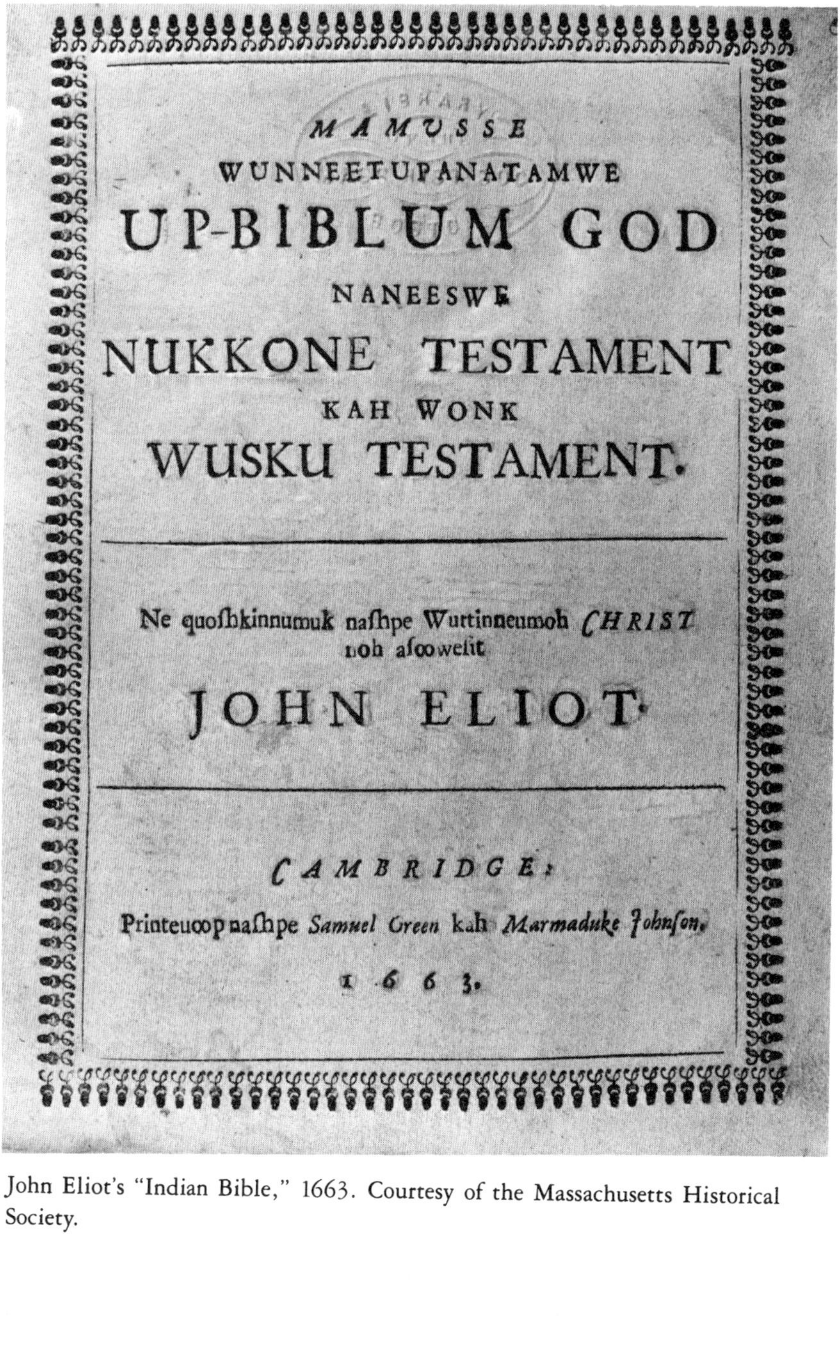

MAMUSSE

WUNNEETUPANATAMWE

UP-BIBLUM GOD

NANEESWE

NUKKONE TESTAMENT

KAH WONK

WUSKU TESTAMENT.

Ne quoſhkinnumuk naſhpe Wuttinneumoh *CHRIST*
noh aſoowefit

JOHN ELIOT·

CAMBRIDGE:

Printeuꝏp naſhpe *Samuel Green* kah *Marmaduke Johnſon.*

1 6 6 3.

John Eliot's "Indian Bible," 1663. Courtesy of the Massachusetts Historical
Society.

kapog. Meanwhile, on the island of Martha's Vineyard, Thomas Mayhew took the Gospel to hundreds of natives. On Cape Cod, Richard Bourne had similar success among the Nausets.

The most difficult task facing Eliot and his fellow missionaries was in the field of education. The Roxbury minister began the boggling task of developing a written version of the Algonkin language so that he could translate the books so important to white Christians—catechisms, tracts, and most significantly, the Bible itself. First editions of minor works appeared in the 1650s. With financial assistance from the SPGNE his translation of the Bible steadily progressed, appearing in its final form in 1663. Eliot's edition was the first to be translated into any native language and was in fact the first to be published in America in any language. Eliot and his assistants continued to produce religious works in Algonkin for several years thereafter, until by 1672 an impressive Indian library was available for those natives willing to learn how to read. To expect real progress, however, a more comprehensive system of education had to be developed. Harvard constructed an "Indian College" building in the mid-1650s but, not surprisingly, only a handful of native youths matriculated during the seventeenth century, and only one completed the four-year curriculum. More to the point was the free admission of Indian children to the elementary schools of the colony and the establishment of such institutions in the praying towns, staffed in part by Christian Indians from Natick.

On the eve of King Philip's War in 1675 about eleven hundred Indians professing Christianity were living in fourteen praying towns scattered throughout the colony. Most were of the Massachusets tribe but Pennacooks and Nipmucks were also included. Two of the towns boasted fully accepted churches, and congregations in several other villages strove toward recognition. Under the benevolent guidance of Daniel Gookin, the Superintendent of Indian Affairs appointed by the General Court in 1656, the native villages managed their own civil affairs with a skill equal to that of the white communities around them. Whether one considers the work of Eliot, Mayhew, Bourne, Gookin, and others to be "successful" depends, of course, on what goals one establishes for a race destined to minority status within an alien culture. The acceptance by perhaps one-third of the commonwealth's native population of the white man's religion and customs was recognized by Eliot's contemporaries in England as a remarkable achievement. Surely their peaceful coexistence among the whites was preferable to the fate that befell the Pequots in

1637 and would soon overtake the Wampanoags. Whatever chance there might have been for a "middle way" was eliminated as far as New England was concerned, however, by the events of the 1670s.

*   *   *

For almost forty years after the Pequot War relations between Indian and Englishman had remained relatively peaceful throughout New England. The confederation gave at least the appearance of unity among the major colonies of the region, while feuds between the powerful Narragansets and neighboring tribes kept the Indians apart. Whenever minor incidents threatened to erupt into violence, the United Colonies' commissioners succeeded in defusing the crisis. To the casual observer, perhaps, peace might have continued indefinitely, but beneath the surface lay ominous conditions. During the half century since the arrival of the Pilgrims at Plymouth, the Wampanoags had steadily lost territory to the expanding English colony. Massasoit had accepted this development primarily because he needed Plymouth's support against his arch-enemies, the Narragansets. By the time Massasoit's son Philip became sachem in 1662, however, the balance of power had drastically changed. Now the whites outnumbered the Indians; their weapons were more powerful; their way of life was more aggressive. And that way of life had gradually encroached upon the lands of the Wampanoag. The white man kept the peace but almost always on his own terms.

Philip brooded over the gradual loss of his power and influence over the lands and people of his tribe. As time passed the morale of his own warriors sagged perceptibly; young hotheads seemed ready to take the warpath themselves. During the winter and spring of 1675 Philip endeavored to cement relations with other New England tribes, including the Nipmucks, Pocumtucks, and even his old enemies, the Narragansets. While there is no hard evidence that Philip was conspiring against the Plymouth Colony at this time, the rumor mill ground out reports that the Wampanoag chief was about to go on the warpath. Then in June 1675 some of his braves began harassing the inhabitants of Swansea, a frontier village on the edge of Indian territory. Within days, looting turned to murder. Whatever Philip's intentions, he could no longer control his braves, and the war that would ever after bear his name was on.

Military security in the English colonies depended entirely upon the trainbands of militiamen composed of the able-bodied men of each community. They were armed for the most part with the clumsy matchlock musket, although the more efficient flintlock had begun to appear. The training they underwent conformed to the well-established maneuvers of professional European armies. None of them could be described as professional soldiers, however, and few had had any actual military experience, either in Europe or in America. Veterans of the Pequot War were now past military age; more recent skirmishes had involved only a handful of militiamen. But as war came, the whites had numerous advantages. First, they outnumbered the Indians of the region by at least two to one. Second, they held the interior lines and the better communications that went with such an advantage. Furthermore, their colonies were better able to sustain a long war. Food, clothing, gunpowder, and other essential supplies could be furnished the fighting men, although with some difficulty at times. For these reasons, time was clearly on the side of the colonists.

But the Indians also enjoyed some advantages of their own. They were more familiar with the forest and from generations of experience as hunters knew better how to survive in it. Almost always on their side was the advantage of surprise, which gave them the choice of time and place of attack in accordance with no predictable pattern. Intermittent warfare among neighboring tribes had kept the braves in fighting trim. They possessed muskets, too, but they also had the skills and weapons necessary for hand-to-hand combat. The prospect of fighting Indians petrified most colonial militiamen, whose unenviable task it was to defend their villages against Indian attack and, even worse, to counterattack through the dense forest. Thus the Indians enjoyed as well a considerable psychological advantage, at least in the early months when confronting inexperienced settlers.

Soon after the Wampanoags struck at the western settlements of Plymouth Colony, counterattacking forces from Plymouth and Massachusetts nearly captured Philip and his retinue at the end of June, but the Wampanoag chief escaped to Nipmuck territory between Boston and the Connecticut valley. There he persuaded the Nipmucks to join the fray. In August they attacked Brookfield and other settlements in the area. From there the fighting spread farther north and east around the salient of white settlements into the Merrimack valley. These events isolated Hatfield, Deerfield, and other settlements in the Connecticut

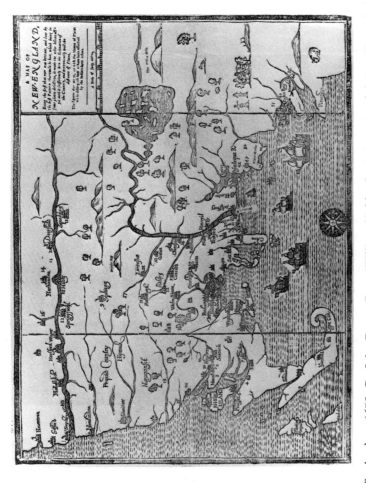

New England, c. 1675. By John Foster. From William Hubbard, *A Narrative of the Troubles with the Indians* (1677). Courtesy of the Massachusetts Historical Society.

valley, where the Pocumtucks lived. Here John Pynchon, William's son and successor to the family holdings at Springfield, took charge of the colonists' defense. He received reinforcements from both Connecticut and Massachusetts and prepared for the worst. The northernmost village of Squakeag (now Northfield) was abandoned, and then Deerfield, but there the evacuees were ambushed at Bloody Brook, where sixty-four men were slain. Next the Indians put Springfield to the torch, a stroke that seriously jeopardized the other valley towns.

Of greatest concern to the leaders of Massachusetts and Plymouth were the intentions of the Narragansets, by far the most powerful of the tribes in southern New England. When they failed to live up to the letter of their agreement with the settlers, rumors spread that they were planning to go on the warpath. The commissioners of the United Colonies decided, therefore, to send an expedition into Narraganset territory to ensure their continued neutrality. It is not surprising that this operation should have had the opposite result. In a scene reminiscent of the massacre of the Pequots four decades before, the whites stormed the Narragansets' fort in mid-December and burned it to the ground. Over seventy militiamen perished in the Great Swamp Fight, as it was called, but several hundred Narraganset men, women, and children died that day, and the Indians lost almost all of their food supplies as well. Thereafter the Narragansets would fight to the death against the whites, but death came as often from starvation as from the bullets of their enemies.

The Nipmucks did not wait long before resuming hostilities on the periphery of their territory. In February they attacked Lancaster, then Medfield less than twenty miles from Boston, and even Weymouth, on the very shores of Boston Bay. By spring the theater of war had spread southward to Simsbury in Connecticut and the outskirts of Providence. But within a few months the tide began to turn in favor of the settlers. Canonchet, the Narraganset sachem, was captured and executed in April. A force of militiamen killed over a hundred Indians on the Connecticut River at what is now Millers Falls. Another expedition killed over two hundred Narragansets in Rhode Island. In June the leaders of Massachusetts were sufficiently confident to issue a general declaration of leniency to those warriors who would turn themselves in. Hundreds took advantage of the opportunity to avoid starvation. Finally, Captain Benjamin Church took charge of a special group of whites and Indian allies to track down King Philip himself, who had reportedly returned to his native Mount Hope peninsula with his remaining warriors. There on August 12, 1676, King Philip met his death ironically, at the hands of one of Church's Indians. The war was over.

King Philip's War had devastating effects on New England. Over one thousand colonists lost their lives in the fight and undoubtedly a far greater number of Indians. Thirteen English settlements were totally destroyed and another half dozen partially burned. The expansion of Plymouth and Massachusetts came to a complete halt, and in some areas the frontier of 1675 would not be reached again for another generation. Furthermore, the war severely affected the welfare of New England's Christian Indians and tribes like the Mohegans who remained neutral. Even those Indians who fought alongside the colonists suffered from the general animosity toward Indians that swept through New England society. Whatever hope there may have been in 1675 of a racial accommodation, either on John Eliot's terms, or on any other, disappeared in the smoke of King Philip's War.

7

END OF AN ERA

If ever a man stood astride the changes that swept through his lifetime, it was Samuel Sewall of Boston. Samuel's father, Henry, had first come to Massachusetts in 1634 to represent a group of English investors, including his own father, who planned to establish a cattle-raising company among the rich meadowlands along the Parker River, thirty miles north of Boston. The company was comprised mostly of Puritan businessmen, whose interest in New England was more financial than religious. Due to mismanagement, the company was disbanded and its assets divided up among the associates as individuals. Henry married Jane Dummer, a neighbor's daughter, and settled down in what became the town of Newbury. Soon the young couple grew discouraged, and they returned to England in 1646. There Jane bore a number of children, including Samuel, and there they might have remained, but in 1659 Henry inherited all of his father's considerable holdings in Newbury. Once more he made the perilous journey across the Atlantic, this time to settle permanently, and two years later he sent for his wife and children. Thus began the New World life of nine-year-old Samuel Sewall. Over the next seventy years he would become a leading merchant of Boston, one of the judges in Salem's witch trials, and a keen diarist, whose journal recorded his views of the momentous changes that marked the end of seventeenth-century Massachusetts.

* * *

Because the Puritans strove to establish and maintain not only a church but an entire society in accordance with their view of God's word, they had never had much difficulty discovering evidence of nonconformity around them. One source of concern had always been the influx into the province of immigrants who had no strong religious motive for coming. At first the Puritan majority had few problems in dominating these people, but with the end of Puritan immigration after 1640, the balance of numbers swung slowly in favor of those who did not necessarily share the high religious purposes of the colony's founders. Even among the first generation of Puritans there had been many men and women who, like the Pynchons, observed the letter of their faith while leading lives that to some seemed contrary to the spirit of placing service to God before all else. But perhaps the most disturbing problem came from the sons and daughters of the first generation, most of them either American-born or babes in arms when their parents arrived in the New World. As they grew to adulthood many of this younger generation seemed to lack the commitment to the religious goals that had inspired their parents to leave their homeland and cross the sea. What was worse, most of them did not seem to care about such ideals.

The problem of uncommitted children deeply disturbed members of the older generation. In theory the only way one could gain membership in the church was by a describable conversion experience; that is, by the demonstration that one possessed God's grace. In most cases, the children of church members were baptized as a matter of course, so that they might be encouraged to attend church and prepare for their own conversion as they came to maturity. But what if they in turn never did become church members? What then would be done with *their* children? That is, could the children of baptized but unconverted persons be baptized themselves even though their own parents were not church members? That was the problem facing ecclesiastical leaders by the middle decades of the seventeenth century. The solution, which came to be known as the Half-Way Covenant, was adopted in Massachusetts by the synod of 1662. This compromise established, in effect, two kinds of church membership. One was for those who met the test of a converting experience and were therefore admitted to full standing, which included the freedom of taking communion. For the godly but unregenerate there was a qualified membership which entitled them to own the covenant and to have their own children baptized, but not to participate in communion. The synod's decision had a devastating effect on the churches throughout the commonwealth, as ministers and congregations disagreed on

Samuel Sewall (1652–1730). Painting by John Smibert. Courtesy of the Essex Institute, Salem, Mass.

whether to accept the doctrine. The turmoil that resulted from the solution was every bit as disturbing to the populace as the original problem.

Equally troubling to the Puritans were the changes brought by a generation of commercial expansion. Boston's bustling harbor attracted mariners, artisans, and tradesmen from all over the Atlantic world whose presence threatened "to mar the worke of Christ," as Edward Johnson put it. The General Court therefore tightened its regulation concerning strangers, requiring them to register before two magistrates upon arrival and, if they stayed more than two months, to take an oath of allegiance to the government of the Bay colony. Merchants and other tradesmen recognized from the outset that such a suspicious attitude was bad for business. In 1646 a group of entrepreneurs called for an easing of standards for both the franchise and church membership, but their petition came to nought. In 1652 William Pynchon's tract *The Meritorious Price of Man's Redemption,* which sought greater understanding for the man of trade, was publicly burned; shortly thereafter Pynchon left for England in disgust. Yet the commerce of Massachusetts continued to expand, and through the port of Boston poured a flock of newcomers eager to share in the material promise of the commonwealth.

Clerical leaders viewed these changes with alarm. In the decades after mid-century they warned their flock of impending doom in sermons and writings called "jeremiads"—after the Old Testament prophet who foretold the troubles that would befall that older chosen people, the ancient Hebrews. Ministers had noted the alleged backsliding of their flocks before and since, but few spoke of impending doom with such conviction. Read the words of the Salem minister John Higginson who, in a sermon of 1663, reminded the inhabitants of the colony's second largest seaport that "New-England is originally a plantation of Religion, not a plantation of Trade."* To those who predicted final doom for Massachusetts Bay there were signs aplenty of God's displeasure. Frequent epidemics of smallpox carried off hundreds of victims. A prolonged drought in 1662 inspired Michael Wigglesworth to write "God's Controversy with New England," in which the Lord wonders aloud:

> What shall I do with such a stiff-neckt race?
> How shall I ease me of such Foes as they?

---

* Bailyn, *New England Merchants*, 140.

And answers His own questions:

> I'le surely beare their candlestick away.
>   And lamps put out. Their glorious noon-day light
> I'le quickly turn into a dark Egyptian night.

In the midst of King Philip's War, Increase Mather addressed *An Earnest Exhortation to the Inhabitants of New England* . . . (1676), claiming that

> . . . that woful neglect of the Rising Generation which hath been amongst us, is a sad sign that we have in great part forgotton our *Errand* in this Wilderness; and then why should we marvail that God taketh no pleasure in our young men, but they are numbred for the Sword, the present judgment lighting chiefly upon the *Rising Generation*.

The fact that Wigglesworth's poem *The Day of Doom* (1662) sold over eighteen hundred copies upon publication to a population of less than fifty thousand indicates that many inhabitants were gravely concerned about the future of their commonwealth.

Increase Mather catalogued the misdeeds of Massachusetts in the "Reforming Synod" of 1679–80. Fancy hairdos, naked breasts, mixed dancing, and other "light behaviour and expressions" had corrupted the youth of the colony, he charged. In its report the synod noted shortcomings within the commonwealth that included profanity, pride, breaking of the sabbath, intemperance, inordinate passions, and a want of truth. More serious, the ministers found an "inordinate affection to the world. . . . There hath been in many professors [of the faith] an insatiable desire after land and worldly accommodations. . . . Farms and merchandising have been preferred before the things of God." In their pursuit of their own gain, men had lost the public spirit, and had permitted schools and other public concerns to decline into "a languishing state." Most annoying perhaps to the ministers seeking to reform society was the opposition that hampered their efforts. "Although the Lord hath been calling upon us, not only by the voice of His servants," the ministers wrote, "but by awful judgments, that we should return unto Him who hath been smiting us . . . , yet men *will not* return every one from his evil way." To the magistrates who had failed, in Mather's view, to take up the cause of reform, he had already predicted in 1677 that "God will *change* either *you*, or your Government *ere* long."* The decade of the eighties would prove him a sound prophet.

*   *   *

In the latter half of the seventeenth century the political world offered its own evidence, for those who would read such signs, that God had judged Massachusetts and had found it wanting. The first indication of difficulty came in 1664, when England's Restoration government sent a commission to New England to investigate numerous complaints that the colonies were ignoring the duties and responsibilities of their charters in general and of the Navigation Acts in particular. The presence on the commission of Samuel Maverick, to the Puritans an old gadfly and now a principal critic, prompted the General Court to withhold its cooperation. Although instructed to avoid involvement in provincial factionalism, Maverick stirred up as much turmoil as he could in an effort to drive a wedge between the Puritan leaders and those who disagreed with them. In large measure he succeeded. Maverick found fruitful ground in Maine and New Hampshire, where many inhabitants had long rankled under Puritan rule, and among the merchants of the seaports. One result was a petition signed by many of the leading entrepreneurs calling upon the General Court to cooperate more fully with the commission. Upon its return to England the group filed an unfavorable report. Only the outbreak of serious difficulties at home, including the plague of 1665 and the London fire in the year following, prevented England from taking corrective measures. But these catastrophes simply delayed the moment when Massachusetts Bay would be dragged most unwillingly into England's version of an empire.

In the dozen years after 1664, Massachusetts continued on its solitary way. But in 1676 the man arrived who paved the way for a complete change in the colony's imperial relationship. Edward Randolph was a relative and protégé of Robert Mason, an heir to the old Mason and Gorges claims to New Hampshire and Maine, which Massachusetts had ignored in taking over the two northern provinces. The Lords of Trade had chosen Randolph to investigate the situation in New England gener-

---

* "Reforming Synod" quoted in Vaughan, *Puritan Tradition*, 311–12; Mather quoted in Middlekauff, *The Mathers*, 116.

ally and to call upon Massachusetts to send agents to London for further discussion of the matter. Randolph's arrogance generated the same sort of resistance that had greeted the commissioners of 1664. Within a week he had concluded that the colony's affairs were in the hands of "inconsiderable mechanicks" and religious fanatics. He observed numerous violations of the acts of trade but was told by Governor John Leverett that Parliament's laws were not binding on New England. Like Maverick before him, Randolph had no difficulty finding numerous complainants among the Bay colony's neighbors, particularly among Anglicans in New Hampshire and Maine. Upon his return to England Randolph filed his report. In it he concluded that "the Bostoners . . . have formed themselves into a commonwealth, denying any appeals to England." For evidence he cited their refusal to take the oath of allegiance, their practice of coining money, their opposition to the commission of 1664, and their control of Maine and New Hampshire. Most significantly, Randolph charged that "they violate all the acts of trade and navigation, by which they have engrossed the greatest part of the West India trade, whereby your Majesty is damnified in the customs £100,000 yearly."*

As a reward for his services Randolph was appointed Collector of Customs for New England in 1679. Before assuming his new duties he helped persuade the Lords of Trade to separate New Hampshire from the jurisdiction of Massachusetts and to award it to his friend Mason as a proprietary grant. Randolph also succeeded in gaining broad powers of appointment over an enlarged customs establishment in New England and even arranged to have an Anglican minister set up a church of that persuasion in the heart of Puritan Boston. Rarely has a civil servant begun his career with such promise of opposition. During his first year in Boston, Randolph prosecuted ten cases of alleged trade violations, but each time local juries acquitted the defendants, who then filed countersuits against him. Although there was some truth to his charge that Boston juries were biased against him, Randolph weakened his own cause by repeatedly violating the legalities of prosecution.

In 1681 Randolph returned to England in search of still greater authority, including some powers which even his English counterparts did not enjoy. But Randolph did not believe that the colonists should be given the rights of due process accorded English defendants. Randolph not

---

* Randolph's report in Vaughan, *Puritan Tradition*, 315–16.

only looked down on the colonists under his jurisdiction; he also had his eye on a share of any seized cargoes to augment his meager salary of £100 per year. In these respects he was the harbinger of scores of subsequent customs racketeers who would follow him out to the colonies for nearly a century to come. Boston merchants violated the Navigation Acts for the same reason that English merchants did—to enhance their profits; but in Massachusetts Bay there was a larger issue at stake as well: many of the merchants there refused to recognize Parliament's power to legislate for them and to appoint officials to collect the customs. In 1682 the General Court itself adopted all of the major provisions of the Navigation Acts and established its own collectors to enforce them. This was no subterfuge to cloak the continuation of illegal commerce; it was a claim that only the General Court had the authority to make binding laws for Massachusetts Bay. In one dispatch to its London agents the court pointed out that the colonists had no representation in Parliament and that therefore "the laws of England were bounded within the four seas and did not reach America."

The constitutional issue came to a head in 1683, when Charles II was persuaded to institute *quo warranto* proceedings against the Bay colony preparatory to revoking its charter of 1629. The General Court voluntarily refused to submit the charter for revision. The Puritan leadership had most to lose, for among the grievances listed by Randolph were the Bay colony's requirement that only church members could qualify as voters and its denial of toleration to other religious sects. Increase Mather spoke for his fellow Puritans when he likened their situation to David "when he chose to fall into the hands of God rather than into the hands of men." What have neighboring colonies gained by submission, he asked? But by then the Bay colony had run out the string of resistance, and in the spring of 1684 its charter was unilaterally revoked by the mother country. Establishment of royal government was delayed by the death of Charles II, during which time Governor Simon Bradstreet and the General Court continued to rule. Then in 1686 the Dominion of New England was established, consolidating the provinces of Massachusetts, New Hampshire, Maine, and Plymouth under the direction of a president and council. Members of the last General Court held a prayer meeting in May at old Governor Bradstreet's house. There they thanked God for His guidance over the past fifty-six years and wept as they voted to "adjourn" (not dissolve) until autumn. The appointment of Joseph Dudley, son of ofttime Governor Thomas Dudley, as first president was a temporary expedient. Under his leadership the merchants of Boston dominated the council and totally neutralized the influence of the old Puritan faction on the provincial level. The fears of Increase Mather and the other saints of New Zion had surely come to pass. But the worst was still ahead.

In December 1686, James II's choice as president of the Dominion of New England, Sir Edmund Andros, arrived in Boston accompanied by one hundred English redcoats. Andros had been chosen in part because he had had some acquaintance with American affairs but largely because he was a professional soldier, with many years of loyal service to the Stuarts to his credit. Soon the Dominion's jurisdiction was expanded to include the colonies of Rhode Island, Connecticut, New York, and the two Jerseys, in addition to the four northern New England provinces. Over this territory "Captain General and Governor in Chief" Andros and a council of twenty-eight, also appointed by the Crown, exercised absolute rule. His commission granted Andros full power, with the advice and consent of the council, to make all laws and statutes for the Dominion, to assess and to raise such taxes as they deemed necessary for the support of government, continuing taxes that were then in force in the various colonies until they had reason to make changes.

Andros's exercise of these powers seems to have been well intended; there was little of the self-serving pettiness so evident in the behavior of Edward Randolph. In less than a year's time, however, Andros had succeeded in uniting both religious and commercial leaders against him. The governor won no friends among the Puritans of Boston when he insisted on using the Old South Meetinghouse for Anglican services. Samuel Sewall and others personally told the governor that "the Land and House was ours," but Andros insisted and ultimately had his way. One can imagine the anger of Boston's Puritans as they were occasionally forced to wait on the street outside their beloved meetinghouse until the governor and his retinue had finished their idolatrous worship. But perhaps Sewall carried the dispute a bit too far in refusing to sell a parcel on Cotton Hill for an Anglican church, suggesting that it would be an improper use of the late John Cotton's land.

A far greater threat to New Englanders lay in Andros's effort to establish English land laws in the territory of the Dominion. If taken literally, the new policy meant that virtually all of the transactions by which towns had distributed land to settlers were null and void as were all purchases of land from the Indians. Land properly patented was subject to a quitrent. Furthermore, all of the unsettled lands within Massachusetts Bay had reverted to the king upon nullification of the Charter of 1629. No issue could demonstrate more effectively the true meaning of Massachusetts Bay to its inhabitants than the crisis over land tenure. True enough, it was a New Zion to the Mathers and their family; and of equal truth, it was a land of commerical opportunity for the Sewalls and their descendants. But what was much more important, Massachusetts Bay had become a territory *possessed* by the thousands of men and women who had cleared its forests, worked its soil, and fished its waters. To challenge the claim to territory thus earned by three generations of settlers was to strike at the heart of a people. It was in fact a threat to his property holdings (on Hog Island), not commercial restrictions or Anglican churches, that prompted Samuel Sewall to return to his native England in 1688, there to argue the case against the change in land policy.

*　*　*

Throughout the winter of 1688–89 tensions grew steadily within the Bay colony. In his vigorous prosecution of a contest against the Indians Andros had called up hundreds of militiamen to wage a grim war throughout the northern winter. Other militiamen were assigned to dreaded garrison duty in the numerous forts constructed by the governor. Worst of all, English professionals commanded these outposts rather than the officers elected by the colonists themselves, as was the New England custom. The men of Massachusetts had no serious objection to an Indian war as such, but Andros proved to be an unusual Indian fighter—provoking hostilities to begin with, releasing prisoners outright instead of holding them for exchange, and suspending the lucrative Indian trade. Bostonians were particularly bitter about the many deaths of colonial militiamen from sickness during the war. These military actions put northern New England on edge during the winter and stirred up a sense of restlessness in Boston itself, where a handful of Andros's troops occupied the Fort Hill garrison and the English frigate *Rose* rode at anchor in the harbor. "'Twas never so in Boston before," Sewall confided.

What little news there was from England added to the atmosphere of crisis. Bostonians had greeted the accession of James II in 1685 with loyalty if not elation, but the birth of his Roman Catholic son three years later renewed their concern for a future under the Stuart monarchy. During the winter of 1688–89 rumors of William's invasion of England and James's flight to France increased the general restlessness. Some even suspected that Andros would support the fallen Stuart cause by somehow joining the Dominion of New England with the French in Canada. In late March 1689 Andros himself sensed trouble and hurried back to Boston from the northern frontier. "There is a general buzzing among the people," he admitted to a friend, "great with expectation of their old charter, or they know not what."

On the 18th of April a company of militia who had deserted from the northern campaign arrived in Boston. Their friends rallied around to prevent their arrest. At about the same time a mutinous band from the *Rose* seized the frigate's captain while he was ashore in the North End, and the rioting spread rapidly through the town. Numerous Dominion officials were seized, some by the militia and others by a crowd of armed citizens, and they were all jailed. Andros himself holed up with the garrison on Fort Hill, which was surrounded by several thousand inhabitants. Hundreds of additional militiamen poured into Boston from the countryside and still more stood ready to cross over from Charlestown if needed. Meanwhile a coalition of civic leaders, which included old Governor Bradstreet together with several sympathetic Dominion councilors, met at the townhouse. From the gallery they read a declaration of grievances against the Andros government, justified the seizure of his officers pending instructions from England, and called upon Andros to surrender himself to their protective custody. After an abortive attempt was made by loyal mariners on board the frigate to rescue the governor, Andros conceded the inevitable and turned himself in. With the surrender of the fort itself the next day and the neutralization of the *Rose*, Boston's version of the Glorious Revolution ended without the shedding of one drop of blood.

Now the provisional government had "a wolf by the ears," as one of its members put it. Unsure of what Dominion forces in New York intended, the rest of the militia was recalled from Maine, thus exposing the whole northern frontier to devastating Indian attacks. The French also took advantage of the situation to regain much of their lost territory along the coast. In Boston a Council of Safety brought together twenty-two respectable citizens under the presidency of Governor Bradstreet, now approaching ninety years of age. The council convened an *ad hoc* meeting of representatives from the various towns to decide what to do next. Many of the merchants preferred a continuation of the interim government, in which they had a disproportionately large voice, but sentiment from the country strongly favored a restoration of the old charter government. Conservatives cautioned that such a move might be viewed in London as an act of defiance, inasmuch as the charter had been revoked three years before, but the will of the people's representatives prevailed. In mid-May Governor Bradstreet and the former council resumed their positions, along with a newly elected House, and familiar statutes were put back on the books.

Various inhabitants hastily wrote to English correspondents in explanation of their recent doings. In addition to charging the Andros regime with numerous abuses, the colonists pleaded for understanding. "We have always endeavored to approve ourselves loyal to the crown of England," Thomas Danforth claimed, "and we are not without hopes but that before you do receive these lines we shall receive from their royal majesties the confirmation of our charter. . . ." But the silence from London authorities continued. Meanwhile a special committee of seven sifted through a list of complaints against the Andros government submitted by the towns. Several of them cited the efforts of Edward Randolph and other officials to help themselves to various lands around the Bay colony. A group of Ipswich residents, including the Reverend John Wise, protested their incarceration for opposing the Dominion's tax policies. Other charges seem, from a twentieth-century perspective, somewhat petty, such as the complaint that Andros had given a ring to an allegedly unfriendly Indian or that he had threatened Joseph Wood with hanging. Charges against Joseph Dudley, Edward Randolph, and several other officials accompanied those against Andros himself.

The colonists would have done better had they concentrated on more immediate problems. Not all the inhabitants accepted the authority of the new government, and enforcement of the laws was in many instances ineffective. From his jail cell Edward Randolph reported, perhaps with considerable bias, that Boston and Salem were wide open to pirates, smugglers, and other illicit traders. By the summer of 1689 the frontier was aflame from the coast of Maine to the Connecticut valley and beyond. Pemaquid fell to the French and their Indian allies in August, and soon thereafter all other settlements east of Falmouth (now Portland) were abandoned. In an effort to recoup these indignities Massachusetts launched an attack under William Phips against the French settlement of Port Royal, in Acadia. His success was only temporary, however, and the colony had to levy onerous taxes and ultimately turn to paper money to finance these and other expeditions. Meanwhile, in May 1690 the French attacked Falmouth and burned it to the ground, killing more than seventy men, women, and children. By 1691 morale in the Bay colony had reached a low ebb.

Authorities in London had enough on their minds during the first months of 1689 not to bother immediately with what might be happening in the colonies. Increase Mather had arrived the previous summer, after slipping out of Boston in disguise to avoid Randolph's effort to prevent his trip. Mather brought with him the case of Massachusetts against Andros and his government and was witness to the historic events of that year in England. With William Phips, Samuel Sewall, and other Bostonians who had traveled to London with their own grievances, he appealed to the new king for the immediate removal of Andros and the restoration of the old government. In Mather's absence from Boston the people there had already solved the first problem. In early 1690 Andros, Dudley, Randolph, and others of the deposed officials were sent to England along with a complete set of the accusations against them. None of the charges was deemed serious enough for prosecution, and after a hearing all the accused were released to serve another day as Crown officials in the American colonies. Fortunately for New England, William III showed no interest in reestablishing the Dominion, but he was equally opposed to returning the old charter to Massachusetts. Mather tried to sneak it through with a bill concerning English borough charters, but the scheme failed when Parliament adjourned.

During the winter of 1690–91 the Committee for Trade and Plantations began drafting a new charter for the Bay colony. The resulting document was dictated by conditions of empire at the end of the seventeenth century as much as by the governmental theories of those who had a hand in writing it. By 1691 England was engaged in all-out war with France, the first of a series of struggles between these two nations that would dominate much of the eighteenth century. William III therefore wanted a government in New England able and willing at least to hold its own against the French in Canada. The Committee for Trade and Plantations was fully committed to the principle of mercantilism and sought a colonial government in Massachusetts that would cooperate in enforcing the Navigation Acts. Perhaps a third ingredient was William III's own preferences for civil and religious toleration. Together these factors resulted in a charter for Massachusetts Bay that turned its back on the seventeenth-century combination of a semiindependent commonwealth and a religious paradise. It provided instead for a colony that was to take its place as part of Great Britain's reorganized empire.

William III decided that the governor of Massachusetts Bay should be appointed by the Crown with veto power over the General Court. Mather argued long and hard on these points to no avail, but after he had explained the particular religious preferences of his colony to the king in private audience, William graciously sought the advice of Mather and the other agents concerning an appropriate candidate for governor (Sir William Phips was the choice) and for the first group of councillors. The governor had broad appointive powers within the militia establishment and the judiciary. A council of twenty-eight members was selected by the General Court (instead of appointed by the king as in other royal colonies) and had the dual functions of a governor's council and an upper house of the legislature. Its membership was so constituted as to represent various geographical sections of the province. Far more important was a new definition of the franchise. No longer could church membership be required as a qualification (that provision had in fact been greatly modified by the General Court itself in 1690). Thenceforward male inhabitants possessing a forty-shilling freehold or other property worth £40 sterling qualified to vote for representatives in General Court. Another significant change confirmed the Bay colony's claim to the province of Maine (but not New Hampshire), gave to it the islands off Cape Cod (Nantucket, Martha's Vineyard, and the Elizabeths), and incorporated within it all of Plymouth Colony.

In effect the new charter strengthened the role within the government of two groups at opposite extremes of the political spectrum—the lowly farmers of the interior communities and the exalted officials of Whitehall. The ministers and merchants of the commonwealth would have to find new ways to influence public affairs, and in this regard the lords of the counting house would prove far more successful than those of the meetinghouse. Neither could match the power gained by the king, however: the right to name his own man to the greatly strengthened position of governor, his right to review all acts passed by the General Court, and most important, a free hand within the colony for a myriad of customs officials, admiralty court judges, and surveyors of the woods, all appointed by the Crown. Whatever the merits of the Bay colony's independent ways during the first sixty years of its existence, in 1691 Massachusetts became a part of the English empire for good, or so it seemed at the time.

But the political settlement of 1691 did not quiet the troubled Bay colony. Differences between generations, between religious conservatives and liberals, between economic and social groups, and between political factions continued to mount through the last years of the century. These tensions exploded in the infamous Salem Village witchcraft trials of 1692. In their idea of witchcraft the Puritans of Massachusetts merely accepted a common belief of their times, no more, no less. The world of the seventeenth century, as Milton so vividly painted it in *Paradise Lost,* was seen as an immense battleground between the forces of God and those of Satan. From earliest times the Hebraic-Christian tradition had attributed to the Devil the most devious tactics, among which was his practice of working through possessed individuals called witches. When Increase Mather returned from London in the early months of 1692, having labored three years to prepare for the future of Massachusetts Bay, he found his neighbors indulging themselves in one of the most lamentable practices of the past—a witch hunt. Ironically, Mather discovered that Samuel Sewall, with whom he had worked in London for a new charter, had been taken in by the mania.

Salem Village (now Danvers) was a small agricultural community on the outskirts of the bustling seaport north of Boston, whose inhabitants had long since earned a reputation for disputatiousness among themselves. By 1691 they had had a succession of ministers, of whom Samuel Parris was the latest. In the winter of 1691–92 his daughter and niece fell ill with what would be clinically diagnosed today as hysteria. But their fits, shrieks, and periods of severe withdrawal suggested to Mr. Parris that the girls had become possessed by the Devil. When asked "Who torments you?" the girls accused the servant Tituba, who had been telling the girls and their young friends strange tales from her native Caribbean home. They also charged that two other women of the village had sent their specters to entice the girls into signing a pact with the Devil. The torments they suffered, it was believed, had resulted from their resistance to these demands. Within weeks more accusers, almost all of them unmarried girls under the age of twenty, leveled similar

Trial of George Jacobs for Witchcraft, 1692. Painted by Tompkins Matteson (1855). Courtesy of the Essex Institute, Salem, Mass.

accusations against suspected witches, mostly married or widowed women in the forty- to sixty-year age bracket.

The accepted procedure in such matters was the appointment of a judicial court to try the accused, and upon his arrival in Massachusetts Bay in May 1692 the new governor, Sir William Phips, appointed seven councillors to comprise the court. Among them was Samuel Sewall. By the time the court convened in early June, more than one hundred persons suspected as witches were in jail awaiting trial. One of the first to be brought before the court was Bridget Bishop, an unpopular woman suspected of immoral habits. Alleged victims stepped forward to testify that Bridget's specter had tormented them by choking, pinching, and biting in an effort to force them into signing the book. One claimed that Bridget's specter had beaten her with iron rods; another charged that he had been hit on the head; and still another testified that fourteen years earlier a shape resembling the defendant had entered his home and so tormented his child that it languished and died soon after. Bridget was even accused of bewitching a sow her husband had sold. She reportedly suckled her specter from a "preternatural teat" which had been discovered on her body, but a subsequent examination revealed no such appendage. Other evidence included the so-called test of "sight and touch," whereby the accusers seemed to fall into a swoon under the gaze of the defendant, whose touch alone could thereafter bring revival.

No one seriously denied that the hand of the Devil was behind these strange doings. The only real question was whether the accused was actually responsible. Chief Justice William Stoughton insisted that the Devil could appear only in the specters of those who gave him their consent; that is, of those who were in fact in league with the Devil. To deny such consort, as most of the accused did, of course, simply confirmed the devious ways of Satan. Those who in fact "confessed" that they were witches, such as Tituba herself, were not executed. Having "blown their cover," as it were, they were of no further use to Old Ned. But for the likes of Bridget Bishop, who denied her pact with the Devil, both the Bible and the laws of the commonwealth called for death. By the end of the summer nineteen citizens of Salem Village and vicinity were hanged from the gallows. Still another victim, Giles Corey, had refused to plead either innocence, for which he would have been hanged with the others, or guilt, for which his estates would have been confiscated. For his obstinacy the old man was pressed to death under heavy fieldstones.

When he returned from the frontier, where he had been leading colonial forces against the Indians, Governor Phips found Massachusetts in turmoil. By now members of several prominent families, apparently including his own wife, stood accused of witchcraft. But now also others began to speak out against the proceedings of the special court. Boston merchant Thomas Brattle denounced the test of "sight and touch," and suggested that many of those who had confessed themselves witches were "deluded, imposed upon, and under the influence of some evil spirit." Still more effective was the somewhat belated intervention of Increase Mather. In a manuscript subsequently published as *Cases of Conscience Concerning Evil Spirits Personating Men* (1693), Mather protested against the court's acceptance of spectral evidence. The ways of the Devil were too devious to conclude that he could assume the appearance of a person only by consent. Mather catalogued a long list of happenings to demonstrate that life was fraught with mysteries which could not be logically explained. Mather did not doubt the existence of witchcraft or the sincerity of the court in attempting to stamp it out. Rather, he simply called into question its procedures. But with the support of other ministers, this was enough. Accepting Mather's conclusion that it was better to let ten witches go free than to condemn one innocent person, Governor Phips dismissed the court at the end of October. Most of the remaining accused were immediately freed on bail and all were ultimately exonerated or pardoned.

Aside from twenty corpses in Salem, what was the legacy of the witchcraft episode? For Samuel Sewall, it was a deep remorse, which led him to present a bill of contrition to a special fast-day meeting of his church in January 1697. "As to the Guilt contracted, upon the opening of the late Commission of Oyer and Terminer at Salem," Sewall confessed, "he is, upon many accounts, more concerned than any that he knows of, [he] Desires to take the Blame and Shame of it, Asking pardon of Men, And especially desiring prayers that God . . . would pardon that Sin and all his other Sins."* For the vast majority of the colony's inhabitants, who had stood by as the witchcraft mania swept through Salem Village, there was no such acceptance of guilt. Most of them probably agreed with the view of John Higginson, minister at Salem, who declared that the

---

* Halsey M. Thomas, ed., *The Diary of Samuel Sewall*, 2 vols. (New York, 1973), I, 367.

witches had been sent by God as a punishment for the sins of a faltering people.

* * *

For Samuel Sewall the more the world changed around him in the last decades of the seventeenth century, the more it remained the same within him. He had already made all of the major decisions of life. Marriage to the daughter of John Hull, one of Boston's richest merchants, gave him both a wife and a calling as well, not to mention a handsome dowry of £500, equal, it was said, to his bride's weight in pine tree shillings. Shortly thereafter he became a member of Old South Church. Sewall's business activities as a Boston merchant seem to have continued with little interruption through the tumultuous years that followed his father-in-law's death in 1683. His vessels carried fish and provisions to the West Indies, naval stores and timber to England, and most of these commodities to the Atlantic islands as well. Imports from the mother country included a vast assortment of cloth goods and other manufactured articles such as farm tools, firearms, gunpowder, and glass. He conducted his English business, as did most Bostonians, through a relative, his wife's cousin Edward Hull. Most of his imports Sewall sold retail through his store or wholesale to country shopkeepers, but he also ordered a variety of English goods for the use of his own family.

For all his wealth and position Samuel Sewall was a man of simple habits. He scorned the high fashions of other merchants in Boston and felt even more out of place among the upper circles of London during his brief visit there in 1688–89. He remained what he always had been, a devout Puritan "at peace with both God and man," as the historian Bernard Bailyn has aptly put it. By the early 1690s, when he was just past forty, Samuel Sewall deserved to be called "old fashioned," and old fashioned he would remain until his death in 1730, a reminder of what seventeenth-century Massachusetts had been, both at its best and, perhaps, at its worst as well.

8

PROVINCIAL POLITICS

In the acquisition of Plymouth Colony under the new charter of 1691 Massachusetts Bay not only gained miles of valuable territory and shoreline but it acquired as well thousands of hardworking inhabitants. Some of them, such as the members of the Otis family, had originally settled within the boundaries of the larger colony, but like so many others they had moved on to less crowded areas in search of a more promising future. Fresh from England's West Country, the Otises had come to Hingham in 1631, and there they remained for about thirty years. But the middle years of the century—the same period that saw the Rices move from Sudbury, Increase Mather return to England, William Pynchon leave Springfield, and the Sewalls move down from Newbury— brought change to the Otises too. John Otis II left Hingham in 1661 to settle his expanding family on a commodious farm in Scituate, within the boundaries of Plymouth Colony. His son John in turn moved on to Barnstable, where the Otis family would remain the town's most prominent residents for over a century. There James Otis, Sr., was born in 1702. Like so many other successful men of his time he combined a prosperous business career with an active political role within and beyond his community. His own rise to influence paralleled the maturing of politics in Massachusetts Bay itself. By the middle of the eighteenth century both James Otis, Sr., and his native province would take significant parts in the power politics of the British Empire.

* * *

The charter of 1691, as we have seen, established Massachusetts Bay on a unique footing among the American colonies. As in other royal provinces a governor appointed by the king headed the political establishment in place of the elected executive of the seventeenth century. Other appointed officials included the lieutenant governor (who exercised full powers during the frequent absences or vacancies in the governor's office), a secretary, the surveyor of woods, the collector of customs, and a number of minor posts. But the twenty-eight members of the governor's council were chosen annually by the General Court with the approval of the governor, instead of by the king. This was a significant departure from the practice in other royal colonies, where the king had retained for himself the power to appoint this body. The council served in a dual capacity. As adviser to the governor its assent to appointments and other executive acts was required. But it also sat as the upper house of the bicameral legislature, where it passed judgment on the acts of the lower branch. The House of Representatives retained much of the legislative initiative it had acquired during the seventeenth century, although its base within the various towns was altered and its powers were considerably restricted, at least in theory.

Political life in eighteenth-century Massachusetts began on the local level. Most political leaders made their start locally, rose to prominence as delegates to the House of Representatives, and, in some cases, moved on to the council, the bench, or, occasionally, the governor's chair. Although the provincial level of government became increasingly important through the century, the basis of actual political power remained firmly rooted on the local level. It is there one must begin the effort to comprehend the politics of provincial Massachusetts.

During the Dominion period Governor Andros had threatened the very existence of local town government. He challenged the practice of allocating land through towns, ruled that town meetings could be held only once each year and then only for the purpose of electing local officers, and, in fact, denied that towns had any legal right to existence at all. In recognizing it as the basis for representation in the General Court, the charter of 1691 reasserted the importance of the town, but it remained for the General Court to enact the legislation which spelled out in greater detail the future role of towns in the political life of the province. Adopted in 1692, this statute reaffirmed town boundaries, many of which had been challenged by Andros and his subordinates, and continued most of the political practices that had functioned successfully throughout the seventeenth century. Of greatest importance, the statute established a low property qualification for voting in town affairs. Expressed in extremely confusing language, the law provided that all adult males "ratable at twenty pounds estate" in addition to the poll tax were entitled to vote. As refined by subsequent legislation the law required the voter to possess within the town taxable property assessed for at least £20. The value of real estate for these purposes equaled the total rent it could earn in six years. Personal property included tools, livestock, clothing, and household effects assessed at a reasonable market value. Income from trade, money at interest, or professional employment was also liable to assessment and thus could be counted toward the £20 needed for qualification.

Perhaps no topic in the historiography of early America has generated more heat, along with enlightenment, than the subject of the franchise and its significance to colonial society and politics. The revisionist work of Robert E. Brown has corrected the view shared by a host of earlier writers that only a small minority of adult males could meet the franchise requirements of town meetings. Although Brown's figures have themselves been criticized for statistical and inferential errors, the outcome of his findings remains substantially intact: at least three out of four adult males could qualify to vote in the town affairs of eighteenth-century Massachusetts. Other investigations have shown that those disenfranchised were mostly younger men in their twenties who either still lived at home with their parents or had just begun a trade of their own and had not yet acquired sufficient property to meet the qualifications. Paupers, ne'er-do-wells, and other public charges seem to account for only a small fraction of the total, and as for independent farmers too poor to be voters, there seems to have been only a scattering.

The statute of 1692 provided also for annual election meetings (to be held in the month of March) to choose the selectmen and other officials. In theory these officers did not have to be qualified voters but in practice almost all were, if only because none but young adults and near paupers could not meet the standard. The new law subjected the conduct of town affairs to various other rules and regulations. Procedures for dealing with the poor, admitting new residents, assessing property, and providing public education were among the many matters included in this and subsequent statutes of the General Court. While many decisions were left to the initiative of the local town meeting, that body was by no means autonomous. In fact, the statute of 1692 provided that all orders and bylaws were subject to the approval of the Court of Quarter Sessions before taking effect, although enforcement quickly became lax. The day of the independent community had surely passed in Massachusetts. Instead the eighteenth-century town would become the fundamental part, but a part nonetheless, of an overall governmental structure. Meanwhile, another local institution underwent drastic modification. The proprietors of each town had, in the seventeenth century, exercised a free hand in all matters pertaining to the common and undivided lands of the community. By the end of the century, few of the original proprietors in the older towns survived; their heirs and descendants often fell to wrangling as the group came to represent a narrowing segment of the community. Disputes between town meetings and the proprietors led to still more bad feeling. By the middle of the eighteenth century most of the common lands had been divided, and the proprietors were no longer an effective force.

One development enhancing the importance of towns in the eighteenth century was their greatly increased numbers. Eighty-three towns comprised the tax list of 1695. All but about twenty of them were located within a day's travel from Boston, exceptions being those situated on Cape Cod and the islands, along the coast of Maine, and in Hampshire county. By the end of Queen Anne's War twenty-three new towns had joined the province, some carved out of common lands of the interior like Sutton and Northfield, others the result of divisions within established towns, such as the formation of Needham out of Dedham in 1711. With the coming of peace in 1713 settlement expanded rapidly westward beyond the frontiers previously established as far back as King Philip's War. Not only did the county of Worcester gain fifteen new communities but the first settlements in the distant Berkshires took root, at Sheffield and at Stockbridge. Meanwhile, in the more settled areas the process of division created still more towns, until by 1765 the total had reached 186, more than double the number at the beginning of the century.

The political significance of this expansion lies in the total commitment to the town as the basic unit of public life in the province. It is not surprising that people moving into vacant lands sought incorporation as towns since that was a common pattern in the seventeenth century. But the dissidents living in the outlying districts of established towns also sought separate status. Two-thirds of the towns incorporated after 1700 were in fact subdivisions of earlier communities. One such division illustrates the phenomenon for all. The town of Newbury, established in 1635, soon developed within it several distinct areas of settlement. One was the original town site along the banks of the Parker River; another was "the waterside," a few miles to the north along the southern edge of the Merrimack. Old-towners were almost exclusively farmers harvesting the salt hay of the marshes and raising cattle, as the Sewall family had done. But the waterside people had chosen an ideal site for a seaport. The gently sloping bank provided a firm foundation for shipbuilding from the timber of the hinterland; the broad mouth of the Merrimack protected by Plum Island formed a safe harbor. Divergent economic interests gradually separated the two population centers. Further expansion during the middle decades of the eighteenth century brought frequent quarrels over the location of a new school, a firehouse, roads, and other improvements, arguments that the Merrimack community almost always lost to the more populous farming region. The establishment of the third parish church at the waterside in 1747 paved the way for political division. Control over its own church encouraged the maritime community to seek autonomy in political matters as well. A petition for incorporation as the town of Newburyport finally gained approval of the General Court in 1764; what had been one town now became two, each with its own town meeting, local officers, and representatives to the legislature. One need only consider the fact that the original town of Dedham has become six different towns to visualize the extent to which the process of splitting off could preserve the machinery of government in the hands of local interests.

At the end of the seventeenth century significant forces were already changing the balance of political power within the towns of Massachusetts Bay. In earlier years a small number of selectmen managed local affairs, but grassroots power began gradually to shift to the town meeting itself. By the 1720s towns like Dedham were holding four or five meetings a year instead of only one or two, and for the first time groups of inhabitants regularly exercised their right to convene a meeting themselves rather than relying on the initiative of the selectmen. Each meeting elected a moderator to chair the session, a further erosion of the selectmen's authority. In some towns the agenda was even subject to amendment from the floor. Executive powers formerly monopolized by the selectmen were increasingly parceled out among such newly created positions as assessors, constables, and treasurer. As elected officials these men reported directly to the annual town meeting rather than to the selectmen. One significant sign of these changes in the town of Dedham was that fewer selectmen served for long periods: the annual turnover increased from 27 percent before 1686 to 40 percent in the period 1687–1736. The cumulative experience of the incumbents fell by half, from fifty years to twenty-five during the same period.

One major reason for these changes was simply that the business of managing rapidly growing towns required more time than most selectmen could afford. Just when many of the founding generation's leaders were dying off, the expanding population began to provide a greater number of men able and willing to assume positions of leadership within their communities. Yet the odds of any one of them becoming a selectman narrowed each year. Increasing the number of officials not only spread the burden of leadership more equitably but also provided new opportunities for leadership.

The dispersal of population into unsettled parts of established towns had a major effect on local politics. In many cases the outlanders found that selectmen paid little heed to their special circumstances, and so they increasingly turned to the wider forum of the town meeting. By so doing they injected a diversity of interests and opinions into a political procedure which had long been accustomed to working by consensus. In town after town majority rule increasingly replaced consensus as the means of reaching a decision. Local issues occasionally became so heated as to divide the town into irreconcilable camps, as happened in Sudbury during the 1650s and in Newbury a century later. The once sacred principle of unity, so vital to the survival of an infant community in the wilderness, gradually gave way. Now particular groups, such as Newbury's waterside merchants and mariners, placed a higher premium on getting their own way than on preserving agreement with farmers. Only when a group despaired of winning such a voice did they take the ultimate step of secession. And sometimes, as in Danvers and Salem, it was the old farmer group that seceded, having lost control of what had once been its own town meeting.

And yet in another sense the establishment of a new town such as Newburyport was itself the result of a new consensus which embraced merchants, shipbuilders, artisans, shopkeepers, and shipwrights of varying wealth and sophistication. The sense of community that had been lost between the farmers and mariners of the old town was regained in the birth of the new one. For several decades thereafter, Newburyport's town meeting made its own decisions by consensus, as men of different social and economic positions reached for common political ground in open town meeting. Not until the intense partisan politics of the Federalist era did majoritarian rule overthrow consensus politics in Newburyport. By some sort of dialectical process, the division of original towns like Newbury into warring factions led to the formation of new communities and preserved the principle of consensus by a continuing process of rebirth. Towns that would not, or could not, divide were thereby doomed to political divisiveness.

In addition to their function as local governing bodies the towns of Massachusetts Bay comprised the principal foundation on which the legislature was based. In 1694 the General Court required that all of its members be residents of the towns they represented. Since the establishment of the lower house more than sixty years before, most towns had in fact sent only residents as delegates. By barring any exception to this practice, the statute of 1694 underscored the principle of actual representation. The English House of Commons, on the other hand, was founded on quite another theory. Members of Parliament sat not as delegates representing territorial constituencies but as the representatives of the various interests which in the English view constituted the realm. Thus one would find country gentlemen in profusion reflecting the predominant interest of that group within the nation. A scattering of merchants and manufacturers, several career military and naval officers, a few churchmen and university types rounded out the Commons. Members did not have to live in the boroughs or counties that elected them and some perhaps had never set foot in their districts. Some of the so-called rotten boroughs had few if any residents so that the electorate itself did not live there! What made the legislature of Massachusetts Bay and of most other American colonies distinctive was the fact that their members exercised a power delegated to them by their friends and neighbors.

Various statutes enacted under the charter of 1691 established the specific rules by which the towns of the province were to be represented in the General Court. Any incorporated town, no matter how small, was entitled to send one delegate; those with forty or more qualified voters (the figure was raised to sixty in 1726) were required to choose a representative. Towns with at least one hundred twenty voters could send two delegates if they wished, and Boston was entitled to four. Many of the smallest towns did not bother to send a representative at all, and because of absenteeism some sessions saw only half the towns participating. By eighteenth-century standards the basis of representation was extremely broad. Had they exercised their right to send delegates the inhabitants of the smallest communities would have been vastly overrepresented compared to those living in larger towns. The dozen or so larger communities could at best send only about thirty delegates altogether, even though their aggregate population far exceeded that of the thirty smallest towns. Delegates were often given specific instructions by their local town meetings. Strong ties between towns and delegates were further maintained by annual elections. Each year, usually just before the March town meeting, those qualified to vote for representatives made their choice in open session. This provincial franchise was in fact somewhat less restrictive than that for town meeting. Adult males with a forty-shilling sterling freehold (real estate that could be rented for at least £2 per annum) or who owned other property worth at least £40 met the qualification. Fluctuating currency and occasional changes in interpretation altered the effect of this requirement somewhat, but throughout most of the eighteenth century about 60 percent of the adult males living in the larger towns could vote for provincial delegates, while over 80 percent of most small-town residents likewise met the qualification. As in the case of town elections the exceptions seem to have been mostly younger men not yet established in life, along with a scattering of older people who were permanently dependent on others for support.

In the years after 1691 the House of Representatives moved quickly to consolidate its position within the political spectrum of the rechartered province. Its members claimed the rights and privileges of the House of Commons concerning freedom of debate, election of its own speaker, and freedom from arrest while the legislature was in session. The lower house claimed the sole right to impose taxes and to control the expenditure of public funds. The General Court itself enjoyed the power to appoint officers to a large number of posts and also to specify their salaries. What was more, the General Court claimed the further right to control the governor's salary and those of other Crown appointees. Although the Privy Council disallowed many of these demands, the legislature nevertheless succeeded in maintaining a strong political position during the eighteenth century. For one thing, the General Court had already established its right to initiate almost all legislation affecting the inhabitants of Massachusetts at a time when the assemblies of a few other colonies had barely moved beyond the advisory stage. Like the members of Parliament whom they tried in so many ways to emulate, the legislators of Massachusetts Bay believed that their primary function was not to create new law but rather to apply the familiar principles of accepted common law to the particular matters before them. The law was, in short, both singular and permanent, not plural and subject to change. Nor did the General Court perform this role solely in what we today might describe as its legislative mode. It also had considerable judicial and executive functions—settling boundary disputes, appointing officers, and occasionally hearing civil cases. While the statutes enacted by the legislators were subject to the governor's veto and the royal disallowance, that body deftly avoided such action by putting many of its decisions in the form of resolutions and orders not subject to review.

A glance at some of the business before the House during the first decade of James Otis's service as a representative from Barnstable (1745–54) illustrates the range of powers and interests of the General Court. King George's War had already erupted in North America, and much of the legislature's business involved support for the military effort. Funds were needed for the siege of Louisbourg, the construction of forts along the interior front, and soldiers' pay. Otis steered a bill through that provided a bounty on Indian scalps, supported a protest against the impressment of American sailors on board British naval vessels, and took a stand against profiteering by the bakers of Boston. But much of his effort was focused on responding to the numerous petitions from individuals that reflected day-to-day life in Massachusetts Bay. Special permission to sell parcels of land, compensation for a constituent who lost a sum of money in a fire, several divorce actions, and benefits for a wounded war veteran were among the mundane affairs considered by the House. Otis served on numerous committees, from the prestigious committee of war and the supply committee to one preparing a response to the governor's annual message. Then there were instructions to be drafted for the colony's agent in London, the interminable measures to regulate currency, drawing up new policies toward the Iroquois and other Indian tribes, and legislation to encourage the fisheries. Throughout his career Otis constantly strove to balance the special interests of his Barnstable constituents with the overriding welfare of the province, all the while trying to maintain an abiding faith in the common law, on the one hand, and his political allies, on the other.

Surely the most unusual power exercised by the lower house was its right to select, while sitting with the outgoing council, the members of the incoming council, subject to the governor's approval. The council in turn served both as an upper house of the legislature and as an advisory body to the chief executive. In this latter role, the council of Massachusetts proved an annoying check on the governor on numerous occasions. Not only was the governor of Massachusetts deprived of the patronage enjoyed by his counterparts in other colonies in nominating councillors, but the council itself reviewed all of the governor's appointments. Governor Thomas Pownall's judgment that the council was "little other than an annually elected committee of the General Court" exaggerated the matter somewhat, however, for councillors were on the whole men of considerably greater wealth and position than the average representative. But almost all had come from similarly common backgrounds, unlike the titled aristocrats who sat in England's House of Lords or in the Privy Council. Nor could the governor regard the councillors as political allies, since they depended upon the will of the House of Representatives for reappointment.

During the eighteenth century yet another level of government gained considerable strength in Massachusetts. In 1699 the legislature reorganized the court structure of the province, establishing a Superior Court of Judicature. Each county was provided with a general sessions court for handling criminal cases and a court of common pleas for civil matters. In addition each county had its own probate court to accept wills, care for wards, and resolve disputes over the property of those dying intestate. By English tradition jury trials were guaranteed for accused criminals who preferred such a procedure, and the jurymen were selected each year from among the electorate of each town in the county. Counties also supported jails, sheriffs, highways, and bridges, and occasionally provided a convenient basis for informal conventions of delegates from its member towns to take positions on matters of common interest. The costs of maintaining county courts and other institutions amounted to a significant part of the total tax burden. It had become clear that the locus of government which helped to shape the terms of everyday life was gradually shifting away from the local townhouse to a point somewhat more remote, as the powers of both the General Court and the county expanded during the eighteenth century.

Despite all the restrictions upon his power exercised by the House of Representatives and the council, His Majesty's royal governor stood firmly at the head of government in Massachusetts Bay. No other single official commanded so much political influence, military power, and social prestige. The stronger governors could get their own way much of the time, and even the weakest were men to be reckoned with by all other political figures. The governor, in fact, enjoyed a number of powers which by the eighteenth century were denied the king himself. His power of absolute veto influenced the legislative process even though occasionally circumvented by the General Court. The governor also had the right to call the House of Representatives into session at the time and place of his choice and to prorogue it at will. His powers of appointment extended beyond the usual executive positions to include all of the judges, from local justices of the peace to those who sat on the Superior Court of Judicature and included the authority to remove them at his pleasure. The governor could also establish new courts and jurisdictional bounds whenever he deemed such action appropriate. While subject to council approval, the governor nevertheless held the initiative in these activities against an often divided opposition. Furthermore, he represented the king in governmental as well as in ceremonial matters. While few inhabitants of eighteenth-century Massachusetts were ideological royalists, most of them respected the Crown and what it stood for. Reminding all branches of government of this relationship, including the governor himself, were the numerous royal instructions which he received from Whitehall.

Offsetting these advantages, however, were numerous obstacles facing the governor beyond the various limitations of power imposed by the charter. One of the most serious difficulties was the very impermanence of the appointment. During the first decade after the arrival of Governor William Phips in 1692 the province experienced four different administrations. In the next eighteen years—to 1730—the situation improved somewhat with five administrations, including the thirteen-year tenure of Joseph Dudley. A further degree of stability in the office finally came with Jonathan Belcher, who served from 1730 to 1741, followed by William Shirley's seventeen years of service. The executive office lost momentum whenever a vacancy occurred, for it often took a year or more for a new appointment to be made and additional months before the new governor arrived. Meanwhile, the lieutenant governor headed a caretaker administration with all the disadvantages that such status implied. Each new governor required time to become accustomed to the province, its charter provisions, political leaders, and particular traditions. By contrast, changes in membership of the General Court came gradually, only a few each year, so that it steadily gained momentum. Time worked against the governor in another way. Bound by royal instructions that reflected the views of British officials three thousand miles away, he could not match the alacrity with which the General Court reacted to changing circumstances in the province. Six months or more might pass before the governor received new instructions.

In naming Sir William Phips the first royal governor of Massachusetts in 1691 William III took the advice of Increase Mather. Phips had been a Boston shipmaster with a bent for warfare and had already led the colony's forces in the capture of Acadia and an assault on the French base at Quebec. Upon his appointment Phips renewed the war with equal vigor but considerably less success. Meanwhile the witchcraft mania had reached its highest frenzy in Salem. Phips returned to Massachusetts, wisely adjourned the court, and ultimately put an end to the crisis by freeing most of the accused. As a man of action Phips could react to crises with admirable decisiveness, but he lacked the statesmanship necessary to build an effective administration. He fell to quarreling with the General Court over nominees for the council, and he arbitrarily spent public funds contrary to the purposes for which they had been appropriated. He frequently lost his temper and finally, in 1694, his job. Under his temporary successor, Lieutenant Governor William Stoughton, the war took a turn for the worse, and political affairs continued to drift. Stoughton put an end to the squabbling that had plagued his predecessor's administration only by giving the General Court its head in governmental affairs. The appointment of the Earl of Bellomont to serve simultaneously as governor and military commander of New Jersey, New York, Massachusetts, and New Hampshire was a clear effort to facilitate prosecution of the war against French Canada. But Bellomont died in 1701, and the office once more reverted to the ineffective William Stoughton. During this first decade of government under the new charter neither the General Court nor the executive had succeeded in developing a permanent working relationship with the other. Indeed, they had largely failed even to determine the significant points of difference between them that required resolution.

Friction was never in short supply during the long administration of

Joseph Dudley, appointed governor in 1702. In the decade after his unceremonious departure from Massachusetts as one of Sir Edmund Andros's henchmen, Dudley had looked to the day when he might return to his native province in triumph. During his years of exile he had served as a member of Parliament, as lieutenant governor of the Isle of Wight, and had acquired a keen sense of what England expected of its royal governors. He wasted no time in conveying these views to the General Court. Immediately upon his arrival Dudley pointed out that Massachusetts was the only English colony failing to provide a fixed and adequate salary for the governor and other appointed officials. The General Court professed surprise at the suggestion and voted instead a present of £500 for the current year. In the next session the General Court announced that "it is not convenient (the circumstances of the province considered) to state salaries, but to allow as the Great and General Court shall from time to time see necessary." When in 1703 Queen Anne specifically instructed Dudley to pursue the matter further, the governor presented the royal letter to the General Court. This time the House of Representatives reached far back into English constitutional history for its response. Since the reign of Henry III, said the delegates, it had been "the just and unquestionable right of the subject to raise and dispose how they see cause, any sum of money by consent of parliament. . . ." The settling of permanent salaries for the governor, the House concluded, would be prejudicial to Her Majesty's good subjects. Not only did the House of Representatives thereby identify itself with the House of Commons but in so doing it also asserted its freedom from royal instructions sent to the governor.

Dudley crossed swords with the General Court on several other issues as well. He vigorously exercised his right to veto nominations for the council, refusing to confirm five candidates in 1703 alone. Among the men he blackballed was Elisha Cooke, an influential and popular leader of the House of Representatives, whom he rejected three years running. Here Dudley stood on solid ground, but when he attempted to veto the House's choice of Thomas Oakes as its Speaker in 1705, that body persisted in its choice and finally prevailed. Dudley struggled unsuccessfully for funds to rebuild the fort at Pemaquid, and without authorization from the House he paid the lieutenant governor a small sum as commander of Castle William. But, in large measure, the General Court cooperated fully with the governor in military matters. When he was finally recalled in 1715, Dudley seemed to have established a working relationship with the General Court that permitted the colony to survive the difficult years of Queen Anne's War, but which left unresolved the major points of difference between the executive and the legislature.

Dudley's immediate successor, Colonel Elizius Burges, was forced to resign even before taking up his duties. His replacement, Colonel Samuel Shute, arrived in 1716 in the middle of a raging controversy over a proposal to establish a land bank for the circulation of paper money. Its strongest supporter was Elisha Cooke, Jr., a Boston merchant whose father had been blocked by Dudley thirteen years earlier. Shute had been chosen partly for his opposition to the land bank scheme, and he immediately joined battle with its proponents. First, he fell into a dispute over the timber preserves in Maine. Next he attempted to control the infant press of the colony with no better success. Then in 1719 he refused to approve the election of Cooke as Speaker of the House and rekindled all of the animosity that this issue had generated under Dudley fourteen years before. Perhaps because he was a professional soldier Shute lacked even the modicum of tact that Dudley had acquired in working with civilians, and the tug of war over Cooke took a serious turn. As before, the House vehemently denied the governor's right to interfere in such matters. Now it retaliated further by cutting £200 from Shute's salary. In the next session the House put its power of the purse to the full test by insisting that the governor sign all the bills passed by the General Court before voting him any salary at all. When the House tried the same tactic again in 1721, Shute countered by holding up the appointment of several officers. Again the House waited for assurance that all bills had been signed before granting the governor the same reduced salary. When Shute departed to plead his case at Whitehall in 1722, he left behind an unpromising legacy for the governors who would follow.

In Shute's absence Lieutenant Governor William Dummer, a respected country gentleman from Newbury, headed an interim administration that lasted for nearly six years. Dummer's hand was somewhat strengthened in 1725, when a new "explanatory charter" gave the governor the express power to veto the choice of House Speaker and to adjourn the General Court at will. But the document failed to mention the salary issue, and soon Dummer ran into the same difficulty as his predecessor. The arrival in 1728 of Governor William Burnet brought the salary dispute to a new head. Burnet had been instructed to demand a perpetual salary, and he promptly informed the House that its refusal would be regarded by the king "as a manifest mark of their undutiful behavior to us" and could well lead to corrective action by the Parliament. The House refused to comply, offering instead a sizable allowance, and Burnet referred the matter to Whitehall. But it soon became obvious both to the governor (through a private letter from the Duke of Newcastle) and to the House (through its London agents) that parliamentary action was unlikely. Once again expediency overcame principle, and Burnet accepted the salary granted him. Before the matter came up the following year, however, Burnet died, and another interim period postponed further controversy.

As the son of a wealthy Boston merchant, Jonathan Belcher longed for the power and prestige that appointment to the governorship would bring. But he had been an opponent of Burnet in the House and was even serving as one of the colony's agents when news of the governor's death reached London. Nothing daunted, he managed to persuade the authorities at Whitehall that as a native son he might succeed where others had failed in securing a permanent salary for the chief executive. When he took office in 1730, however, Belcher had already gone on record suggesting that royal instructions constituted an insufficient basis for such demands and that Parliament was unlikely ever to interfere in the dispute. Eager to enhance his own wealth Belcher had little heart for the fray and sought permission to accept the generous grants that the House offered him on the usual year-to-year basis. When Whitehall matched the governor's acquiescence with its own, the battle over administrative salaries went by default to the House of Representatives. Except for an occasional and desultory effort by some of Belcher's successors, the dispute became a dead issue.

Few governors had as great an opportunity to establish their administrations on a firm footing as did Belcher, but his initial advantage soon fell before a series of quarrels with the General Court. One such issue concerned the House of Representatives' insistence that public funds could be expended only for the specific purposes it designated. Belcher vetoed all such encumbered appropriations, and a long wrangle ensued which kept provincial finances at crisis level. Another controversy centered on the northern pine forests. Like several of his predecessors, Belcher was governor of New Hampshire as well as of Massachusetts Bay and was therefore responsible for protecting the king's timber reserves.

But when the ambitious young advocate general, William Shirley, discovered that several of Belcher's friends were systematically raiding the woods, the governor made himself new enemies of Shirley, David Dunbar, the surveyor general, and Samuel Waldo, a principal supplier of masts for the Royal Navy. All of these men had important connections in London and did not hesitate to use them in opposition to the governor. Meanwhile, Belcher's own patron, Lord Townshend, had been forced from the ministry and another London friend, Samuel Shute, had died. His relentless campaign against the land bank scheme of 1740, while ultimately successful in shutting down the plan to provide paper money for the colony, earned him the everlasting enmity of the influential men who lost heavily as the result of the governor's opposition. The political turmoil that followed caught him short, without sufficient political support at home to weather the storm. When Belcher's career in Massachusetts came to an abrupt end in 1741, it was English as much as American politics that brought him down.

* * *

Looking back on the early career of William Shirley, one might easily conclude that from the moment of his arrival at Boston as a young lawyer fresh from England in 1731 he was destined to become the governor of Massachusetts Bay. During his first years in Boston he developed a prosperous and influential legal practice with the help of Governor Belcher. But he and his ambitious wife, Frances, had their sights set on a far higher station that that of a mere provincial lawyer. Like so many Englishmen who had come to America primarily for personal gain—William Pynchon and Henry Sewall among them—Shirley could not fully commit himself to the New World. Instead he relied on his Old World contacts to press for a place in the British colonial establishment. In 1733 he talked Belcher into appointing him advocate general of the admiralty court. He pursued his new duties with such vigor, however, that he soon found himself prosecuting some of Governor Belcher's closest allies among the merchant-smugglers of timber and foreign goods. Before long the young lawyer decided that his relationship with the governor was more liability than asset. He strengthened his ties with Belcher's opponents in New England and sent his wife back to the old country, where she sought to undermine the governor's support. As Belcher's position weakened, his enemies pressed their case against him with mounting energy. Among Shirley's advantages were his Anglican orthodoxy, his skill as a prosecutor in the king's cause, and most particularly, his friendship with the Duke of Newcastle, whose political star was in rapid ascendancy. When in the summer of 1741 Whitehall was finally persuaded that Belcher had outlived his usefulness, William Shirley was not waiting demurely in the wings—he was already striding across the stage to take over the leading role in Massachusetts Bay.

The new governor moved almost immediately to solidify his political base within the province by transforming the common opposition to Belcher into support for himself. He refused to criticize the disappointingly small salary granted him by the House. He bent every effort to ease the financial shock accompanying the dissolution of the land bank and with some reason could boast in a letter to Newcastle in the fall of 1741 that the "malignant spirit is now vanished." Early the next year the governor accepted a compromise arrangement with the House that allowed for a moderate expansion of the currency with at least some protection against inflation. An important first step toward a stable currency had been taken. Now Shirley was ready to take up the ancient cause of a permanent salary. Throughout the months-long discussion with the House the governor maintained a moderate demeanor which enabled him to accept a vastly increased grant, albeit on the same old annual basis. Thereafter, he let the matter drop for the remainder of his term without the loss of face suffered by most of his predecessors. In 1743 Shirley came to grips with yet another prickly issue—the enforcement of laws reserving white pines for the royal mast-yards. To strengthen his hand Shirley and his allies could offer lucrative contracts to William Pepperrell and others who had previously opposed reforms. Shirley had more difficulty enforcing the Navigation Acts. Here he was able to make some headway by exploiting a split among the merchants of Boston, but his vigorous prosecution generated strong opposition, and in the end he was forced to relax enforcement. It is significant, however, that Shirley had the wisdom to compromise on minor issues in order to preserve the political base he needed for major undertakings like the war against French Canada.

In his effort to establish and maintain support for his policies within the House of Representatives Shirley depended on local politicians for whom he could do a good turn. The Otises of Barnstable proved most amenable to the governor's favors. James Otis, Sr., was elected to the House in 1745 with the help of his brother-in-law Isaac Little and neighbor Sylvanus Bourn, both of whom were Shirley men in the council. James's brother John received the governor's approval as a councillor in 1747 and also enjoyed the lucrative post of king's attorney for Barnstable county. As for James himself, these connections with the governor, indirect though they were, marked him as a man of influence within the House and contributed to his appointment to several important committees during his first years as a representative. As a hard-money man, Otis welcomed the governor's support of a measure to put the province's currency on a silver standard in 1749. Otis also appreciated the governor's strong anti-French stance. In anticipation of war Otis bought up whaleboats and ship timber throughout Cape Cod and the islands and then made a good profit when they were needed on the inland rivers and lakes of New York. As a consistent supporter of Governor Shirley, Otis had reason to hope that loyalty might result in a more permanent reward—say a seat on the governor's council. But a politician makes enemies while serving friends, and those whom Otis had antagonized through the years blocked his election in the House.

For nearly half of Shirley's long term England was at war with either Spain or France or both. As a strong advocate of empire, the governor encouraged the inhabitants of Massachusetts Bay to support the naval and military campaigns of the mother country to the utmost. While the details of these wars will be traced in another chapter, it should be noted here what skillful use Shirley made of the opportunities they offered him. It was the governor who conceived and planned the assault on the French base at Louisbourg in 1745 and to him as much as to William Pepperrell and Admiral Peter Warren belonged credit for the victory. Only political considerations in England deprived Shirley of the honors he deserved. The establishment of defensive forts along the interior front gave Shirley the patronage of numerous military appointments. Even more useful were the contracts for constructing and supplying these and other fortifications during both King George's and the Seven Years' War that followed. His own war profits went into the construction of an elegant country seat in Roxbury, but his wife unfortunately died before they could finally enjoy together a life-style both had sought for so long in provincial Boston.

For the next several years Shirley busied himself with imperial matters that took him to London and Paris. In his absence opposition within the House of Representatives gained considerable strength, generated in part perhaps by the vitriolic attacks against him in Boston's first opposition newspaper, the *Independent Advertiser*. When he sought to rebuild the interior forts against the possible renewal of war, the House refused to vote sufficient funds. More embarrassing though less harmful was its adamant opposition to compensating him for his extra expenses while abroad. Approaching war strengthened the governor's position once more, however, and a successful expedition into the interior of Maine checked French aspirations there and greatly enhanced his prestige at home. He made further gains by his adroit handling of a bill to raise a revenue on the manufacture of liquor. Then in 1755 General Edward Braddock put him at the head of an expedition to capture Fort Niagara and made him second in command of the British army in North America. With Braddock's ambush and death, Shirley became commander in chief of all the king's forces. Frances would have been proud of her husband at the pinnacle of his career, but she might also have shared his misgivings, for Shirley was no professional soldier. The tasks ahead proved too much for him. He was unable to fend off his adversaries in New York, in Massachusetts, and ultimately in England. The first signs of trouble came in the spring of 1757, when Shirley's merchant allies in Boston and London lost a series of major contracts to political and commercial rivals. The military campaigns in America had thus far proved disastrous, and the ministry was badly in need of a scapegoat. Shirley's patron, Newcastle, had serious political difficulties of his own and was in no position to prevent Shirley's recall both as commander in chief and as governor. As a combination of English and American politics had made Shirley governor in 1741, now sixteen years later a similar combination brought about his downfall. The citizens of Boston gave him a warm farewell as he left for his homeland. Few governors of any American colony had earned such respect and affection.

Governor Shirley in fact left behind a more significant legacy than his fine mansion house, a town named in his honor, and pleasant associations. In the coalition he had formed around Jonathan Belcher's opponents he had laid the foundation for a system of party politics. According to John Adams, there had always been a court and a country party in the Bay colony, but more recent analysis suggests that such a system did not reach full development until the administrations of Thomas Pownall and Francis Bernard in the decade 1757–67. Entire towns rather than individual politicians comprised the essential units; in this sense few towns aside from Boston had a genuine two-party structure within them, although some communities changed their allegiance over a period of years. Generally speaking, the delegates from "court party" towns supported the royal governor and were closely related to various executive and judicial functions of government. Most of the county seats, for instance, were court-party towns, as were the leading maritime and market centers. They were both economically and socially more diverse, more adaptable, and more prosperous than the country-party towns.

With a large share of the colony's lawyers and merchants, the leadership of the court-party towns became increasingly elitist by mid-century. They sought to control the House of Representatives by electing the Speaker and dominating the major committees. But their primary fulcrum of power lay in the governor's council. Not only did control of the council give these towns a voice in governmental decisions but membership in the council was itself a choice political plum with which to reward faithful supporters of the governor. Political power rather than ideological goals provided fuel to move the group. When James Otis, Sr., reached the inescapable conclusion by 1757 that Thomas Hutchinson had succeeded in cutting him out of the party altogether, the Barnstable leader took his town and much of his county over to the "country" party. Otis and the new governor, Thomas Pownall, needed each other to counteract the rising political fortunes of Hutchinson, who now became lieutenant governor. Pownall approved the election of Otis as Speaker of the House and promised him the next vacancy on the Superior Court. But before the alliance could develop further, Pownall was accepted for the governorship of South Carolina. When his replacement, Francis Bernard, named Hutchinson to the court vacancy instead, Otis led his country party back into its traditional role of opposition to the governor. It was a lonely battle for six years. Then the controversy with Great Britain brought a partial realignment and expansion of Otis's group into what came to be known to its opponents as the popular party. With this change a difference of ideology would appear for the first time in the politics of Massachusetts Bay.

9

PROVINCIAL LIFE

Thomas Hancock was born just a few years after the beginning of the eighteenth century, the second son of Lexington's pastor. His older brother had already decided to follow in his father's footsteps and attend Harvard in preparation for a career as a minister. Young Thomas might have become a cordwainer like his grandfather Nathaniel, but the Hancocks were apparently more ambitious. Just short of his fourteenth birthday in 1717, the youngster was sent off to Boston like so many other country boys before and since. There he was indentured as an apprentice to Samuel Gerrish, a bookseller in Cornhill. During the next seven years Thomas learned how to bind books, sell stationery, and stock the great variety of reading materials in demand among the customers of a busy seaport like Boston. At the age of twenty-one, perhaps with a little help from his father, young Hancock went into the bookselling business himself at the Sign of the Bible and Three Crowns in Ann Street, on Boston's waterfront. He became a specialist in binding and within three years had a well-established business selling Bibles, psalms, singing and school books, and volumes on history, navigation, poetry, and divinity, among other subjects. He also sold account books and a full range of stationery supplies.

While many artisans, like shoemakers or tailors, retailed their own products, Hancock took one important step further. He combined a particular manual skill, bookbinding, with a retail trade, bookselling. The potentialities for growth were considerably greater because of the diversity of his business and because of the variety of men he met in his shop. He began to invest in a number of minor business ventures, such as a paper factory, which a group of Bostonians had begun in 1728. His marriage in 1730 to the daughter of Thomas Henchman connected him with one of Boston's most enterprising businessmen. As a bookseller Hancock was almost totally dependent on London suppliers for his stock. He faced the same difficulty confronting almost all American businessmen in the eighteenth century—how to pay for the goods he bought in England. Like so many other shopkeepers in Boston, Salem, and Newburyport, Thomas became a merchant so that he could find his own "returns," as exports used to purchase goods in England were called. With his fellow businessmen, Thomas Hancock would in time enjoy both the headaches and the rewards of such an undertaking.

*　*　*

For every young man who followed Thomas Hancock into the larger towns to learn a craft or become a tradesman at least five others remained in the countryside as farmers. The environment kept the agriculture of Massachusetts as diversified as it had been in the seventeenth century. Few farmers owned the expanse of tillable land required for specialization to begin with, nor did they have the necessary labor force to work extensive fields. And the most marketable crop, wheat, suffered so severely from the infectious plant disease, blast, that it was virtually given up well before 1700. From then on Massachusetts imported virtually all of its wheat and flour from New York, Pennsylvania, and by the mid-eighteenth century, Virginia. Families that could not afford wheat relied on rye and that old New England staple, Indian corn. Other vegetables flourished in most sections of the colony, but none bore much promise as major market crops. If the Bay colony had any agricultural specialty at all, it was livestock. From the time Henry Sewall and his associates began their cooperative venture in Newbury, the farmers of Massachusetts realized that their land could support considerable numbers of cows, horses, oxen, sheep, and swine. Valuation figures disclose that in 1735 the province as a whole supported thirty-six cows, ninety sheep, and eighteen horses per hundred persons. Of course, each farm family had at least one cow and a horse for domestic use so that surplus livestock reached only modest proportions, but the sheep represented a promising investment in the production of wool and mutton for market. Livestock required not only pasturage but for the long winter months considerable amounts of hay, which became a valuable product in itself. A report

Thomas Hancock (1703–1764). Painting by John Singleton Copley. Courtesy of the Harvard University Portrait Collection, gift of John Hancock, 1766.

made in 1767 on the nonwoodland acreage of Norfolk, Essex, and Middlesex counties described only one out of eight farm acres as arable land, somewhat more than two out of eight as hay fields, and the remainder as pasture, except for a small amount of orchard land.

Natural conditions in some of the inland regions were more encouraging, but until the development of better roads, lack of access to markets prevented the full exploitation of these lands. The Connecticut valley from Longmeadow to Greenfield proved an exception. There the river not only brought rich alluvial soil to the lands along its banks but provided a natural route to the market towns of Northampton, Springfield, Hartford, and Middletown. The river was navigable by deep-water vessels as far as Warehouse Point above Hartford and by flat-boats, with a few portages, all the way to Turner's Falls, near the New Hampshire border. As in all other areas of the colony most farmers lived close to the subsistence level and produced only a small excess each year. But as the eighteenth century progressed these surpluses began to accumulate in sufficient quantities to encourage country merchants to look for markets. A little wheat and other grains, specialty crops like butter and cheese, and the ubiquitous sheep and cattle were the principal produce of the region. In their spare time some farmers made pot and pearl ashes directly for export; others cut shingles, clapboards, hoops and staves, and a number of them sent down apple cider and other fruits. Few farmers profited very much from these activities, but their surpluses did permit them to purchase manufactured articles otherwise unobtainable. Thus in their small way they contributed to the ever-increasing specialization that marked the eighteenth-century economy.

In many of the older communities of eastern Massachusetts the generation coming to maturity at the beginning of the eighteenth century faced an obstacle unprecedented in the American colonies—a shortage of land. In Dedham, for instance, the turning point came as early as 1713, when the proprietors made the last division of the common lands. Those vast stretches of forest and meadow which had first attracted settlers to the area in 1636 were now altogether in private hands. By the first decades of the eighteenth century the town's population had so increased that the average holding shrank to about a hundred acres, adequate to support a single family in comfort in cropland, meadow, and woodlot, with enough left over to allow a field or two to lay fallow each year. But one hundred acres was not enough to apportion among several sons, as partible inheritance rather than primogeniture remained the custom. Furthermore, some of this land had been farmed almost continuously for nearly a century and had lost its fertility. By the 1790s some farmers would begin to apply scientific methods to rejuvenate their fields, but those techniques were still unknown in mid-century Massachusetts. Much of the remaining land had not been particularly productive to begin with. As a result the price of good land began to rise beyond the level that most young men could afford. In the southeastern town of Norton, for instance, the real price of land rose from 15.5 shillings an acre in 1711–15 to 21.7 shillings in 1736–40, while the actual price of wheat was declining. Now with the disappearance of the common and undivided lands the young men of the early eighteenth century in Norton, Dedham, and other towns founded at about the same time faced an uncertain future. After a century of hard work and sacrifice by succeeding generations of colonists whose principal motivation had been to make a better world for their descendants, their very success had produced, in its burgeoning population figures, the seeds of its own destruction.

The irony of their situation was probably lost on most of the victims. It often is. But the rising generation in Dedham must have sensed that their lives would be different from those of their parents and grandparents. For some of them the change meant leaving Dedham altogether for opportunities elsewhere. The percentage who decided to move varied widely from town to town. Only two out of ten young men chose to leave Dedham during the early eighteenth century, while members of the same generation moved out of Andover at twice that rate. Perhaps the explanation for this wide variation lies in the fact that immigration was such a personal matter. Family ties have always been strong among conservative rural families; familiar neighbors and surroundings contrasted strongly with the strangeness of new territories to the west and north. The possibility of Indian attacks was a further restraint for some; the formidable prospect of breaking virgin forest constrained others. Just as push-pull drew a few away from Dedham each year, contentment combined with anxiety about moving kept most others at home. Of course the land held some of them; the ones who remained to help their parents eventually inherited the family homestead. Those sons who did not have to share the land with too many brothers could expect to lead lives as comfortable as those of the older generation. And the young farmers who marketed specialty crops in Boston and other seaports might do even better. But most of Dedham's farmers struggled to eke out an existence on the marginal lands far beyond the village center. By mid-century many of them could no longer meet the property qualifications for voting in their own town. One out of four adults failed to do so in 1750, one in three later in the century. In these middle decades the town of Dedham discovered that poverty did not dwell among widows, orphans, and the simpleminded alone. For the first time inhabitants began to refer to "the poor" among them as an impersonal group rather than as familiar individuals.

A few farmer sons abandoned the fields to become artisans in the village, a trend which had begun in an earlier generation when yeomen skilled at one craft or another found it profitable to spend more time at blacksmithing, say, than at farming. What started as a part-time avocation for a father might be continued as a full-time business for his son. And so it began, the gradual flight from the land, imperceptible at first, of course, because the land was still being worked. But no longer did everybody work the land. In Norton farmers declined from 56.2 percent of the population in 1711–20 to 37.1 in 1731–40, while artisans rose from 31.2 to 40.8 and laborers even more sharply during the same period. For Winthrop's generation, which believed in a static world, God had so ordered society that some were rich and others poor. But this rationalization could not explain why in the dynamic world of the eighteenth century some individuals grew richer while others became so poor they could no longer participate in community decisions. Yet as growth, change, diversity, and tension threatened to replace stability, order, unity, and tranquillity, these older traits remained as values still worth pursuing far into the future for Dedham as for Massachusetts and the emerging nation.

And what about those who decided to leave the eastern towns during the middle decades of the eighteenth century? A recent study of Andover indicates that, unlike Dedham, a large percentage of third- and fourth-generation adults (those coming to maturity in the periods 1705–35 and 1735–65) moved away from the town of their birth. Of the second generation only one in five men left, but with a sharp increase in population at the turn of the century, two in five third-generation sons moved away, and over half of the next generation likewise sought their fortunes elsewhere. Most of these people settled in western Massachusetts, eastern Connecticut, or New Hampshire, where land was cheaper. Members of the third generation have been traced to twenty-two different towns, while the larger number of fourth-generation migrants were scattered through at least fifty-two communities. Occasionally they traveled together to establish a new town among old friends. Windham county in Connecticut became an enclave of expatriates from Andover, but just as often the men moved off singly to settle among strangers. Not all of the immigrants intended to continue as farmers, of course, and some of them headed for other settled towns to become craftsmen or shopkeepers.

The experience of a single Andover family offers an extreme example of third-generation mobility. George Abbot was a tailor who probably did a little farming on his sixteen-acre homestead. The eldest of his six sons, George Jr., became a blacksmith and lived successively in Cambridge, Framingham, and Hardwick. The second son, Uriah, was a shoemaker. In exchange for agreeing to care for his widowed mother, he inherited his father's estate and remained in Andover throughout his life. He was the only son to do so. Jacob established himself as a carpenter in West Brookfield, where his brothers Moses and Peter later joined him. The last son, Obed, was a weaver who first moved to Salem and then to Billerica. The young men who moved away obviously gained a greater degree of freedom from their parents than those who stayed. In many cases they were able to become economically independent sooner and to marry earlier than the brothers who stayed behind.

But the wrench of family separation brought its own anguish, as the experience of the fourth generation of Chandlers illustrates. Josiah Chandler had worked his ninety-acre Andover farm with the help of his sixth son, David, to whom he willed all of his real estate, stock, and equipment in exchange for a promise to care for the widowed mother. The eldest son had moved to New Hampshire, where he was a carpenter. Another operated an inn in Bradford, and the third had become a minister, first in York and then in Gloucester, after his graduation from Harvard. Three other sons died in young adulthood. As long as the parents were alive the sons did their best to maintain family ties. They gathered in Andover on the occasion of their brother's death at Louisbourg in 1745 and to attend another brother's funeral in 1752. After the death of their parents, the fourth generation's ties with Andover rapidly dissolved. Even before this event, the minister, Samuel, had begun to write the genealogy of his family, an undertaking that would hardly have been necessary a generation or two before, when almost all of the Chandlers lived in Andover, next to the graves of those who had departed.

The experience of the Abbot and Chandler families indicates that not only were the third and fourth generations dispersing geographically but, even more important, they were discovering new and different ways of making a living. Sixty Andover men of the third generation, for instance, pursued fourteen different occupations in addition to farming. This diversification had numerous implications for men and women of the eighteenth century. Now for the first time significant alternatives to life on the farm were possible. Instead of the natural work cycle geared to the seasons, the hours of daylight, and the needs of the livestock, a man could set his own schedule, no less demanding perhaps, but considerably more autonomous. A home in the village or town meant, for better or worse, closer neighbors in place of the farmstead's comparative isolation. It also brought a degree of independence from parental control, even for those sons who remained in the same town as their fathers. The sale of one's skills and wares provided a new degree of economic freedom, for cash could purchase a far wider variety of goods and services than could the farmer's meager surplus.

In reality, however, the artisan merely exchanged one set of restrictions for another. When a young man left the farm, he lost the security of a roof over his head and enough food in the cellar to feed his family. He now ran the risk of losing both house and larder, for success depended on his skill at using the tools and knowing the materials of his craft. Unlike the family farmer he was also at the mercy of other factors far beyond his control. First he had to find a master craftsman willing and able to teach him the trade. Then he needed capital with which to rent or purchase a shop, buy his own tools, and acquire the necessary raw materials. Through the first months or even years of business, he could expect lean times while competing for customers with other craftsmen. No wonder many a young artisan failed to meet the property qualifications for voting. As he continued to perfect his own skills, he had to master the mysteries of the marketplace, how to price his wares, advertise his business, and carry an inventory. He had to decide when to extend credit and on what terms, what goods to take in exchange when cash was scarce, and how to deal with the varying currencies in circulation during the period. As his business expanded, the craftsman also became an employer, responsible for apprentices or hired assistants. During the course of his career, an artisan might concentrate on a single aspect of the craft. The carpenter's trade split into cabinetmakers, chairmakers, carvers, upholsterers, and joiners. Tanners, curriers, saddlers, and harnessmakers shared the work formerly done by the general leatherworker. Specialization, which became the keynote of the eighteenth-century economy, reached its peak in the seaports on the eve of the Revolution. Newburyport's seven hundred adults pursued a total of sixty-three different occupations in 1773.

The principal link joining the farmers and small-town artisans of the interior with the larger commercial world was the local storekeeper. Members of the Dwight family operated a store in Springfield from about 1750 until well into the next century. During one six-month period they did business with customers living in twenty different communities from neighboring Westfield to distant Stockbridge. The Dwights sold a wide range of commodities—especially drygoods, hardware, groceries, and spirits. They obtained West Indian goods from merchants in Hartford and Middletown but went to Boston for their English and European wares. The small size of the operation did not justify entering the import business themselves. In a given year Josiah Dwight purchased about £1,000 worth of goods from one Boston importer. The store also carried items of domestic manufacture such as ironware, paper, hats, and especially rum purchased from nearby sources. At first almost all of the Dwights' business was retail, but over the years the family established branch stores in neighboring towns staffed by former clerks, some of whom had married into the family. These stores the Dwights supplied at wholesale along with a few peddlers and other small retailers in the area.

Goods sold for cash went at around 10 percent below those sold in exchange for country produce. Accounts paid within a short time, usually a month, earned a similar discount, while debts outstanding for a year or more were charged interest of around 6 percent. The Dwights' customers could buy their goods in any of three ways. About six out of ten paid in money, another three in goods, and the last in work. Currency payments were not simple. In a single year the storekeeper might deal with ten different coins of four nationalities, and he had to know the current equivalents of each in the lawful money of Massachusetts. Worse still was the jumble of paper money circulating in an area like the Connecticut valley. Storeowners had to keep track of at least five different colonial issues, all of which were depreciating at varying rates. Dwight would have welcomed payment in produce. Not only could he charge the higher "credit" prices for his wares bought in exchange but the produce itself provided the returns he needed with which to purchase imported goods. Yet another method of payment was through such labor and services as transporting goods by boat or cart, slaughtering animals, dressing furs, and making barrels. Most frequently the arrangement came at the initiative of the storekeeper who, needing certain work done, preferred to pay for it by credit at his store rather than in cash.

The more prosperous storekeepers like the Dwights and the Elys in fact provided many of the financial services that banks would later offer to the community. They lent money to customers, arranged for drafts on merchants in neighboring towns, and accepted notes and bonds drawn on other businessmen. They even collected debts between customers by transferring credits on their books. Josiah Dwight had other economic activities beyond the store. He operated both an ironworks and a potash manufactory, and he put out wool yarn among the farmers' wives for the weaving of stockings. Like other storekeepers he probably owned several small boats for transporting goods along the river. It is difficult to know just how successful a storekeeper like Josiah Dwight was, for we know little of his capital possessions at the outset of his career. But when he died around 1767 his net worth totaled £8,200, of which about £1,200 was reckoned as bad debts. Such an estate placed him among the wealthiest residents of the Connecticut valley.

Beyond the Dwights' general store in Springfield stretched a complex commercial network which, by the middle of the eighteenth century, joined together the most distant parts of the world's most prosperous empire. In the decades since the 1660s English mercantilists had refined the system by numerous additional regulations, particularly in 1696. The colonial governors were now required to enforce the laws on pain of both fine and removal from office. The new law authorized the appointment of customs officers in the colonies with broad power of search and seizure. Suspected violators could be tried without jury in admiralty courts, where they had to prove their own innocence. The broken voyage evasion was specifically eliminated as were all other colonial laws which contravened the intent of the Navigation Acts.

Generally speaking the patterns of trade already established in the seventeenth century continued to characterize the commerce of Massachusetts throughout the eighteenth. Coastwise trade with the other continental colonies climbed most rapidly, as New England towns became more dependent upon importations of wheat and flour. At the same time

Yankee merchants acquired in the southern plantations enumerated commodities like tobacco, indigo, and rice with which to purchase goods in England. The West Indian trade continued at a lively pace, fish, wood products, and provisions being exchanged for sugar, molasses, rum, and a scattering of other tropical produce. The Atlantic trade was dominated by the main run to England and a side commerce with the ports of southern Europe and the wine islands. Beyond these legal trade routes lay the hazy world of illicit commerce, involving the exportation of enumerated articles directly to the continent and the importation of manufactured goods from either Holland or France. After 1733, with the imposition of a heavy duty of sixpence per gallon on molasses from the foreign West Indies almost every New England importer was obliged to find one means or another of evading full payment of what was a prohibitive levy.

Small shopkeepers in the port towns had the opportunity to expand their activities into this world of overseas commerce, and around 1730 the young bookseller Thomas Hancock did just that. He was initially interested in discovering a ready means of paying for the books and other stock he ordered in London, the bills of exchange he sent over having proved difficult to negotiate. The long-range solution lay in finding American goods suitable as returns. There was little demand in London for the fish, peas, and pork which New England produced. Nor did Englishmen pant for the Puritan sermons Hancock optimistically dispatched. Gradually the neophyte merchant learned that he had to send the country produce with which his customers purchased his books to a demand market such as the West Indies or the southern plantation colonies, where he could then purchase goods that might sell in the mother country. Hancock discovered one New England product in great demand on the London market—whale oil and bone. He and his partner, William Tyler, purchased these commodities from the whalemen of Nantucket and other fishing ports and then sent them along to be marketed by their principal London agent, Francis Wilks. The proceeds were invested in the various English goods which Hancock sold at retail in his Boston store.

The whalemen often landed much of their oil at Newfoundland, where Hancock had already established contact with the increasing numbers of fishermen settling there. By the mid-1730s he regularly sent to Newfoundland vast quantities of rum, flour, bread, and staves to be exchanged for whale oil, skins, and cod. The fish was of first quality,

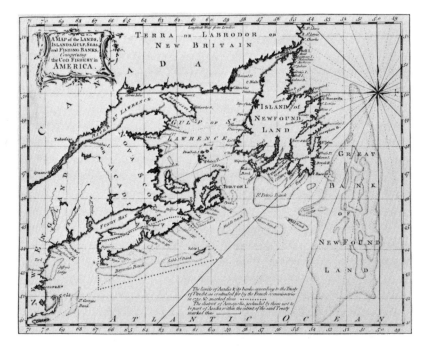

North Atlantic Fisheries in the Eighteenth Century. Engraved by Thomas Kitchin. In William Bollan, *The Ancient Right of the English Nation to the American Fishery . . .* (1764). Courtesy of the Massachusetts Historical Society.

suitable for Spain or Portugal, where Hancock sent cargoes each year to obtain much-needed specie and sound bills of credit. As he became more involved in the import-export trade Hancock discovered the advantages of owning his own vessels. Like most merchants he preferred to spread his risks by purchasing shares in several different vessels. Ownership gave him greater control over the timing of his shipments and allowed him to give his captains flexible instructions to take advantage of the best local situations. The vessels themselves could be built quite inexpensively in New England and were in considerable demand in England, where Hancock and Tyler sold a number of ships after a few years' hard use.

One of the major challenges facing American merchants of the eighteenth century came from the various wars that raged through much of the period between England, France, and sometimes Spain. All of these struggles involved privateering and naval warfare on the Atlantic, and most of them included hostilities between the northern colonies and French Canada. Rumors of war between England and Spain swept through the commercial community in the early months of 1739. In preparation, Hancock sold several of his vessels to reduce his liabilities and sent off a conditional order for one hundred half-barrels of gunpowder. When the Cartagena expedition was fitting out at Boston the following year, Hancock secured one of the contracts to provide it with beef and pork. As hostilities broke out in earnest Hancock joined with other Boston merchants to form a privateering company to prey on Spanish shipping and shared in the earnings of the successful *Young Eagle*.

In 1744 King George's War, as it was known in the colonies, spread to include France, which possessed a far more effective navy and privateering fleets than did Spain. Hancock took full advantage of the opportunity to furnish supplies for the northern expeditions against French Canada, including four vessels loaded with bricks to improve English fortifications in Newfoundland. In this business Hancock worked closely with Christopher Kilby, a Yankee opportunist then living in London as agent for the Bay colony. Profits and politics, as always, went hand in glove during these wars. Hancock bent every effort to have a share in supplying the Louisbourg expedition, but the competition was keen. His efforts were rewarded by appointment as an agent of the British Board of Ordnance for the outpost at Louisbourg. The position offered a wide variety of ways to increase his profits. By war's end in 1748 Thomas Hancock was probably richer by £15,000 to £20,000.

Another source of considerable profit for Hancock and his fellow merchants came from outside the British empire altogether. Most of Hancock's illegal trade was with various Dutch possessions—Amsterdam of course, Surinam, and particularly the island of St. Eustatius in the Caribbean. Hancock's vessels carried such enumerated goods as sugar and indigo to Holland, where his captains purchased homeward cargoes of various European manufactures including paper, fancy piece goods, and sailcloth. Sometimes a Dutch house shipped these illegal wares to St. Eustatius, where a Hancock vessel would pick them up. King George's War disrupted illicit commerce along with its legal counterpart, but after the return of peace Hancock renewed his smuggling activities. He ordered large quantities of tea in Amsterdam, where it was much cheaper than in London, and gave his captains careful instructions on how to avoid interception on the return passage. A successful voyage might net the shipowner as much as two or three times a similar cargo of legal goods, but the risk was far greater.

Colonial merchants smuggled not to defy the law as a matter of principle but to enhance their profits. When regular trade patterns became sluggish, Hancock felt obliged to keep his business moving by going outside the system. Years later Thomas Hutchinson bitterly attributed Hancock's rise in fortune to his smuggling of tea. True enough, he had profited from illicit commerce and even more from the war contracts he had obtained through the heavy use of influence. But Hancock ran a profitable house through the years of peace as well as war, and most of this commerce remained strictly within the English mercantile system. In the final analysis, as the merchant-historian Hutchinson had to admit, the secret of Hancock's wealth was that he "made easy and advantageous remittances." In short, the Boston bookseller turned merchant became more successful than most of his competitors in finding the returns necessary to make his English purchases.

*   *   *

The rise of overseas commerce from the last decades of the seventeenth into the eighteenth century wrought a profound change on the towns of eastern Massachusetts. What had begun as farming and fishing communities were gradually transformed into busy seaports. The shoreline from Boston Bay north and eastward was blessed with numerous natural harbors: Boston itself, along with the smaller towns that shared the bay—Lynn, Marblehead, Salem, Beverly, and Gloucester, all under the protecting arm of Cape Ann; then Ipswich, Chebacco (later Essex), and Newbury's waterside, each shielded by the sandy stretch of Plum Island. Increasingly the inhabitants of these and other seacoast communities looked across their snug harbors and out to sea for their livelihood. As they grew impatient with their ties to an agrarian past, they severed these bonds. Thus Salem probably welcomed the secession of its interior village, which became Danvers in 1757, and Newburyport broke off from its parent Newbury in 1764. Thereafter, the commercial interests became masters of their own houses.

By the end of Queen Anne's War in 1713 Salem's commerce had already begun to expand from its original dependence on the fisheries. From the shops of the port's various merchants one could purchase southern wheat, hides, tallow, and tobacco; from the West Indies came molasses and sugar; and wine, salt, and assorted fruit from the Iberian peninsula. As in other ports English cloth goods, hardware, and other manufactures lined the shelves of the shops along Essex Street and other principal ways of the town. Two or three wharves reached into the harbor from the southern edge of town, and others had been built along the North River, on the opposite side of the peninsula. Shipyards, ropewalks, and fishflakes covered other waterfront areas. During the next several decades Salem became the principal entrepôt for the region between Boston and the Ipswich River. The West Indian trade expanded rapidly, as did the overseas commerce with the mother country and the Iberian peninsula. Several merchants rose above their fellows in activity and wealth; in the last half of the century the Ornes, Pickmans, and Derbys vied with the Lyndes and the Brownes for social prominence.

Wealthier inhabitants began to build fine homes along the main street in the mid-eighteenth century, but one could also find shops interspersed among homes throughout the residential areas of town. A visitor in 1750 reported that the town consisted of about four hundred and fifty houses "several of which are neat buildings, but all of wood . . ., being at a convenient distance from each other with fine gardens back their houses." Salem depended upon wood boats from the coast of Maine for lumber to construct its half dozen new buildings each year and for sufficient fuel for heating and cooking. Architectural styles were noticeably evolving away from the heavy influence of medieval England and simpler floor plans and roof lines, such as the gambrel. In 1754 the seaport's population stood at 3,462, of whom 1,710 were females, including 205 widows. One hundred twenty-three blacks, numerous French Huguenots and Scots-Irish along with a few Germans, Irish, and Scotsmen brought a degree of relief to the town's predominantly English stock. Because of its peninsular site, Salem had little room for expansion. A bridge over the North River built in 1742 made the "North Fields" more accessible.

Commercial activity meant modest prosperity to the many shop-keepers and craftsmen of Salem, but to a small group of merchants it brought opulence. A group of about fifty families emerged by the middle of the century as the social leaders of the town. Some of their sons formed what they called "the Civil Society" in 1745. A few years later a group of three judges, two ministers, and a doctor organized another club, which in 1760 led to the establishment of the Social Library. Its list of twenty-seven charter subscribers included all the prominent names of the community—Pickman, Orne, Curwen, Holyoke, Pynchon, Browne, Derby, and Cabot, among others. Thirty-two original shares provided a fund of about 160 guineas with which to purchase books in London as a basis for the institution. Its founding suggests that Salem's social leaders had not only money for such an undertaking, but leisure as well. Several of the town's wealthiest inhabitants had already indulged in that most conspicuous of all possessions, the country seat. Earlier in the century Benjamin Lynde chose a rocky prominence south of town for his estate. Later Judge William Browne built a luxurious mansion on a high hill six miles north of Salem. "Browne's Folly," the common folk called the place. The main building formed a large "H" with wings forty-five feet long joined in the middle by a Grand Hall thirty-five feet in length. Hardly a mansion by English standards, or perhaps even in the eyes of southern planters, but a magnificent structure for an eighteenth-century New Englander. Broad lawns led the eye to a view of the ocean to the east and of fields and mountains to the west and north. Salem had come a long way in the century since John Endicott and Roger Conant had laid one of the colony's earliest foundations.

Everything that can be said about Salem in the eighteenth century must be multiplied several-fold for Boston. While the town was not yet the "hub" of the entire commonwealth, it was already becoming the center of a maritime half-wheel whose spokes led to the north and south shore ports as well as directly out to sea. At the close of the seventeenth century, Bostonians owned 124 vessels, six times as many as Salem, and more than three-quarters of the colony's entire fleet. During the next half century shipbuilding flourished in several of the outports, particularly on the Merrimack at Newbury and on the North River at Kingston, but Boston merchants continued to dominate the ranks of shipowners. Generally speaking, Boston merchants maintained a strong lead in the trans-Atlantic runs, leaving a little more room for the outport merchants in the fishing and coastal trades and the West Indies commerce. Even in these activities, however, Boston became the focus. Most of the colony's English imports entered there, and a flow of commodities for export came in by water to the entrepôt. Boston's merchants supplied not only inland storekeepers like the Dwights of Springfield but many of the out-port retailers as well.

Topographically, Boston would at first glance appear to be a most unlikely site for a major settlement. Nestled along the edge of a hilly peninsula jutting out into the bay between the mouths of two meandering rivers, the location offered virtually no room for growth. Yet Boston remained the largest community in the English colonies until after mid-century. An exact census in 1743 gave Boston a population of 16,382 against Philadelphia's estimated 13,000 inhabitants and New York's 11,000. By 1760 Philadelphia had taken the lead with 23,750, ahead of New York with 18,000, while Boston's population had actually fallen somewhat, to 15,631. On the eve of the American Revolution the total remained at about 16,000. A major reason for its stable population was the town's restricted area. The principal settlement developed along the waterfront bordering the eastern edge of the peninsula from Windmill Point around the Great Cove to the North Battery. By the end of the colonial period the eastern half of the peninsula was densely populated, particularly the North End. The western half, including Beacon Hill, remained more open, except for one or two large estates overlooking the spacious Common and a small grid of streets at the West End. The principal artery ran from the tip of Long Wharf, a magnificent structure that stretched two thousand feet into the harbor, straight up King Street past the townhouse (rebuilt after a fire in 1747 as the Old State House), to Cornhill, whence it reached out via Marlborough, Newbury, and Orange streets over the narrow Neck to the countryside beyond. Lesser streets radiated from the townhouse to other parts of the penin-

A Northeast View of Boston, c. 1723. Attributed to William Burgis. Courtesy of the Essex Institute, Salem, Mass.

Thomas Hancock House, Boston, 1736. Courtesy of the Massachusetts Historical Society.

sula. The construction of a magnificent building in 1742, the gift of the merchant Peter Faneuil, provided the town with much-needed new market space. A few years later Thomas Hancock and three associates built three large warehouses. Other wharves and commercial structures were erected during the first half of the century to serve the needs of Boston's expanding commerce.

The experience of living in eighteenth-century Boston was as intensive and varied as the town itself. The mariners, longshoremen, carters, and other day laborers of the town worked long hours at low pay with uncertain employment. Many of them lived in abysmal surroundings. A carter named Edward Grater dwelt in a small wooden two-family house on the waterfront, but many others called a dingy boardinghouse or a backyard shed their home. Artisans were considerably better off, the majority of them living in a room or two over their shops, while a few others had separate houses or at least a part of one in a more residential section of town. Furnishings were simple yet adequate, with some china, perhaps a few books, glassware, and pewter to relieve the plainness of the surroundings. Craftsmen's families seem to have eaten well, the housewife going each day to the market stalls around Faneuil Hall and to one of the numerous bakeries. Middle-class Bostonians had begun to develop a liking for tea, coffee, or chocolate with which to vary their meals, and the more prosperous among them might occasionally treat themselves to other imported foodstuffs like fruit or sugar. Many such households of the middle class might also boast a servant girl, perhaps a youngster serving out her indenture or a country lass working for wages.

Conspicuous consumption had already become a way of life for some of Boston's wealthier merchants and government officers. To signal his success in business Thomas Hancock and his wife, Lydia, purchased in 1735 an acre of land on Beacon Hill, then considered to be on the outskirts of town. First he laid out his gardens, on the south side of the hill, sending to England for bulbs and flower seeds, nut trees, cherry, plum, peach, and other fruit trees. The house itself was constructed in 1736, Thomas and Lydia fussing like other homebuilders over every detail of its furnishings. He returned a clock whose carvings failed to satisfy him and complained that his trees and flowers did poorly. But at length the house was complete and the couple moved in, thereafter to take a leading role in the social whirl of the provincial town. Governor Shirley's mansion in Roxbury marked the move to the suburbs beyond the peninsula. Cambridge's "Tory Row" would attract a dozen or more merchants seeking the pleasant environment of the college, while others chose sites in such outlying towns as Medford, Dorchester, and even distant Milton, where the Hutchinsons established a seat in 1743.

Prosperous colonists who lived in country towns far removed from the seaports could easily match the physical possessions of their urban cousins—housing, furnishings, and clothing. But rural dwellers were deprived of the broad range of cultural activities and entertainment that could be found in commercial centers like Boston, Salem, and Newburyport. Into the seaports came a constant stream of travelers from the other American colonies, from the mother country, and from foreign lands as well. And the seafarers who called these ports home returned with strange tales and mementoes of faraway places. A Salem youngster was likely to know more about Cadiz than Concord, and more likely to visit the Spanish port as well. That cosmopolitan style of life which has long been associated with urban centers began to develop in Massachusetts during the middle decades of the eighteenth century. Town and country would never be the same thereafter, and the differences would make their indelible marks on the inhabitants of each kind of community.

*   *   *

The most significant change taking place in mid-eighteenth-century Massachusetts was the gradual modernization of towns and villages from self-sufficient farming communities to complex societies increasingly dependent on the world around them. Everywhere stability slowly gave way as the dynamic pursuit of progress challenged the earlier commitment to order. Men began to take risks to improve their situation in life. All over the province emerged a generation of merchants, land speculators, and paper-money advocates willing to sacrifice the stable certainties of the present for the more rewarding possibilities of the future. And yet the old ways died hard. For decades the traditional values of community and order remained the official ideology even as individualism and progressive change became the actual values by which men lived. And this difference between what men believed and how they acted brought a new tension to life in Massachusetts, a conflict that would emerge in the religious upheaval of the Great Awakening and the political turmoil of the American Revolution.

The long debate over currency illustrates very well the kind of change that was in the wind and the effects these new activities had on the institutions and people of the eighteenth century. A chronic shortage of specie had long plagued the American colonies, and several attempts to provide a more flexible currency had been made in Massachusetts as elsewhere even before the end of the previous century. A number of Boston merchants proposed a private land bank, but in 1714 the General Court established a public land bank instead. This institution issued bills of credit which were lent out and circulated as legal tender throughout the province. The system worked for a time but could not keep pace with new demands. Not only was the economy expanding but at the same time it grew increasingly complex and therefore more dependent upon a circulating medium of exchange in place of the goods and services that had once dominated economic relations. Another problem was the growing scarcity of land. New farmers were increasingly forced to purchase their homesteads from merchants and other businessmen who were investing some of their mounting profits in large tracts in western Massachusetts and eastern Maine. These transactions increased the demand for currency at a time when long-term credit was tightening. Finally, inflation itself required a larger amount of circulating money.

The currency situation reached a crisis in 1739 when Whitehall instructed Governor Belcher to order the retirement of all outstanding public bills (then amounting to £250,000) within two years and to limit future issues to about £30,000. Such a severe contraction seriously threatened the continued expansion of the economy. The new instructions did not prohibit private parties from issuing bills of credit, however, and two schemes were immediately put forward. Nearly four hundred subscribers sought a charter for the Land Bank or Manufactory Company, which proposed to issue £150,000 worth of bills secured by the borrowers' land, annual payments to be made in bills or particular manufactured articles such as hemp, bar iron, or sawn lumber. In opposition to this plan a number of Boston merchants formed the far more conservative silver bank, which would emit bills to the amount of £120,000 ultimately redeemable in silver. In the absence of legislative action by the General Court, both institutions began to issue their bills in the late summer of 1740, but Parliament intervened the following year to outlaw both banks.

Supporters of the Massachusetts land bank came from many different towns throughout the province. Such seaports as Boston, Salem, and Ipswich had strong representation along with such inland communities as Sudbury, Uxbridge, and Mendon. Merchants, farmers, innholders, professional men joined in the scheme with only one discernible characteristic in common. They were for the most part prosperous members of their respective communities. Supporters of the silver bank were far fewer in number, mostly concentrated in Boston, and almost without exception among the wealthiest men of the province. The line between the two groups remains difficult to define. It was not that of debtor versus creditor, nor inflationist versus deflationist, for both groups were dominated by men of means who proposed to expand the currency by issuing paper money. The difference lay in the respective foundations for the bills. Almost any landowner could obtain a loan from the land bank by mortgaging his real estate and making payments in the various commodities enumerated. The proposal would appeal particularly to farmers who needed additional capital with which to purchase more land perhaps or to establish a store, inn, or craftsman's shop. In short, the land bank combined the traditional value of real property as the basis of wealth with the modern need to borrow money to improve one's economic position. The land bank therefore seemed to appeal more to men on the rise, while the conservative silver bank suited those who had already reached the top.

Significantly, the land bankers received broad political support in the elections of 1740; the scheme collapsed only because of the determined opposition of Governor Belcher and the Crown, not from lack of popular backing. The fact that large numbers of people preferred a currency based on land and commodities to one founded on silver specie is one measure of their willingness to accept risk in the pursuit of prosperity. In a larger sense the land bank scheme symbolized the break already taking place from an older pay-as-you-go economy in favor of a modern system built on credit and a faith in future growth. The battle between land bankers and silver bankers also marked a shift in the arena of political decision-making from the local to the provincial level of government. By mid-century only the General Court could deal with such complex problems as the currency. Furthermore, speculators and men on the make increasingly looked to the provincial government for favors that only it could give—land grants, war contracts, and prestigious appointments. And because of Belcher's staunch opposition to the land bank the battle helped to polarize the politics of provincial Massachusetts. Many of the bank's supporters, like Samuel Adams, Sr., united against Belcher to form the basis of the country party, while silver bankers, like the Hutchinsons, became the nucleus of the court party.

In 1764 the merchant Thomas Hancock died. He left behind an estate worth about £100,000. The way to wealth for Hancock was a route theoretically open to many other youngsters from the small country towns of Massachusetts. Only a few would take that road in the mid-eighteenth century, and fewer still would be successful. But the opportunity seemed to be there, and it was the vision of opportunity that became the hallmark of the new era. And yet one cannot overlook the cold facts of economic life resulting from this quest for wealth. A study comparing the distribution of wealth in Boston for the year 1771 with that of 1687 is revealing. While the total population of the town doubled in the period, the number of men without property increased fourfold. And among the propertied population itself still further changes had taken place. The share of property owned by the bottom two quarters of the group fell from 12 to 10 percent, while that of the third quarter dropped even further, from 21 to 12½ percent. The winners could be found in the top quarter, where the share of wealth increased from 66 to 78 percent. Still more spectacular were the gains made by the elite 5 percent at the pinnacle. In 1687 the fifty men in this category had owned 26.8 percent of Boston's property. In 1771, eighty-five such men held 44.1 percent of the wealth. Perhaps the bottom three quarters of Boston's property holders on the eve of the Revolution should have taken consolation in the fact that they were as a whole far better off than their counterparts of the previous century. But men do not compare themselves with their great-grandfathers. They compare themselves with other contemporaries, and Bostonians of the late eighteenth century could not escape the conclusion that while they lived in a time of greater opportunity, the rewards seemed to be going to a smaller percentage of the people.

10

PROVINCIAL CULTURE

Jonathan Edwards was a true son of the Connecticut valley. His father's side of the family had come to Hartford in the 1640s, and Jonathan himself was born at East Windsor in 1703. His mother was a Stoddard, daughter of Northampton's famous minister, Solomon Stoddard. Jonathan's father was also a minister, and as the only son among eleven children, Jonathan too was destined for the pulpit. In a break with family tradition, he went to Yale instead of Harvard, and there the young scholar read deeply in the works of John Locke and Isaac Newton. For a few years after his graduation Jonathan served a Presbyterian church in New York, returned to Yale as senior tutor, and then in 1727 was called to Northampton to assist his aging grandfather. When Solomon Stoddard died two years later, young Jonathan took full charge of the parish. By family heritage an orthodox Puritan, Jonathan Edwards nevertheless became the most articulate voice of the Enlightenment in colonial America. At the same time, as minister at Northampton, he also became the leading spokesman of the Great Awakening in New England. However paradoxical these diverse currents have appeared to subsequent historians, Jonathan Edwards made them the foundation for a new way of looking at the nature of man and the world during the middle decades of the eighteenth century. In this sense Edwards was the first modern American.

The young men and women of Edwards' generation were born into an era of great promise. With the witchcraft ordeal and the worst of the Indian wars behind them, they could look forward with optimism to years of increasing prosperity. Surely the many blessings enjoyed by this generation were a sign that God continued to smile upon His favored people of Massachusetts. Yet just beneath the surface of this rapidly expanding society lay numerous fault lines which might suggest to a more discerning observer that all was not well within the Bay colony. Disputes broke out between the proprietors and other inhabitants over the common lands in numerous towns. The number of lawsuits between private parties rose sharply. Whole communities divided over local issues such as the placement of schools and provincial matters like the land bank. Some of these arguments split existing towns completely asunder, and all of them left enduring tensions among the people of the eighteenth century.

A religious person might have further cause to doubt the purity of his society when he saw his fellow Christians relentlessly pursuing material rewards in an effort to improve their God-given station in life. Worse still was the state of God's church in Massachusetts. Surely the Puritans of his grandfather's generation had led more pious lives and devoted themselves more fully to the services of the Lord than those he saw about him in the early decades of the eighteenth century. Halfway covenanters and their children seemed to abound, and in many parishes whole groups of them "owned the covenant" together in mass open meetings without giving witness to any converting experience or being examined by any committee of church members. When the Reverend Solomon Stoddard went so far as to admit such people to the sacrament of the Lord's Supper, many pious folk were deeply disturbed. Stoddard called these gatherings his "harvests," altogether five in number, which began in 1679 and recurred every decade or so until 1718.

A few years after succeeding to his grandfather's parish Jonathan Edwards reported to his fellow ministers the details of a remarkable revival at Northampton in 1735, one of many local "awakenings" that were occurring in various Connecticut valley towns during the period. Young and old, rich and poor, all seemed equally affected by a regeneration of spirit. "All the talk in companies and upon occasions was upon the things of religion, and no other talk was anywhere relished," Edwards wrote. Those in town who had been the greatest sinners seemed gravely concerned about their spiritual welfare, even those accustomed to ridiculing religious experiences in others. The effects of this revival on the individuals concerned were truly remarkable. "The looser sort are brought to forsake and to dread their former extravagances," reported Edwards. Even more astounding, people who had hitherto pursued material goals were now "ready to run into the other extreme of too much

Jonathan Edwards (1703–1758). Painting by Joseph Badger. Courtesy of the Yale University Art Gallery.

neglecting their worldly business and to mind nothing but religion."
They sought out former opponents to settle old quarrels; contention
among the inhabitants seemed to disappear almost completely. Several
people even claimed that "they could freely die for the salvation of any
soul of the meanest of mankind, even of any Indian." People seemed to
have a love for all mankind. "This town," Edwards concluded, "never
was so full of love, nor so full of joy, nor so full of distress as it has lately
been. . . ."

It was easier for Edwards (and for us) to describe the revival than to
account for it. Of course, he attributed it in the first instance to God, "an
extraordinary dispensation of providence" which "seized" people and
"brought off" many from their former complacency to a new sense of
longing to be free of sin. Edwards was struck by the universality of the
revival. Not only were almost all the inhabitants of Northampton affected, but skeptics who had come in from other towns went away "with
wounded spirits," carrying the torch of revival home with them. " 'Tis
extraordinary as to the extent of it, God's spirit being so remarkably
poured out on so many towns at once and its making such swift progress
from place to place," he wrote. Edwards hastened to disavow the more
extreme manifestations of the revival that had led some to envision
Christ in heaven shedding blood for sinners. These extreme imaginings
Edwards attributed to the Devil, who was up to his old tricks of
"endeavoring to mimic the work of the spirit of God and to cast a slur
upon it." Satan was so enraged at the revival, according to Edwards, that
he had even taken advantage of Jonathan's uncle, Joseph Hawley, and
had driven him to suicide during a moment of melancholy. Edwards
hastened to assure his correspondents that in his view all these happenings could be accounted for by orthodox beliefs—"there are no new doctrines embraced . . ., no new way of worship affected."

What Edwards observed in Northampton was but the forerunner of
the "Great Awakening" that swept through the American colonies and
had counterparts in England and Europe as well during the middle decades of the eighteenth century. His reports, in fact, encouraged the
spirit of reform wherever they were published and read. By the 1740s
itinerant preachers traveling through the southern and middle colonies
aroused extraordinary zeal among the thousands of ordinary people who
flocked to hear their sermons. The greatest of them was the English
minister George Whitefield, who first came to Massachusetts in the fall

of 1740. During his first week at Boston he preached no less than ten sermons, generally to audiences of several thousand at a time. When the crowd at the Summer Street Church became so unruly that several people fell out of the gallery to their deaths, Whitefield moved to the Common. Up the eastern seaboard he went, through Ipswich, and Newbury, and on to York, and then back to Boston via Salem. Thirty thousand Bostonians reportedly turned out to hear Whitefield's farewell sermon. As he departed for the Connecticut valley, the preacher left behind "great numbers . . . happily concerned about their souls . . . and their desires excited to hear their ministers more than ever." At Northampton Whitefield held four meetings in two days. "Our Lord seem'd to keep the good Wine till the last," Whitefield concluded. "My soul was much knit to these dear people of God . . . , and though their former fire might be greatly abated, yet it immediately appeared, when stirred up."

"Stirring up" was precisely the mission of the revivalist preachers. Whether by the startlingly realistic imagery of Edwards' sermons, or by Whitefield's somewhat warmer approach, they appealed less to the minds than to the senses in bringing their audience to conversion. Herein lay what was new in the Great Awakening. Edwards in particular among the revivalist preachers used words not to convey the sterile ideas of orthodox Christian thought, distilled through centuries of tomes written by scholastics hidden away in their studies, but to arouse the senses, to force upon his listeners the idea of hell, as he did in the following passage from his sermon "Sinners in the Hands of an Angry God," delivered at Enfield, Connecticut, in 1741:

> . . . imagine yourself to be cast into a fiery oven, all of a glowing heat, or into the midst of a glowing brick-kiln, or of a great furnace, where your pain would be as much greater than that occasioned by accidentally touching a coal of fire, as the heat is greater. Imagine also that your body were to lie there for a quarter of an hour, full of fire, as full within as without as a bright coal of fire, all the while full of quick sense; what horror would you feel at the entrance of such a furnace! And how long would that quarter of an hour seem to you . . .! But what would be the effect on your soul if you knew you must lie there enduring that torment to the full for twenty-four hours! And how much greater would be the effect, if you knew you must endure it for a

whole year; and how vastly greater still, if you knew you must
endure it for a thousand years! O then, how would your heart
sink, if you thought, if you knew, that you must bear it forever
and ever! That there would be no end! That after millions and
millions of ages, your torment would be no nearer to an end,
than ever it was; and that you never, never should be delivered!

"Imagine" is the key word here, compelling the audience to sense the
meaning not only of hell but of eternity, two words that had become
lifeless terms in the sermons and writings of orthodox ministers.
Through the voice of Jonathan Edwards, however, they are given new
vitality, as the preacher appeals to the sensory experience of his listeners.
A new kind of religious man gradually took form, one whose being was
shaped as much by feelings and affections as by reason.

Something else was new about the Great Awakening. The historic role
of the minister changed from one who offered logically correct proofs of
some theological truth or other to a leader who figuratively at least and
often literally as well got down out of the pulpit and led his people into a
religious experience which they could share together. Edwards had reported in 1736 that the Northampton revival had put "an end to the
differences between ministers and people." Of his own visit to Northampton Whitefield noted that "dear Mr. Edwards wept during the whole
time of exercise—the people were equally, if not more affected, and my
own soul was much lifted up towards God." Ministers who appealed to
the feelings of their congregations had been rare enough in Puritan Massachusetts; those willing and able to share in the expression of those
feelings were virtually unknown.

In most communities the ministers were accorded respect out of defer-
ence to the authority of their positions, and most ministers had accepted
the duty of reinforcing the authority of other officials of town and province. Family status, learning, and even wealth had become the de facto
evidence of one's right to lead. But in 1748 Jonathan Edwards proposed a
revolutionary new set of criteria for leaders of both church and state.
They must have enhanced their natural abilities not only by study and
learning but, more important, by observation and experience in order to
gain "a great understanding of men and things, a great knowledge of
human nature, and of the way of accommodating themselves to it."
Abstract theory and dogma were no longer enough; the ruler must adjust

himself to the welfare of his people. Edwards also had in mind the business leaders of the Connecticut valley. From his pulpit he attacked "those
of a narrow, private spirit that may be found in little tricks and private
intrigues to promote their private interest." He particularly criticized
entrepreneurs who "will shamefully defile their hands to gain a few
pounds, are not ashamed to nip and bite others, grind the faces of the
poor, and screw upon their neighbors." And Edwards singled out those
who "will take advantage of their authority of commission to line their
own pockets with what is fraudulently taken or withheld from others."

In one sense the Great Awakening was a reaction against beliefs and
practices that had become entrenched within the churches of Massachusetts. Not surprisingly, leaders of the orthodox establishment staunchly
opposed the religious revival that was sweeping through the province.
One point of contention revolved around the belief among many ministers that individuals might actively bring about their own salvation.
This development had its roots in the doctrine of "preparation," the
seventeenth-century practice of making oneself a fit receptacle for God's
grace if and when it came. By the middle of the eighteenth century,
however, some ministers seemed to suggest that men could, by their
rational powers alone, discover God's will in respect to themselves and
then consciously choose to fulfill it. Such a belief, in Edwards' opinion,
ran counter to the basic Puritan tenet of "justification by faith alone" and
bordered on the heresy of Arminianism. A related issue grew out of the
practice which Jonathan's own grandfather had pursued in Northampton
of encouraging virtually all of the inhabitants to join the church, whether
or not they had experienced a conversion. Even before the initial spirit of
revival began to wane, Edwards recognized how flimsy a church resulted
from such members. In 1742 he insisted that a covenant be drawn up
binding all members to a strict code of behavior, particularly in business
affairs. Two years later he repudiated his grandfather's leniency by re-
stricting participation in communion to those making a profession of
faith. The controversy that followed led ultimately to Edwards' dismissal
from the Northampton church in 1750.

Over the years Edwards' most articulate opponent was Charles
Chauncy, minister of Boston's First Church. Chauncy spoke for the
supremacy of reason over the passions to which he thought Edwards and
other "enthusiasts" appealed. "In nothing does the enthusiasm of these
persons discover itself more than in the disregard they express to the

dictates of reason," Chauncy complained. "They are above the force of argument, beyond conviction from a calm and sober address to their understandings." Chauncy objected not only to the revivalists' style but to their beliefs as well, particularly their view of God as condemning vast numbers of people to hell. But the significant difference between the rationalists, or liberals, and spokesmen for the Awakening lay in their conflicting concepts of man. Edwards believed with Locke in the unity of the human personality, that mind and feelings were inseparable, and that understanding is acquired only through sensory experience. Chauncy, on the other hand, clung to the older belief that man's reason, affections, and senses were separate faculties, and that man's reason could and should control his emotions. The final irony was that Chauncy relied on an old-fashioned view of man to espouse his modern rationalism, while Edwards turned to modern psychology to defend his old-fashioned Calvinism.

As the revival subsided in the 1750s it left behind a number of permanent changes. The spirit of harmony proudly reported by Edwards in 1736 crumbled before charges of "Arminian" and "enthusiast" that tore parishes apart and led to the founding of new sects and denominations. Revivalist preachers established a new relationship with the people and admonished civil officers to do the same with their constituents. Edwards regarded the rapid spread of the Great Awakening as a divine call for the reform of social behavior throughout America. More accurately, perhaps, he recognized that social change was in fact under way and that ministers and other leaders should be in the vanguard rather than in opposition. In putting Christianity back into the business of judging men's relations with each other, he established the welfare of the people as the goal. In this respect, the Great Awakening led away from the European concept of society as a hierarchical structure toward a uniquely American view of the supremacy of the people.

*   *   *

While controversy tore apart the religious establishment of the colony, educational institutions experienced comparative calm. Toward the end of the seventeenth century, Massachusetts could boast of at least twenty-three public schools, more than twice the number to be found in any other colony, and yet there were many towns that had still not provided even a basic education for its youngsters. In 1692 the General Court enacted new legislation designed to correct this situation. This law required towns with fifty or more householders to provide a schoolmaster to teach reading and writing, and those communities with more than one hundred families to maintain a grammar school as well. But in less than a decade the court increased the fine for noncompliance from £10 to £20 and required that the grammar instructor be full-time. In 1718 the fine was raised still further. Clearly, most towns had continued to ignore the law of 1692.

Some communities, however, did respond to this prodding from their representatives. Even as it paid a fine in 1702, the town of Sudbury, for instance, hired a grammar-school master. For an annual remuneration of about £25 he was to teach "all children sent to him to learn English and the Latin tongue, also writing and the art of Arithmetic." At that time, like many towns its size, Sudbury had no schoolhouse, lessons being taught in private homes and in the meetinghouse. Even after the construction of the first school building in 1702, the question of where to hold classes was complicated by the dispersal of population through the various sections of town on both sides of the river. By the 1730s the annual budget for instruction was divided between sessions at the schoolhouse itself and "in the out parts or quarters" of the town, but this "moving school" concept proved unsatisfactory to those families living away from the village center. In 1735 a petition to move the grammar school to an outlying area was turned down, but five years later the town agreed to offer grammar-school instruction "in the five remote corners of the town" for a part of the coming year, and this arrangement continued for a number of years. The final solution adopted by Sudbury, Dedham, and other rapidly expanding towns was to build schoolhouses in the outlying areas. By mid-century Sudbury had eight schoolhouses altogether, in which reading and writing sessions were held as well as grammar-school instruction.

The seaport towns, less susceptible to population dispersal, nevertheless had the problem of providing adequate education for their increasing numbers of youngsters. In Salem a combination of funds drawn from tuition payments, income from gifts, the rental of public lands, as well as taxation, supported the public-school system. Gifts ranged in size from £5 to the munificent sum of £240 given by Colonel Samuel Browne in 1729. Browne's generosity may have had a particular purpose to it, for he stipulated that his funds be spent for schools "to be kept in or near the Town House Street in Salem now so called being in the Body of the Town." Such an arrangement well suited the vast majority of Salem residents, but the decision added fuel to the demand of those living in Salem Village to be made a separate town, an action finally taken in 1757.

The new educational requirements established at the beginning of the century improved instruction in all but the smallest communities throughout the colony. Scholars from towns like Dedham could now become adequately prepared for entrance at Harvard, while at the other end of the scale, illiteracy virtually disappeared among men by the eve of the Revolution. In the period 1760—75 male signatures on Dedham legal documents outnumbered marks seventy-one to two. Since no provision was made for the regular instruction of young women, it is remarkable that only nine of thirty-eight women were unable to sign their names. Between the standard of college preparation on the one hand and the ability to sign one's name on the other lies the vast area of what education is all about in any society at any time. For John Adams, himself a product of Braintree's local schools, the purpose was to train young people "to virtue [and] habituate them to industry, activity, and spirit." If John himself was any proof, the local schools of Massachusetts were capable of achieving such goals by the mid-eighteenth century.

Those students willing and able to continue their education beyond grammar school invariably went on to Harvard College. Colonial colleges, as well as churches, were affected by the Great Awakening, but Harvard avoided much of the controversy that swept over Yale during the era and which led to the establishment of the College of New Jersey at Princeton. Harvard did refuse to invite George Whitefield to speak, which turned the revivalist's ire upon the college and led to an institutional counterattack against Whitefield. But the controversy soon died down, and when Harvard lost much of its library in a fire twenty years later, the famed preacher was among the major donors, an act that earned his portrait a place on the hallowed walls of liberal learning. By 1760 Harvard had achieved such a level of self-confidence that it even permitted its students—with parental permission—to attend Episcopal services rather than those at the Congregational church.

Numerous changes took place in Harvard Yard during the thirty-two years of Edward Holyoke's presidency, from 1737 to 1769. Older Aristotelian texts were replaced by more modern works. The teaching of

Harvard College, 1760. Engraving by Paul Revere. Courtesy of the Essex Institute, Salem, Mass.

science under the leadership of Professor John Winthrop became thoroughly updated. Public exhibitions twice a year sharpened the debating and oratorical skills of upperclassmen. Most significantly, in the 1760s faculty members were permitted to specialize. One tutor handled all the instruction in Latin, another in Greek, still another in Logic, Metaphysics, and Ethics, while a fourth taught Natural Philosophy, Mathematics, and Astronomy. All four tutors were expected to teach English.

Educational activities changed in other ways as well. Political questions began to take their place alongside the more traditional moral and religious topics of commencement theses. President Holyoke gave strong support to the study of science. Professor Winthrop carried on electrical experiments, organized the first American expedition to observe the transit of Venus in 1761 from Newfoundland, and established the first American laboratory for experiments in physics. Students occasionally performed various plays in college halls, but not without running the risk of punishment for blasphemy. Nevertheless, Harvard, like all institutions, resisted change. Scholars still arose at six, faced four hours of morning lectures, and had a brief two-hour recess for dinner and recreation before spending the rest of the afternoon studying in their chambers. Discipline was stern, although flogging was outlawed early in the century. Upperclassmen continued to lord it over their inferiors, and sophomores, as always, regarded themselves as the most sophisticated of young men.

What is sometimes difficult to remember is how few young men actually attended college at all. The largest class of the colonial period, sixty-three, graduated in 1771, and there would be no equal for another forty years. In view of this fact, it is the more astounding that so many of the colony's leaders during the Revolutionary era were Harvard graduates. In his search for a relationship between the college's curriculum and the politics of patriotism, historian Samuel Eliot Morison concluded that it was in their study of the classics that young Harvard scholars were most likely to find inspiration to resist the real or imagined tyrannies of George III. Why a knowledge of Cicero's *Orations* and Plutarch's *Lives* failed to have the same effect on Thomas Hutchinson as on Samuel Adams is not answered by this explanation. The point to be made, perhaps, is that the Harvard curriculum, originally designed to train ministers, by the mid-eighteenth century provided excellent preparation for political leadership, whatever the ideological orientation of the graduate.

Youngsters not destined for Harvard might by the eve of the Revolution find a number of other educational opportunities, mostly in the seaport towns of Massachusetts Bay. Private tutors offered instruction in navigation, bookkeeping, foreign languages, and several other skills, often at night so that ambitious young workers could take advantage of the chance to improve their lot. Women had more difficulty acquiring an education even in Boston, but by the 1770s it had become fashionable for daughters of the rich to acquire "female embellishments," if not further education, from private instructors. Young ladies from families who could not afford such arrangements had no educational opportunities whatever, for the Boston public schools did not admit women on a regular basis until 1789, although in other towns such discrimination was not always enforced.

Professional training followed the pattern of earlier years. A young Harvard graduate such as John Adams, who wished to pursue the practice of law, sought out an established barrister willing to take him on as an apprentice for two or three years. John read law in the office of James Putnam, a graduate of Harvard and a successful practitioner in Worcester, where Adams had taught school for a year after graduation. Admission to the Suffolk County bar, his formal acceptance into the profession, came after two further years of study on his own following his return to Braintree, during which period he undertook several legal assignments. Physicians pursued a similar course of apprenticeship and self-education. John Jeffries, of the Harvard Class of 1763, studied under Dr. James Lloyd for a year or two and did a stint at the smallpox hospital on Castle Island. Unlike most of his fellow physicians, however, Jeffries improved upon his American training by spending a year working in Guy's Hospital in London before returning to establish a practice in Boston. Not until the end of the eighteenth century would Massachusetts have a medical school.

In September 1762 a Boston artist wrote to the famous Genevan painter, Jean Étienne Liotard, to order a set of the best Swiss crayons. "You may perhaps be surprised that so remote a corner of the Globe as New England should have any demand for the necessary utensils for practicing the fine Arts," John Singleton Copley admitted, "but I assure you, sir, however feeble our efforts may be it is not for want of inclination

Paul Revere, c. 1767. Painting by John Singleton Copley. Courtesy of the Museum of Fine Arts, Boston.

that they are not better." Copley went on to express the hope that despite the recent years of war and desolation America "will one day become the school of fine arts." Within five years, however, the Boston painter complained to a friend that America had no taste for painting. "The people generally regard it no more than any other useful trade, as they sometimes term it, like that of a carpenter, tailor, or shoemaker, not as one of the most noble arts in the world."

Copley perhaps overstated the case against his fellow Americans, but not by very much. The first distinguished painters in Boston were transplanted Britons, such as the Scottish emigré John Smibert who settled in 1730 and painted over two hundred canvases before his death twenty-one years later. Yet even he was forced to open a print shop in order to support his family. In addition to his paintings Smibert left his mark upon the work of native American artists, particularly Robert Feke and John Singleton Copley. The young Copley also profited from the work of another English artist resident in Boston, Joseph Blackburn, and from his stepfather, Peter Pelham, he learned the art of engraving. But the young Bostonian was greatly talented in his own right. Before the age of thirty Copley could write that "I have a large room full of pictures unfinished, which would engage me these twelve months if I did not begin any others." His painting "The Boy with the Squirrel" was exhibited in London in 1776 and won him election to the Society of Artists in Great Britain. His reputation made abroad, Copley thereafter grew increasingly discontented with his lot in provincial Boston. This fact, combined perhaps with his distaste for the town's raucous political behavior, led to his permanent departure in 1774. In his last ten years in Boston Copley painted the portraits of virtually every prominent New Englander, which netted him an annual income of about £300.

There were numerous more popular forms of art in Massachusetts as in the other colonies, including the work of such engravers as Peter Pelham, who sold likenesses of famous men, prominent buildings, historic scenes, and maps to enthusiastic if not always discriminating customers. Increasing numbers of newspapers, almanacs, and magazines required woodcuts and engravings for illustrations and proved a great boon to the cartoon style of popular art. Families unable to afford a Smibert or Copley portrait could settle perhaps for a silhouette. Whether by established artists or common limners, Americans received unusually frank and realistic works, unembellished by fanciful imaginations, which, in the parlance of a more recent era, told it "like it is."

The art forms most familiar to inhabitants of Massachusetts Bay—architecture, furniture, and other forms of practical craftsmanship—were far more utilitarian than was their portraiture. Domestic architecture in the eighteenth century continued the trend established earlier—away from the Old World forms that the first settlers brought with them. Increased affluence in the older centers of populations encouraged larger homes. The older four-square designs were more frequently expanded than before by the addition of lean-tos out back which resulted in the well-known saltbox profile. Kitchen ells with sleeping chambers upstairs and the raising of roof lines to make two full stories were other common alterations. In many of the new homes built after 1750 the bulky center chimney of an earlier era gave way to a pair of end chimneys, making room for larger chambers, a center hallway, and a more generous staircase to the floors above. In most of the seaports and interior market towns affluent merchants and landowners could now afford to display their new fortunes by the construction of truly magnificent homes, as Thomas Hancock, Isaac Royall, and a few others had already done. One need only amble along Newburyport's High Street, Brattle Street in Cambridge, or the many streets of Ipswich to see examples of such splendid architecture. In the presence of these buildings it is difficult to remember that at the same time frontiersmen were living in rude huts no better than those inhabited by the first settlers in Plymouth or Salem more than a century before. A cursory inspection of Williamstown's replica of a 1753 "regulation house" will illustrate the point (see p. 208).

Because of the danger from fire many eighteenth-century buildings in Boston were built of brick, and as a consequence a number have survived to this day. The graceful Pierce-Hichborn house in North Square built by a glazier was later owned by a boat builder. Its fine interior details suggest that craftsmen could also afford good taste. Hopestill Capen's three-story building, once a dry-goods store, is now occupied by the Union Oyster House. Another brick building, still standing as the Old Corner Bookstore at Washington and School streets, was built by an apothecary immediately after the Great Fire of 1711.

Still more striking developments appeared in the design of public buildings during the eighteenth century. Christ Church in Boston's North End, now called Old North Church, was built in 1723, perhaps from the designs of William Price. Its magnificent high spire dominated the Boston skyline for many years. On present-day Washington Street, almost hidden from view by surrounding commercial buildings, is the graceful Old South Meeting House, also of brick. One of the few buildings in Massachusetts constructed of stone was King's Chapel, designed by Newport's Peter Harrison, and built in 1749 of Quincy granite. Lack of funds prevented the completion of its Ionic portico until after the Revolution and its lofty steeple never was erected, but on the strength of its magnificent interior alone King's Chapel is nevertheless one of the finest examples of Georgian architecture in America.

If architecture is any indication, eighteenth-century Bostonians cared as much for commerce and politics as for religion. One would expect to find in Boston, the province's capital and wealthiest community, finer examples of public architecture than in other communities of the colony. When the affluent merchant Peter Faneuil wished to give the town a much-needed new market house in 1740, for instance, he called upon the artist John Smibert to execute the plans. The result was a two-story structure with nine open arches on the ground floor to house market stalls and with rooms for the selectmen as well as a hall for town meetings on the floor above. The dormered roof was topped by a domed cupola with a magnificent grasshopper, which has survived through earthquakes, fires, and vandalism to serve Bostonians as a weather vane for two centuries. When the fire of 1711 burned down the old townhouse at the head of King's Street, the colony erected the brick building now known as the Old State House. Itself gutted by the fire of 1747, it was rebuilt the following year and stands today as another fine example of Georgian architecture, with handsome carved ornamentations adorning its belted facade.

The art form most suited to the American emphasis on use was that of furniture making. Yet here the craftsmen of Massachusetts were even more strongly influenced by English styles than were the architects of public buildings. Furniture in the first half of the eighteenth century reflected the Queen Anne style so popular in England, with its graceful cabriole leg, rococo ornamentation, and decorative work such as inlays, shells, and pendants. By the 1760s American furniture makers had joined the move to the Chippendale style, named for the author of *The Gentleman and Cabinet Maker's Director,* published in London in 1754. These larger, somewhat heavier pieces featured ornamental carving and imaginative variations such as blocked, bombé, or serpentine fronts, techniques especially characteristic of Boston and Newport craftsmen.

Faneuil Hall, Boston, 1742. From the *Massachusetts Magazine* (1789). Courtesy of the Massachusetts Historical Society.

Furniture of the Connecticut valley reflected slight regional variations, as did the work of furniture makers in Salem and other seaports north of Boston.

Silverworking was another useful craft that met with enthusiastic support throughout eighteenth-century Massachusetts. Silverware was not only useful and decorative but served as an investment as well, a fact greatly appreciated by affluent and ostentatious merchants. The advent of tea-drinking in the colonies by the beginning of the century gave silvermakers opportunity to display their talent and imagination far beyond the cups and candlesticks of the previous era. The ornamental technique of gadrooning was introduced by a Boston craftsman, Jeremiah Dummer, and was further developed by his student Edward Winslow. Another one of Dummer's apprentices was John Coney, perhaps the most skillful silversmith of colonial America. Coney in turn trained the father of Paul Revere, surely the most famous of such craftsmen. With these and other silversmiths Boston maintained its position of leadership in the craft throughout the eighteenth century.

Of the various major art forms practiced with increasing skill throughout western Europe in the eighteenth century, music was the one least well developed in Massachusetts Bay, as it also was elsewhere in America. Even so, that colony's *Bay Psalm Book*, first printed in 1640, was in its ninth edition by 1692. Church singing had fallen upon ill times by the early eighteenth century. Samuel Sewall had difficulty as a deacon of his church in setting the right tune to be sung, and Cotton Mather was frank to complain about having to suffer through "an odd noise" from more than one congregation. Matters became so bad in Wilbraham that a committee was appointed in 1723 to consider "the broken state of this town with regard to singing." But the Reverend John Tufts of West Newbury had already published *A Very Plain and Easy Introduction to the Art of Singing Psalm Tunes,* which contained numerous melodies in three-part harmony designated by letters (for fa, so, la, etc.) rather than by notes. The book was immensely popular and helped generate a proliferation of singing schools, singing-masters, and ultimately trained choirs.

The first American to make music his profession was Boston's William Billings, born in 1746. Billings developed what he called his "fuguing" style of composition, with notes "flying after each other, altho' not always the same sound." In 1764 he opened a music shop in Boston and six years later published his *New England Psalm Singer.* With greater energy and enthusiasm than talent, Billings nevertheless advanced the state of his chosen profession by his compositions, publications, and the introduction of the pitch pipe, the cello, and a crude metronome of his own invention. His most successful composition, "Chester," appeared in 1770 and when joined by patriotic lyrics in 1778 became the most popular war song of the Revolution. Boston was also the scene of the first musical concert performed in the colonies, in 1731, presented by Peter Pelham, the versatile engraver, dancing-master, and stepfather of John Singleton Copley. Concerts were regularly performed in Faneuil Hall until the construction in 1755 of a concert hall in Queen Street. For all their crudity of composition and performance these first colonial musicians, like artists in other fields, expressed a form which at least partially broke away from the standards established in eighteenth-century England and Europe.

As we have seen, Massachusetts Bay had already established a strong literary tradition before the close of the seventeenth century. The eighteenth century opened on an even stronger note with the publication in 1702 of Cotton Mather's magisterial *Magnalia Christi Americana,* by far the best work of history written up to that time in the colonies. Whatever one's opinion of Mather—who has been the subject of more abusive commentary than almost any other colonial American figure before Thomas Hutchinson—he was the first truly American genius native born of native-born parents (Increase Mather and Maria Cotton, the daughter of John). In *Magnalia* Mather was ostensibly writing an "ecclesiastical history" of New England, but he in fact included numerous biographical sketches of the great and not-so-great, action-packed descriptions of Indian fights, natural disasters, and other dramatic events, and lengthy political commentary. This prolific writer, with a total of 450 printed works to his credit, was also one of the Bay colony's leading scientific writers, although he could not match the stature of John Winthrop, Harvard's distinguished scientist. Before his death in 1728 Cotton Mather had published essays on phenomena of both macrocosm and microcosm, and with his father and brother helped establish a receptive frame of mind for the intensive scientific inquiry that would come in the decades to follow.

Mather's history, while comprehensive in subject matter, was nevertheless religious in its explanation of why things happened. This point of view was found in the historical writings of others. Although himself a cleric, the pastor of Boston's South Church, Thomas Prince, expressed a new faith in historical fact. He wrote his *Chronological History of New England in the Form of Annals,* published in 1736, "not in the specious form of a proper history, which admits of artificial ornaments and description to raise the imagination and affections of the reader," he explained, "but of a closer and naked register comprizing only facts." Like so many other "factual" histories, however, Prince's work was somewhat dull and colorless. A far more interesting account, though laced throughout with monumental prejudices against the provincial Americans, was written by William Douglass, a transplanted Scotsman who had settled in Boston in 1718. Douglass was far more a chronicler than historian, and except as the personal views of a perceptive and witty observer of the times, his writings have little value today.

Not so the work of colonial America's best historian, Thomas Hutchinson. Accompanying his *History of the Colony and Province of Massachusetts Bay* Hutchinson published a two-volume collection of documents, or "original papers." "He who rescues from oblivion interesting historical facts is beneficial to posterity as well as to his contemporaries," wrote Hutchinson. His first volume, covering the seventeenth century, appeared in 1764 and despite the fact that his partially completed manuscript was thrown into the street during the Stamp Act riots of August 1765, he published a second volume in 1767, bringing the history down to 1750. Volume III (1750–1755) was written in England but did not appear in print until long after his death. In addition to the anger of his patriotic neighbors, historian Hutchinson had also to cope with the fact that numerous documents had been destroyed in the periodic fires that swept through Boston. Hutchinson used the sources available to him judiciously and faithfully, showing great respect for the record and permitting himself few liberties of expression. The result, at least in the first two volumes, is a reliable narrative of his beloved colony's first 120 years. Yet his writing, too, was nearly as devoid of human interest as Prince's had been thirty years before. As he himself conceded, "I have no talent at painting or describing characters. I am sensible it requires great delicacy. My safest way was to avoid them and let facts speak for themselves."

Among the most widely read works in eighteenth-century Massachusetts Bay were the scores of sermons and other religious tracts that appeared each year from the presses of Boston's printers. The Great Awakening generated a larger number of controversial pamphlets than the decades before and after. The exchange between Boston's liberal Charles Chauncy and the revivalist Jonathan Edwards was but one running battle of the era. In 1742 Chauncy denounced the religious enthusiast as one who "has a conceit of himself as a person favored with the extraordinary presence of the Deity." According to Chauncy, "he mistakes the workings of his own passions for divine communications and fancies himself immediately inspired by the Spirit of God, when all the while, he is under no other influence than that of an overheated imagination." In a rebuttal published under the title *A Treatise Concerning Religious Affections* in 1746 Edwards responded that "gracious affections do arise from the mind's being enlightened, rightly and spiritually to understand or apprehend divine things. Holy affections are not heat without light," he continued. "The child of God is graciously affected, because he sees and understands something more of divine things than he did before." This and other controversies between New Lights and Old Lights reached wide audiences through the printed page and kept alive an interest in theological questions throughout the remainder of the colonial period.

Despite the continuing popularity of religious tracts, by far the most significant development in eighteenth-century literature was its increasing secularization. In 1704 Boston gave birth to America's first successful newspaper, the *News-Letter,* and in fact supported a second before Philadelphia or New York had their first. The *News-Letter* and the *Gazette* were joined by still another journal, the *New England Courant,* in 1721. Thereafter Boston had at least three and sometimes as many as five newspapers through the remainder of the colonial period. Salem, Newburyport, Worcester, and Cambridge all had journals of their own before independence. A circulation of three hundred copies weekly was considered good in the earlier decades, while a few newspapers exceeded five hundred copies by mid-century, each copy, of course, being handed around among several readers. Newspapers meant printers, and these craftsmen kept their presses busy with other publications: religious tracts, philosophical essays, broadsides on various subjects, and, particularly after 1760, political pamphlets. Almanacs, introduced in the previous century, became increasingly popular with the inhabitants of the more secular eighteenth century.

A newspaper served the community in several ways. By reprinting the news from the London journals brought in by shipmasters, the editors helped break down the sense of isolation from Europe which had characterized earlier generations. Printers were often postmasters or sometimes tavern keepers as well, both excellent sources of information from the other colonies. News of New York, Philadelphia, and other centers to the south gradually familiarized Bostonians with ways different from their own. But still more significant was the regular publication of notices that advertised numerous goods and services offered by local merchants and craftsmen. This information stimulated business not only among Bostonians themselves but, because each issue reached the inhabitants of outlying towns, these newspapers helped make Boston an entrepôt for a wide interior region. And when controversial issues arose, resolutions adopted by Boston's town meetings and letters to the editor written by its inhabitants gave the town greater political influence as well.

One of the most accomplished of almanac publishers was not a printer at all. Nathaniel Ames practiced medicine in Dedham, kept a tavern there in later life, and in 1725 issued his first almanac, eight years before the appearance of Franklin's *Poor Richard* in Philadelphia. At its height of popularity Ames's almanac sold sixty thousand copies a year. Ames included the usual astronomical tables and predictions of weather in his annual, along with excerpts from the writings of famous essayists and poets. He also included a sprinkling of the kind of aphorisms that would make Franklin's almanac so famous to later generations. Warned Ames: "All Men are by Nature equal, / But differ greatly in the sequel." But Ames was a writer, too, and his own verse and short essays, often on scientific matters, appeared throughout his almanac. Thus he brought to the vast majority of his readers who rarely saw newspapers their only contact with contemporary writing of any kind.

In newspapers, almanacs, and occasionally in separately printed volumes the small number of American poets printed their work. It is difficult to find in Massachusetts any eighteenth-century verse with the simple charms of Anne Bradstreet's or Edward Taylor's poetry of the previous era. The temptation to imitate the writing of Dryden, Pope, and other English masters of the form was too much for American poets to resist. The results in most cases were feeble copies of the original. Yet the works of Mather Byles, for instance, enjoyed considerable popularity throughout the Bay colony despite, or perhaps because of, conscious aping of English forms. Byles wrote on a vast range of subjects, including religious themes, and he had a noted reputation as a wit and punster. His arch rival in this latter role was Joseph Green, a Boston merchant, with whom Byles had friendly exchanges for many years. Neither governors nor Masons nor ministers were safe from Green's sharp pen. But whether serious or satirical, poetry, like music, did not show off the minds of Massachusetts to best advantage.

To describe the various forms by which the creative people of Massachusetts expressed themselves in the eighteenth century is far easier than to explain the deeper meaning of their work in philosophical or cultural terms. One theme is already apparent. Attention was gradually shifting away from God toward man and his world. And yet God was not forsaken in the process. An excerpt from Nathaniel Ames's "Essay upon the Microscope" reflects the subtlety of the change:

> If thro' an Optick Glass
> You view a spire of Grass
> That in the Road is trod,
> With Admiration you may gaze
> On Veins that branch a thousand ways,
> In nice proportion wrought.
> Which truly to th' assisted Eyes are brought,
> That he who is not void of common sense
> Or fill'd with daring Impudence,
> Must own its Maker truly to be GOD.*

A greater interest in what went on around them, in science, in war and politics, and in the world of commerce characterized the generations of eighteenth-century Massachusetts. The interest in history, in newspapers and almanacs, and the popularity of the Indian captivity stories attest to that. It was an era, furthermore, that could tolerate Professor John Winthrop's thoroughly scientific explanation for earthquakes, even though Winthrop repudiated the Reverend Thomas Prince and his *Earthquakes the Works of God*.

Interest in war and politics focused on matters of direct concern to

---

* From the almanac of 1741, in Sam Briggs, ed., *The Essays, Humor, and Poems of Nathaniel Ames* (Cleveland, 1891), 146.

America. A sense of America as something more than a geographical expression for the first time shaped the outlook of Bay colony inhabitants. Not that New Englanders saw much that they admired in the residents of other colonies, but recognition was an important first step toward the acceptance of differences and awareness of similarities. Probably no artist or writer consciously strove to establish an "American" style in his work, and yet conditions peculiar to America nevertheless influenced the result. Certainly the most significant fact of life in eighteenth-century Massachusetts was the dominant position of the middle-class farmer and artisan, the so-called common man. To him the revitalized religion of Jonathan Edwards had greatest appeal. For him the towns maintained their elementary and grammar schools, and for him the printers published their newspapers and almanacs. The Great Awakening had successfully challenged the authority of established church leadership. In its wake the ordinary people of the colony would challenge other authorities as well—in town meeting, in the legislature, and ultimately in the empire itself. When Edwards insisted in 1748 that rulers must adjust themselves to the welfare of the people, he was in fact giving voice to the demands of those people. Ironically, he himself fell victim to this exacting principle in 1750 when he was removed from his Northampton parish against his will. But his concept of leadership lived on.

11

MASSACHUSETTS AND THE EMPIRE

The "compleat" British-American is how one might describe Thomas
Hutchinson, Jr., merchant, councillor, judge, and governor of Massachusetts Bay during the middle decades of the eighteenth century. Born
in 1711 in the North End mansion of his parents, Colonel Thomas and
Sarah Foster Hutchinson, young Thomas was descended through his
father from one of the colony's oldest Puritan families, although his
great-great-grandmother, Anne Hutchinson, had found it necessary to
seek religious freedom in Rhode Island. The colonel was a member of the
Provincial Council, a staunch ally of Judge Samuel Sewall, and a
parishioner of Increase Mather, in whose church Thomas was baptized.
His father's library interested the youngster in his early childhood, and
he immersed himself among the various volumes of English history he
found there. After preparing at the North Grammar School under John
Barnard, he entered Harvard at the age of twelve, where he continued his
interest in history. Upon graduation with the Class of 1727, in which he
ranked only behind the two Browne brothers from Salem, Hutchinson
joined his father's mercantile house. In 1734 he married one of the
daughters of Rhode Island's Governor Peleg Sanford, by which match he
gained a dowry of about £5,000. Shortly thereafter he began a long and
distinguished public career.

The world that Thomas Hutchinson entered, both as a merchant and
as a political leader, reached far beyond Massachusetts Bay to London,
the center of the British empire. Before his death in 1780 he would come
to know that world far better than most of his fellow colonists. He would
work with representatives from neighboring provinces, meet with other
colonies at the Albany Congress in 1754, travel to London in a futile

effort to win a favorable decision for his colony, and he would die an exile in the empire's capital after his native country had repudiated that empire. Thomas Hutchinson was as "British" as a man born in Massachusetts at the beginning of the eighteenth century could possibly become.

*   *   *

Soon after Massachusetts Bay was reorganized in 1691 as a royal colony, binding it more closely to the British empire, the central administration of that empire itself underwent considerable change. At the beginning of the new century Great Britain began to rule her colonies with significant new authority. In 1696, King William III created a Board of Trade to collect information concerning the colonies and their potential contributions to the mother country and ultimately to administer those colonies in furthering the best interests of the empire as a whole. Largely on the strength of Edward Randolph's unfavorable impressions of the American colonies (especially Massachusetts Bay), which he reported in 1695, Parliament adopted additional legislation the following year. The Navigation Act of 1696 strengthened earlier laws by closing loopholes, establishing vice-admiralty courts in the colonies to try accused violators, giving the colonial governors a large role in enforcement, and authorizing the treasury office to enlarge the number of customs officers stationed in America. For the first time, the king appointed a single cabinet-level official, the Secretary of State for the Southern Department, to be responsible for colonial affairs.

Structure, on the one hand, and the way things really worked, on the other, were and are rarely the same thing in matters concerning governmental administration. The colonies were regarded as dependencies of the Crown and not of Parliament, although that body enacted legislation from time to time affecting the colonies as parts of the British empire. By the issuance of royal charters, commissions to royal governors, and especially royal instructions, the Crown made its will known throughout the empire. Indirectly, the customs service, the military establishment, and the naval authorities gave the Crown supplementary lines of power into the colonies, especially during wartime. For their part, the governors corresponded with the mother country through the office of the Secretary of State for the Southern Department. And the

Thomas Hutchinson (1711–1780), c. 1741. Painting by Edward Truman. Courtesy of the Massachusetts Historical Society.

colonial agents, men appointed by the legislatures of the various colonies to serve as lobbyists in Great Britain, also focused their attention on the Board of Trade and other administrative offices. Despite the preponderant influence of the Crown, however, the Parliament could and did from time to time intervene in colonial affairs, especially by enacting various regulations of imperial trade or colonial economic activity.

Maritime interests within Massachusetts Bay felt the indirect effects of British colonial policy far more frequently than did inland peoples. Virtually every aspect of the Navigation Acts affected the merchants and mariners of the Bay colony. By 1710 the colony's ports were divided into two customs districts, one at Salem and Marblehead covering the North Shore, the other at Boston, embracing the other harbors of the colonies from Lynn all the way around to Dartmouth (now New Bedford). The collector at Boston had the help of a comptroller and two tidewaiters and often hired further assistance on his own. The collector earned a salary of £100; and the comptroller, £70.

Given the attitude in Massachusetts toward matters like customs duties, these officers deserved every penny of their remuneration, especially after the passage of the Molasses Act of 1733. This legislation was an effort of Parliament to manipulate patterns of trade by affixing a duty of sixpence per gallon on molasses and ninepence per gallon on rum imported from the foreign West Indies. The act protected both the planters and distillers of the British West Indies, and contrary to general belief, the customs service at first made a determined effort to enforce the law. But in time geography triumphed over all. "The Sea Coast of the Province is so extensive and has so many Commodious harbours," Governor Belcher explained in 1737, "that the small number of Customs House Officers are often complaining they are not able to do much for the preventing of illegal Trade." And Belcher ruefully concluded: "Nor does the Sugar Act take any great Effect; great Quantities of foreign Molasses are still brought into this Province, and much of it by way of Rhode Island." If the evidence from Salem is indicative, most customs officers agreed with the merchants to levy the duty on only a small fraction of each cargo of foreign molasses.

The merchants and shipmasters were second to none in discovering ways to avoid the payment of customs duties on importations. Next to foreign molasses, tea and other India goods from Holland were favorite items of contraband. Meletiah Bourne, of Plymouth, managed to break several laws in one voyage when he sent the schooner *Sally* to Amsterdam with rice, an enumerated commodity that could legally be exported only to England (or by special license to ports south of Cape Finisterre). At Amsterdam, the captain exchanged his rice for a cargo of tea, which when sold in Boston brought Bourne a net profit of over £250. Francis Bernard wrote in utter exasperation soon after becoming governor in 1761 that "I receive from divers persons intelligence that there is a great quantity of Dutch Teas stirring about this town; that carts and other carriages are heard to be continually going about in the dead of the night, which," he concluded, "can be for no other purpose than smuggling." Governor Shirley had predicted as far back as 1743 that unless something were done about smuggling it would weaken "the Dependance which the British Northern Colonies ought to have upon their Mother Country." Tightening the sysem would come, but not until the 1760s, when it became intertwined with the new policy of collecting a revenue from the colonies.

As far as the generality of Massachusetts inhabitants was concerned, only through the agent appointed by their delegates in General Court did they have even indirect contact with the mother country. At the end of the seventeenth century, Massachusetts had sent Increase Mather over in an effort to secure a liberal new charter for the colony, and thereafter the colony retained a permanent agent in London to represent its interests. Prototype for agents in the early eighteenth century was Jeremiah Dummer, a Boston native and Harvard graduate who reversed the usual formula by going to England to seek his fortune, in his case as a lawyer. In 1721 he published an influential pamphlet entitled *Defence of the New England Charters* and served as agent for both Massachusetts and Connecticut for the better part of twenty years. Dummer's influence depended on his personal connections: his mistress was the daughter of Bishop Burnet, and he curried the acquaintance of such minor officials as the secretary to the Board of Trade, an aide to the Duke of Newcastle, and in time the duke himself. And he was particularly close to London's "American merchants," the men who traded with the colonies Dummer represented. At the end of our period, William Bollan served the General Court from 1745 until relieved in 1762. In contrast to Dummer, Bollan was a native of England who practiced law in Massachusetts, where he married the daughter of Governor Shirley. In 1745 he went to London in an effort to win repayment of the money Massachusetts had spent in capturing Louisbourg. After succeeding in this undertaking, he stayed on and by taking advantage of the many connections he had established, he served his adopted colony well.

Through royal instructions to the governors, the efforts of the customs officers to enforce the Navigation Acts, and the lobbying activities of its agents in London, the inhabitants of Massachusetts Bay received intermittent reminders of their subordinate place within the British empire. Whatever later historians have concluded, "salutary neglect" is not a phrase that most colonists would have thought descriptive of Great Britain's policy toward them in the first half of the eighteenth century. Yet despite serious disputes such as those concerning the land bank or the governor's salary, the reins of empire tugged but lightly upon the inhabitants of Massachusetts Bay. In their view, the system worked.

In addition to governmental ties with the mother country, Massachusetts had numerous less formal bonds as well, some of which have been noted in other contexts. For one thing, in the course of their business correspondence with English houses, the merchants of the Bay Colony discussed a wide range of subjects including some with only a peripheral bearing on the world of commerce. The possibility of war (or peace) with France and Spain, the progress of rebellions in Scotland, Ireland, or in the West Indies, the state of European diplomatic affairs were all matters of great interest to the colonial merchant, and his English correspondent proved a useful if not always accurate source of information. American merchants often shared with the rest of the community these more general portions of the letters they received by offering them to the local printer. "An excerpt of a Letter from a Gentleman in London to his Correspondent in Boston" would then appear in a subsequent issue of the newspaper, offering such news as "It is beyond a doubt that a concerted effort will be made in the spring for the reduction of the Havannah." The printer had numerous other sources of news of English and general European affairs, and his clients never seemed to tire of reading about happenings great and small in the Old World.

On a different plane, well-to-do residents eager for good literature frequently ordered books directly from London. They and others could also purchase a wide variety of reading materials from Boston's many bookstores. During the middle decades of the eighteenth century Boston ranked second in the empire behind London itself as a center for the selling of books. Its thirty-odd bookshops sold by auction and at wholesale to shopkeepers throughout New England. Soon after mid-century Boston lost its primacy to Philadelphia but remained the regional center for the rest of the period, despite the establishment of bookshops in Salem and Newburyport. Boston's John Mein maintained a stock of ten thousand volumes in the 1760s, many of them novels, plays, and general magazines in addition to the sermons and religious and philosophical tracts popular in the eighteenth century. In the absence of copyright laws, printers like Edes & Gill were free to bring out their own editions of English works. Thus Americans could purchase inexpensive editions of Johnson, Defoe, Chesterfield, and other notable English authors. Works of science and various textbooks became increasingly popular on the eve of the Revolution.

In addition to personal and literary connections with the mother country, a number of Americans maintained ties to various religious institutions in England. After the accession of William and Mary in 1689 and especially with the founding in 1701 of Thomas Bray's Society for the Propagation of the Gospel in Foreign Parts, American colonists became the objects of intensified missionary work by the Anglican Church. Professors of the Anglican faith could be found among the inhabitants of numerous Massachusetts communities in the seventeenth century, but not until the arrival of the Reverend Robert Ratcliff in 1693 were Anglican services conducted on a regular basis in Boston. Within a short time the SPG had made enough converts among New Englanders to spread alarm among the region's Congregational ministers. They sought advice and support from Dissenters in England and closed ranks against the invaders. In 1725 the Reverend Timothy Cutler, a graduate of Harvard and a member of its Board of Overseers, declared religious war against his alma mater, writing a friend in Cambridge, England, that "here is a snotty town of the same name where are near 300 scholars among who[m] a ch[urch]man durst hardly say that his soul is his own, and I think it will never be well untill that College become an Episcopal College." Harvard successfully fought off the assault, as did Massachusetts in 1732 when the Anglicans attempted to disestablish the Congregational church. But for the remainder of the colonial period, the SPG in London waged a steady campaign for the establishment of a bishop in the American colonies, which was regarded as "ecclesiastical imperialism" by mid-century.

Other denominations maintained somewhat less tempestuous ties with the mother country. New England's Quakers corresponded regularly with Dr. John Fothergill and other English Friends. Baptists, Presbyterians, and Methodists depended upon the moral and sometimes financial support of their English connections. Surely the Great Awakening itself would not have spread so rapidly or widely throughout Massachusetts without the visits of England's great itinerant preacher George Whitefield. Ministers and other men of learning on both sides of the Atlantic carried on extensive correspondence throughout the eighteenth century, commenting on theological or philosophical issues of mutual interest. The letters of Cotton Mather, Samuel Sewall, and Thomas Hutchinson among others suggest that these Americans, at least, could exchange ideas on an equal footing with their English friends without becoming objects of the condescension or worse to which many provincials were subjected.

People themselves constituted yet another line of communication between Massachusetts and the British Isles. Shipmasters made frequent voyages to London or Bristol, although they did not remain long and were often preoccupied with commercial matters. Merchants and other well-to-do inhabitants occasionally visited England on various affairs of business and, at times, young men continued their education in the mother country after finishing grammar school or college in Massachusetts. But the principal flow of people was westward. After the initial Puritan migration of the 1630s, not many Englishmen came to Massachusetts until after the Restoration in 1660. Even then, for the remainder of the century, the colony received few newcomers, aside from a handful of seamen who deserted their vessels or fishermen whose captains deserted them. One exception was the settlement of some forty French Huguenots at New Oxford in 1686. Although troubles with the Indians soon drove them out, the Huguenots resettled in Boston and became the nucleus of a significant addition to the community, which included the families from which James Bowdoin, Paul Revere, and others came.

A combination of various events in the early decades of the eighteenth century encouraged further immigration into Massachusetts. The end of almost twenty-five years of intermittent warfare in 1713 made migration for dissident groups possible. About one thousand Scots-Irish arrived at Boston in 1718 from their adopted homes in northern Ireland, where recent crop failures prompted them to look for new lands. Massachusetts was not altogether cordial to these new arrivals but saw in them a means of maintaining a buffer along the frontier. One group settled in Worcester, where they began to build a church. When local inhabitants burned it down, many of the Scots-Irish left for other parts, settling in Sutton, Rutland, and Ware. In 1738 a group migrated to Pelham and later still others would found Colrain. Meanwhile, another spearhead pushed north of Boston, to Dracut, Andover, and finally into Maine, where their arrival helped Falmouth and other communities recover from years of Indian warfare. In succeeding years numerous Scots-Irish communities sprang up around Casco Bay and along the Kennebec River. A few Scotsmen also came to Massachusetts, usually as individuals determined to establish themselves as schoolmasters, ministers, merchants, or shopkeepers.

Not all the immigrants into eighteenth-century Massachusetts came from the British Isles. In 1740 Samuel Waldo, a Boston merchant of German descent with extensive investments in lands along the Maine coast, attracted forty families from Germany to settle around Broad Bay, east of Casco Bay. There they founded the town of Waldoborough. Although reinforced by the arrival of 150 fellow countrymen two years later, the Germans suffered severely. The climate and soil gave little encouragement to the agriculture with which they were familiar and they knew little of fishing as a means of subsistence. A devastating Indian attack in 1746 wiped out the village altogether; yet after the war, survivors returned to reestablish the community on a stronger footing. Except for the occasional arrival of newcomers, these various communities of French, Scots-Irish, and Germans had little contact with the old country; nevertheless, their presence in Massachusetts Bay provided a reminder of the European past shared by all of its inhabitants.

* * *

Surely the most dramatic reminders of their British ties came to the inhabitants of Massachusetts Bay during the frequent warfare between France and the mother country that dominated the years from 1689 to 1763. Indeed, the colony of Massachusetts Bay was in a state of war for forty-six of that period's seventy-five years. Only in New York, perhaps, were so many inhabitants directly exposed to the attacks of the French and their Indian allies as were the people of Massachusetts Bay. They fought not only within the colony itself, but in Cape Breton and Nova Scotia, Quebec, New York, and as far away as Cuba and Cartagena. At home and abroad they fought and died, for no other conscious reason than to protect their community, their province, and their nation, probably in that order of priority.

The new century had hardly begun when the uneasy peace that had terminated King William's War in 1697 abruptly collapsed. In 1702, the War of the Spanish Succession broke out in Europe and erupted as Queen Anne's War in the colonies soon thereafter. As in the previous war the French made firm alliance with the Abnakis in Maine, who fell upon the communities along the eastern frontier from Casco Bay to York during the summer and fall of 1703. On the western frontier a band of French and Indians surprised the fortified town of Deerfield in late February 1704, killing more than forty inhabitants, burning seventeen houses, and carrying off one hundred captives. Altogether less than half of the town's inhabitants escaped death or capture. The town's pastor, John Williams, lost his wife and two children in the attack and was marched three hundred miles overland to Montreal with his five remaining children and other townspeople. Of this group about fifty, including Williams himself, survived the ordeal to be ransomed and ultimately returned to their New England homes. One of the minister's captive daughters remained in Canada, however, embracing the Catholic faith and marrying an Indian, to the utter consternation of her family.

Queen Anne's War dragged on for nearly another decade, during which the frontiersmen of Massachusetts bore the brunt of the battle with little help from other colonies. It was even said that goods taken by the Indians from frontier homes in Massachusetts turned up for sale in the shops of Albany. Constant alarms of impending attack and long periods of garrison duty made farming both difficult and hazardous. More than once men working in distant fields fell victim to marauding war parties. "Many of us are driven from our homes. Much of our stock is killed by the Heathen. Many of our able men are removed from us," complained the inhabitants of one town, "and we daily grow more and more feeble and deplorable; daily walking and working with fear, trembling, and jeopardy of life."* Occasionally Massachusetts forces

---

* Douglas E. Leach, *The Northern Colonial Frontier, 1607–1763* (New York, 1966), 122.

went on the offensive, as in the expedition led by old Benjamin Church along the coast of Maine which destroyed the French settlement at Grand Pré in Nova Scotia. After several failures a joint Anglo-American expedition finally succeeded in capturing the French stronghold at Port Royal in 1710 and with it all of Acadia fell, a loss confirmed in the Treaty of Utrecht, which officially ended the war in 1713.

The treaty secured an uneasy truce between France and England that lasted for nearly thirty years. New Englanders looked forward to a period of peace that would enable them to regain at least some of the territory they had abandoned along the coast of Maine. But the French under the Marquis de Vaudreuil and the Jesuit priest Sebastien Rale had other ideas. Rale was missionary to the Abnakis at Norridgewock on the Kennebec, and he determined to prevent the expansion of English settlement into that valley. The confrontation broke out into full-scale war in 1722, after the Indians had attacked the town of Brunswick at the head of Casco Bay. Governor Dummer's War, as it was called, continued for three years, during which the settlers adopted tactics every bit as barbarous as those of the Indians. Bounties offered by the General Court on Indian scalps gave encouragement to bands of frontiersmen. But the slaughter of Captain John Lovewell and many of his men at Pigwacket in the spring of 1725 somewhat dampened the Yankees' appetite for this sort of activity, and peace was restored at year's end.

When the English decided in 1741 to attack the Spanish bastion of Cartagena, the continental colonies were asked to contribute to the expedition. Massachusetts sent five hundred men, of whom all but fifty perished, mostly from yellow fever and other diseases. The fact that most of the men enlisted more in hope of booty than out of patriotism in no way lessened the shock of such casualties. Meanwhile, in the New England interior Massachusetts tried with some success to regularize the fur trade through its so-called truck-house system, which operated through a series of government-owned trading houses and ships. The goal was to eliminate the abuses perpetrated by private traders as well as to draw the Indians of northern New England away from the French. The operation fulfilled these objectives reasonably well for a number of years. But by 1744 the Anglo-Spanish quarrel had broadened into a renewal of the struggle between England and France, known as the War of the Austrian Succession in Europe and as King George's War in America.

Once more Massachusetts found itself in the front lines of warfare on both land and sea. The French had used the intervening years to replace their lost base at Port Royal with a far stronger bastion at Louisbourg, on Cape Breton Island. Now, in the spring of 1744, they took the English garrison at Canceau and seriously threatened to recapture Annapolis Royal itself, as the British had renamed Port Royal. New Englanders feared the havoc that privateers operating out of Louisbourg might wreak among their fishing and mercantile fleets and urged Governor Shirley to authorize an assault against the French stronghold. The task seemed impossible at first—walls thirty feet high, surmounted by 250 cannon and guarded by two other batteries. But returning prisoners reported that the French garrison was undermanned and could be taken. Shirley was persuaded. He arranged for help from the British Commodore Peter Warren and from sister colonies as far south as Pennsylvania. He then chose as commander of the expedition William Pepperrell, president of the colony's council and a popular merchant from Kittery, Maine.

The New England contingent left Boston in early April 1745 and rendezvoused with Commodore Warren at Canceau. Instead of trying to force their way into the harbor of Louisbourg itself, an almost impossible task, the expedition landed against feeble opposition about two miles from the fortified town. The next day a force of New Englanders marched overland and occupied one of the outlying batteries, which the French had abandoned in the belief that it could not withstand an assault from the land. Repeated efforts to take the second battery, on an island in the middle of the harbor, resulted only in mounting casualties and dissatisfaction among the Yankees chosen for these suicidal missions. Relations between Pepperrell and Warren worsened as the siege continued, and morale among the troops sank further when some of the cannon burst among the gun crews. Then at the end of May, Warren, with the help of two New England vessels, captured an approaching French warship loaded with powder, cannon, and supplies for the beleaguered garrison. The Yankee gunners increased their bombardment, and the troops prepared to launch a joint attack with Warren on the 17th, but on the eve of the assault the French capitulated.

To the inhabitants of colonial Massachusetts the capture of Louisbourg was their finest hour. Only 101 New Englanders were killed along with about 30 others who died of disease (although the force that occupied the fort lost 1,200 men over the next winter by sickness). Furthermore, Pepperrell had refused to play second fiddle to Commodore Warren and

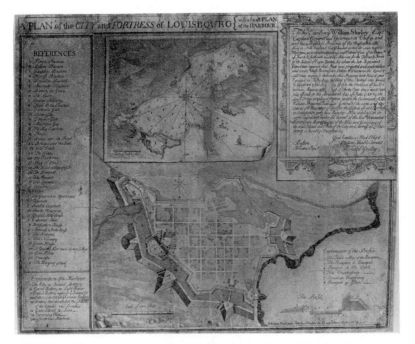

Plan of Louisbourg, 1745. Engraved by P. Pelham after Richard Gridley. Courtesy of the Massachusetts Historical Society.

the British regulars, some of whom were unbearably arrogant, and therefore Yankees could rightfully claim much of the glory from the bottom ranks to the top. Pepperrell was in fact created a baronet (the first American-born colonist thus honored). Characteristically, the inhabitants of Massachusetts gave most of the credit to God. In recounting the various pieces of good fortune that favored the Anglo-American force, Seth Pomeroy, who served as a major of artillery, concluded that "God has gone out of the way of his common Providence in a remarkable and almost miraculous manner." The Reverend Charles Chauncy, from his Boston pulpit, proclaimed that "I scarce know of a conquest since the days of Joshua and the Judges wherein the Finger of God is more visible. . . ." But the New Englanders were not so humble as to think that God was *entirely* responsible for the victory. The conquest of Louisbourg greatly bolstered the confidence of the Yankees as soldiers and became a symbol of what determined citizen-soldiers could do. The return of Louisbourg to the French by the Treaty of Aix-la-Chapelle in 1748 stunned New Englanders. This decision too became a symbol—of Old World politics and cynicism. Neither the military conquest of Louisbourg nor its loss at the diplomatic table would be forgotten by the next generation in Massachusetts.

Meanwhile, King George's War raged on along other fronts. In the very northwestern corner of the colony a French and Indian force overwhelmed the undermanned Fort Massachusetts, the first in a chain of bases established to protect the vulnerable Connecticut valley. Massachusetts contributed the largest share to a joint colonial expedition against Quebec, but troops promised from England never arrived and the attack was canceled. Then rumors of a French invasion fleet aimed at New England forced the colony onto the defensive. More than three thousand troops were in fact headed for North America, but storms and disease so wracked the fleet that the expedition lost over twenty-four hundred men without even sighting their foes before staggering back to France. But the French took Grand Pré and repeatedly assaulted Fort Number Four, now Charlestown, New Hampshire, on the Connecticut River, both of which were manned by Massachusetts men. When peace came in 1748, the Bay colony welcomed the end of hostilities if not the actual terms of settlement. As the Boston merchant Thomas Hancock succinctly put it: "I think a general peace may be for the Good of the Nation, tho I don't think it will prove so to this Country."

Regulation House, 1753, Fort West Hoosac (Williamstown). Replica built in 1953. Courtesy of Henry N. Flynt.

No one expected the frontier to remain quiet for long, but for once the next round of warfare in America did not start in New England. Rather it began at the forks of the Ohio River, on the site of present-day Pittsburgh. There a force of Virginians was repulsed in the spring of 1754 followed by the defeat of an expedition under George Washington in July. Colonel Israel Williams, in charge of the forts protecting northern Massachusetts, saw "a very dark and distressing scene opening" and urged Governor Shirley to construct two new fortifications against anticipated attacks by French and Indians. Meanwhile, the French were pressing their claims to much of Nova Scotia. In the late spring 1755, Governor Shirley sent two thousand militiamen to repel the French, which they succeeded in doing by summer. The French Acadians inhabiting Nova Scotia had resisted British rule ever since their province had been surrendered by the Treaty of Utrecht in 1713. Despite the freedom to practice their religion and exemption from both militia service and taxation they refused to swear allegiance to their new sovereign. Out of exasperation British authorities ordered nearly seven thousand Acadians removed from their ancient homeland and dispersed among the other English colonies of North America, a tragic episode known to later generations of Americans through Henry Wadsworth Longfellow's epic *Evangeline*.

At the same time that he dispatched two thousand troops to the very eastern regions of English territory, Governor Shirley had also planned two massive attacks on the western frontier, one against Crown Point, the French fort on Lake Champlain, the other against Fort Niagara. Nearly five thousand men from Massachusetts enlisted for these campaigns, one out of eight men of militia age. Veterans of the Louisbourg victory such as Seth Pomeroy and Moses Titcomb, professional militiamen like Ephraim Williams, and skilled artisans like shipwrights from Newbury were gradually assembled. William Johnson of New York commanded the Crown Point expedition, while Governor Shirley, who had temporarily become commander of all British forces in America upon the death of Braddock, took charge of the push toward Niagara. Neither commander reached his objective. South of Lake George a scouting force of Massachusetts men under Williams was ambushed in early September by French and Indian forces, and Johnson's drive stalled. Shirley at least reached Lake Ontario at Oswego, but lack of support from New York authorities and the approaching winter persuaded him to postpone further campaigning that year. Before he could renew the offensive in the spring of 1756, Shirley was recalled to London and was replaced as commander in chief by the ineffectual Earl of Loudoun and as governor of Massachusetts by Thomas Pownall.

The spring of 1756 finally brought a formal declaration of hostilities between France and England, called the Seven Years' War in Europe and the French and Indian War in America, an imprecise term since all the wars since 1689 had been against the French and Indians. Loudoun managed to fritter away the entire year of 1756, losing Fort Oswego to his energetic French counterpart, the Marquis de Montcalm, who also encouraged the completion of a new French stronghold at Ticonderoga, which controlled the portage between Lake George and Lake Champlain. When Loudoun asked for militia from Massachusetts to join in an assault against Quebec planned for 1757, the General Court was understandably skeptical of this blundering English aristocrat. Like most of the colonial assemblies, they decided to leave military activities to the British regulars until the future became clearer. Loudoun's invasion of Canada was shelved in favor of an effort to recover Louisbourg, which was in turn scrapped because of bad weather and superior French forces. Another year ended with nothing accomplished on the Anglo-American side except the loss of Fort William Henry south of Lake George in August. There the French made no serious effort to restrain their Indian allies until they had slaughtered over two hundred troops, including many New England militiamen, and had carried off an equal number of prisoners. French callousness and Indian savagery had accomplished what Loudoun could not, a reawakening of the Yankees' determination to destroy the menace from the north. But now the frontier of Massachusetts lay open to attack. The only hopeful sign was the recall of Loudoun himself.

Campaigning in 1758 began inauspiciously, when a force of British regulars under their new commander, James Abercromby, was repulsed with fearful losses before Ticonderoga. The Massachusetts men present were appalled at the carnage. "I have told enough to make you sick, if the relation acts on you as the facts have on me," wrote an officer in his account of the battle. The British met with better success to the east, where generals James Wolfe and Sir Jeffrey Amherst recaptured Louisbourg in a campaign modeled on Pepperrell's victory thirteen years before. A few hundred Massachusetts men were among the victorious army. At long last the tide began to turn in favor of the Anglo-American forces.

Enlistment Certificate with Scene of South Battery, Boston, c. 1760. Engraved by T. Johnston. Courtesy of the Essex Institute, Salem, Mass.

In August they regained control of Lake Ontario when a force of provincials captured Fort Frontenac. Amherst landed in Boston with his Louisbourg veterans and marched the length of Massachusetts to reinforce the army north of Albany. Nothing further was accomplished that year, but the stage was set for an all-out offensive against Canada in 1759.

The plan called for Wolfe to storm Quebec by sailing up the St. Lawrence with an army composed mostly of regulars but which included some four hundred men from Massachusetts. Amherst was to close in by way of Lake Champlain. His advance was so slow, however, that he never did reach Quebec, and Wolfe alone won the decisive battle and a hero's death on the Plains of Abraham. In the spring of 1760, Amherst and his mixed force of regulars and provincials pressed down on Montreal. After a summer of campaigning he accepted the surrender of Montreal and with it the rest of French Canada. Seventy years of struggle for the control of North America had at length ended in victory for the English and their American allies. Even before the final victory, Governor Pownall had, in a report to William Pitt, praised Massachusetts as "the frontier and advanced guard of all the colonies against the enemy in Canada." During the year 1758, the colony maintained seven thousand troops and contributed another twenty-five hundred to British units. It had incurred a debt of well over £300,000 by 1758, only a small part of which was reimbursed by Parliament. But with the Treaty of Paris in 1763 the French scourge was at last removed from the waters off Nova Scotia and from the backwoods as well.

Even more significant was the measure of pride and joy expressed by the inhabitants of Massachusetts Bay in the glorious victory of their parent nation. "As British subjects," Boston's liberal minister Jonathan Mayhew asserted in 1761, "we must acknowledge that providence has in this respect favored us above most *other* protestants." Along with Americans in other colonies the people of Massachusetts were proud to be a part of the British empire. In the years that followed they would look back to 1763 as the high-water mark of contentment.

*   *   *

Just as membership in the British empire involved the colony of Massachusetts in the foreign affairs of the mother country, so too did it lead to closer ties with other British colonies on the American continent. We have already seen the importance of coastal trade in the commercial activities of a merchant like Thomas Hancock. By the eve of the Revolution about 40 percent of all Massachusetts shipping was engaged in such commerce, for almost all cargoes and passengers bound to the middle and southern colonies went by sea. Water transportation was cheaper, more comfortable, and often faster than by land. By the eighteenth century, however, three major overland routes connected Boston with Connecticut, New York, and the other provinces farther south. One led west through Worcester to Springfield and then down the Connecticut River valley to Hartford and Middletown. There it left the river for New Haven, where it joined the post road running along the southern Connecticut shore to New York. Another route led from Boston to Providence, thence to New London, across the Connecticut River at Saybrook, and on to New Haven and New York. A third route lay between these two, passing through Milford and Uxbridge to Coventry, Connecticut, and thence westward to join the first route at Hartford. A postal service established by Andrew Hamilton in 1693 soon provided once-a-week service between Boston and New York during the summer months, and once a fortnight in winter. By the mid-eighteenth century, postal service greatly improved under the direction of Benjamin Franklin and William Hunter. Yet travel was still restricted to horseback, for in places the roads were too narrow and soft for vehicles. Not until the very eve of the Revolution did regular stagecoach service connect Boston and New York.

Boston merchants engaged in intercolonial commerce relied on merchants in other American ports to handle their affairs. By the mid-eighteenth century this dependence led to other intercolonial undertakings as well. Boston's John Wendell held real estate in New York City and considered investing in a new town along the Connecticut River with a group of New Yorkers he knew. Even more significant was the movement of population from one colony to another. Already Massachusetts farmers had begun to look for better lands in New Hampshire, New York, and occasionally as far away as New Jersey and Pennsylvania. Merchants, lawyers, ministers, and other professional men sought to establish themselves in distant communities, where they generally married and settled down permanently. Skilled artisans moved from one colony to another whenever opportunity appeared sufficiently attractive. The Americans' restless pursuit of "greener pastures" had long since become a habit, and it affected merchants and artisans as well as farmers. By the middle of the eighteenth century wherever a person of Massachusetts traveled he might very well encounter a distant cousin or former neighbor. Intermarriage spread family ties still further. Fayerweathers of Boston were tied to Shippens of Philadelphia, while New York Wendells claimed connections with the Quincys and Hancocks of Massachusetts.

But ideas travel more easily than people, and the establishment of a reliable postal service in the eighteenth century widened the network of intercolonial communication formerly confined to the seaports served by coastwise commerce. Books and pamphlets published in New York and Philadelphia reached Boston in a week or so, where they were reprinted and given still wider distribution. Enterprising printers of newspapers often combined their publishing business with the management of a tavern or the office of postmaster, in order to enhance their access to news sources. Even these more aggressive printers helped themselves to whatever items of interest they found in newspapers brought by ship-masters and travelers from other towns. For this reason a reader of, say, the *Boston Gazette,* could usually learn more about events in other colonies than about those that occurred in Boston itself. The intercolonial book trade added its contribution to the development of an American mind. Boston's *New England Primer* was probably the most widely re-printed school book in the colonies, Franklin alone issuing thirty-seven thousand copies during the middle years of the century. The development of libraries, both public and private, broadened the distribution of printed matter still further. And the fact that inhabitants of all the colonies shared a common interest in English newspapers, magazines, and other printed matter bound the colonists together in somewhat more subtle fashion.

As lines of communication between the colonies improved during the eighteenth century, so too did the idea of establishing closer military and political ties. Occasional and temporary arrangements helped coordinate the defense of the northern colonies during the numerous wars with France, but by mid-century some commentators had a more permanent union in mind. In his *Summary, Historical and Political . . . of the British Settlements in America* (1749–51), the Boston physician and historian William Douglass suggested that a colonial council be established in London to draw up a uniform system of government for all the colonies, subject to parliamentary approval. At about the same time, other colonists, including Archibald Kennedy of New York and Benjamin Franklin of Philadelphia, pondered the advantages of colonial union in dealing with the Indians. In September 1753, the Board of Trade proposed that commissioners from the colonies most concerned about relations with the Iroquois meet to draw up a single treaty with the Six Nations. The following spring, Governor William Shirley urged the General Court of Massachusetts to support the plan. "An Union of the Several governments for the mutual defense and for the annoyance of the enemy has long been desired by this province," the court responded. It appropriated £300 for expenses, including a gift to the Indians, and chose a five-man delegation to represent the province at a meeting in Albany. Thomas Hutchinson and Oliver Partridge were its most distinguished members.

Even before the conference convened, several commissioners discussed by correspondence and in person the prospects for establishing a permanent union at least among the northern colonies. In early June, Franklin sketched an outline—"Short Hints," he called it—for such a union. As the delegates assembled, the topic of union immediately superseded that of an Indian treaty as the subject of first priority. Hutchinson was chosen to join with Franklin and several other commissioners to draft a plan for the consideration of the whole body. But first the committee had to establish the need for such an innovation. Hutchinson, therefore, drafted "a representation of the present state of the colonies," in which he traced alleged encroachments by the French into parts of North America claimed by the English. "It is the evident design of the French to surround the British colonies . . . , to take and keep possession of the heads of all the important rivers, to draw over the Indians to their interest, and," he concluded, "to be in a capacity of making a general attack on the several governments." In language that would become common to Hutchinson's opponents twenty years later, the future royal governor of Massachusetts urged that "speedy and effectual measures be taken to secure the colonies from the slavery they are threatened with." Among other proposals, Hutchinson recommended that "there be a union of His Majesty's several governments on the continent." After minor revisions, the congress meeting at Albany adopted Hutchinson's "representation" on July 9, 1754.

Meanwhile, the committee made Franklin's "Short Hints," and perhaps suggestions of other commissioners as well, the basis for its consideration of a plan of union. After discussions lasting several days, the plan was ready for presentation, and the congress adopted it on July 10, 1754. One historian of the period, Lawrence H. Gipson, has suggested that Hutchinson himself submitted the draft prosposal which became the basis for the final plan, but the evidence is conjectural at best. On one occasion, fifteen years after the event, Hutchinson apparently did claim authorship, but on three separate occasions thereafter he assigned the responsibility where it almost certainly lay, with Benjamin Franklin. Hutchinson, nevertheless, strongly endorsed the plan as adopted by the congress.

Support from Hutchinson and the other commissioners sent by Massachusetts could not assure adoption of the proposal by the General Court, however. Even though that body had authorized its delegation to work toward such a scheme, in the end the General Court voted down the Albany plan. The issue was somewhat clouded by the consideration of various compromise measures, but the main reason for rejection was made clear in a letter to the colony's London agent, William Bollan. "In its operation it would be subversive of the most valuable rights and liberties of the several colonies included in it; as a new civil government is thereby proposed to be established over them with great and extraordinary power to be exercised in peace as in war."

*   *   *

As Thomas Hutchinson looked back upon the close of the last French and Indian War in his *History of Massachusetts-Bay* he noted what he considered a portent for the future. Governor Francis Bernard had, upon learning of the conquest of Quebec in 1760, congratulated the General Court on this final victory over the French. He took the occasion to remind that body of "the blessings they derive from their *subjection* to Great Britain, without which they could not now have been a free people. . . ." In its response, the assembly repeated the term "subjection" but hastened to add that "the whole world must be sensible of the blessings derived to Great Britain from the loyalty of the colonies in general and from the efforts of this province in particular." The legislators went on to point out that for more than a century, Massachusetts Bay had spared neither blood nor expense in repelling the French "without which effort Great Britain at this day might have had no colonies to defend." And the council was even more pointed in rejecting implications of the governor's choice of words. "To their *relation* to Great Britain," not their *subjection,* did they owe their freedom. "These addresses have the appearance of caution," Hutchinson concluded in his *History,* "which I have not before met in any publick papers since the revolution [of 1688]."

Writing from the perspective of his English exile in 1776, Hutchinson could safely declare that the cession of French Canada to Great Britain thirteen years earlier would in time bring about the independence of the continental colonies. But he had the objectivity to recognize that at the time of that cession, in 1763, the people of Massachusetts were genuinely proud of their membership in the British empire. With more than a touch of irony, however, Hutchinson, the historian, could not resist choosing to quote from the town meeting speech of his arch foe James Otis, delivered upon receipt of the final peace with France. "We in America have certainly abundant reasons to rejoice. . . . The British dominion and power may now be said, literally, to extend from sea to sea, and from the great river to the ends of the earth. . . . The true interests of Great Britain and her plantations are mutual, and what God in his providence has united, let no man dare pull asunder."

But irony proved to be a two-edged sword for Thomas Hutchinson. In the decade after 1763, the man who had symbolized the political and cultural ties between Massachusetts and the mother country became instead the symbol of British "tyranny" over his native province. And the colonial union which he had tried in vain to bring about in 1754 came to fruition twenty years later at Philadelphia, in no small measure the inadvertent result of Thomas Hutchinson's own governorship.

12

THE GATHERING STORM

In the years immediately following the peace of 1763 Boston was in serious difficulty. It had reached a peak of commercial activity in the 1740s and thereafter experienced little of the growth enjoyed by Philadelphia and New York. To make matters worse came the postwar depression of the 1760s. Nearly 30 percent of Boston's adult males had neither property nor a secure place within the community. Most of these men depended entirely upon master mechanics and craftsmen for whatever jobs they could get and hold. Others were mariners who shipped out when they could find berths but who spent much of their time "on the beach," waiting for the next opportunity. Many of these men drifted out of the seaport to search for jobs elsewhere, only to return after a few months. Unemployment and its companion, underemployment, were no strangers to the urban poor of Boston in the 1760s.

To find a representative member of this large group of men presents a difficult task to the historian, for little more than their names has remained on record. And yet to treat them as mere statistics is in itself demeaning. Perhaps we can know something of these people through the man many of them accepted as their leader in the 1760s, Ebenezer Mackintosh. Descended from a Scots Highlander captured by Cromwell's army and deported to Boston in 1652, Mackintosh was born in Boston in 1737. His father Moses was an illiterate who, during the course of his life, was warned out of Boston and neighboring towns on numerous occasions. The father's only known employment was as an occasional soldier at Castle Island, in Boston harbor. Young Ebenezer apparently learned the shoemaker's trade under apprenticeship to an uncle, after which he presumably took up residence in Boston's South End.

In 1758 Ebenezer enlisted in the expedition against Canada, taking part in the futile assault against Ticonderoga under the leadership of General James Abercromby. Mackintosh was among the survivors of that disastrous affair and returned to Boston in November. He soon became well acquainted with the South End through his position as engineman in one of the fire companies, a vocation he could easily combine with that of cordwainer. Rival fire companies often fought in competition for the bonuses awarded by the town for especially meritorious service. Mackintosh undoubtedly earned his spurs as the leader of the South End through his experience as an engineman. The Pope's Day celebration on November 5 had become the annual occasion for a major parade which almost always degenerated into a brawl between inhabitants of the North End and the South End of town. After the 1764 affair, a particularly vicious battle in which a child was run over, Ebenezer Mackintosh was among the men arrested. The young cordwainer had, at the age of twenty-seven, clearly won his position as the leader of Boston's South End.

*   *   *

One of the most serious problems confronting British authorities in Massachusetts, as in other maritime colonies, was enforcement of the Navigation Acts. Like merchants elsewhere, Americans smuggled goods in order to increase profits; there were no political implications in the practice. In Massachusetts molasses from the French islands probably comprised the most popular article of illicit goods. As a general rule, merchants reported only a small portion of their cargo at the customs office or by other ruses, often with the connivance of officials, paid a fraction of the sixpence duty owed on each gallon. Other cargoes, such as Dutch gin, French cloths, wines, and tea, were landed under cover of darkness in any one of the many coves along the coast. Thomas Hancock was only one of many shipowners who instructed their captains how to avoid detection as they approached the coast. In early 1754, Hancock ordered a shipment of tea from Amsterdam sent to the Dutch island of St. Eustatius and, later that year, dispatched his trusted captain Simon Gross in the schooner *Lydia* to pick it up. He instructed Gross to take on a legitimate cargo at Montserrat before returning home. Upon his arrival off Boston he was to "stop at the lighthouse where you shall have a letter for your further proceeding." Gross landed his tea safely, earning Hancock a net profit of £200.

British authorities became particularly annoyed when Americans continued to trade with the French and Spanish West Indies during the various colonial wars which made these islands enemy territory. As the last war ground ever onward, Prime Minister William Pitt needed additional funds, and he concluded that the American customs service could contribute a greater revenue by tighter enforcement of existing regulations. One of the traditional instruments used by customs officials in Massachusetts was the so-called writ of assistance, which permitted them to search private buildings for illicit goods without a specific court order. With the death of George II at the end of 1760 all such writs, like most other commissions, had to be renewed. A group of Boston merchants engaged the legal services of James Otis, Jr., and Oxenbridge Thacher to oppose the issuance of new writs. The veteran lawyer Jeremiah Gridley represented the customs house in late February 1761 before the Superior Court of Massachusetts, Thomas Hutchinson, presiding.

From the first, the case was heard against a bitterly partisan political backdrop. For shortly after taking office in September 1760, the newly appointed governor, Francis Bernard, had repudiated a promise made by his predecessor, Thomas Pownall, to appoint James Otis, Sr., to the next vacancy on the Superior Court bench. Bernard named Thomas Hutchinson to the post instead. The Otises, father and son, promptly withdrew from the court party and swore vengeance against both Bernard and Hutchinson. The writs of assistance case was only one of a series of confrontations between the Otises and their new allies, on the one hand, and the new governor and his lieutenant, on the other.

"Otis was a flame of fire," John Adams later described the young attorney's conduct of the case. "Then and there was the first scene of the first act of opposition to the arbitrary claims of Great Britain. Then and there," he concluded with more than a little exaggeration, "the child Independence was born." When Gridley focused his defense on the fact that Parliament had authorized such writs at least since the reign of Charles II, Otis carried the argument onto constitutional grounds. Noting that Gridley's precedent had been established during "the zenith of arbitrary power" under the Stuarts, Otis pointed out that writs of assistance violated the constitutional principle that every Englishman was entitled to be "as secure in his house as a prince in his castle," safe from unreasonable search. Citing *Bonham's Case* of 1610 as his own precedent, Otis claimed that common law could set aside laws against common right or reason. The writs themselves and the Navigation Acts, of which they served as instruments, were, in Otis's view, void. Hutchinson ignored the thrust of Otis's argument altogether, choosing instead to decide the case by determining what current British practice was. When after many months he confirmed the fact that English courts regularly issued such writs, he found in favor of the customs service. Otis may have lost his case, but he introduced a new issue into the political maelstrom of Massachusetts—the rights of Americans under British law. Relations with the mother country would never be the same thereafter.

In later years many Americans would look back to the days before 1763 with evident nostalgia. For it was in that first year after the close of the French and Indian War that George Grenville, England's new prime minister, undertook an unprecedented series of changes in the way the empire worked. Better enforcement of the Navigation Acts had been a matter of concern in Great Britain for some time. But Grenville was interested in revenue as well as regulation, especially since he realized that evasion of the Molasses Act alone cost the treasury an estimated £200,000 every year. Fear of French efforts to regain their North American losses ran far higher in London than in the colonies and seemingly demanded that a large military force be permanently garrisoned along the frontier. Such an army, numbering around ten thousand men, would cost over £200,000 a year to support. Other members of the ministry had an additional project for an American revenue: establishment of a civil list to free various colonial officials of their dependence on the legislatures. And better enforcement of the Navigation Acts would itself cost money. Never doubting Parliament's right in the matter, Grenville therefore proposed a number of statutes calculated to raise a revenue in the American colonies.

The first new law of significance to Massachusetts was the Sugar Act of 1764. Among its forty-odd provisions were numerous clauses that greatly improved the terms under which merchants of the Bay colony conducted their business. Abolition of the duty on whale fins imported into England encouraged the whalers of Nantucket and Dartmouth; a prohibition against the importation of foreign rum into America protected the distillers of Medford and Newburyport; rice could now be carried into the foreign colonies of the Caribbean, giving traders to the West Indies an additional cargo. Fur traders profited from the reduction of the duty on beaver skins entering the mother country. But the Sugar Act of 1764 was not remembered in Massachusetts for any of these provisions. Instead attention in a general sense focused on the preamble, which proclaimed that "it is just and necessary that a revenue be raised" in the colonies. The clause that drew the most notice in Massachusetts was that which lowered the duty on foreign molasses from sixpence to three. This fact combined with the language of the preamble and numerous other clauses tightening customshouse procedures made it abundantly clear that Great Britain intended to collect its threepence duty on each and every gallon of French molasses. The measure would cost the importers, distillers, and consumers of Massachusetts over £30,000 each year. New duties were levied on the importation of Madeira, coffee, and foreign indigo and sugar as well. An elaborate system of bonds and certificates added to the red tape of doing business, and the establishment of a vice-admiralty court at Halifax boded ill for shipowners. So too did the clause broadening the Royal Navy's role in enforcement. All in all, the Sugar Act of 1764 provided for major changes in the way the merchants of Massachusetts had customarily conducted their business during the mid-eighteenth century.

The Sugar Act came at a particularly bad time for the merchants of Massachusetts. Along with other provinces, the Bay Colony had been in the throes of a depression since the end of hostilities in 1762. Concern for the future prompted nearly one hundred and fifty merchants and traders of Massachusetts in 1763 to form the Society for Encouraging Trade and Commerce within the Province of Massachusetts Bay. Anticipating the renewal of the Molasses Act in some form, the society prepared a "State of the Trade" to explain the importance of the West Indies commerce to the commercial prosperity of the colony. Various delays prevented this document and an accompanying protest drafted by the General Court from reaching England before passage of the Sugar Act. It is not likely it would have affected the legislation in any event. When official notice of the new law reached Boston in May 1764, the merchants were dismayed to learn of its terms. Not only did it seem that their own prosperity was at stake, but so too was the future livelihood of hundreds of mariners, distillery workers, and others associated with the colony's commerce. Already about one out of four adult males in Boston had neither property of his own nor a place within a propertied family. Many of these men were unemployed; most others could find only occasional work. Any further threat to the precarious state of commerce would have serious consequences within the social and economic structure of the seaport towns. In fact, within less than a year the financial collapse of Boston's Nathaniel Wheelwright sent tremors like an earthquake through the business community and set off a wave of other failures. For a time, Governor Bernard feared that a general bankruptcy would occur.

In the face of such impending catastrophe the merchants of Boston couched their ensuing protests against the ministry's new policies primarily in economic terms. A curtailment of the prosperity of Massachusetts could only adversely affect the prosperity of the West Indies and the mother country itself. The ability of Massachusetts merchants to purchase English manufactures depended on a complex series of commercial transactions, for like most other New England colonies, Massachusetts produced virtually nothing that could be exported directly to Great Britain. The molasses trade, they wrote, "is the great spring to every branch of business among us, such as the fishing, the lumber trade, and shipbuilding, because molasses is distilled into rum, as well as our trade to Africa."

While the merchants protested the Sugar Act for its probable economic effects, others in Massachusetts took a different approach. The instructions to Boston's newly elected representatives in May 1764, drawn up by a committee which included Samuel Adams, expressed apprehension that the Sugar Act might presage further taxation by Great Britain. "For if our trade may be taxed, why not our lands? Why not the produce of our lands and everything we possess or make use of?" the committee asked rhetorically. "This we apprehend annihilates our Charter right to govern and tax ourselves. It strikes at our British privileges . . . ," for "if taxes are laid upon us in any shape without our having a legal representation where they are laid, are we not reduced from the character of free subjects to the miserable state of tributary slaves?" There, clearly expressed in May 1764, was the essence of the constitutional dispute which, left unresolved for the ensuing decade, would contribute so much to the ultimate destruction of the empire.

Few contemporaries read Boston's instructions of 1764, but the writings of another Bostonian, James Otis, gained wider circulation that year. His pamphlet *The Rights of the British Colonies Asserted and Proved* moved inexorably, if somewhat more circuitously, to the same conclusion: "The imposition of taxes . . . in the colonies [by Parliament] is absolutely irreconcilable with the rights of the colonists as British subjects and as men." Yet Otis admitted that the colonists had no recourse at law. "The power of Parliament is uncontrollable but by themselves, and we must obey," he acknowledged. "They only can repeal their own acts." To refuse obedience was treason. Otis was confident that the members of Parliament would in fact see their error and repeal those statutes that violated God's natural laws and the principles of the constitution. On the grounds of justice, if not expediency, then, Otis confidently awaited redress. "See here the grandeur of the British constitution! See here the wisdom of our ancestors."

In October 1764, the House of Representatives drafted a petition to the king protesting the new duties as a tax "which we humbly apprehend ought not to be laid without the representatives of the people affected by them." But the council under the prodding of its presiding officer, Lieutenant Governor Hutchinson, watered down the final version so drastically that even Governor Bernard approved it. All suggestion of right disappeared altogether; only the appeal to economic expediency remained. And as if to recognize the special authority of the House of Commons, the final petition was addressed to that body as well as to the king. Stronger language from the General Court of Massachusetts would have to await further provocation.

The occasion was not long in coming. From the first disclosure of the Sugar Act Americans had learned from one of its clauses that the Grenville ministry intended to levy a stamp tax on the colonists similar to an English revenue measure of long standing. Contemporary observers, as well as historians, have speculated as to why the first minister announced his intentions so far in advance. The agent for Massachusetts, Jasper Mauduit, seemed convinced that Grenville meant to give the colonies an opportunity to propose modifications of the plan or an acceptable alternative scheme of taxing themselves. When Boston's representatives to the assembly sought the advice of Governor Bernard in the matter, he was unable to offer them much encouragement in forestalling parliamentary action altogether. But in a revealing letter to Richard Jackson, one of Grenville's assistants, Bernard expressed the hope that the General Court be given "the liberty of enacting internal taxation themselves: which I have no doubt, but that they will readily do, when it shall be positively required of them." Bernard's reading of what the legislature of Massachusetts might be willing to do was perhaps no better than the next man's; but at least he seemed convinced that the Boston delegation, primarily consisting of future "patriots," would support a plan of self-taxation. But Massachusetts, like other colonies, was never given the opportunity to consider such an alternative.

Bernard's discussion and subsequent plea were to no avail, however, because it soon became obvious that Grenville's primary reason for delaying consideration of the Stamp Act was to allow time for the careful preparation of its various terms. Indeed, the stream of colonial petitions denying Parliament's claimed right of taxation seemed only to have hardened the minister's intention of offering an American Stamp Act to the next session. As finally enacted in March 1765, the law imposed on a large number of legal documents stamp duties ranging from threepence to ten shillings, levies of up to ten pounds on various licenses and franchises, and taxes on deeds which varied from one shilling six pence to five shillings. Perhaps the most provocative duties were those levied on printed matter such as pamphlets, broadsides, almanacs, and newspapers. Unlike the Sugar Act, the burden of which fell primarily on the merchants, the Stamp Act would affect inland as well as coastal communities, farmers along with mariners, landholders, and shipowners. The first crisis of empire was at hand.

In late June 1765, the inhabitants of Massachusetts read somewhat exaggerated accounts of staunch resolutions against the Stamp Act reportedly adopted by Virginia's House of Burgesses the previous month. These resolves contrasted sharply with the tame petition sent by Massachusetts the year before. Governor Bernard's bland assurances that the Bay Colony's respectful plea would gain a hearing in London rang with bitter hollowness now that Parliament had gone ahead without so much as considering the appeals from America. Oxenbridge Thacher growled on his deathbed that at least the Virginians were men, and the patriots of Boston cursed their own "frozen politicians" who had insisted on replacing Thacher's original petition with "a certain tame, pusillanimous, daub'd insipid thing, delicately touched up and called an Address." Throwing caution aside in early June, the Massachusetts House of Representatives wrote a circular letter to the other colonial legislatures proposing that they all send delegates to a congress to be held in New York the following autumn. Its avowed purpose was to consider the drafting of a united appeal for relief from the Stamp Act.

Among the twenty-seven delegates from nine colonies who met in

October were James Otis, Oliver Partridge, and Timothy Ruggles, the latter two included at the apparent insistence of Governor Bernard. Ruggles, a future loyalist, was chosen chairman of the congress instead of Otis, who himself had unaccountably repudiated, at least in public, his earlier opposition to British taxation. Even so, the delegates adopted with only a few changes a set of strong resolves drafted by Pennsylvania's John Dickinson. They asserted that it was "the undoubted right of Englishmen that no taxes be imposed on them but with their own consent." Because of their location Americans could not be represented in Parliament and therefore it was unconstitutional for the people of Great Britain "to grant His Majesty the property of the colonists." The more radical delegates also fought off an effort by the conservatives to assert in positive terms what authority they did recognize Parliament to have over the colonies. After two weeks of wrangling the majority finally adopted the general admission that the colonists simply owed "all due subordination" to the British Parliament. But Timothy Ruggles, along with only one other delegate, refused to sign the final resolution and thereby earned the censure of the General Court for his position.

A few days after the Stamp Act Congress finished its business in New York, the Massachusetts House of Representatives unanimously adopted its own resolves in opposition to the British measure. The document might well have served as the mold into which local and county resolutions would be poured for the next generation. The delegates asserted, first, their belief in certain common rights of mankind, founded in the law of God and nature and embodied in the British constitution, which no law of society could abrogate. On one of these natural rights, that "no man can justly take the property of another without his consent," was based the right of representation in the body levying taxes. These rights were guaranteed to Englishmen by the Magna Carta and conveyed to the inhabitants of Massachusetts through their royal charter. Because American representation in Parliament was impractical, only their general assemblies could legitimately levy taxes. The resolves closed with an acknowledgment of loyalty to the king and "the greatest veneration" for the Parliament.

Long before the Stamp Act Congress met at New York in October, violence had broken out in Massachusetts. Bostonians had been long used to civil disturbances, especially on Pope's Day and other celebrations each year. Except in the case of the Revolution of 1689, however, these outbreaks had little to do with politics. In most cases, they were primarily a way for a narrowly confined urban population to let off a little steam. Yet the potential significance of violence, particularly as a means of bringing about change, was not lost to Americans. Whig ideology of the late seventeenth and early eighteenth centuries stressed that the first sign of tyranny called for prompt measures in defense of liberty. By the 1760s the great English constitutional authority William Blackstone could confidently write that the people's right to remove the legislature, while still valid, was no longer a practical or a necessary option. Americans did not uniformly share this optimistic view of the English Parliament, however. The young Massachusetts lawyer Josiah Quincy, Jr., asked himself upon reading Blackstone's argument "whether a conclusion can be just in theory that will not bear adoption in practice." Quincy's fellow citizens soon put that question to the test.

Opponents of the Stamp Act had the problem of preventing enforcement of the law until such time as, they hoped, Parliament would repeal it in response to American protests. During the course of the summer a small group of Boston shopkeepers and artisans, calling themselves the Loyal Nine, met together to consider this problem. One of them was Benjamin Edes, co-printer of the *Boston Gazette,* in which had appeared many articles opposed to the new law. Except for John Avery, from an old Harvard family, the others were virtually unknown to the community at large. The group decided on the tactic of preventing the stamp distributor, by force if necessary, from performing the duties of his office. That person, they thought, was to be Andrew Oliver, currently secretary of the colony, a member of the governor's council, and a relative by marriage of Thomas Hutchinson. To persuade him to resign, the Loyal Nine apparently engaged the services of Ebenezer Mackintosh, leader of Boston's South End gang. On the morning of August 14, 1765, Mackintosh's men hanged Oliver in effigy on what subsequently became known as Liberty Tree. After a crowd had gathered, it set off for a new building Oliver had constructed on his wharf. On the assumption that he planned to make his stamp office here, members of the crowd demolished the structure. Next they headed for his fine mansion, there to demand his resignation as stamp distributor. When they discovered that Oliver had already fled the premises, the people attacked the house itself, ripping out the woodwork, smashing all the windows, and breaking up the fine furnishings. Hutchinson and the sheriff attempted to calm the crowd but were driven off. Not surprisingly, Oliver resigned from the office of stamp commissioner even though he had not yet been officially appointed to the position. With no official to distribute the stamped paper when it arrived, Boston seemed safe.

But Mackintosh and his crew, or the Loyal Nine, or both had apparently resented the "interference" of Thomas Hutchinson in the affair. Besides, the lieutenant governor's previous success in watering down the General Court's petition against the Sugar Act had made the province look weak and vacillating in comparison with other more resolute colonies like Rhode Island. On the night of August 26, Hutchinson paid a terrible price for his unpopularity as his own luxurious home in Garden Court Street became the target. As he described the consequences a few days later:

> Not contented with tearing off all the wainscot and hangings and splitting the doors to pieces they beat down the Partition walls . . . cut down the cupola . . . and began to take the slate and boards from the roof. . . . The garden fence was laid flat and all my trees &c broke down to the ground. . . . Besides my Plate and family Pictures household furniture of every kind my own my children and servants apparel they carried off about £900 sterling in money and emptied the house of everything whatsoever . . . not leaving a single book or paper in it and have scattered or destroyed all the manuscripts and other papers I had been collecting for 30 years together besides a great number of Publick papers in my custody. . . .*

Reaction to the Hutchinson affair almost universally condemned the excessive manner in which the Bostonians had dealt with the lieutenant governor, and for what it was worth the town met at Faneuil Hall the next day to express its "utter detestation" of the episode and to offer the town's officials aid in suppressing such disorders in the future. Although a few inhabitants were indicted for the riot, none was brought to trial, not even Mackintosh himself, who had been seized but released when supporters apparently threatened to destroy the customshouse.

---

* From Hutchinson's letter to Richard Jackson, 30 August 1765, in Edmund S. Morgan, ed., *Prologue to Revolution: Sources and Documents on the Stamp Act Crisis, 1764–1766* (Chapel Hill, 1959), 108–9.

In the estimation of Governor Bernard, inhabitants of the country towns seemed even more adamant in opposition to the Stamp Act than those in Boston and the other seaports. "They talk of revolting from Great Britain in the most familiar manner," he later reported. Bernard had confidently expected that economic necessity would compel compliance with the Stamp Act and predicted that if the courts and seaports were closed there would be "an insurrection of the poor against the rich." Perhaps even a famine would ensue before the end of winter. But Bernard did not understand that the people of Massachusetts did not intend to suspend all legal and commercial transactions until repeal of the Stamp Act. They intended to proceed with their daily affairs as though there were no Stamp Act at all. And when November 1 arrived, that is precisely what they did, as royal officials nervously passed the responsibility of enforcement from one to another.

Meanwhile, the merchants of Boston joined in still a different means of protest. Building upon the momentum of an earlier movement encouraging more economical buying habits during the lingering depression, merchants in most of the major ports agreed not to import British manufactures until the Stamp Act should be repealed. Here Boston followed the lead of New York and Philadelphia and was promptly followed by Salem, Marblehead, Plymouth, and Newburyport. The idea of an economic boycott became one of the most popular means of mercantile protest against British policies in the decade to follow. By exerting such economic pressure the Americans hoped to force English merchants into demanding a repeal of the Stamp Act. But the principle did not receive a fair test; before its effects could be felt the new ministry under the Marquis of Rockingham repealed the iniquitous legislation in February 1766. The good news reached America first by one of John Hancock's vessels. Soon afterward the colonists learned that the molasses duty was reduced from threepence to one penny per gallon but made applicable to English as well as French varieties. Since they imported relatively little molasses from the English islands, and the new law did lower the duty on French molasses, it was difficult for the merchants of Massachusetts to make immediate protest. Besides, for a time at least, the entire issue seemed trivial in comparison with repeal of the Stamp Act.

In their joyous response to repeal, Bostonians acquired several erroneous lessons from the Stamp Act crisis in general. In the first place, they gave too much credit for the victory to the merchants' boycott, which had little real effect on the matter. Furthermore, in welcoming the help of Isaac Barré, William Pitt, Rockingham, and their political allies, Americans overestimated the motives and strength of the so-called "friends to liberty" in Great Britain. Finally, they confidently assumed that repeal meant recognition of the American argument that Parliament had no right to tax the colonists. Such a conclusion could be reached only by ignoring or misinterpreting the 1766 Declaratory Act, which proclaimed Parliament's right to make laws binding the colonists "in all cases whatsoever." Yet hundreds of inhabitants of Massachusetts must have agreed with James Otis when he confidently asserted in Boston town meeting that the Declaratory Act had nothing to do with taxation. Adding to the strength of this viewpoint was the fact that the colonial agents in London played down the implications of the new law, probably to focus more attention on the very real accomplishment of repeal. Furthermore, inaccurate reports of William Pitt's speech in Parliament, in which he allegedly limited the House of Commons's jurisdiction by distinguishing between legislation and taxation, added to the false impressions. Yet a perceptive colonist like John Adams could still wonder "whether they will lay a tax in consequence of that resolution, or what kind of a law they will make." Adams did not have to wait long to find out.

Meanwhile, other unresolved matters continued to create friction between the mother country and her colonies. One was the recently passed Quartering Act, which required colonial legislatures to provide certain commodities for the support of British troops stationed within their boundaries. Its impact fell most heavily on New York, and when the assembly of that colony dragged its feet, the legislature was suspended until it agreed to make adequate provision for the troops stationed there. Massachusetts, among other colonies, also strove to avoid direct compliance, for, as Sam Adams queried, was the law "not taxing the colonys as effectually as the Stamp Act?" When a storm drove about seventy British troops into the harbor by accident at the end of 1766, however, even Adams could not turn his back on their needs, not wishing to be "so wanting in humanity, or in regard to our sovereign as to refuse to grant him the aid with our free consent." The implication of Adams's wording was clear: the legislature was careful to point out that it was acting in response to previous custom without mentioning the Quartering Act itself.

Another problem resulted from Parliament's insistence, at the time of the Stamp Act repeal, that all persons suffering damage during the various riots be indemnified for their losses. After long delay, in January 1767, the General Court of Massachusetts finally moved to comply with "his [Majesty's] desire to forgive and forget," as the bill put the issue in its preamble. The General Court offered Hutchinson £3,194 in compensation and lesser amounts to Andrew Oliver and other officials suffering property losses during the Boston riots. But the court proceeded to apply the king's principle of "forgive and forget" to the rioters as well by extending full pardon for "all burglaries, felonies, rescues, and breaches of the peace whatsoever" committed during the tumults, with similar amnesty for all who stood accused of abetting or advising others. Not wishing to deprive the victims of their compensation, Bernard let the measure become law. Later in the spring, however, the Privy Council disallowed the measure, but fortunately for Hutchinson he and the other victims had already been paid before word of the British action reached Massachusetts.

In the view of the merchants of Massachusetts, serious problems continued to disturb the world of commerce. They resented the myriad of cockets, bonds, and other documents required by the Sugar Act of 1764; they sought total repeal of the duty on molasses; and they renewed their objections to recent restrictions on the wine trade. A crackdown by a new commodore-governor in Newfoundland against whalers and codfishermen in those waters brought further protests. In January 1767, a committee of the merchants' Society for Encouraging Trade and Commerce finally sent a long petition concerning these and other grievances to Dennys DeBerdt, one of the Massachusetts agents in London. Although the waters had been badly muddied by an outspoken petition from New York, the Massachusetts document brought promise of modest reforms. But major grievances remained. The British navy enforced provisions of the Navigation Acts with a vengeance, in the opinion of the Americans. They believed that a statute dating from 1708 made impressment of colonists illegal, but the navy ignored the law. When several crew members deserted from the armed sloop *Gaspée* in late 1764 at Falmouth, Maine, the lieutenant in charge impressed four local sailors. But a mob promptly kidnapped the naval officer and forced him to release his captives, and he returned to Halifax with his vessel badly undermanned. After 1766, however, Massachusetts had less trouble from the British navy than did Rhode Island, for its merchants seemed more willing to comply with the revised molasses duty.

Still another grievance of the maritime community focused on the establishment of a new vice-admiralty court in Halifax, whence customs officers could bring cases for trial free from the popular pressures that had made convictions difficult to obtain in the court at Boston. Ever the lawyer, John Adams had labeled the new court "the most grievous innovation of all," for admiralty cases were tried before a single judge, without a jury, a procedure which Adams considered "directly repugnant to the Great Charter itself." Then in June 1767, Parliament authorized the establishment of an American Board of Customs Commissioners in order to tighten enforcement of the Navigation Acts in the colonies. The ministry chose Boston as the new board's headquarters. By a stroke of bad timing the commissioners landed on November 5, 1767—Pope's Day—but to everyone's surprise no riot greeted their arrival. The occasion was not entirely ignored, however. The traditional Pope's Day parade met the officials at the wharf and escorted them through the streets. Signs bearing the legend "Liberty, Property, and no Commissioners" conveyed adequately enough the mood of the crowd. And an effigy of the Devil bearing a remarkable resemblance to Charles Paxton, the most disliked of the new commissioners, was burned at the end of the festivities. Otis called upon his fellow townspeople to remain calm and avowed his confidence in the effectiveness of "humble and dutiful petitions and remonstrances."

Shortly after their arrival the commissioners sought to strengthen their hand in anticipation of trouble by asking Commodore Samuel Hood to station a warship in Massachusetts waters (where none was then based). They also urged Governor Bernard to ask for some troops from General Thomas Gage at New York. Although Bernard demurred, Hood sent his fifty-gun flagship *Romney*. Whether because of, or despite these precautions, tensions in Boston gradually mounted during the winter and spring of 1768. One Daniel Malcom infuriated the officials by managing to slip in a cargo of wine without detection. On the anniversary of the Stamp Act repeal two commissioners were hanged in effigy, and the mob threatened to tear down the house of one of them. The customs commissioners had quickly become symbols of all the petty irritation, anger, and helpless frustration the mariners of Massachusetts seemingly suffered under strict enforcement of the commercial regulations. Many contemporaries and some historians have noted numerous episodes of "racketeering" on the part of minor customs officials throughout the colonies. On top of these concerns came the heavyhandedness of the Royal Navy. For instance, upon his arrival at Boston, the captain of the *Romney* began to impress sailors off incoming vessels. The General Court lodged a strong protest, and Governor Bernard asserted his moderating influence, but more effective perhaps was the stone-wielding crowd that forced a press gang to give up the sailor it had collared in early June. Hutchinson shared the general indignation against peacetime impressment and pointed out that "the fear of it prevents coasters as well as other vessels coming in freely and it adds more fewel to the great stock among us before."

The explosion came in June 1768. Earlier that spring, John Hancock's sloop *Liberty* had arrived from Madeira with a cargo of wine, the captain entering only twenty-five pipes, well below the vessel's normal capacity. Hancock had boasted that he intended to defy the law, but the customs officials could find no witnesses or other evidence to suggest that he had in fact committed a violation. There the matter rested for several weeks, while Hancock ordered an outward cargo of whale oil and tar loaded aboard for London. But a commonly ignored legal clause required shipowners to apply for a permit before loading any vessel, and technically, Hancock had broken the law. Seeing their chance for revenge (and the opportunity to obtain both the vessel and its valuable cargo), the customs officers ordered the *Liberty* seized. When Collector Joseph Harrison, his son, and comptroller Benjamin Hallowell boarded the vessel on June 10, however, an ominous crowd began to gather along the waterfront. A boat crew managed to tow Hancock's ship out under the guns of the *Romney*, but the Harrisons and Hallowell were not so fortunate. The crowd pursued them through the streets of the waterfront, stoned their homes, roughed up young Harrison and burned a pleasure craft belonging to his father. Next day, these and other royal officials sought refuge aboard the *Romney* and soon thereafter took up residence at Castle William, in the middle of Boston harbor, a safer but hardly more effective place from which to conduct their business.

The customs establishment was not through with Hancock, however. One of the officers who had been on board the *Liberty* when it first arrived in early May, and who had denied seeing any suspicious activity, now changed his testimony to claim that he had heard sounds of the cargo being secretly unloaded. Now Hancock was charged with smuggling, a far more serious offense, and one that made him liable for triple damages—amounting altogether to over £50,000. John Adams agreed to represent Hancock, and after many months of delay, the case was dropped by the authorities. Hancock lost his sloop, after all, but gained a continental reputation as the latest victim of "customs racketeering."

*   *   *

Meanwhile quite a different issue broke upon the relations between Great Britain and its American colonies. In the spring of 1767 the Chancellor of the Exchequer, Charles Townshend, proposed to Parliament a new means of raising a revenue in America. In order to help defray the cost of defending the continental colonies and also to establish a civil list for various officials, the Parliament adopted the Townshend Act, imposing a series of duties upon the importation of goods into the colonies. Notable among the charges was a threepence per pound levy on tea, and taxes on various sorts of glass, paper, and painters' colors. Of these various levies the duty on tea bore heaviest, for by the late colonial period that commodity had become immensely popular in Massachusetts as elsewhere in America. Had the annual imports of about two hundred fifty thousand pounds continued to enter the colony, the merchants would have contributed to the British treasury over £3,000 each year on that commodity alone, enough to meet the governor's salary and those of several other officials as well.

Reaction to the new scheme of parliamentary taxation came slowly at first. A town meeting held at Boston in October 1767 voted to send around a paper binding those who signed it to give preference to American over British goods. The proposal did not appear to be aimed particularly at the Townshend Act but was rather part of a general effort to reduce the consumption of luxury goods during continuing hard times. Indeed, Governor Bernard reported that the once fiery James Otis had asserted that opposition to the Townshend duties would not have been prudent at that time, "when every other town . . . in America seemed to acquiesce in them." None of the other major towns of Massachusetts seemed to take notice of the new measures, but many of them did respond positively to Boston's nonconsumption agreement. Because homespun was cheaper than English cloth and tea was regarded as a luxury, the movement did have some effect on trade with Great Britain.

Meanwhile, however, John Dickinson's *Letters from a Farmer in Pennsylvania* began to appear in Boston's newspapers. The lawyer who had two years earlier drafted the resolves adopted by the Stamp Act Congress wasted little time in asserting that the Townshend duties were "as much taxes, upon us, as those imposed by the Stamp Act." He cautioned his readers not to succumb to the argument that these were "external" duties rather than taxes or that they were too small to cause alarm. "If they have the right to levy a tax of *one penny* upon us, they have the right to levy a million. . . ." By the beginning of 1768 the leaders of Massachusetts had come to hold the Townshend duties in similar light. In mid-January the House of Representatives began to address a series of letters to various British officials, including such former "friends" as Rockingham, Camden, and William Pitt, now the Earl of Chatham, and to the king himself, seeking repeal of the Townshend duties. Then in mid-February the House sent a circular letter drafted by Sam Adams addressed to the Speakers of the House of Representatives in each of the other colonies. Here the legislators of Massachusetts outlined the constitutional and economic reasons for protesting the Townshend Act and seeking its repeal. Although the authors did not specifically suggest that the other assemblies take similar action, they drew attention to the new taxation and hoped to assure that colonial responses, if any, "should harmonize with each other."

The Massachusetts Circular Letter generated little immediate response from other assemblies. But it did set off an explosion in Whitehall, where the newly appointed secretary for the colonies, the Earl of Hillsborough, feared that other provinces would unite to endorse the Bay colony's denial of Parliament's right to tax Americans. He, therefore, sent off a circular letter of his own, with orders to each colonial governor to take whatever measures were necessary to prevent support for Massachusetts in his own assembly. He also instructed Bernard to demand that the General Court rescind its February action on pain of dissolution. Faced with this sort of challenge, one assembly after another drew up encouraging responses to the Massachusetts letter. The Massachusetts House itself refused to recant by the overwhelming margin of 92 to 17. Hillsborough's tactics had backfired; the unity he had sought to avoid had in fact been encouraged by his highhanded interference, and the colonists had a new group of heroes, "the Glorious 92," toasted at banquets, hailed in song, and honored along with John Wilkes's "45" by Paul Revere's masterpiece, the liberty bowl. Every

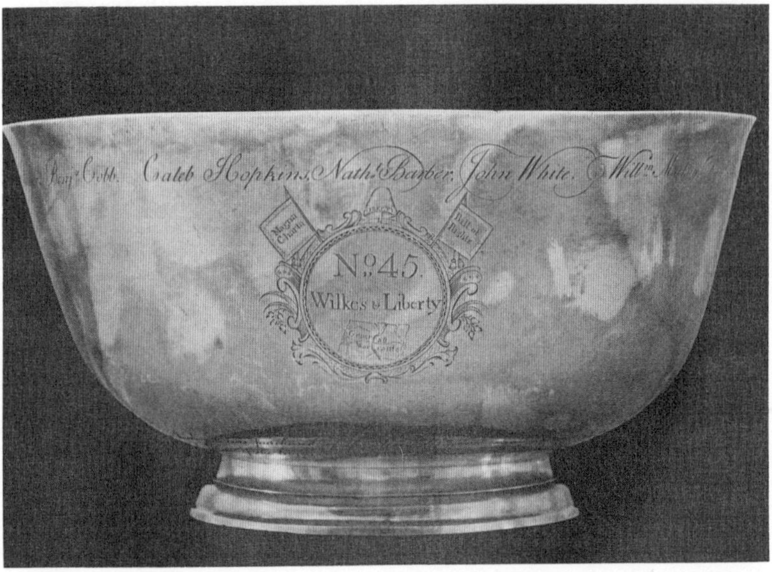

Liberty Bowl. Courtesy of the Museum of Fine Arts, Boston.

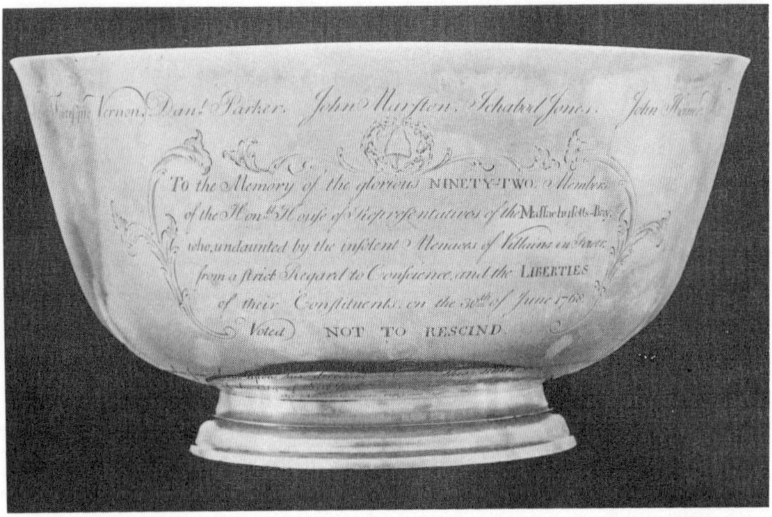

popular movement needs its mystical element and special symbols: the Glorious 92 became a part of the revolutionary lexicon, not only in Massachusetts but in other colonies as well. Thus, Philadelphia's patriotic poet Rusticus could urge his readers:

> With Resolution still your Plan pursue,
> Support the glorious Number Ninety-Two . . .

Hillsborough himself gained an unwanted immortality when patriots called the excrement they daubed on their opponents' houses and shops "Hillsborough paint."

Circular letters and poetry and night soil would not force repeal of the Townshend duties, but perhaps another round of economic boycott would. Remembering the apparent success of the threatened boycott of 1766, about one hundred merchants of Boston met at the British Coffee House to draw up an agreement not to import any but a few English goods (only those items needed in the fisheries) for one year or until repeal of the Townshend duties. Merchants in Salem, Marblehead, and Newburyport supported the scheme, the traders in the last town endorsing the plan despite the fact that the town itself had only recently rejected a similar scheme. Newburyport's merchants felt strongly about the matter of parliamentary taxation, if the correspondence of Jonathan Jackson is representative of the group. A boycott on British goods might well force repeal of the duties in Jackson's view: "No one thing will give [the common people of Great Britain] so convincing a proof of what importance America is to them, as ceasing to import their manufactures will." But the movement collapsed even before it could begin, because the merchants of Philadelphia refused to join. In August 1768 the merchants of Boston tried again, this time with an agreement not to import English goods that would take effect on the first of January following. The Philadelphians finally concurred in April 1769, long after most of the merchants of New England and New York had curtailed their trade with the mother country.

It was one matter to make an agreement and another altogether to enforce it. To be effective, of course, the boycott required the adherence of all major importers within the area; to allow exceptions put the cooperating merchants at a competitive disadvantage. Despite vigorous campaigns in newspapers, town meetings, and church gatherings, consumers still sought the finer English cloth goods, Sheffield hardware, and East India Company tea. Imports of the last commodity were particularly difficult to block at Boston, for smuggled Dutch tea was scarce there. Not only did public demand for tea continue, but several mercantile houses that specialized in the tea trade were among those refusing to sign the nonimportation agreements. One such partnership was Thomas & Elisha Hutchinson and their friends and colleagues, Richard Clarke & Son. Still another was John Mein, a merchant who was also publisher of the conservative *Boston Chronicle*. When patriots proscribed him as an enemy to his country for refusing to comply with the boycott, he released customshouse figures citing chapter and verse on the full extent of noncompliance at Boston. The fact that most of the offenders were, like Mein himself, ideologically opposed to nonimportation did not make the record look any better to those who expected Boston's boycott to be watertight. A Worcester shopkeeper protested that "I will not sacrifice my interest to serve the publick any longer" when he learned of the violations at Boston. During the single year 1769 the Hutchinson brothers imported over fifty thousand pounds of dutied tea until they finally bowed to public pressure in early 1770, only a few months before the boycott itself collapsed. What annoyed the patriots of Massachusetts even more than the obstinance of a few merchants was the obvious fact that the inhabitants of the colony continued to purchase dutied tea when available.

It was not enough to discourage consumption by anti-tea campaigns or to intimidate merchants by threats of violence. To be effective, militant Bostonians learned, any boycott would have to stop the dutied goods at the water's edge. The lesson would be remembered three years later.

In the autumn of 1769 the more zealous patriots among the merchants of Boston overreached themselves. Noting how illogical it was to accept parliamentary duties on molasses, sugar, and wine, they proposed to the merchants of New York and Philadelphia that the nonimportation movement should continue until those levies were repealed as well as the Townshend duties. Their colleagues elsewhere refused to go along with the suggestion, however, and it is doubtful that other merchants in the Bay colony would have accepted the plan, for too much depended upon the continuing importation of molasses, and besides these duties had long been accepted in the public mind as a legitimate means of regulating trade, even though they had since become revenue measures. Boston's merchants backed off and concentrated on the serious problem of enforcing their original agreement.

In early March 1770, the new chief minister, Lord North, brought about the repeal of all Townshend duties save that on tea. North and his faction had considered the levies "inexpedient" to begin with, for most of the articles taxed were British manufactures, whose sale in the colonies was adversely affected by the added tax burden quite apart from the boycott of these and other goods. But North insisted on retaining the duty on tea, "to keep up the right," as he put it, despite the strong urgings from the colonial agents and members of the loyal opposition. Partial repeal of the Townshend duties put the American patriots in a quandary. They had originally agreed to maintain their boycott until all of the Townshend duties were repealed, but realists among them began to argue that four-fifths of a loaf was better than none. New Yorkers weakened first, in mid-summer 1770, followed shortly thereafter by the Philadelphians. The merchants of Massachusetts made an effort to hold out a few weeks longer, but by mid-October they too bowed to the inevitable, just in time to get orders out for spring goods. The great nonimportation movement had at last come to an end.

It is almost impossible to determine by commercial statistics just how effective the boycott in Massachusetts was during the two-year period of its enforcement. New England as a whole reduced importations from the mother country from an average of over £425,000 for the five-year period 1764–68 to £208,000 in 1769 and a two-year average of £300,000 for 1769–70. In the final analysis the nonimportation movement probably had more effect on the American colonists than on the ministry and Parliament of Great Britain. For despite the petty jealousies and suspicions, the movement did represent a greater degree of sustained cooperation among the inhabitants of the several colonies than had previously been achieved. The 1769–70 movement provided a foundation on which patriots would build a far more effective boycott four years later.

*   *   *

The historical record tells us little of the activities of Ebenezer Mackintosh in the years after the Stamp Act crisis. Was he among the crowd that chased Joseph Harrison and his companions through the streets during the *Liberty* affair in June 1768? How many doors of shopkeepers who refused to sign the nonimportation agreement did he smear with "Hillsborough paint"? Was he among the group of men who menaced the loyalist printer John Mein and his partner in King Street one autumn night in 1769? Perhaps he helped to tar and feather one George Gailer, seized on the night of the Mein incident for allegedly having informed the customs office of an attempt to smuggle wine. Whether Ebenezer Mackintosh himself took part in such activities is of little importance. What is significant is the fact that, from the time of the Stamp Act onward, hundreds of Bostonians asserted themselves not by orderly votes in town meeting but by taking to the streets of their own town and forcing their will upon men of both high station and low, from Hutchinson and Oliver to Mein and Gailer. Such behavior cannot be cast aside as mere "hooliganism" by the rabble, nor can it be explained away as the activity of simple citizens led astray by the machinations of "propagandists." The truth is that hundreds of Bostonians felt oppressed by an economic and social establishment which seemingly prevented them from earning a full day's wages and recognition as decent human beings. British officials and the Americans who supported them seemed natural enemies; when the crisis with the mother country brought charges of "English tyranny," the men of Boston struck out at their oppressors. In so doing they did not always observe fine distinctions, but it is nonetheless remarkable that with few exceptions only the persons and property of British sympathizers were harmed.

13

CONFRONTATION

In the midst of the Townshend Act crisis, in August 1769, Governor Francis Bernard was recalled to England. Lieutenant Governor Thomas Hutchinson thereupon assumed the responsibilities of chief executive officer until promoted to the position of governor in his own right in November 1770. But the honor came too late, for by the time he took over, circumstances had intervened to make the office almost unbearable. A man of lesser talent or will would have abandoned the post long before Hutchinson was in fact forced to retire, in May 1774. Not only was the continuing quarrel with Great Britain troublesome in itself, but the patriots of the colony were determined to shackle Hutchinson's political power in every way possible. The man most responsible for developing a grassroots counterweight to the power of the royal governor was Samuel Adams.

Adams was a native of Boston, born in 1722 as one of twelve children of a prosperous and prominent brewer. Like the father of Thomas Hutchinson, the elder Adams also had an active if less significant political career, one in which he served intermittently as selectman and member of the General Court. Like Thomas as well, young Samuel was prepared for Harvard, where he graduated in 1740, ranked fifth socially in his class (Hutchinson had ranked third thirteen years before). And like Hutchinson, Adams tried his hand at mercantile pursuits, but there the similarities ended, for Adams was a dismal failure. He failed also in efforts to succeed in business for himself and frittered away an advance of £1,000 from his father. After the elder Adams's death in 1748 the son soon lost the rest of his inheritance as well.

Meanwhile, Sam Adams had discovered a new avocation—politics. In

1748 he and a group of friends established a club and launched a short-lived newspaper, the *Independent Advertiser,* in opposition to Governor William Shirley. To Adams, the governor evidently symbolized an ostentatious materialism which had seemingly arisen in Massachusetts at the expense of an older Puritan emphasis on simplicity. Adams and his friends also attacked many of the wealthier merchants and minor governmental officials who formed the nucleus of the court party of the 1750s. Some of these men, like Thomas Hutchinson, had been staunch opponents of the land bank scheme of 1741, of which Sam's own father had been a prominent backer. It was the belief of Adams and the country party that only the legislature stood as bulwark against the power of the governor and the awesome authority he represented. In their view the General Court of Massachusetts possessed powers parallel to those enjoyed by the Parliament itself, powers requiring constant protection against encroachment by the governor, whether William Shirley, Francis Bernard, or (and especially) Thomas Hutchinson. On more than one occasion Samuel Adams reduced the controversy between Great Britain and the American colonies to a personal confrontation between Thomas Hutchinson and himself. The ultimate result was the downfall of Hutchinson and the hastening of royal government's demise in Massachusetts.

*   *   *

The disturbances that had culminated in the *Liberty* riot of June 10, 1768, prompted Governor Bernard to seek military assistance from General Thomas Gage at New York. In response Gage ordered two regiments of troops down from Halifax. At about the same time the Earl of Hillsborough authorized the transfer of two regiments from Ireland. These forces, the first to be stationed in colonial America for the purpose of keeping civil peace, converged on Boston in early autumn 1768. The patriots of Massachusetts took alarm. To make matters worse, Bernard had dissolved the General Court in June for its refusal to rescind the assembly's circular letter of the previous February, as Hillsborough had ordered. Deprived of their legislature at this critical time, the patriots cast about for alternative courses of action. At a special town meeting in Boston in mid-September, James Otis, by now given to frequent periods of irrationality, reportedly urged the inhabitants to resist the landing of the troops by force of arms. Instead of distributing the town's four

Samuel Adams (1722–1803), c. 1772. Painting by John Singleton Copley. Courtesy of the Museum of Fine Arts, Boston.

British Troops Landing at Boston, 1768. Engraved by Paul Revere after Christian Remick. Courtesy of the American Antiquarian Society.

hundred muskets, however, the town meeting issued a call for a "convention of towns" to meet in lieu of the canceled fall session of the legislature.

Response to Boston's call from the towns compared favorably with the number that regularly sent representatives to the General Court: about one hundred communities participated in the Convention of 1768 when it met at Boston later that month. Although the gathering was technically not a meeting of the assembly and made no attempt to behave as a legislature, Governor Bernard was nevertheless irritated by this blatant challenge to the executive's prerogative to call the General Court into session. Nothing substantive came of the convention, but the very fact that so many towns participated gave testimony to their belief in the right to regular legislative sessions. Furthermore, it demonstrated a faith in orderly if "extralegal" procedures in time of crisis.

On the first day of October 1768, the troops from Halifax began to disembark at Boston's Long Wharf. For the moment all thought of resistance was put aside as the inhabitants turned out en masse to witness the spectacle. Up King Street the soldiers marched, banners and flags leading the way with the tall grenadiers of each regiment close behind. The bright autumn sun highlighted gold and silver trim on the soldiers' uniforms and caught their gleaming accoutrements and polished brass. Rank after rank they came, marching to the beating drums and whistling fifes, past the customshouse, into Queen Street and on to the Common, where they all drew up in parade by late afternoon. Meanwhile, out in the harbor lay His Majesty's warships, ready to swing their broadsides into position to cover the waterfront if necessary.

Bostonians knew enough not to oppose such an overwhelming display by force. They turned instead to more subtle tactics. Governor Bernard had expected to quarter the troops in what was called the Manufactory House, but the tenants absolutely refused his demand to vacate the building. Lieutenant Colonel William Dalrymple sought the assistance of the selectmen of the town but to no avail. As long as the season remained mild at least one regiment could camp out on the Common. Others found temporary quarters in Faneuil Hall and the townhouse, but such arrangements made it difficult for the officers to retain rigid discipline. Some of the troops began to desert, and petty squabbles broke out between soldiers and civilians. When the regiments arrived from Ireland in November, the problem became more desperate. Finally, General

Gage, who had come up from New York to solve the crisis, found enough warehouses and other buildings to get all his men under cover just before the first bad winter storm. One regiment was forced to remain at Castle William, in the middle of the harbor, where its effectiveness as a peace-keeping force was considerably reduced.

The winter of 1768–69 passed in remarkable quietude considering both the circumstances and Boston's past record for tumult. The inhabitants resented being challenged by military patrols on the streets of their own community, and many found the public executions and whippings administered to soldiers on the Common distasteful in the extreme. Sam Adams and other patriots maintained a running account of all incidents between the citizens and soldiery, which was published in New York and elsewhere as a "Journal of the Times." The entry for December 12, 1768, is not unrepresentative:

> A married lady of this town was the other evening, when passing from one house to another, taken hold of by a soldier; who otherways behaved to her with great rudeness; a woman near Long Lane was stopped by several soldiers, one of whom cried out seize her and carry her off; she was much surprised, but luckily got shelter in a house near by; Another woman was pursued by a soldier into a house near the north end, who dared to enter the same, and behave with great insolence. . . .*

Hillsborough was nevertheless pleased by the apparently mollifying effect of his decision to station troops in Boston, and in June 1769 he authorized General Gage to remove some or all of the regiments there "if you shall judge it expedient." It was decided to withdraw two units that summer, and Gage wrote that "I hear of no riots or commotions in any of the colonies . . . and I know of no reasons at present that should induce me to detain the two [remaining regiments] any longer in this country." But Gage needed time to arrange transportation and find alternative quarters. Besides, Bernard was about to leave for England and wished to avoid responsibility for approving a complete withdrawal; nor was Hutchinson eager to rush into that decision after Bernard had departed.

---

* *New York Journal,* 29 December 1768, in Oliver M. Dickerson, comp., *Boston under Military Rule . . . as Revealed in a Journal of the Times* (Boston, 1936), 34.

Two regiments therefore remained at Boston, not as the result of a positive decision to keep them there but by the failure to carry out a decision to remove them.

From the summer of 1769 on, incidents between troops and civilians increased in both frequency and intensity. Soldiers were assaulted with stones, brickbats, and "Hillsborough paint" while on their posts. The law restrained them from retaliating, for the only weapons they possessed were classified as "deadly," and they sought revenge instead during off-duty hours. When brought into court soldiers frequently found themselves before the patriot judge Richard Dana who almost invariably sided with the Bostonians lodging the complaints. Tensions were further increased in September by a coffee-house brawl between James Otis and one of the customs commissioners. Another episode that winter caused the accidental death of a young boy, Christopher Seider, whose public funeral became a patriotic rally against the continuing presence of soldiers in Boston. And in early March 1770, a clash between ropewalk workers and a group of soldiers presaged an explosive showdown. It came on the 5th of March.

In the thin pale moonlight of early evening one could see bands of inhabitants clustered about various street corners, armed with clubs. Small groups of soldiers prowled the streets as well. In front of the customshouse in King Street a young apprentice got into an argument with the sentry on duty, Hugh White. Finally, in exasperation, White struck the youth with the butt of his Brown Bess musket. Soon after a church bell began ringing. "Fire . . . fire" rent the chilly air, the recognized rallying cry of the street crowd. A gang of youths closed in on White, yelling, "Lobster son of a bitch! Damned rascally scoundrel lobster son of a bitch!" White backed off until he could retreat no farther, and the boys began throwing snowballs and chunks of ice, chanting, "kill him, kill him," and daring White to fire his musket into the gathering crowd. The sentry yelled for the main guard to turn out. Someone else ran along the street calling upon the "town born" themselves to turn out.

Summoned by these and other cries, the clanging of church bells, and sound of tumult, a large crowd began to gather in front of the customshouse. The captain of the watch, Thomas Preston, ordered out a squad of six grenadiers and a corporal to rescue White and followed them through the press of people. There they formed a line around the sentry's post, loaded their muskets, and tried to stand their ground against the three or four hundred people crowding in. Preston took every possible precaution to prevent his men from firing, but suddenly a club hurling through the air struck one of the grenadiers and knocked him down. Upon recovering, he fired his musket, apparently into the air, but other shots followed. Before Preston could restore order, five men lay dead or dying on the snow-covered street. There was Samuel Gray, a veteran of the ropewalk battle some weeks before, killed by a ball from the musket of Mathew Kilroy, who had also fought at the ropewalk. Two bullets hit Michael Johnson, the towering black who was also known as Crispus Attucks. A young apprentice named Samuel Maverick, related by marriage to Ebenezer Mackintosh, was killed by a ricocheting bullet as he fled the scene.

Only the quick and courageous action of the authorities prevented further bloodshed. Despite great personal danger, Thomas Hutchinson worked his way through the streets to the townhouse. From the balcony overlooking King Street he urged the crowd to go home, giving his assurances that "the law shall have its course; I will live and die by the law." Hutchinson then suggested to one of the army colonels that the inhabitants would disperse if he ordered his soldiers back into their barracks, and the soldiers and civilians began to drift away. By his quick action Hutchinson had in all likelihood prevented a bloodbath that night. The next day, under intense pressure from the selectmen, the council, and a special committee organized by Sam Adams, the governor officially requested the withdrawal of all British troops to Castle William. Colonel Dalrymple, eager to prevent further trouble, agreed.

As preparations to try Captain Preston and the grenadiers got under way, the patriots made certain that their view of the episode gained wide circulation. Paul Revere contributed a highly speculative print of the scene. Under the direction of James Bowdoin, a member of the governor's Council, nearly one hundred depositions and other "eyewitness" accounts were compiled into *A Short Narrative of the Horrid Massacre in Boston*. Although the document made considerable impact throughout the colonies, the loyalists at least scored a newsbeat in England by publishing their own account before copies of the patriots' pamphlet arrived there. The trial of Preston finally got under way in September 1770, after many months of delay and procrastination on both sides. But by the time Gilbert Deblois and Philip Dumaresq found their way onto the jury, Preston's acquittal was virtually assured, for both men were avowed

Boston Massacre, 1770. Engraved by Paul Revere after Henry Pelham. Courtesy of the Essex Institute, Salem, Mass.

loyalists unlikely to join in the unanimous vote necessary for conviction. John Adams and his fellow defense attorney, Josiah Quincy, had only to avoid any major blunders, and to no one's surprise the British officer was duly acquitted in late October. A separate trial of the soldiers involved found two men guilty of manslaughter only; the rest were freed. Under the circumstances prevailing in Boston in 1770 it is doubtful that the British soldiers could have received a fair trial in any case. But the patriots had no need for a courtroom triumph. In driving the regulars from the town they had won a far more significant victory, for once again the streets of Boston belonged to the people.

The Boston Massacre also gave the patriots a distinct advantage in the struggle for men's minds. Americans had always been suspicious of standing armies, and in the lexicon of Whig politics the use of military force against civilians had long ranked high as an indication of governmental tyranny. Succeeding anniversaries of the Massacre were marked with ringing reminders from public orators and writers of the horrors of standing armies. In such a climate, Hutchinson had no choice but to see that the troops remained in Castle William. Indeed, during the three years and more after the troops' withdrawal, a degree of calm unknown since passage of the Stamp Act settled over Boston and the other seaports of Massachusetts. "There seems now to be a pause in politics," wrote Samuel Cooper to his friend Benjamin Franklin in January 1771. Superficially at least, Cooper was right. With the end of the nonimportation movement in November 1770, trade between England and America resumed on a greater scale than ever before. In the first year alone, over £1.5 million worth of British goods poured into New England, mostly through the ports of Massachusetts. In the three-year period, 1771–73, over five hundred thousand pounds of dutied tea entered Boston despite a nominal continuation of the boycott against that article. In the single year 1772, collections under the Sugar Act and tea duty at Boston and Salem amounted to nearly £16,000. Massachusetts seemed to have settled back into a comfortable and profitable relationship with the mother country.

But some among the inhabitants of Massachusetts remained suspicious of the British ministry nevertheless. In the summer of 1772, they learned that the salaries of the governor and other executive officials of the colony were to be paid out of revenues collected by the customs service. Worse still was word that the Crown intended to support in similar fashion the justices of the Superior Court. "Is it not enough to have a governor, an avowed advocate of ministerial measures . . . totally independent of the people over whom he is commissioned to govern?" asked Sam Adams in October. "Is life, property and every thing dear and sacred to be now submitted to the decision of *pensioned Judges,* holding their places during the pleasure of such a governor . . . ? Let not the iron hand of tyranny ravish our laws and seize the badge of freedom. . . . Let every town assemble. Let associations and combinations be everywhere set up to consult and recover our just rights," Adams concluded.

Although he could do little at first about other towns, Adams did succeed in drawing the attention of Boston to what he considered a new threat to American freedom. In November 1772, a town meeting adopted his suggestion that a committee of correspondence be appointed "to state the rights of the colonists and of this province in particular" and to communicate these views to the other towns and the world at large. On November 20, Boston endorsed two statements, largely drafted by Adams himself, one entitled "The State of the Rights of the Colonists" and the other an "Enumeration of the Violations of our Rights." The first document outlined now-familiar theoretical rights claimed by patriots as men, Christians, and British subjects. It was the second statement, however, that reopened the quarrel with the mother country.

"The Boston Pamphlet," as it was soon called, was sent to each of the colony's 260 towns and districts. Here Adams called attention to the appointment of numerous Crown officials "invested with powers altogether unconstitutional" and supported by fleets and armies in their collection of revenues without the consent of the people. Worse still, these monies were being used for "the most destructive purposes," rendering governor, judges, and attorney general totally independent of the people's representatives and thus destroying the delicate equilibrium "without which we cannot continue a free state."

In pointing out how British policy had diminished the power of the legislature, Adams had struck a sensitive cord among the towns which viewed that body as their principal defense against real or imagined ministerial tyranny. For the first time, people on the grassroots level throughout the colony were asked to take a stand on the issues between mother country and the colonies. A surprisingly large number of communities—over half by the summer of 1773—would respond in some positive fashion to the Boston Pamphlet. Many of these towns had never publicly expressed their views on the crisis with Great Britain. Pownallborough was perhaps making up for lost time when it avowed that "our Forefathers soon as they landed here considered themselves as beyond the jurisdiction of the supream authority of the relm of England." Most towns contented themselves with the desire to keep in touch with Boston on developing affairs, in many cases by establishing their own committees of correspondence. During the course of the winter and spring of 1773, the patriots of these communities helped to build the foundations for future unity.

Another significant consequence of Adams's Boston Pamphlet was the effect both the document itself and its surprising popularity had on Thomas Hutchinson. Worried that the infection spread by the pamphlet would reach epidemic proportions if not immediately countered, he called the General Court into special session in early January 1773. The governor then proceeded to lecture the assembled delegates on his interpretation of the British constitution in general and the place of the colonies under it in particular. Hutchinson's rash action set off a series of heated exchanges between the governor and each house of the legislature which ran unchecked for two months until Hutchinson adjourned the session in early March. Both sides attempted to enlist the aid of outsiders—Daniel Dulany and John Dickinson by the assembly; James Bowdoin and others by the governor. As collected and published first in the *Massachusetts Gazette* and then in pamphlet form, the debate reached a wide audience throughout the colonies. Hutchinson persuaded himself that his argument would win support for the British cause, but John Adams was far closer to the truth when he confided in his journal that Hutchinson's "ruin and destruction must spring out of it, either from the ministry and Parliament on one hand, or from his countrymen on the other."

Hutchinson's principal argument was familiar. There could be only one supreme authority within a government and in the British empire that authority resided in Parliament. He attempted to place the opposition into the seemingly untenable position of either accepting the supremacy of Parliament or of claiming total independence, "for I know of no line that can be drawn [between these alternatives], as it is impossible there should be two independent legislatures in one and the same state." He then challenged the General Court to find "any other constitutional dependence than what I have mentioned." Neither house hesitated to take up the gauntlet. The council argued that no man-made institution such as the Parliament enjoyed unlimited authority but refused to offer a more advanced alternative.

The House of Representatives showed no such reluctance. Sam Adams, John Hancock, and Joseph Hawley of Northampton drafted a vigorous response to the governor's challenge. They wisely rejected Hutchinson's formulation of the problem by refusing to draw a line between insubordination and independence. Nor would they consider doing so without the consent of the other Assemblies "in Congress," they retorted. But if, as the governor suggested, no such line existed, then the authors concluded Massachusetts was either in a state of vassalage to Parliament or it was in fact totally independent of that body. Surely independence was less dreadful than total submission to an "absolute, uncontrolled power," they logically concluded. The patriots closed with the promise that as long as the people of Massachusetts could enjoy all the liberties granted in their charter, "there would be no danger of an independence on the Crown." Here was new ground in the debate. Parliament was left without so much as the general superintending power over the empire which most patriots had conceded up to that time. Forced, as it were, by Hutchinson's either-or argument, the men of Massachusetts chose the "or," and made their choice known throughout the colonies.

The enormity of Hutchinson's blunder lay not so much in giving the patriots of Massachusetts the chance to express their extreme position; they could have done that on their own. Rather it lay in the devastating effect his own "either-or" formulation of the controversy had on moderates in both America and England. If Hutchinson, the leading colonial spokesman for the mother country, saw no middle ground between total submission to, or total independence from, Parliament, where could those thousands of colonists now stand who distrusted the ministry but who trembled at the thought of an empire consisting of so many independent states bound together only by allegiance to a common sovereign? John Adams was right: Hutchinson "would not be thanked for this." The new secretary of state for the colonies, Lord Dartmouth, swallowed his official pride and attempted by private letter to persuade the Massachusetts Assembly to rescind or modify its statement, but to no avail. At the same time, he dispatched a stunning rebuke to the governor and summarily ordered him to avoid such questions in future, "the

agitating of which has already produced such disagreeable consequences."

The patriots of Massachusetts now had Hutchinson on the defensive,
and a stroke of good fortune (for them) would soon put an end forever to
his effectiveness as governor. Shortly after his return to England in 1769,
former governor Francis Bernard had launched a vindictive campaign to
tighten the reins of imperial government in Massachusetts by alterations
in the charter. To bolster his case before the ministry, Bernard had assembled various documents, including a number of letters written by
Thomas Hutchinson, Andrew Oliver, and Charles Paxton to Thomas
Whately, a British official in the Grenville ministry. By a curious combination of circumstances, these letters, which argued in favor of Bernard's
general goal, fell into the hands of Benjamin Franklin. The wily agent
for Masssachusetts saw in them confirmation that the real enemy of
American liberties was not the ministry but groups in America like
Hutchinson's clique of self-serving officials. To alert the patriots of Massachusetts, Franklin sent the letters to Thomas Cushing, Speaker of the
House of Representatives, with strict instructions that they not be published but only circulated privately among his friends and associates. The
letters arrived in March 1773. But exaggerated rumors of their contents
soon spread, making continued confidentiality difficult to maintain. Finally, in June 1773, circumstances forced Cushing to authorize their
publication, first in the newspapers and then in a pamphlet which went
through ten editions.

In one of the letters, Hutchinson had asserted that in his opinion
"government had been too long in the hands of the people in Massachusetts." In another he urged that Parliament punish its opponents in the
colony. The governor's most damaging statement was that "there must
be an abridgment of what are called English liberties" in the colonies for
it was impossible for colonies "3,000 miles distant from the parent state
[to] enjoy all the liberty of the parent state." But it was not so much *what*
Hutchinson had written that caused such a sensation; his views were after
all a matter of public record. It was the fact that he had urged these views
upon members of the British ministry through a secret correspondence
that was so disturbing. Patriots had long suspected the existence of a
conspiracy to deprive Americans of their freedom; now the evidence of
such a plot was seemingly at hand.

In mid-June, the House of Representatives adopted a series of resolu-

tions condemning the governor and petitioning the king to remove both
Hutchinson and Lieutenant Governor Oliver from their offices:

> There has long been a combination of evil men in this province,
> who have contemplated measures and formed plans to raise their
> own fortunes and advance themselves to posts of power, honor,
> and profit. . . . The said Thomas Hutchinson and Andrew
> Oliver have been some of the chief instruments in the introduc-
> tion of a fleet and army into this province, to establish and per-
> petuate their plans; whereby they have not only been greatly
> instrumental in disturbing the peace and harmony of the gov-
> ernment and causing unnatural and hateful discords and
> animosities between the several parts of His Majesty's Domin-
> ions, but are justly chargeable with all that corruption of morals
> in this province, and all that confusion, misery, and bloodshed
> which have been the natural effect of the posting of troops in a
> populous town. . . .*

The millstone of the Boston Massacre hung heavy upon the neck of
Thomas Hutchinson, the man whose quick and courageous action had in
all likelihood prevented a holocaust that night. "The people are highly
incensed against the two impeached gentlemen," reported Samuel
Adams a few days later. "Even some of their few friends are ashamed to
countenance them."

*   *   *

Even before the episode of the letters Hutchinson had wearied of his
duties as governor of Massachusetts Bay Colony. In the spring of 1773, he
planned to seek a leave of absence to visit England in search of a less
onerous appointment, one that might provide a comfortable income of
£600 with plenty of time for travel and relaxation. Sam Adams would
probably have welcomed such a solution, but the two antagonists seemed
almost destined for yet another confrontation, this time of deed as well as
word. Its outcome would drive Hutchinson from office and point Mas-

---

* Harry A. Cushing, ed., *The Writings of Samuel Adams* (New York, 1907), III:
45–48.

sachusetts toward the road to independence. The crisis began innocently enough. Severe financial difficulties coupled with a large surplus of tea prompted the East India Company in the spring of 1773 to seek permission to export some of its tea directly to America. In passing the necessary legislation Parliament followed Lord North's advice in refusing to rescind the threepence Townshend duty, despite a prediction from the opposition leader that "if he don't take off the duty, they won't take the tea." By September the shipments were ready, and vessels bearing six hundred thousand pounds of duties tea headed out across the Atlantic toward Charleston, Philadelphia, New York, and Boston. There the cargoes were to be consigned to selected merchants who would sell the tea in wholesale lots at public auction, assuring a low price for consumers, a commission for themselves, and a minimum of competition from smuggled Dutch tea.

Word of the plan reached New York and Philadelphia first. Patriots there warned that if the East India Company succeeded in establishing a monopoly of the tea trade, it might soon control the importation of all British goods into the colonies. Furthermore, submission to the tea duty might once again invite wholesale taxation by a revenue-hungry ministry. Because merchants in both ports had ready access to ample supplies of smuggled Dutch tea they had imported almost no duties English tea since passage of the Townshend Act. But opposition to the East India Company's scheme reached far beyond the smugglers. Local patriots launched a major campaign in the newspapers and through mass meetings to require the consignees to resign their commissions and agree to send the tea back to England. Before a pound of company tea had arrived at either New York or Philadelphia, the consignees backed down. At Charleston, where the first ship arrived in early December, the cargo was confiscated by cooperating customs officials and stored in their warehouse for the duration of the crisis.

The situation at Boston was quite different, as the vessels neared their destination in late autumn. Partly because of continuing anxiety about the matter of judges' salaries, the patriots there were surprisingly slow to recognize the threat inherent in the shipment of duties tea. But in late October their campaign against duties tea got under way. From the start, they viewed the scheme as a conspiracy between company, ministry, and perhaps the governor as well to force recognition of parliamentary taxation. Among the consignees were Thomas & Elisha Hutchinson, sons of the governor, and their close friends, Richard Clarke & Sons. In addition to their connection with the governor, both of these firms had angered and embarrassed the patriots by their continued importation of dutied tea during the nonimportation agreement of 1769–70. Letters to the newspapers threatened "the two children" with revenge from "a betrayed people" and promised destruction of the company's tea if it was not returned. Unlike their counterparts at New York and Philadelphia, however, the Boston consignees had no intention of caving in under public pressure. Instead, Richard Clarke wrote a strong defense of the undertaking, asking how his fellow citizens could object to the tea tax while they continued to pay duties on sugar, molasses, and wine as well as on English tea itself. Another writer threatened to disclose the names of all the customers who regularly purchased dutied tea in his shop, among whom, he intimated, were numerous patriots. To make matters worse, a letter from Philadelphia doubted the Bostonians' ability to hold the line against the scheme and predicted that their noncompliance "will confirm many prejudices against them and injure the common cause."

In early November the patriots attempted to force the consignees to resign without success. Then town meeting issued its own demand, but to no avail. In mid-month one of the Clarke family who had been in England arrived, along with the report that the company's tea was indeed on its way. That evening a small band of patriots gathered at the Clarke family residence in protest. When someone fired a pistol at the demonstrators, they responded with a barrage of stones and brickbats, inflicting considerable damage to the house, but the Clarkes remained firm.

Late in the evening of November 27, the ship *Dartmouth*, Captain James Hall commanding, arrived off the harbor mouth with the first of Boston's consignment of tea. Next morning the vessel beat its way up the channel, past Castle William, and came to anchor under the stern of Admiral Montagu's flagship, a few hundred yards off the waterfront. Later Thomas Hutchinson would claim that he tried to prevent the *Dartmouth* from actually entering the harbor and that somehow Sam Adams had forced Captain Hall to bring his vessel in. But examination of the ship's journal shows no evidence to support this accusation. On the contrary, the governor had no reason to oppose the *Dartmouth*'s entry, for once in the harbor its cargo became liable to payment of all duties within twenty days on penalty of confiscation. With British troops in charge of the Castle and the navy commanding the harbor, the ship could not possibly escape without a clearance. Only the customs officials or the governor could issue such permission, and Hutchinson had no intention of passing up the chance for revenge which these circumstances had presented him.

Boston's committee of correspondence met Sunday morning, the 28th, and succeeded in persuading young Francis Rotch, son and representative of the *Dartmouth*'s owner, not to enter the ship at the customshouse until Tuesday, hoping that the delay would somehow facilitate the vessel's immediate departure. The committee also called its counterparts in neighboring towns to a mass meeting the following day. So many people gathered at Faneuil Hall on Monday that the meeting moved to Old South Church, where over five thousand inhabitants of Boston and vicinity met to demand that the consignees resign and the tea be returned. Instead of complying, the Hutchinsons and Clarkes sought protection from the council. When that body refused to intervene, they took refuge in the Castle, free from popular pressures. As the meeting reconvened the following day, Hutchinson sent the sheriff with orders to disperse the crowd in the name of the king. Sam Adams taunted the absent governor. "He, he? Is he—that shadow of a man, scarce able to support his withered carcase or his hoary head. Is he a *representation* of *majesty*?" And the meeting continued. Finally Rotch and Captain Hall agreed for their part to return the tea, but the consignees sent word that they could not or would not be a party to such a solution.

As the meeting of the 30th broke up in frustration, it became increasingly obvious that Hutchinson had no intention of backing down, and without his compliance, owner, shipmaster, and consignees were equally powerless. The public saved their choicest rhetoric for the hated governor. "Can you deny, Mr. Hutchinson, that an absolute despotism is establishing itself here?" challenged one writer. "Ruthless barbarian . . . !" screamed another. "You cry Peace! Peace! But there is no peace, saith my God to a trampler on the rights of his country." Amid the threats and epithets that rained down upon him Hutchinson stood firm, confining himself for safety's sake to his Milton estate. Time was surely on his side. The twenty-day period would expire on the 17th of December. If the duties were not paid by then, the customs officials could take over the vessel, with the help of the navy if necessary, and land the tea. Even though the ship had been brought up to Griffin's Wharf and a guard of

twenty-five men put aboard, the patriots would have had difficulty resisting the seizure. Meanwhile, two more vessels with tea arrived, the
ship *Eleanor* and the brig *Beaver,* while the brig *William* was cast ashore at
Cape Cod, a total loss. As the days slipped by, letters in the newspapers
became more bellicose, and one resident reported that " 'twould puzzle
any person to purchase a pair of p[isto]ls in town, as they are all bought
up with a full determination to repell force with force." Admiral
Montagu maneuvered his ships into position to block all channels out to
sea, and the garrison at Castle William had reportedly charged its cannon
ready for action if necessary.

As the deadline approached, Rotch backed off from his ill-advised
promise to return the tea. Dispatches from New York and Philadelphia
confirmed the fact that the consignees had resigned there. "You have
failed us [before] in the importation of tea . . .," taunted one Philadel-
phian, "and we fear you will suffer this to be landed [also]." The patriots
were in a desperate position. On the 14th, Sam Adams escorted Rotch to
the office of Collector Richard Harrison, there to seek a special clearance.
The official took the matter under advisement. Perhaps it was irrelevant
that, along with his father, Harrison had been a victim of the *Liberty* riot
more than five years before and had no reason to do Sam Adams a favor.
But in any event, Harrison announced the next day that to grant a clearance was in his view "utterly inconsistent" with his duty. Another effort
at nonviolent solution had failed.

Thursday, December 16, was the last day in the period of grace.
Thousands of inhabitants from Boston and surrounding towns crowded
into Old South Church, uncertain of what to expect. The meeting instructed Rotch to ask the governor for a special permit to allow the
Dartmouth and other tea ships past the Castle. The hapless young merchant could hardly refuse this further demand. While he undertook the
fourteen-mile round trip to Milton, the meeting recessed. Rotch found
Hutchinson resolute in his determination not to back down just as victory was seemingly in his grasp. The governor had written to Lord
Dartmouth just two days earlier that "it is time this anarchy were restrained by some authority or other." Giving in to the patriots' demands
was impossible.

It was already dark when Rotch returned to Old South Church with
word of Hutchinson's refusal. "A mob! A mob!" rang through the hall as
he made his grim report. After the crowd was quieted with a few more

speeches, Sam Adams rose to say, as later recalled by those present, "As for me, I shall go home, set down and make myself as easy as I can, for this meeting can do nothing further to save the country." The words apparently gave signal to others standing by. An Indian war whoop rent the air, then another. "Boston harbor a tea-pot tonight!" "Hurrah for Griffin's Wharf!" With that the doors burst open and the crowd swept out into the street. "You'd have thought that the inhabitants of the infernal regions had broke loose," recalled a merchant living nearby.

From various side streets and alleyways small bands of men and boys roughly disguised as Indians converged on the procession. Some were members of the Masons' Lodge of St. Andrews, others of various political clubs. Many were young, teenagers or barely in their twenties, apprentices, laborers, mariners, or men without jobs at all. A handful of wealthier men joined the throng—merchants and shopkeepers or well-to-do artisans. When they reached Griffin's Wharf, where all three ships then lay, the men broke into parties of about twenty-five and boarded the vessels. Systematically they broke open the hatches, hoisted out the heavy chests of tea by block and tackle, smashed them apart, and poured the contents into Boston harbor. Within less than three hours 340 chests of East India Company tea, worth about £10,000, were destroyed in Boston harbor. Hutchinson was apparently taken by complete surprise. Neither the troops in Castle William nor the ships of Montagu's fleet were given authority to interfere. Had the soldiers (and the governor) remained in Boston, perhaps the outcome would have been different.

The Boston Tea Party resulted only in part from the patriots' opposition to having dutied tea crammed down their throats, as they put it. It was equally the result of Hutchinson's refusal to permit the ships to take their unwanted cargoes back to England. When the ship *Polly* entered the port of Philadelphia at the end of December, Governor John Penn made no attempt to interfere. There the patriots succeeded in driving the ship out of the harbor, tea and all. The attitude of the governor made all the difference, and Hutchinson was not about to bend the rules as his counterpart in Pennsylvania would do to avoid a showdown. Yet even in this last confrontation he failed to defeat his lifelong opponents. To the end, he remained convinced that he had made the right decision, and by his own lights he most certainly had. But as usual, Sam Adams got the last word. Writing to Arthur Lee in London, he enthused: "You cannot imagine the height of joy that sparkles in the eyes and animates the

Destruction of Tea in Boston in 1773. Published by Prentiss Whitney. Courtesy of the Essex Institute, Salem, Mass.

countenances as well as the hearts of all we meet on this occasion; excepting the disappointed, disconcerted Hutchinson and his tools."

*   *   *

News of the Boston Tea Party reached London in the latter part of January 1774. George III's reaction set the tone when he regretted that "the instigation of bad men hath again drawn the people of Boston to take such unjustifiable steps." The ministry immediately laid plans to close the port of Boston, seize the ringleaders for trial in England on charges of treason, and move the capital of the province elsewhere. Opinion in the British press ran heavily against the Bostonians; a wide variety of punishments was suggested, some only half seriously perhaps, including several demands that the navy bombard the town into submission. Soon the ministry realized that its proposals required the consent of Parliament and that sufficient evidence for treason indictments could probably not be collected. Despite these setbacks the ministry was ready by early March to propose concrete measures. In his introductory speech, Lord North reviewed the long history of Boston's opposition to parliamentary authority and argued that its inhabitants must be punished as well as reformed. He ended with the ministry's proposal to close the port on June 1 until the East India Company was compensated for its losses, the miscreants brought to justice, and the mother country assured of the town's future good behavior. Until that time (if ever), no vessel would be permitted to enter or clear the harbor except small coasters carrying fuel or provisions. All efforts to hear Boston first or otherwise to intercede in its behalf were summarily brushed aside. By the end of the month the Port Act had become law.

The ministry had other measures in mind as well. In what became known as the Massachusetts Government Act, North proposed that the governor's council be appointed by the king, as in other royal colonies, rather than through the intricate process of election that was called for under the Massachusetts Charter of 1691. The bill greatly increased the governor's appointive powers, altered the method of choosing juries, and restricted the communities of Massachusetts to a single town meeting each year, for the sole purpose of electing local officials. The government had already decided to replace Governor Hutchinson with General Thomas Gage, who was to be backed up with fresh troops. To protect the soldiers and other officials in their task of maintaining peace, still another law was introduced—the Administration of Justice Act—permitting any crown officer who killed a rioter in line of duty to be tried not in Massachusetts but in another colony or in England itself. Finally, a new Quartering Act gave colonial governors increased powers to billet soldiers within American towns; Gage could thus move his troops into Boston proper and seize whatever vacant buildings he needed over the objections of local officials. By early June, the so-called Coercive Acts had been overwhelmingly approved by the Parliament, the opposition unable to collect more than 64 votes against 239 in the fullest division of opinion recorded.

While Parliament discussed the means by which it hoped to restore Massachusetts to a proper subordination, the inhabitants of the Bay colony continued their new-found opposition to dutied tea. Throughout the winter, one town after another held a ritual tea-burning on its Common, and shopkeepers who persisted in selling the article met with the people's "just resentment." When in March 1774, to everyone's surprise, a brig sailed into Boston with twenty-eight chests of dutied tea on private consignment, local patriots wasted no time in dumping it all into the harbor. In other colonies some of the conservative inhabitants regretted the extreme measures taken in Massachusetts, but for the most part Americans generally seemed to recognize the necessity for the tea party. Referring to the East India Company's plan, John Hancock opined that "no one circumstance could have taken place more effectively to unite the colonies then this manoevere of the tea." Massachusetts would soon need all the support it could get.

Word of the Boston Port Act reached Massachusetts on May 10, followed shortly thereafter by the arrival of Governor Gage. "At length the perfect crisis of American politics seemed arrived," wrote the patriot Dr. Thomas Young. "A very few months must decide whether we and our posterity shall be slaves or freemen." The merchants of Newburyport needed somewhat less time to make up their minds. Meeting on the 12th they proposed to draw up all their shipping as a protest against the Port Act and a demonstration of their refusal to profit by Boston's misfortune. Merchants elsewhere failed to respond, however, and the gesture fell through, at least for a time. Boston's shipowners scurried to get their vessels out to sea before the act went into effect, as Gage moved the capital to Salem. Almost unnoticed in the excitement, Thomas Hutchinson prepared to leave the colony of his birth for what would become lifelong exile in England. In some of the major ports, groups of loyalists signed addresses regretting the circumstances of his departure and wishing him well, but in the months to follow, local patriots would force many of these signers to recant their expressions of sympathy. On June 1, the port of Boston shut down. Their town once again an armed camp and deprived of their principal means of livelihood, the Bostonians looked to an uncertain future.

Faced with a reluctance on the part of Boston's merchant community to cancel their fall orders, the committee of correspondence decided to appeal directly to the consumers themselves. In early June, therefore, the committee drafted a "Solemn League and Covenant." Its signers would agree not to purchase any British goods imported after August 31, and to boycott everyone who continued to import or buy such commodities themselves. The proposal proved far too strong for the moderates and conservatives in the community, however. In mid-June the committee found itself in a fight for its very life before a jam-packed meeting of the town. Sam Adams and other patriots hurried back from the General Court session at Salem to participate. After long and heated debate, a loyalist motion to censure and disband the committee was overwhelmingly voted down, and the committee continued.

At the same time, however, Bostonians refused to endorse the committee's proposal of so strict an economic boycott as the Solemn League and Covenant. It soon became clear that other towns in the colony shared this reluctance, and in the large communities especially the question caused serious divisions. Several alternatives to the Boston covenant began to circulate, one of which had been drafted at Worcester, and the inhabitants became increasingly unsure of what course to follow. Loyalists like the Chandlers and Paines of Worcester had considerable evidence to justify their charge that the patriots had created nothing but "disorder and confusion." But the committees of correspondence in the larger towns held fast through the summer crisis, and the smaller towns did not for the most part experience such divisiveness. Gradually, town after town agreed to the idea of nonconsumption in one form or another, partly spurred on perhaps by Governor Gage's denunciation of the Solemn League and Covenant as a "traitorous combination." By midsummer the inhabitants were firmly resolved to resist the Coercive Acts to the fullest possible extent.

Bostonians in Distress, 1774. Mezzotint by Philip Dawe, London, 1774. Courtesy of the Library of Congress.

What gave the people of Massachusetts a particular focus during the summer months was the plight of Boston itself. The new commander of the British North Atlantic Station, Admiral Samuel Graves, in true navy fashion interpreted to the letter his instructions to enforce the Port Act. Vessels bringing in food and firewood were forced to unload at Marblehead or some other outport and to send their cargoes overland in wagons that were quickly dubbed "Lord North's Coasters." Water traffic within Boston harbor was constantly disrupted, and naval crews even harassed the farmers who used offshore islands for pasturing flocks and gathering hay. The town itself became an armed camp once again with troops encamped on the Common. Just before its dissolution in mid-June, the House of Representatives resolved that the people of Boston be given "speedy and constant relief" by the inhabitants of the colony's more fortunate communities. In less than two weeks the first offerings came pouring into Boston, not only from towns in Massachusetts but from those in other colonies from Rhode Island to South Carolina.

Boston set up a committee headed by Sam Adams to cooperate with the Overseers of the Poor in receiving and acknowledging these contributions and in distributing them to needy townspeople. The gifts themselves and the letters that accompanied them gave testimony to the fact that during the summer of 1774 the cause of Boston became the cause of Americans throughout the continent. Each contribution, whether two barrels of flour sent by the hill town of Charlemont, or eleven cartloads of fish from Marblehead, was acknowledged by the Bostonians. And by its responses the committee enhanced the donors' conviction that no matter how far they lived from the scene of trouble they could still make a contribution to the common cause. When the town of Middleborough forwarded eighty bushels of grain, the accompanying sentiments were of equal value to the shipment itself. "The eyes of all the friends of liberty are now fixed on America, and chiefly on your illustrious town," they assured the Bostonians. "Stand firm in the glorious cause of liberty." And the Boston committee wrote back that "your letter breathes a noble spirit and becoming zeal and ardor in the glorious cause of American freedom. . . . It serves to encourage and animate us to persevere in a manly, steady opposition to all tyrants." After such an exchange as this the patriots of Middleborough, hitherto isolated and unable to express their concern, became a part of the larger current that was sweeping across the colony. And before the end of the year 1774 they would join a still broader movement that would unite them with peoples from the district of Maine to the borders of Georgia.

* * *

The role played by Samuel Adams during the critical years from 1770 to 1774 has frequently been described as indispensable. Without Adams, many historians have seemed to say, there would have been no Revolution. Surely he contributed more during this period than any other individual (save Thomas Hutchinson) to the "perfect crisis" of 1774. But neither he nor anyone else was the indispensable man. "Pioneer in propaganda" he may have been, but that is not to say that he controlled the "mobs" of Boston, let alone the thousands of other inhabitants of Massachusetts. The people of the Bay colony could and did think for themselves. When the committee of correspondence sent around its Boston Pamphlet in 1772, for instance, it knew better than to suggest that other towns adopt the resolutions as their own. When numerous communities did respond, they discussed the issues first in town meeting and then expressed their conclusions in their own language. No clearer evidence of the limits constraining Adams's Boston committee can be found than the initial rejection of the Solemn League and Covenant. And yet there exists no better example of his true contribution than in his role as chairman of the committee on donations. For Adams had the knack, as he so well demonstrated on that occasion, of inspiring others to *express* the views they shared in common with so many inhabitants of Massachusetts. By so doing he encouraged them to make a commitment, not only in words but in deeds as well. As a result, by 1774 he stood at the head not of a mob of blind automatons but of an army of well-informed freemen.

14

WAR COMES TO MASSACHUSETTS

Less than a year after the closing of Boston harbor, hostilities broke out in Massachusetts between the British regulars under Gage and the inhabitants of several towns surrounding the beleaguered port. In many wars the burden weighs heavily upon the innocent victims—the women and children left at home and the old folks unable to flee before the advancing enemy. There would be numerous such tragedies in America during the next few years. But in one important respect the war that came in the spring of 1775 was significantly different from the wars that preceded it. Unlike most foot-soldiers before them, who were forced to fight their sovereign's battles, the militia who fought at Lexington, Concord, and Bunker Hill considered themselves the sovereign body of Massachusetts Bay Colony. They and their representatives had had a voice in determining the events that brought them face to face with death on the battlefield. For the most part they fought by choice, not by compulsion.

One such person among the thousands who responded to the call to arms in the spring of 1775 was Captain John Parker of Lexington. There had been Parkers in New England since 1635 and in the town for three generations. His mother's family, the Stones, had been there for four. John Parker had fought at Louisbourg and Quebec during the recent war with France and perhaps served for a time with Rogers's Rangers. After these campaigns he settled down on his farm two miles out of Lexington center. His father had been a selectman of the town and John himself held various town offices. When the local militia asked Parker to be their captain in the winter of 1774–75, therefore, the men chose someone who not only had had considerable military experience but whom they knew and trusted as a friend and neighbor. Many of these men had

shared in the various decisions that step by step took Lexington, along
with other towns in the colony, into conflict with the mother country.
And when that conflict resulted in a showdown on Lexington green they
would be there to accept the responsibility of their decisions.

*   *   *

In the summer of 1774, however, a military confrontation was still ten
months away. Massachusetts was in no position to take on the British
army without some assurance of support from other provinces. Nor were
colonists elsewhere willing to give the Bay colony a free hand. Therefore,
when the Massachusetts House of Representatives resolved, on June 17,
1774, that the colonies should send representatives to a Continental
Congress, many conservatives supported the idea along with more radical colonists. In order to prevent Governor Gage from dissolving the
assembly before it could nominate delegates, the patriots had to work in
secret, completing their selections just as the province secretary arrived,
as expected, with Gage's order to disband. Samuel and John Adams,
James Bowdoin, Thomas Cushing, and Robert Treat Paine were the men
selected to meet at Philadelphia in September with delegates from the
other colonies. All five men had taken active roles in the revolutionary
movement, although Cushing was counted a conservative, and Bowdoin
was rather unpredictable. Although no avowed loyalist was included,
few such men would be found among the delegations of other colonies
either. In short, the Massachusetts representatives (except for the extraordinary reputation of Sam Adams) were not remarkably different
from those sent by other provinces to Philadelphia.

The inhabitants of Massachusetts shared with other Americans a degree of uncertainty about the forthcoming meeting. The word congress
itself had in the eighteenth century only its literal meaning of a "coming
together." Connotations of a legislative function were still in the future.
The only American precedents, the Albany Congress of 1754 and the
Stamp Act Congress of 1765, adopted a few resolutions and adjourned in
a matter of weeks. There was no single pattern for the selection of the
delegates who would gather at Philadelphia. In some colonies they were
chosen by the assemblies, in others by the counties, and in at least one
by the committee of correspondence. No wonder, then, that in mid-
summer the town of Newburyport seriously considered sending its own

delegate but settled for a statement of its interests and pledge of its support. Throughout the summer numerous towns of Massachusetts discussed the crisis at meetings held in defiance of the Massachusetts Government Act. When Salem convened such a session in late August, Governor Gage, who had just established his capital there, ordered its dispersal. Armed men from Marblehead and several other neighboring towns began moving toward Salem, and a confrontation was averted only by the town's tardy compliance. But Gage realized the difficulty of governing the province in such a hostile atmosphere and decided to move back to Boston a few days later. There he proceeded to turn the seaport into an armed camp by fortifying Boston Neck.

Gage had already attempted to put the Massachusetts Government Act into effect by appointing so-called mandamus councillors in place of the officials who had under the charter of 1691 been chosen to the council by the assembly. He also appointed judges and sheriffs under his new authority, but the Massachusetts countryside refused to accept the new regime. Instead, mobs of inhabitants forced several of the new officials to resign their commissions, including Thomas Oliver, the incoming lieutenant governor. They prevented others from taking their oaths of office, and in the western parts of the province blocked the courts from meeting. Governor Gage discovered just how high the spirit of the country was when he dispatched an expedition of troops on September 1 to seize a supply of provincial powder at Charlestown. False rumors of hostilities swept through the colony and into neighboring provinces as well. By the end of the day thousands of militia started out to the scene before learning that Gage's men had already returned to Boston with three hundred barrels of powder from Charlestown along with several cannon from Cambridge. The "Powder Alarm," as it was called, made clear to patriot and government men alike that the New Englanders were ready to fight if necessary to defend their territory. Many loyalists fled their country homes for Boston, and by the end of September the governor's effective authority reached no farther than his fortifications on Boston Neck.

Meanwhile, many of the colony's counties held special conventions to circumvent the ban on town meetings and to take a stand on the state of affairs. By far the most significant of these sessions brought delegates from the towns of Suffolk county to meet at Milton. In the absence of Sam Adams, Dr. Joseph Warren chaired the committee which drafted the convention's resolutions, nineteen in all. The document's preamble set the tone for what followed: "If we arrest the hand which would ransack our pockets, if we disarm the parricide who points the dagger at our bosoms, if we nobly defeat that fatal edict which proclaims a power to frame laws for us in all cases whatsoever . . . , [then] posterity will acknowledge the virtue which preserved them free and happy. . . ." In the resolutions that followed, Warren's committee called upon all inhabitants to ignore not only the Coercive Acts themselves but also the judges and other officials appointed under their authority. As a further act of civil disobedience the convention recommended that all local taxes be withheld from the county treasurers until the government was placed "on a constitutional foundation." It also suggested that a provincial congress be summoned in October to deliberate further on the state of affairs. One of the resolves advised all qualified inhabitants to "use their utmost diligence to acquaint themselves with the art of war as soon as possible" in weekly training sessions. Neighboring towns were to be alerted by written messages in case trouble (i.e., with the British troops) broke out. Not only was Suffolk county ready for war in September 1774 but, judging from the response to the Powder Alarm, its inhabitants would not be fighting alone.

On their way to Philadelphia the Massachusetts delegation had time for a little sightseeing; for most of them it was their first trip outside of New England. An anonymous group had contributed funds to purchase a new wardrobe for Sam Adams, complete to silver-buckled shoes, gold-headed cane, and sleeve buttons embossed with Liberty caps. Cousin John took the measure of people and places he met en route and in Philadelphia itself. New York's Philip Livingston was a blusterer, "a great rough, rappid mortal . . . [who] seems to dread N. England." John Dickinson, with whom Adams would soon feud, seemed "a shadow, tall, but slender as a Reed," while Caesar Rodney of Delaware was "the oddest looking man in the world . . . ; yet there is fire, spirit, wit and humour in his countenance." The first weeks were marked by a seemingly never-ending series of banquets, and by mid-month John was complaining of "the Harry of Business, Visits and Ceremonies which we are obliged to go through."* Within Carpenters' Hall, however, the first

---

* Lyman H. Butterfield, ed., *Diary and Autobiography of John Adams,* 4 vols. (Cambridge, Mass., 1961), II: 107, 117, 121; Lyman H. Butterfield, ed., *Adams Family Correspondence,* 2 vols. (Cambridge, Mass.), I: 158.

days were spent awaiting the arrival of tardy delegates, accepting credentials, and deciding on a number of procedural matters.

Then on the 16th of September Paul Revere arrived from Massachusetts with a copy of the Suffolk Resolves. The effect was electrifying, for
the document focused the attention of all the delegates on the very crisis
that had brought them to Philadelphia in the first place—the plight of
Boston. On the 17th, the resolves were read to the applause of the as-
semblage, which then gave its unanimous endorsement and called for a
continuation of the contributions to the town of Boston. To Abigail,
John Adams wrote that during the discussion he even saw a few "old,
grave, pacific Quakers" weep for the plight of Massachusetts. Although
even Joseph Galloway, the Pennsylvania loyalist, must have voted with
the other delegates, much later he privately voiced his opposition. "By
this treasonable vote, the foundation of military resistance throughout
America was effectively laid," he concluded. Hindsight, perhaps, but
John Adams drew a similar conclusion in his diary entry. "This day convinced me that America will support the Massachusetts or perish with
her." The Suffolk Resolves galvanized the delegates into taking a stand;
next they had to decide on the stand to take.

The Massachusetts delegation supported strong economic measures
against British commerce. The colony's inhabitants had made that position clear by proposing a wide variety of boycotts and nonimportation
agreements. At the end of September the congress agreed to prohibit the
importation of British goods, effective December 1. Southern delegates
reluctantly agreed to end the exportation of their plantation commodities to British ports after September 10, 1775, unless the Coercive
Acts were repealed by then and other grievances redressed. To enforce
these economic measures the congress drew up the Continental Association, which called upon each county and town to elect a committee of
inspection to encourage compliance and to publish the names of those
who violated the code. In Massachusetts and several other colonies these
committees soon led the way toward preparation for war. The congress
also adopted several petitions addressed to the king, to Parliament, and
to the people of Great Britain stating their case and seeking redress.

In almost all of these actions the Massachusetts delegation took a back
seat, letting Virginia's Richard Henry Lee and South Carolina's Christopher Gadsden spearhead the movement toward a firm stand against the
policies of the mother country. This was shrewd politics, for it disarmed

the more cautious delegates who had come prepared to oppose the "radicals" from New England. In one particular matter the strategy paid unforeseen dividends. In early October the congress received a letter from the Boston committee of correspondence reporting on General Gage's latest actions in fortifying the town and disarming the inhabitants. The committee asked for advice: should the inhabitants stick it out or abandon the town to Gage altogether? The congress refused to recommend the latter course, realizing that to do so would have precipitated an effort to recapture the town by force. When hostilities did break out the following spring, it was therefore the British and not the patriots who appeared the aggressors. In contrast to its cautious advice concerning Gage and the troops, the congress unanimously denounced all persons in Massachusetts who had accepted appointments under the recent Government Act as "violating the charter." In recommending that these men should be detested and abhorred "as the wicked tools of despotism," the delegates stopped just short of endorsing the establishment of a provisional government in the Bay colony. Congressmen united as well in the various petitions they addressed to the king, Parliament, and the people of Great Britain. In each letter the delegates made it clear that they stood behind Massachusetts. The patriots of Boston could expect no greater support, at least not in 1774.

* * *

With adjournment of the Continental Congress a decade had passed since the Sugar Act had precipitated the controversy between England and America in 1764. During this period it must have seemed to many contemporaries (as it has to subsequent historians) that most of Massachusetts stood united in protest against the policies and practices of the British ministry. In fact, however, numerous inhabitants refused altogether to support the protest movement. Some had particularly strong bonds to the mother country: nativity or other family connections, oath of office, or church affiliation. Others rejected out of hand the contention that American liberty was threatened by the ministry. These men would become hard-core loyalists. But until the end of 1774 there remained a large middle group which, while disturbed by British policies, nevertheless objected to the American manner of protest. Some of these men had joined the early nonimportation movement and had even petitioned for repeal of the Townshend Act. But this was as far as they would go. When protest turned to intimidation, harassment, and the destruction of property, they concluded that Americans were a greater and more immediate threat than the British.

Until the events of 1774, however, many moderates successfully straddled the fence, objecting to both British policy and American countermeasures. Then came the Coercive Acts, difficult for any colonist to condone. Next the Continental Association with its extra-legal system of government demanding the allegiance of all inhabitants. Then the requirement that all able-bodied men join a militia company and undergo military training. Compliance with these measures suggested a willingness to bear arms against the mother country, perhaps even to revolt. Failure to submit, however, exposed one to condemnation as "an enemy to the country" and to all the harassment and worse that such a position invited. "Those who are not for them [the mob], they say are against them," wrote Customs Comptroller Benjamin Hallowell as early as September 1774. "As I observed to you in a former letter that a neutrality would not be allowed of much longer, the time that I have been expecting is now come." By the end of 1774 the middle ground in Massachusetts had all but disappeared. One was either a "patriot," by which was meant one was willing to defend American "liberty" by whatever means necessary, or one became a "loyalist," stigmatized by support of the "tyrannical" British regime. The term "loyalist" did not properly gain its specific meaning until the year 1774, and in fact was rarely used by contemporaries, for virtually all colonists considered themselves loyal to Great Britain until well into the latter half of 1775. But a conflict of loyalties had long since taken root—a conflict between loyalty to "nation" (Great Britain) and to "country" (Massachusetts, or New England, or finally, "America"). Never fully compatible, as Thomas Hancock had noted in 1748, these loyalties grew further apart after 1763 until by 1775 one could hardly maintain loyalty to both.

While the historian can make no single individual a spokesman for all the loyalists of Massachusetts, one inhabitant of the colony stepped forward into this position during the winter of 1774–75. Daniel Leonard, a native of Bristol county and a practicing lawyer in Taunton, had the necessary credentials to become "Mr. Loyalist" in 1774. He had in fact been chosen to represent his town in the assembly of that year, but in August was selected by Governor Gage to sit on the council. His acceptance of the position earned him the opprobrium of local patriots, and like so many others he was driven into Boston to seek refuge during the autumn. In a series of newspaper articles published during the winter of 1774–75 over the signature MASSACHUSETTENSIS, Leonard undertook to state the case for the loyalist viewpoint, perhaps consciously attempting to fill the void left by Hutchinson's departure earlier in the year.

Leonard's letters introduced no new arguments, perhaps, but they did focus attention on the principles that separated loyalists from patriots and brought his position up-to-date. At the heart of the matter for MASSACHUSETTENSIS lay the argument that the body politic, like the body biological, could be ruled by only one head. Parliament was by necessity the supreme authority within the British empire. Divided sovereignty, *imperium in imperio*, was an absurdity. Furthermore, Leonard asserted, there could be no middle ground between total subjection to Parliament on the one hand or total independence on the other. Leonard carried his position one further step beyond Hutchinson, however, when he suggested that centuries hence, when America became more populous and more powerful than Great Britain "some future GEORGE . . . may cross the Atlantic, and rule Great-Britain by an American parliament." MASSACHUSETTENSIS argued from expediency as well as from principle. Only by continued membership within the empire could Americans be assured of economic prosperity, political stability at home, and protection from foreign attack. British restrictions upon the "democratical" interest such as those embodied within the Massachusetts Government Act were essential to preserve the connection between England and her colonies.

The fact that Leonard's letters provoked a running response from John Adams as NOVANGLUS presents an interesting challenge to the historian. Both men were native-born, members of respectable families of moderate wealth. They were within a few years of each other in age (Adams was the older), and both were Harvard graduates. Each had served his town in the House of Representatives and apparently shared similar aspirations for future political power and prestige. They both tended to view the imperial crisis in absolute terms. For Leonard anything less than complete colonial subordination to parliamentary authority was independence; for Adams anything less than complete freedom from parliamentary authority was slavery. One was a loyalist, forced to leave his home town and eventually the country of his birth; the other was a patriot who ultimately became a president of the new nation he helped to found.

The public exchange between Leonard and Adams furnishes ample evidence of *how* their ideas were different but very little to explain *why*. One contrast seems to emerge in their correspondence, however. Leonard seemed more fearful for America's future than did Adams. He had less confidence in the "democratical" influence within the body politic and placed more dependence on the office of governor and on the courts to prevent anarchy. Furthermore, he seemed fearful of Great Britain's military and naval power. "With the British navy in the front, Canadians and savages in the rear, a regular army in the midst," he prophesied, "we must be certain that when ever the sword of civil war is unsheathed, devastation will pass through our land like a whirlwind. . . ." Adams responded with unbounded optimism. The "hardy, robust people" of the back country were accustomed to defending themselves against Indians. Arms and ammunitions could be manufactured in the colonies or imported. As for the navy: "How many ships can Britain spare to carry on this humane and political war" while Spanish and French fleets threaten the home island, asked Adams. Furthermore, an attack against the seacoast towns of America would provoke the anger of all the colonists. Neither Leonard nor Adams could know for certain what the outcome of such a military confrontation might be, of course. What is significant is that Adams and his fellow patriots were ultimately willing to take the risk; Leonard and his loyalist companions were not.*

Perhaps in the end it was mostly a matter of temperament that separated the two men. Leonard was fearful of the future, eager to postpone the changes that even he recognized were inevitable. Rather than admit that the continued growth of America would ultimately lead to dissolution of the empire, for instance, he suggested that when outnumbered, the British would submit to the authority of an American Parliament. Could Leonard have seriously believed that the proud Britons would subordinate themselves to former colonists? More likely, the suggestion

---

* The Adams-Leonard exchange is conveniently available in a new edition, Bernard Mason, ed. *The American Colonial Crisis: The Daniel Leonard-John Adams Letters to the Press, 1774–1775* (New York, 1972).

indicates the lengths to which he would go to avoid what for him was an unpleasant eventuality. Thirty years ago a wise historian of the colonial period explained the loyalists this way: "They saw the dangers ahead rather than the noble possibilities. They did not have the daring needed to strike for a better future even at the risk of losing a present good. They lacked—many of them—a sufficient faith in mankind, in common, American mankind, to believe that out of disorder and violence, out of an inexperienced leadership and an undisciplined following, could come a stable and intelligent body politic. They were Loyalists, in short," concluded Leonard W. Labaree, "because they had both the weakness and the strength of all true conservatives."

The loyalists of Massachusetts would need all the courage they could muster in the months ahead. They had already been subjected to years of minor harassment, suffering damage to their property, personal indignities, and in a few cases bodily harm. In February 1775 the conservative *Boston News-letter* listed twenty-five incidents of intimidation it claimed had occurred since the previous summer. Some episodes fell little short of outright torture. Israel Williams, a mandamus councillor from Hatfield, was confined all night in a smoke-filled room with no ventilation until he agreed to resign his commission. Others were forced to ride a sharp-edged fence rail which the mob jounced to intensify their victims' discomfort. Tarring and feathering seemed somewhat less frequent in Massachusetts by 1775, but carting was still a featured means of intimidation. One of the most bizarre of all harassments involved slitting an ox's belly and stuffing the hapless victim in among the entrails to be carried from town to town by the howling mob. The fact that no loyalists lost their lives from such assaults in Massachusetts is more a testimony to their hardiness than to moderation on the part of the patriots.

One major disadvantage facing the Massachusetts loyalists was that they were few in number and except for the Bostonians were generally isolated from one another. They had to face their adversaries alone, an act requiring great courage and determination. Occasionally, however, a single town was dominated, at least for a while, by loyalist sympathies. One such town was Marshfield. In late January 1775 some two hundred inhabitants sought the protection of British troops against "the licentious spirit" displayed by "the lower ranks of people" in the colony. Gage sent one hundred troops in response. In February Marshfield town meeting rejected the Continental Association and its call for military preparations. Barnstable adopted similar resolutions at about the same time. But such examples of united action on the part of loyalists were rare indeed. Far more commonly, opponents of the patriots, when they dared to participate in town meeting at all, found themselves hopelessly outnumbered. Had it not been for the refuge created by Gage's control of Boston, the loyalists of Massachusetts would have suffered still more grievously. Their dependence on his protection added a practical reason for their support of the British cause. By the spring of 1775 the isolation of many loyalists from their fellow inhabitants of Massachusetts had become physical as well as ideological, making reconciliation virtually impossible.

The patriot leaders on both local and provincial levels were hardly less concerned about the need for stable government than were the loyalists. Their task after the Coercive Acts went into effect was how to achieve the goal without giving recognition to the Massachusetts Government Act or to officials appointed under its authority. In addition to town meetings held in defiance of the act and county conventions in circumvention of it, a few courts of law such as the Inferior Court of Common Pleas at Newburyport sat "upon the old form of constitutional government," as though the Parliament had legislated no changes in the charter whatsoever. The most blatant disregard for royal authority came in the fall of 1774. To prevent the scheduled autumn meeting of the General Assembly, Gage had canceled the writs of election. But at the instigation of Joseph Warren, most of the previously elected members met at Salem in early October anyway. There they resolved themselves into a Provincial Congress and carried on the business of a legitimate legislature, first at Salem, then at Concord, and finally at Cambridge.

The congress spent much of its first weeks on organizational matters and in denouncing Governor Gage and the men who surrounded him. In response Gage showed remarkable restraint, assuring the congress that he had no hostile intentions and calling upon the delegates to put an end to their own "illegal and unconstitutional proceedings." Privately, however, Gage had already lost much of his earlier optimism. "From present appearances there is no prospect of putting the late [Coercive] acts in force but by first making a conquest of the New England provinces," he admitted to Lord Dartmouth. For its part the Provincial Congress placed preparedness high on its agenda. In late October it called for the acquisition of cannon, shot, powder, and muskets worth over £20,000, enough to equip a force of five thousand men. It then appointed a provincial committee of safety, a commanding officer, and a receiver general to handle financial affairs in place of the loyalist provincial treasurer, Harrison Gray. To this office alone were provincial taxes thereafter to be paid. Finally, the congress called upon all inhabitants to undertake military training. In almost every particular the delegates representing all parts of the colony had adopted for themselves the firm position taken by the convention of Suffolk county in September. Before the end of 1774 Massachusetts stood united in its course toward establishing a revolutionary government.

Many of the older and higher-ranked militia officers in Massachusetts had definite loyalist sympathies, stemming in part from their previous service on behalf of the king in the French and Indian War. In the late summer and autumn of 1774 the patriots viewed this fact with considerable apprehension. Clearly, if the militia were to be an effective defense against Gage and his regulars, a change would have to occur. The Worcester county convention set the pace by suggesting that all militia officers, junior as well as senior, submit their resignations. When the younger men, most of whom were patriots, complied with the proposal, the older field officers had little choice but to do so as well. The way was then clear for the towns to elect their own officers, who in turn would choose their colonels, who were, of course, patriots. The Worcester convention also recommended that each local officer make certain that a third of his force "be ready to act at a minute's warning." In October the Provincial Congress picked up the Worcester idea and urged all of the towns to follow suit. Gradually through the winter and spring of 1775 other communities did so. In the process the minutemen companies, each numbering about fifty men, were organized into separate regiments distinct from the militia proper, with their own elected officers. But progress was slow and by April numerous towns had not yet complied with the new plan. The congress also suggested that each town enlist able-bodied boys and old men into "alarm" companies, who were to become the last line of defense. To complicate matters further, the Provincial Congress decided in mid-April 1775 that this dual system was impractical. In its place was proposed an all-volunteer army, with officers appointed by the congress. Before the change could take place, however, war broke out.

During the winter and spring of 1775 the patriots were busy putting the Continental Association into effect throughout the colony by urging communities to adopt the agreement itself and to elect a local committee to enforce its terms. Although General Gage had claimed in a letter to Lord Dartmouth in November that the association's provisions "astonish and terrify all considerate men" he was forced to admit that it would probably be "generally received" throughout America. In Massachusetts, while numerous towns took no action at all, only a few positively refused to endorse the association. But most towns hastened to comply with its provisions.

Events in the coastal town of Newburyport illustrate how the association affected the lives of the inhabitants. The seaport had already appointed a thirty-man committee of safety, which took over the duty of enforcing the association through newspaper notices and announcements in town meeting. In addition to the ban on British imports, the committee warned local merchants and shopkeepers to hold the line on prices. Nor would it brook interference in its responsibilities by others. When a band of shipwrights destroyed a quantity of tea confiscated by the committee in January 1775 the committee roundly denounced this breach of law and order. Public opinion supported the committee in its enforcement efforts. One merchant was persuaded not to send a cargo of sheep to the West Indies; another agreed to rescind his recent price increases; a lawyer publicly repudiated the address to Governor Hutchinson he had signed the previous May. Merchants who would stay in business had to make swift adjustments. They canceled unexecuted orders for British goods and searched for new opportunities in the coastal trade. Overall, Newburyport's West Indies trade dropped by half in early 1775, while coastal voyages doubled in number. But most shipowners gave their captains standing orders to sell their vessels at the best opportunity. The merchants knew that the days of steady profits within the empire were drawing to a close.

Although the committees of safety in seaports like Newburyport did their best to build up their supplies of war matériel during the winter and spring of 1775, the major responsibility for this undertaking remained in the hands of the provincial committee. In mid-October George III had prohibited the export of arms, ammunition, and gunpowder to America, and British officials strove to enforce the ban, broadly interpreted to mean that no munitions should be allowed into the colonies. At Boston, Admiral Samuel Graves, long on bluster but rather short on effectiveness, deployed his augmented force to inspect incoming vessels for contraband. A number of cargoes of munitions from the foreign West Indies and from Europe nevertheless got through the blockade. One band of patriots even succeeded in getting some cannon out of Boston itself, and in desperation Graves ordered the guns of the north battery spiked to prevent their capture as well. The patriots gradually accumulated military supplies and stored them in the various towns around Boston.

Spies and other informers kept Gage apprised of these developments throughout the winter and spring of 1775. In response to a report of twelve brass cannon secreted in Salem, Gage sent a detachment under the command of Lieutenant Colonel Alexander Leslie in late February. Leslie went by sea, landing his force at Marblehead and marching it overland. When he reached the bridge over North River, however, the British commander discovered that the inhabitants had raised the draw. Militia from Salem and neighboring towns converged at the scene as opposing forces confronted each other across the narrow waters. After long and heated negotiations Leslie finally agreed to make but a short march across the bridge and immediately return. Leslie thus preserved at least some of his honor and the Salemites all of their weapons, which proved to be old ships' cannon being fitted to carriages. As in the case of the Powder Alarm the previous September, the inhabitants of the towns around Boston showed their determination to defend their territory against the British regulars.

Meanwhile, the second Provincial Congress had met at Cambridge in early February 1775. After only two weeks there, however, the session adjourned, reconvening in late March in Concord, where the delegates were somewhat more secure from the possibility of capture. Concern for their safety was no idle fear. In January Gage had asked for authority to seize "the most obnoxious" of the patriot leaders, and when the congress met in February British marine Major John Pitcairn wrote of his longing for orders "to march to Cambridge and seize those impudent rascals." In the interim between sessions the Provincial Congress redoubled its efforts to build up the colony's supply of war matériel. The committee undertook its work with such aggressiveness that Northampton's Joseph Hawley, a firm patriot, feared that it would initiate hostilities and thereby jeopardize the province's standing with other colonies. Upon reassembling in March the congress responded to Hawley's concern by cautioning the committee not to call up the militia unless the British army marched out of Boston in strength. As on earlier occasions, when a difference of opinion threatened the patriots' solidarity, the British government unwittingly restored the Americans' resolve. This time it was news of the Restraining Bill, which would prohibit New Englanders from fishing along the North American coast or on the Newfoundland banks and restrict their commerce to Great Britain and its Caribbean possessions. In an earlier motion, furthermore, Parliament had declared Massachusetts Bay to be in a state of rebellion and urged the king to take effective measures to suppress it. During its two-week session at Concord, the congress responded to these developments by reorganizing the provincial army and calling upon the other New England colonies to lend military assistance when and if needed. On April 15 the Provincial Congress adjourned in anticipation of further developments. They would not have to wait long.

Throughout the winter of 1774–75 both patriots and loyalists shared a sense of foreboding that the crisis in Massachusetts would soon lead to a clash of arms. Thomas Cushing expected that mustering the minutemen would persuade them it was their duty to fight. "For fear of being impeached of cowardice," he concluded, "it is more than probable they will commence hostilities. . . . Once they are begun, they must be continued." As the tension mounted, leaders on both sides found themselves almost hoping for war, having concluded that their objectives could be gained only by violent measures. Thus the loyalist Peter Oliver could write in February that "the sooner it [a military engagement] comes the better—the sooner we shall get to be a peaceable people." Major Pitcairn could hardly contain his eagerness to get at the rebels around Boston. When the will to compromise one's differences by peaceful means breaks down, man turns to his most ancient means of settling his disputes. That time had come in Massachusetts with the approach of spring in 1775.

It is impossible to establish with any accuracy the potential number of Massachusetts inhabitants available for military duty. The limiting factors included scarcity of equipment, distance from possible battle sites, and reluctance to answer the call to arms when issued. Working back from actual events, however, one can estimate the force available for immediate service at about four thousand. Some of these men were equipped with the Brown Bess muskets they had used in the recent

French and Indian War; most others carried nondescript hunting weapons which had been handed down from father to son through several generations. The bayonet was virtually unknown, and artillery pieces mounted in carriages ready for field use were rare. For his part, Gage had about four thousand regular troops and about five hundred marines available for duty in April 1775. They were far better equipped than the Americans, almost all of them with Brown Bess muskets and gleaming bayonets. They were well trained and disciplined, and they were supported by considerable numbers of field artillery. But their morale had sagged through long months of garrison duty among hostile inhabitants. Gage was firmly convinced that he needed a far larger army to reestablish the authority of royal government in Massachusetts. Except for a few marines, however, he would receive no reinforcements until well after the outbreak of hostilities.

On April 14, Gage received a letter from Lord Dartmouth sent out in late January. In it the colonial secretary informed the general that the king and ministry wanted him to seize the patriot ringleaders in Massachusetts if the Provincial Congress met again (as it already had in February) even though such action might be "a signal for hostilities." Gage realized that an attempt to seize the patriots at Concord was impracticable. Besides, the convention adjourned the next day and the delegates were heading for their homes. But the tenor of Dartmouth's letter was clear: the general was expected to take some sort of first step toward the reestablishment of authority in his province. The patriot military stores at Concord were an inviting target, as the powder at Charlestown had been the previous September and the cannon at Salem in February. Gage thereupon detached his grenadier and light infantry units, numbering around seven hundred men, from their regiments and ordered Lieutenant Colonel Francis Smith to seize and destroy the colonial munitions.

Gage took unusual precautions to prevent the premature discovery of the expedition. He provided for a small detachment to precede the main force and seize whomever might be found along the way. The march itself was to begin under cover of darkness and to follow a roundabout route across the Charles River to Phips Farms opposite Boston rather than through the populated centers of Roxbury and Cambridge. But even as the troops embarked for their river crossing in the late evening of the 18th, their intentions were known to the patriots in Boston. At least two couriers, Paul Revere and William Dawes, set forth to alert the inhabitants along the road to Concord. Although neither reached his destination, the news of the British march did, and the countryside was waiting.

In Lexington Captain John Parker turned out with his company of minutemen soon after word of the British march reached the town. For hours, nothing happened, and Parker let his men drift off to the nearby tavern and houses. Then just before dawn word came that the redcoats were about to arrive. Parker hastily assembled as many men as he could, perhaps no more than seventy, and drew them up in two ranks on the village green, about one hundred yards in from the highway. Leading the British advanced guard was Major Pitcairn, the marine officer who had been so eager in February for hostilities to begin. As the British approached, Pitcairn rode ahead and ordered the militia to disperse. Parker later testified that he in fact ordered his men to comply, but as they were withdrawing in orderly fashion, the British made a rushing attack and killed eight colonists by gunfire. Pitcairn finally regained control of his men, broke off the engagement, and proceeded down the road to Concord.

Meanwhile, hundreds of minutemen and regular militia set a converging course to meet the British at Concord. Local inhabitants had scattered as much of the province's stores as they could and then settled down to await the British troops. As the regulars approached, the Americans fell back, finally taking up position on the far side of the Concord River, across North Bridge. Colonel Smith decided to divide his forces, sending one group across the bridge in search of munitions hidden on the outskirts of town, while another secured the bridge itself. A third group remained in the village, rummaging about and burning a few gun carriages and other equipment of possible use to the Americans. Across the river the Concord militia concluded that the British intended to put the town to the torch, as Pitcairn had in fact threatened to do earlier in the year. Spontaneously, it seemed, they decided to return to defend their homes "or die in the attempt," as they later explained. As they started across the bridge, the British detachment opened fire. The Americans replied in kind, driving the redcoats from their position and killing two men, the first fatalities suffered by the British in the Revolution.

Colonel Smith now struggled to reunite his forces, and when he had done so, they set out on the long march back to Boston. But now the route was lined by several thousand militiamen determined to take a heavy toll of the invaders. Fortunately for his men, Smith had asked that a relief column be sent out to cover his withdrawal. In mid-afternoon General Earl Percy's force met Smith's at Lexington, where the day's fighting had begun more than eight hours before. After a brief rest the combined expedition ran the gauntlet back to Boston. A withering fire came from behind the walls and trees lining the route and from houses and barns as well. In their desperate efforts to clear the way, British flankers attacked wherever they suspected the enemy lay concealed, routing out occasional civilians as well as soldiers, burning and plundering numerous homes. As night fell, the exhausted British troops finally reached the safety of Boston. Together the two British forces suffered 273 casualties, including 73 dead out of their combined total of about 1,800. Americans killed numbered 49, with 46 others wounded and missing, of some 4,000 men who at one time or another fought against the British expedition. On that April day of 1775, nearly twelve years of opposition to British policies had erupted into revolution.

As Thomas Cushing had predicted earlier in the year, a peaceful settlement of the dispute would be difficult to achieve once the fighting had begun. For one thing, exaggerated reports of atrocities committed by British troops during the battle stirred up age-old American prejudices against the evils of a standing army. For another, most of the colonists who participated in the day-long battle, and survived, overcame many of the anxieties they must have had about facing the regulars in the field. Having committed the ultimate act of bearing arms against their king, furthermore, these men would no longer be constrained by the fear of being labeled rebels. And the next militia units confronted by advancing redcoats would not dare to fall back. For their part the British concluded that they were in fact faced with a rebellion which could be suppressed only by force of arms. Events of the next two months bore out the fact that both sides were determined upon a military solution.

Responsibility for the military affairs of Massachusetts rested on the committee of safety appointed by the Provincial Congress. General Artemas Ward of Shrewsbury assumed field command of the assorted units which had flocked to his camp at Cambridge. He was assisted by generals John Thomas, William Heath, and John Whitcomb; committee and generals together gradually brought order to the confused melée. The militia were sent home, the minutemen disbanded, and in their places a provincial army of eight thousand men was enlisted for eight months' service. With the reorganization, however, came seemingly insuperable

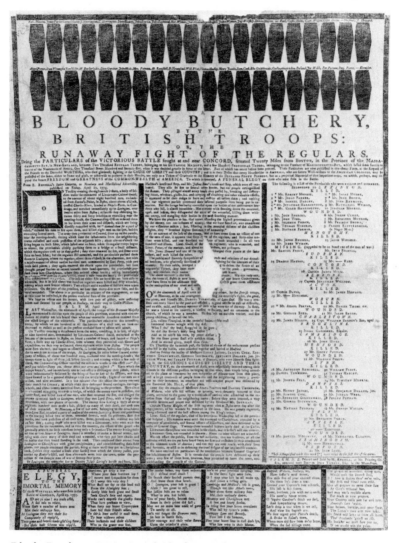

Bloody Butchery, 1775. Broadside from *Salem Gazette*, April 21, 1775, commemorating the Battle of Lexington and Concord. Courtesy of the Essex Institute, Salem, Mass.

problems. Officers refused to accept a lower rank than they had held in the militia; men balked at serving in units other than home-town companies; no colonel could find enough men to fill up the larger regiments prescribed in the original plan. Gradually these problems were overcome, however, and the army took shape through May and June. Meanwhile, the committee of safety sought additional support from neighboring New England colonies, and the Provincial Congress asked the Continental Congress at Philadelphia to take over direction of the army before Boston. Before help could come from outside, however, Massachusetts and its New England allies found themselves once again in combat with the British regulars.

Prompted perhaps by rumors that Gage was planning to take Dorchester Heights to the south of Boston, the committee of safety agreed to fortify Bunker Hill to the north of the town as a countermeasure. Such a position would command both the Charles and Mystic rivers. Although the patriots did not have cannon large enough to take full advantage of the site, they went ahead with their plan on the night of June 16–17, constructing a redoubt not on Bunker Hill but on a somewhat smaller hill named Breed's a little to the south. When the American position was revealed at dawn, Gage wasted no time in planning an assault by both fleet and army. After a morning-long bombardment the British sent 1,500 men under the command of newly arrived General William Howe to make a landing. The redcoats threw one attack after another against the entrenched Americans, only to fall back before a withering fire. Not until the third assault, with the help of 400 fresh men, could Howe's force finally drive the patriots from their position. But the British suffered over 1,000 casualties of 2,400 men committed to battle. All 12 of Howe's staff officers were hit; Major Pitcairn was killed; and only 9 men of Lord Percy's company survived. The Americans lost 140 killed and another 271 wounded out of about 1,500 men.

Bunker Hill changed the nature of the war overnight. Although tactically a defensive engagement for the Americans, the battle resulted from a strategic decision to take the offensive. Furthermore, hundreds of troops from Connecticut, New Hampshire, and distant towns in Massachusetts participated in the effort to harass the British position in Boston. For their part the British learned that the American forces would stand their ground and fight it out in pitched battle when attacked. "The rebels are not the despicable rabble too many have supposed them to be,"

Gage reported to Dartmouth. In the two-month period since Lexington and Concord the American military objective had changed from defense of their villages to the removal of all British presence in the province. The attack on Fort Ticonderoga in early May and plans for an assault against Canada suggested that some New Englanders looked to the prospect of removing the redcoats from the North American continent altogether. With the arrival of George Washington in early July to take command of the troops around Boston, the Continental Congress assumed ultimate responsibility for the direction of military affairs in Massachusetts.

*   *   *

The smoke had hardly cleared from Lexington green before the argument began over who fired the first shot, and historians have been debating the subject ever since. The British claimed that the Americans were guilty of the act, while the patriots laid the blame at the door of the redcoats. And a loyalist accompanying the British expedition deposed that a group of country people had opened fire first from behind a wall. It makes little difference who in fact began hostilities at Lexington, for as Gage, Cushing, and many others had predicted long before, repeated confrontation between the opposing armed forces would eventually lead to warfare. What was significant about the 19th of April was the decision of Captain John Parker and his company of militia to take a stand on their village green against the expedition which Gage had decided to send out into the countryside. The action of Parker and his men was duplicated by a score of other companies throughout the area that early morning. Had the British expedition passed through Lexington without the necessity of exchanging shots they would still have been met at Concord by an imposing array of men determined to defend their village. Nor were the militia and minutemen of Lexington, Concord, Acton, and vicinity the first Americans to step forward in the face of a British advance. What of the men who responded to the Powder Alarm in September, of the men of Salem, Marblehead, and Danvers who met Colonel Leslie at that other, earlier North Bridge?

All of these men collectively were responsible for the outbreak of hostilities in Massachusetts, for they were willing to risk their lives in defense of their homes. When he learned of the British advance toward his village, each man was forced to make a choice between "country" and "nation." Some were undoubtedly conscious of the choice, but many more were not. Together they were responding to an age-old need to defend their territory from the invader. An awareness of the generations who preceded them in Massachusetts had deepened their sense of possessing the land as their own; a decade of strife with the mother country had transformed their sovereign's army into the role of hostile invaders. Surely many must have hesitated even at Lexington and Concord before raising their muskets against the British regulars. But in the end, "country" won out over "nation." In the ensuing months the territory each was willing to defend expanded from the home village to the province and later to the entire New England region. Redefining "country" to include all of the colonies would take a little longer, perhaps. And by that time the idea of a new nation had already begun to develop throughout the American continent.

15

INDEPENDENCE AND
STATEHOOD

"I always expected we should have more difficulty and danger in our attempts to govern ourselves . . . , than from all the fleets and armies of Great Britain." With these words John Adams recalled the critical spring of 1775 in his *Autobiography*. Menacing as was the military threat facing the people of Massachusetts, the political situation was equally serious. While Captain John Parker and thousands of militiamen worried about self-defense, hundreds of other inhabitants were, like John Adams, troubled by affairs of government. Having received a classical education at Harvard and training as a lawyer in the office of Oxenbridge Thacher, Adams combined this background with an intense interest in history to become, by the 1760s, the Bay colony's leading student of constitutional theory. But like most other patriot leaders of the period he had focused his intellectual powers on the problem of justifying the growing resistance of his colony to the measures of Parliament. In his private correspondence, public statements, and in his published replies to Daniel Leonard's MASSACHUSETTENSIS letters, John Adams argued persuasively that successive ministries had led Parliament into repeated violations of the charter of Massachusetts Bay.

It was fairly easy to state the case for opposition against these alleged violations of American rights and to argue the necessity for a provisional authority to maintain law and order until a legitimate government could be restored. But during the winter and spring of 1775, chances for such a restoration were growing steadily more remote. Equally obvious, moreover, was the fact that provisional government under successive provincial congresses could not continue indefinitely. There were too many proper constitutionalists in every town who would insist upon the establishment of some sort of legitimate government. The colony looked to men like John Adams for leadership in reshaping its essentially negative opposition to British rule into more positive form—a new government. The struggle would continue for five years, long after the last British redcoat had left Massachusetts soil. Finally, in the spring of 1780, a new state government emerged to embody the revolutionary goals of the people.

*   *   *

By the spring of 1775 the old charter had proved for most inhabitants of Massachusetts an inadequate protection against the whims of Parliament, and so a return to the *status quo* of 1763 could no longer be satisfactory. Dr. Joseph Warren had suggested to Sam Adams in mid-September 1774 that the people should propose a new compact with the king, limiting their subjection to him, "which he may accept or reject, as he pleases." Because of Governor Gage's role in precipitating hostilities at Lexington and Concord the Provincial Congress declared his office vacant. This made the establishment of a legitimate government doubly urgent, not only to ensure political stability but also to control the army then being raised. But the province could not act alone without alienating the other continental colonies, whose charters, Warren conceded, "have not yet been torn to pieces by the harpies of power." In May, therefore, the Provincial Congress asked for military support from the Second Continental Congress then convening at Philadelphia as well as for advice on whether it should assume the powers of civil government. "We shall readily submit to such a general plan as you may direct for the colonies," the Massachusetts letter offered, or to "establish such a form of government here as shall not only most promote our advantage but the union and interest of all America."

John Adams was sitting in the congress at Philadelphia when the request arrived. He had already pondered the problem of government under the circumstances which then confronted Massachusetts and which would soon face the other colonies. As he later recalled in his *Autobiography,* new structures were called for, to be erected "on the broadest foundations, [but] this could be done only by conventions of representatives chosen by the people. . . . " With that statement in June

John Adams (1735–1826), 1766. Painting by Benjamin Blyth. Courtesy of the Massachusetts Historical Society.

1775, the fertile mind of John Adams gave birth to the single most significant new concept to emerge from the American Revolution—how to put the *idea* that the people were the source of all political power into actual practice. Few of his fellow congressmen were ready for such a radical move as the calling of a constitutional convention in Massachusetts, however, and the committee appointed to draft a response to that province's request for advice made a more conservative proposal. Congress did endorse the removal of Governor Gage but urged the colonists to conform as near as possible to the spirit and substance of their royal charter. Congress went on to suggest that the Massachusetts Provincial Congress issue writs of election for a new assembly, whose members would then choose councillors as before under the old charter. This government was to exercise its powers only "until a governor of his majesty's appointment will consent to govern the colony according to its charter." Far from authorizing the establishment of a new structure, the delegates to the Continental Congress urged the people of Massachusetts to put up only a temporary structure, and upon an old foundation at that. "I can't say that I admire the form of Government prescribed," wrote James Warren to Adams when he learned of the recommendation, "but we are all submission and are sending out our letters for calling an Assembly. I hope we shall have as good an opportunity for a good government in some future time," he ruefully added. The ever-practical John Adams responded that "your government was the best we could obtain for you."

The delegates elected to the new assembly met at Watertown in late July, chose James Warren as its speaker, and proceeded to select a council of twenty-eight men, who because the governor's chair was considered vacant assumed many of the functions of the executive branch. It appointed various judges and other county officers, clearing the way for a reopening of the courts. Working together as a General Court, the new assembly and council confirmed the resolves of the Provincial Congresses that preceded it as lawful and valid acts, and settled down to a long, hard summer of leading the province through its challenging political, military, and economic affairs.

While James Warren and others struggled with the problems in Massachusetts, John Adams did his best to represent his province's interest at the Continental Congress. On more than one occasion his impatience with the caution of other delegates, particularly those from the middle colonies, showed through in his correspondence with Warren. "You will see a strong oscillation between love and hatred, between War and Peace—preparations for War and negociations for peace." But Adams recognized the necessity for going slowly in order to avoid discord and disunion at this critical juncture. Yet he himself had already concluded that negotiation would gain the colonies nothing, except time to strengthen themselves militarily. The colonies should set up governments of their own, he believed, band together, and throw open their ports to the nations of the world. But as he noted to Warren, the other delegates were not yet ripe for such moves.

Warren and his fellow patriots, meanwhile, faced a myriad of problems large and small in their efforts to contain the British army. Numerous skirmishes on the islands around Boston and occasionally along the front lines separating the two armies kept the Americans on edge. Admiral Graves did his best to harass fishermen and coastal traders with his small armed craft, but the patriots retaliated with a small number of privateers and a few armed vessels that Washington had pressed into Continental service. In Boston itself the British army of occupation made life difficult for the common people. The loyalists could not have been comfortable in the beleaguered seaport either, but their welfare received short shrift from Warren. The patriot leader was convinced that the British soldiers were equally distressed, with smallpox and other ills greatly reducing their effective numbers. Yet the Americans were themselves too disorganized to take advantage of the situation, and the military stalemate around Boston continued into the autumn. The replacement of General Gage by William Howe in mid-October did not alter the situation. The only offensive action of significance taken by either side was Benedict Arnold's expedition through the Maine woods to Quebec, which departed from Newburyport in late September with over one thousand men, including numerous Massachusetts volunteers. After an arduous march up the Kennebec River and through nearly impenetrable wilderness, Arnold's force reached Canadian soil but failed in its joint effort with Richard Montgomery's expedition from New York to capture Quebec city. The pitiful remnants of Arnold's force straggled back home in early spring 1776.

Warren's chief concern, however, remained governmental. During the fall the assembly and council squabbled over which body had inherited the governor's power of appointment and other executive functions. "I hate the monarchical part of our government," as Warren termed the council in a letter to Adams in mid-November. "They have got a whirl in their brains, imagine themselves kings, and have assumed every air and pomp of royalty but the crown and scepter." When he learned in mid-November that the congress had authorized both New Hampshire and South Carolina to establish new governments, Warren's frustration at having to work under the old royal charter overflowed. The council backed down in its claim to the exclusive right to choose militia officers but was determined to deviate no further from the royal charter.

Warren and other leaders of the assembly were not alone in their desire to establish the government of Massachusetts on an entirely new footing. From distant Berkshire county came a challenge to the provisional government itself. Convening at Stockbridge in mid-December 1775, the committee of correspondence objected to the appointment of the county's judicial officers by the council and proposed instead that the judges be elected by the people of the various towns. In a closing resolution the committee disapproved of any civil officer not nominated by the county's representatives. A minority of committee members, five of whom had recently received council appointments, voiced their dissent from the resolutions, ostensibly because they tended "to dissolve all government, and introduce dissension, anarchy, and confusion among the people."

At the end of the month, however, the shire town of Pittsfield threw its weight behind the committee by adopting a strongly worded petition of its own to the General Court. In contrast to the years of tyranny under government, they maintained, "we have lived in peace, love, safety, liberty, and happiness" since the suspension of government. Now they feared a return to their former state of oppression. The Berkshire inhabitants especially objected to the nomination of officers "by those in power" instead of by the people. They were quick to point out that the Continental Congress had recently advised both New Hampshire and South Carolina to draw up whatever constitutions were best suited to promote the happiness of their inhabitants. "Certainly the Continental Congress could have no intention of forcing upon us a constitution so detested by the people . . . ," they concluded. The petitioners called for the popular election of a governor and lieutenant governor and the right of each town and county to nominate its own judicial officers. If this right were not to be vested in the people, "we are indifferent who assumes it whether any particular persons on this or the other side of the water." Strong language to direct against the provisional government of the province, moderated only by the petitioners' promise to become "meek and inoffensive subjects" whenever a new constitutional government was established. Until such time the people of Pittsfield preferred to remain in a state of nature. And as if to put its own declarations into immediate practice, the town ordered the quarter sessions court of Berkshire county to desist from future sessions.

Within a month the General Court responded to these challenges with a proclamation of its own. Loyalty to the provisional government was the duty of all moral men. Those who failed to support and assist the courts, which are "necessary for the preservation of peace, virtue, and good order," deserved to be punished as disturbers of the peace. All justices and other officers of the province were urged to encourage by exertion and example a general reformation of manners and to execute the laws. But the General Court had no intention of substituting its own form of tyranny for that of the British. Its proclamation recognized that "the happiness of the people is the sole end of government" and that "the consent of the people is the only foundation of it." Yet neither did the General Court reveal any intention to initiate the establishment of a permanent new government. As spring of 1776 approached, matters seemed at a standstill.

*   *   *

Events beyond the political affairs of Massachusetts Bay itself ultimately affected the question of a new constitution. Conditions within Boston had steadily deteriorated through the winter of 1775–76. Fresh food and firewood grew scarce and almost prohibitively expensive. The political moderate John Andrews later recalled that his family had to burn horse dung for fuel. The loyalists and British forces were hardly better off, although they had first choice of what food and fuel were available. General William Howe had taken over from Thomas Gage in October. In January the inept Samuel Graves was replaced by Admiral Molyneux Shuldham, who proved to be no more successful than his predecessor in maintaining a tight blockade of the New England coast. At least he avoided unnecessarily antagonizing the people as Graves had done when he had ordered the town of Falmouth (present-day Portland, Maine) burned in October. Both Howe and Shuldham seemed content to make themselves as comfortable as possible in their besieged city while awaiting further orders or whatever other opportunity spring might bring.

For his part, Washington showed considerably greater imagination and energy in preparing for an assault against the British forces. He bent every effort to obtain the "unum necessarium," Adams's phrase for gunpowder. American vessels succeeded in capturing occasional British ships with cargoes of powder and other munitions, and the General Court authorized foreign voyages for the purchase of war matériel wherever it could be found. That body also encouraged the manufacture of saltpeter at Stoughton, Newburyport, and other sites. Meanwhile, Washington struggled to keep his army together despite expiring enlistments, tardy pay, and rising desertions. In mid-winter the commander in chief sent his artillery expert, Colonel Henry Knox, to procure the cannon at Ticonderoga and Crown Point, British forts captured the previous spring. Knox was one of the truly remarkable men of his time—an enormous fellow who had learned all he could about artillery from books on the subject among the stocks of his bookstore in Cornhill, Boston. Taking advantage of the winter snows Knox rounded up teams of oxen to haul nearly sixty cannon and mortars to Albany, across the Hudson, and up over the Berkshire mountains, and finally to the outskirts of Boston, where they arrived at the end of January. The next challenge was to place these weapons in position on Dorchester Heights (from which Boston could be bombarded) without alerting the British forces. Only by the most careful planning, along with the coordinated efforts of thousands of men, could the task be done. On the night of March 4, 1776, the emplacements were begun; by the following morning two forts bristling with cannon commanded the beleaguered city and its harbor beyond. Howe planned an all-out attack for the following evening, but a gale sprang up to scatter his assault boats. Already pessimistic about the operation's chances of success, Howe used the excuse of weather to cancel his plans. Instead, he decided to abandon Boston altogether.

Once having made his decision, Howe hastened to carry it out. Although a considerable amount of matériel was loaded aboard outgoing vessels, the British were forced to leave further quantities of goods behind. Soldiers plundered the property of patriots and loyalists alike and stole what they could, despite Howe's best efforts to prevent such mischief. Boston's notorious east wind held up the fleet for several days, first at the wharves, then down harbor. As hundreds of patriots streamed into the city on the heels of the departing British, others enjoyed the sight from various heights around Boston. James Warren watched "the pretty

A PLAN of BOSTON in NEW ENGLAND with its ENVIRONS,

Including MILTON, DORCHESTER, ROXBURY, BROOKLIN, CAMBRIDGE, MEDFORD, CHARLESTOWN, Parts of MALDEN and CHELSEA.

With the MILITARY WORKS Constructed in those Places in the Years 1775 and 1776.

Boston and Environs, 1775–1776. Map by Henry Pelham, 1777. Courtesy of the Essex Institute, Salem, Mass.

appearance" of the enemy fleet from atop Pens Hill. Although it took Howe nearly two weeks to get clear of the land, Bostonians have ever after observed the 17th of March as Evacuation Day (as well as the day of St. Patrick). Despite the worst fears of Washington and other patriot leaders, Howe did not sail for New York or some other vulnerable part of the thirteen colonies. Instead he took his fleet to Halifax, Nova Scotia, there to reorganize his troops and matériel, rid himself of the loyalists, and await reinforcements. With the exception of a few outposts along the sparsely held coast of Maine, the British would never again occupy the soil of Massachusetts.

For the British army, the evacuation of Boston was merely a military matter, an unwanted reversal of fortunes, perhaps, but hardly without precedent. To 1,100 loyalists, however, March 17, 1776, was another matter; it was for most of them their last day as residents of their native land and their first as refugees. For them, departure was the most difficult. Crowded aboard British vessels, they were able to take only a few of their possessions. In most cases they were obliged to pay for their passage to destinations not of their own choosing to face an uncertain future. The price of loyalty now became the onerous task of making a new start in another land—Nova Scotia, New Brunswick, or England, where they were strangers, not always welcomed, rarely understood. Given the intensity of the ideological dispute with the mother country and the social and economic threats to conservatives in general, it is surprising that more men did not declare their opposition to the patriot cause and leave with Howe's fleet or shortly thereafter. Those of loyalist persuasion who remained behind found Massachusetts a far less hostile country than the region around New York, for instance, or the Carolinas, where intermittent civil war continued to take its toll in lives and property for the next half dozen years.

The departure of the British in the spring of 1776 greatly altered the political situation in Massachusetts. Some of the energy and attention previously focused on military affairs could now be given to the need for a new government. Even more influential in this shift of focus was the rising fervor in favor of independence that swept through the colonies. Many inhabitants of Massachusetts had discussed the subject in private correspondence and in letters to the press throughout the previous year, particularly after Lexington and Concord. The outbreak of hostilities was viewed by many as a breach of contract on the part of King George. "Your sword that ought in justice to protect us, is now drawn with a witness to destroy us," wrote JOHANNES IN EREMO. "O George, see thou to thy own house." Yet it was difficult to close the door altogether to the possibility of reconciliation. The reluctance of many members of the General Court to throw aside the royal charter and draw up an original constitution was but one manifestation of this concern. Even Adams and Warren stopped short of calling for an outright declaration of independence until later in the year. Cousin Sam had long since decided upon independence as a long-range goal, although there is little evidence that he tried to win converts while in Congress.

The publication of Paine's *Common Sense* in January 1776 had a galvanizing effect on opinion in Massachusetts as elsewhere. Sam sent a copy to Abigail Adams and urged Warren to read it as soon as possible. By the end of February the copy was passed along to the moderate James Bowdoin, who became an immediate convert to its doctrine. In Massachusetts there was little public debate over the question of independence, for the departure of the loyalists with Howe's army had removed many members of the opposition; without the assurance of British troops nearby, few others dared argue openly against the movement.

Nor was it necessary, as in several other colonies, to persuade the Massachusetts delegation in Congress to press for independence. The recall of Thomas Cushing at the beginning of the year removed the only member who might have held out for another try at reconciliation. Indeed, the problem Adams and the others faced was to avoid appearing too eager. By April, however, Adams felt the time was ripe at last. He suggested to Warren that the General Court ought either to change the province's constitution on its own or petition Congress for consent. "It will give life and activity and energy to all the other colonies. Four months ago," he admitted, "it might have been disagreeable and perhaps dangerous; but it is quite otherwise now," Adams concluded. Furthermore, he urged the Massachusetts court to instruct its delegation to favor a declaration of independence. A few months before such a move would have produced "jealousies and animosities," but no longer.

As spring progressed Adams himself took a larger role in pushing Congress toward a declaration. In mid-May he wrote a strong preamble to the congressional resolution recommending that the various provinces set up new governments. In his draft he pointed the finger of blame directly at George III. "His Britannic Majesty, in conjunction with the

Lords and Commons of Great Britain, has by a late act of Parliament [the Prohibitory Act of December 1775] excluded the inhabitants of these united colonies from the protection of his Crown." The exercise of every kind of governmental authority under that crown should therefore be totally suppressed, he concluded. "Every post and every day rolls in upon us, independence like a torrent," he gleefully reported to Warren a few days later. When John Dickinson made one final effort in favor of reconciliation at the end of June, it was John Adams who summed up the case in favor of an immediate declaration. The decision for independence made on July 2, 1776, owed much to the efforts of the tireless delegate from Massachusetts.

*   *   *

Instrumental in bringing about independence on the continental level, Massachusetts was nevertheless still bound to a provincial government based on its royal charter of 1691. Ironically, the eastern establishment which had led the colony in its long opposition to British policies was subjected to the preachments of western inhabitants who for the most part had only recently contributed to the movement. Even as Adams was working for independence on the continental level, the town of Pittsfield reaffirmed its dissatisfaction with the provisional government in Massachusetts. "We have heared much of governments being founded in compact. What compact has been formed as the foundation of government in this province?" the people of Pittsfield asked. Although they conceded that such a document could be formed by the legislature, a constitution could gain its "life and being" only by the approval of the majority of inhabitants.

Yet another season passed before the General Court was ready to proceed with the task of putting into practice the political principles for which most of its members had risked "their lives, their fortunes, and their sacred honor" in the dispute with the mother country. Finally in September the legislature sought approval from the province's adult male inhabitants for the council and House, sitting together, to draw up a new constitution. The General Court proposed to make public the resulting document "for the inspection and perusal of the inhabitants" before its ratification by the assembly. Towns that had not yet chosen representatives to the current session were urged to do so.

The response of the towns was hardly encouraging. Out of some hundred replies that have been preserved only a handful endorsed the proposal precisely as made by the General Court. The most common amendment was to insist that the constitution be submitted not only for "the inspection and perusal" of the people but for their approval as well. Otherwise, opinion ranged from Wareham's belief that no change should be made in the constitution at least during the war, to Concord's insistence that a special convention be assembled for the task. Since the body drawing up a constitution has the power to change it at will, the town of Concord reasoned, the people would have no security against governmental encroachment under a constitution framed by the legislature itself. Ashfield approved of the proposal in principle but offered a long list of suggestions: the council should have no role making the constitution; there should be no executive branch ("we do not want any Goviner but the Goviner of the univarse"); each town should name its own judges; and all laws passed by the General Court should "be sent to the several towns for their acceptants before thay shall be in force." Some towns disapproved of the proposal out of concern for the many younger inhabitants then in army service whose opinions could not be considered. Bellingham proposed an elaborate plan for the formulation of the constitution. The state was to be divided into temporary districts, to which each town would send its own idea for a constitution. There a "district" proposal would be agreed upon and then returned to the towns for amendment. Finally, a statewide convention of town delegates (one for each sixty inhabitants) would meet in Watertown to choose one of the district proposals as the state's constitution. That document in turn would then be submitted to all of the towns for their final approval.

If the towns replying to the General Court in the autumn of 1776 agreed on nothing else, almost all of them strongly believed that the people, voting through their town meetings, should at least have the right to review any proposed constitution. Indeed, a convention of Worcester county towns belatedly endorsed the Concord suggestion of a special constitutional convention, but when the General Court finally got around to considering the matter in March 1777, it rejected the idea by a wide margin. Instead, the court finally agreed in early May to recommend that the towns specifically empower their representatives soon to be elected to form a constitution. That document would then be laid before the towns for the approval of their inhabitants. Oddly enough,

John Adams, who had been perhaps the first proponent of a constitutional convention, now considered it "a pity" that the new document would have to be laid before the people. "It will divide and distract them. However, their will be done," he concluded, "if they suit themselves they will please me." Warren was thankful that the constitution was at least not to be drawn up by a convention.

In June 1777, almost one year after the Declaration of Independence, the General Court of Massachusetts resolved itself into a convention to draw up a new frame of government. A committee of seventeen members, including James Warren, met under the chairmanship of Thomas Cushing to draft the actual document. When little progress had been achieved by September, the General Court, meeting once again as a convention, prodded its committee "to sit at every opportunity." Yet that group still had nothing to report until mid-December. Even then it sought permission to continue sitting, but the convention had wearied of the long delay and was eager to get at the draft itself. For yet another two months the whole body worked its way through each article and section until finally, on the last day of February 1778, it offered a new constitution to the people of Massachusetts. Inexperience in the mysteries of putting political theory into practice, rather than lack of conscientious effort or deliberate delaying tactics, accounted for the extraordinarily long period of gestation for the new frame of government.

The Constitution of 1778 followed what had become a traditional form of governmental structure: three branches, theoretically independent of one another; a bicameral legislature; and property qualifications for officeholders. The men voting for representatives needed only to be free, white, twenty-one, and taxpayers. Those voting for governor and senator, however, required £60 estate. The governor was to be elected annually and was given no veto over legislation, but he did head the militia with broad powers over its activities. In an effort to solve a perennial problem the document assured every incorporated town at least one representative, with larger communities entitled to additional members. A complicated districting system was to produce a senate of twenty-eight members. To assure continuity with the past the constitution provided that all the laws of the provisional government, the common law, and those English and British statutes commonly practiced in Massachusetts be continued in full force until specifically altered.

Throughout the spring the towns of Massachusetts met to consider the proposed constitution. By overwhelming margins in almost every town the people rejected the scheme. Although in most cases the returns gave no reasons for the decision (none were asked for), the fact that the legislature rather than a special convention drew up the plan seemed to be a common objection. Some of the smallest towns took the opportunity to explain at length why their inhabitants voted against the proposed constitution. In some cases their criticism focused on minutiae: the low number of representatives required for a quorum; the provision for probate courts; or procedures for impeaching civil officers. But most of the stated complaints dealt with fundamental issues. One of the most commonly cited was the exclusion of Negroes, Indians, and mulattoes from the right to vote (Georgetown had only contempt for the exclusion of men "being born in Afraca, India or ancient American or even being much Sun burnt"). Another common objection centered on the governor's control of the militia; still another on the property qualifications for gubernatorial electors. Underlying several of the returns was a continuing suspicion of government in general. Greenwich complained that the proposed constitution "intirely divests the good people of this state of many of the priviledges which God and nature had given them, and which has been so much contended for. . . ." Sutton objected to the absence of any clause against corruption and bribery. A number of towns specifically cited the necessity for a bill of rights so that, as Lexington put it, "Not only that government, and the persons in authority might know their stated limits and bounds; but also the subjects . . . might know when their rights and liberties are infringed or violated."

In addition to the actions of individual communities, the towns of Essex county assembled at Ipswich in late April to voice their objections in a manifesto subsequently published as *The Essex Result*. Largely the work of Newburyport's young lawyer Theophilus Parsons, the document catalogued eighteen specific objections to the proposed constitution and then set forth what the delegates believed to be the correct principles for a frame of government. First, the individual's unalienable rights should be specifically guaranteed by a bill of rights; second, the legislature should represent the two elements of society—people and property—in balance; and the legislative, judicial, and executive powers should be independent of each other. The report concluded with a proposed new constitution, in narrative form, putting these principles into a more practical form. But *The Essex Result* expressed the views of a particular

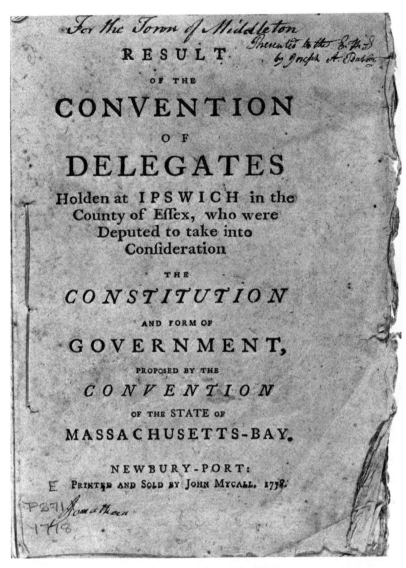

For the Town of Middleton
Presented to the E. H. S
by Joseph A. Peabody

RESULT

OF THE

CONVENTION

O F

DELEGATES

Holden at IPSWICH in the
County of Essex, who were
Deputed to take into
Confideration

THE

CONSTITUTION

AND FORM OF

GOVERNMENT,

PROPOSED BY THE

CONVENTION

OF THE STATE OF

MASSACHUSETTS-BAY.

NEWBURY-PORT:
PRINTED AND SOLD BY JOHN MYCALL. 1778.

The Essex Result, 1778. Pamphlet by Theophilus Parsons summarizing arguments against proposed Constitution of 1778. Courtesy of the Essex Institute, Salem, Mass.

segment of Massachusetts only—the eastern seaboard, in which the interests of merchants, well-to-do artisans, and professional men carried great weight. Nevertheless, the document well summarized the case against the Constitution of 1778. From Maine's Blue Hill Bay (26 in favor and 0 against) to Egremont in the southern Berkshires (14 in favor, 30 against) the freemen of Massachusetts voiced their opinions. Sometimes the language was confident and sophisticated like *The Essex Result*; more often it was hesitant and simple: "If there is Aney thing that we have ommetted in the return I would have you let us know . . . ," pleaded the chairman of Blue Hill Bay's committee, "for we are so as it ware out of the wourld that we dont hardley know wither we do rite or rong but we mean to do as well as we can."

* * *

For almost a year after the verdict was in on the Constitution of 1778, no further action was taken on the matter of reform. The provisional government, much as it had for the previous three years, remained primarily concerned with military affairs and public finances. And the Berkshire constitutionalists continued their objections to that government. The town of Pittsfield had in fact voted in favor of the 1778 proposal, not out of enthusiasm (it objected to three specific articles) but because of its insistence on some sort of replacement for the old royal charter. In August 1778 the westerners met once again at Pittsfield, asked that a constitutional convention be called, and voted against reopening their courts until a new constitution was accepted by the people. If their request was rejected, the Berkshirites threatened, they might join one of the other states "which have constitutions [and] who will we doubt not, as bad as we are, gladly receive us." Worcester county rejected Berkshire's quest for support, however, and Hampshire county made no response at all, having already reopened its courts. But throughout the remainder of that year and into the next the people of Berkshire persisted in their refusal to recognize the provisional government or its courts.

By February 1779, however, the General Court was prepared once again to bring up the matter of a new constitution. This time it sent round to the various towns a two-part inquiry: whether they chose at this time to have a new constitution; whether they would authorize their representatives to vote for the calling of a special constitutional convention. Well over two-thirds of the towns responding favored another try, and although a smaller number specifically supported a convention, there was no significant opposition to the idea. In June the General Court called for the election of delegates to a constitutional convention, each town entitled to as many delegates as it had representatives, all adult freemen being allowed to participate in the choice. The resulting document was to be submitted for the approval of the freemen, two-thirds of those voting being necessary for ratification. The convention would then meet once more to bring the constitution into conformity with the people's will, and ratify the resulting document. At last the people of Massachusetts, or more accurately, the free male adults, wielded constituent power in fact as well as in theory.

Freemen not only had the right to select their delegates but to instruct them as well. A number of towns reminded their representatives that a bill of rights was essential. Pittsfield called for the election of judges; Douglas wanted a constitution as close to Connecticut's as possible; Sandisfield supported "the free exercise of religious principles . . . and liberty of conscience," but only for Protestants. The town of Gorham rejected the idea of a governor and council, recommending instead a single house of the people's representatives with its Speaker serving also as president. Stoughton, on the other hand, argued for a bicameral legislature, one house to represent the people, the other to represent the property of the state, with an additional council of censors meeting every three years "to pass publick censures, to order impeachments, and negative laws enacted contrary to the principles of the Constitution."

On the first day of September 1779, the convention met at Cambridge, chose a committee of thirty to make a draft, and settled down to seven months of concentrated effort. As is often the case in such procedures, much of the actual work was done by a subcommittee of three— James Bowdoin, Samuel Adams, and John Adams, with the last drawing up the basic frame. John was in his element, having at last been given the opportunity to put into practice the governmental theories he had cherished all his life. If the accumulation of political principles from Locke, Montesquieu, and the British constitution was his anvil, then his hammer was the experience of having witnessed the misapplication of these principles in the American colonies by the ministry in the years since the end of the Seven Years' War. During the autumn and winter of 1779–80 Adams would work a foundation for government in Massachusetts that (with numerous amendments) is still in existence today, two centuries later.

The convention profited greatly from the procedural shortcomings made in previous efforts. Most significantly the document it finally sent to the towns for approval in March 1780 was accompanied by a lengthy address explaining the principles upon which it was based and urging its adoption. Only "by accommodating ourselves to each other, and individually yielding particular and ever favorite opinions of smaller moment to essential principles and consideration of general utility," the convention pleaded, would Massachusetts soon "be blessed with such a constitution as those are intitled to, who have struggled hard for freedom and independence." The delegates darkly hinted that "there may be among us some persons disaffected to that great cause for which we are contending, who may be secretly instructed by our common enemy to divide and distract us. . . ." Once again, individuals were asked to give way, except in matters of conscience, to the will of the majority "for the sake of union."

In its preamble the Constitution of 1780 set forth the basic political principles upon which it was based. The end of government was to give the members of the body politic the power of enjoying "in safety and tranquillity their natural rights and the blessings of life." The body politic itself was viewed as a voluntary social compact in which each individual covenanted with his fellows to be governed by law for the common good. In a Declaration of Rights were catalogued those basic principles which had, by the late eighteenth century, become regarded as "natural, essential, and unalienable rights." Here were to be found such concepts as free elections (within the qualifications established by law); equal protection of the laws; trial by jury and the right to confront one's accusers; freedom from unreasonable search and seizure; liberty of the press (Adams had proposed a freedom-of-speech clause which was dropped by the convention); the right to bear arms, and the freedom of assembly and of petition. The third article of the Declaration, which would prove the most controversial, provided funds for the "public protestant teachers of piety, religion, and morality." In most cases, of course, this meant the local Congregational ministers. Inhabitants who attended services of other Christian denominations could earmark their contributions for their own church. But the monies of nonchurchgoers went to support the ministers of the local parish. The final article as-

A

CONSTITUTION

OR

FRAME OF GOVERNMENT,

Agreed upon by the DELEGATES of the People of the State of
MASSACHUSETTS-BAY,

IN

CONVENTION,

Begun and held at CAMBRIDGE on the First of *September*, 1779,

AND

Continued by Adjournments to the Second of MARCH, 1780.

[Revised and Corrected.]

═══════════════════════════════

BOSTON:
STATE OF MASSACHUSETTS-BAY,
Printed by BENJAMIN EDES & SONS, in State-Street,
M,DCC,LXXX.

Constitution of 1780. Courtesy of the Essex Institute, Salem, Mass.

serted the principle of separation of powers "to the end that it be a government of laws and not of men."

That government was itself of traditional form: three branches, with an executive, a bicameral legislature, and an independent judiciary. Each house had a check on the other; the governor possessed a suspensive veto over legislation, and the judiciary, although appointed by the governor, enjoyed office during good behavior. Serving as a check upon the governor was a council of nine members, chosen by the General Court from among the men elected as senators. Officeholders were required to possess varying amounts of property (the governor an estate of £1,000; senators, £300; and representatives, £100). There was a property qualification for electors as well: real estate valued at £3 per annum, Massachusetts currency, or other property worth £60. Taking currency devaluation into consideration, this requirement about equaled the forty-shilling freehold qualification of the royal charter. In addition to the Declaration of Rights protecting the individual from overweening governmental power, the constitution also concluded with other security against tyranny. One clause prohibited plural officeholding (so well developed in colonial years by the Hutchinson-Oliver faction); the writ of *habeas corpus* was guaranteed; and the General Court was ordered to convene a second constitutional convention in the year 1795 to consider whatever revisions might be needed to improve the frame of government.

During the spring of 1780 the towns of Massachusetts Bay once again met to consider a proposed constitution. The convention had asked for detailed explanations of any article failing to receive support from a majority of adult freemen present and voting, and they were not disappointed. The clause most commonly objected to was the third article of the Declaration of Rights, providing support for public worship, Congregational style. The town of Ashby, for instance, listed seven reasons for its opposition to this clause, including the separation of church and state. Other objections were based on the principle that no man should be compelled to support any religious sect against his wishes.

The requirement that the governor be merely a Christian likewise met considerable opposition, for many towns believed it should specify that he be a Protestant. At least a third of the towns responding felt that the next convention should meet sooner than fifteen years. A considerable number of communities objected to property qualifications for voting.

Mansfield wondered how many "young men neither profligates nor idle persons, for some years must be debar'd that priviledge? how many sensable, honest, and naturly industerouss men by numberless misfortins never acquire and possess property of the value of sixty pounds?" Considering the fact that all adult males (without respect to property) were entitled to express their opinions on the article, it is surprising that the restriction did not meet with more opposition. Some of the poorer freemen might very well have voted to exclude themselves from the ranks of electors. Some towns objected to having a governor, others to having a Senate, and still others thought the House would become too large by allowing bigger towns to send several representatives.

When the convention met again in mid-June to consider the returns, it faced an impossible task. Although several articles had apparently failed to gain the approval of two-thirds of the voters, the objectors themselves offered such a variety of alternatives (or none at all) that it was impossible for the convention to alter any deficient article "in such a manner as that it may be agreeable to the sentiments of two thirds of the voters." Nor did the delegates have much incentive for further changes. Their proposal had in substance met with overwhelming approval; they were not required to resubmit the document to the people; and they were undoubtedly satisfied that they had already done their best. On June 16 the convention therefore declared the Constitution of 1780 ratified, to become effective in October 1780. At long last Massachusetts had a constitution befitting its status as a free and independent state.

*   *   *

The work of the Massachusetts Constitutional Convention in one sense completed a process that had begun 160 years before. The people who had settled with William Bradford at Plymouth in 1620, at Boston ten years later with John Winthrop, or at Sudbury, or Newbury, or Agawam—all of these men and women had come to possess the land that Massasoit and his fellow Algonkins once occupied. Their act of possession was the act of thousands of individuals who cleared the land, built their homes, planted crops, and gave in turn what they had possessed to their children. To many of them, like Edmund Rice and William Pynchon, their new lands meant the opportunity to make a comfortable living from the soil. For others, such as Samuel Sewall and Thomas

Hancock, opportunity was found not in the land itself but in the sea it bordered. But these men and their fellow inhabitants did not strive for material comfort alone. Like Jonathan Edwards, they also sought the spiritual well-being that came from living according to God's holy ordinances. At the same time such men as Richard Mather and Thomas Hutchinson led Massachusetts toward a cultural self-sufficiency by their support of public education and by their own writings. For James Otis and John Adams, among many others, self-sufficiency came to mean self-government. And when this self-sufficient community was threatened by the British ministry after 1763, men like Ebenezer Mackintosh, Samuel Adams, and John Parker were ready to sacrifice their lives for its preservation.

To a remarkable degree the Constitution of 1780 reflected the values and endorsed the aspirations expressed by the generations of inhabitants who had helped to build the commonwealth. The very first article of the Declaration of Rights asserted that among the natural rights of men was that of "acquiring, possessing, and protecting property." Landowners enjoyed a special position in the government that was created by the Constitution of 1780. They could more easily fulfill the qualifications for voting than could those with personal property only; they alone could hold the offices of governor, senator, and representative. Furthermore, their property was itself represented, at least in theory, by the upper house of the legislature. Ownership, not occupancy or tenancy, of land constituted the important bond between inhabitant and territory and served as the basis for government in the new commonwealth of Massachusetts.

The Constitution of 1780 recognized other special relationships as well. The fact that the Congregational church was assured public support underscored concern for the contribution of formal religion to the well-being of society. The president and fellows of Harvard College were also accorded special guarantees in their corporate capacities. The constitution also gave particular recognition to the place of "wisdom and knowledge" by enjoining governmental officials "to cherish the interests of literature and the sciences, and all seminaries of them. . . ." The state's right of self-defense was reflected not only in the article concerning the bearing of arms but in provisions for a militia. And throughout the entire document ran the most significant theme of all—the principle of self-government. For the Constitution of 1780 recognized no sovereign other than almighty God and the people of Massachusetts themselves.

John Adams had never doubted the superiority of republicanism over monarchy as a form of government. But on the eve of independence he had had serious doubts whether Americans were a good enough people for republicanism. Writing to the remarkable Mercy Otis Warren in March 1776, he noted that "public virtue cannot exist in a Nation without private, and public virtue is the only foundation of republics. . . . Men must be ready," he continued, "to sacrifice their private pleasures, passions, and interests . . . when they stand in competition with the rights of society." Yet as he looked about even his beloved New England, Adams saw "such selfishness and littleness" as to make him doubt whether his people had virtue enough to maintain a successful republic. All around him the "spirit of commerce" corrupted even the farmers and tradesmen of New England.

What threatened the public interest, in Adams's view, was not the ownership of property but rather men's seemingly insatiable urge to acquire more and more wealth, particularly by trade. The very forces of expanding ambition that had led to the growth of Massachusetts Bay from its beginnings along the coast seemed now to haunt the author of its republican constitution. The very problem that had rent asunder the community of Sudbury in the mid-seventeenth century—the urge to acquire ever more property and wealth—now threatened the new republic. If Massachusetts was truly to become the "Commonwealth" that the title of its constitution implied, then the men who possessed its wealth in their private capacity would have to subordinate their private interests to the public good. As he looked to the future, John Adams could only hope that the spirit of community upon which the original settlers had founded the colony 150 years before might live again in the hearts and souls of their successors.

BIBLIOGRAPHY

I. GENERAL

There are only a small number of general histories available to the student of colonial Massachusetts, perhaps the most useful as a reference work being that of Albert B. Hart, *Commonwealth History of Massachusetts,* Vols. I and II (New York, 1927–28). D. L. Marsh and W. H. Clark, *The Story of Massachusetts*, 4 vols. (Boston, 1938) is somewhat less satisfactory. Valuable both as document and history are Thomas Hutchinson, *History of the Colony and Province of Massachusetts Bay,* 3 vols., ed. Lawrence S. Mayo (Cambridge, Mass., 1936) and George R. Minot, *Continuation of the History of the Province of Massachusetts. . . . 1748 to 1765*, 2 vols. (Boston, 1798–1803). For Plymouth Colony, George D. Langdon, *Pilgrim Colony: A History of New Plymouth, 1620–1691* (New Haven, 1966) is a fine survey. For both colonies the relevant sections of Charles M. Andrews, *The Colonial Period of American History*, 4 vols. (New Haven, 1934–1940) are excellent accounts. Douglas R. McManus, *Colonial New England: A Historical Geography* (New York, 1975) fills an important gap in our understanding.

Both William Bradford, *Of Plymouth Plantation, 1620–1647*, ed. Samuel E. Morison (Boston, 1952), and John Winthrop, *History of New England*, 2 vols., ed. J. K. Hosmer (Boston, 1908) should be considered essential sources for the early settlement of Massachusetts Bay.

Other important printed sources, not otherwise cited in this bibliography, include *The Acts and Resolves of the Province of Massachusetts Bay* [1692–1786], 21 vols. (Boston, 1869–1922); W. H. Whitmore, ed., *Colonial Laws of Massachusetts* (Boston, 1889), and the *Record of the Court of Assistants of the Colony of Massachusetts Bay, 1630–1692*, 3 vols. (Boston, 1901–1928); as well as Nathaniel B. Shurtleff, ed., *Records of the Colony of New Plymouth* [1620–1692], 12 vols. (Boston, 1855–1861) and the *Journals of the House of Representatives of Massachusetts* (Boston, in progress).

The *Publications* of the Colonial Society of Massachusetts (Boston, 1895–) and both the *Collections* (1792–) and *Proceedings* (1859–) of the Massachusetts Historical Society contain a wealth of articles and other historical material of great value. Both organizations have also published a large number of documentary materials too numerous to be listed separately here.

II. BIOGRAPHY

The historian of colonial Massachusetts is more fortunate than most of his colleagues in that there are numerous fine biographies of the men and women who, in Morison's phrase, were "builders of the Bay Colony." The best of these studies, along with printed collections of personal papers, are listed alphabetically by subject.

Lyman H. Butterfield, et al., eds., *Diary and Autobiography of John Adams*, 4 vols. (Cambridge, Mass., 1961)
————, *Adams Family Correspondence,* 4 vols. (Cambridge, Mass., 1963, 1973)
Zoltan Haraszti, *John Adams and the Prophets of Progress* (Cambridge, Mass., 1952)
Peter Shaw, *The Character of John Adams* (Chapel Hill, N.C., 1976)
John C. Miller, *Sam Adams, Pioneer in Propaganda* (Boston, 1936)
H. A. Cushing, ed., *The Writings of Samuel Adams*, 4 vols. (New York, 1904–1908)
Bradford Smith, *Bradford of Plymouth* (Philadelphia, 1951)
Helen S. Campbell, *Anne Bradstreet and Her Time* (Boston, 1891)
Larzer Ziff, *The Career of John Cotton: Puritanism and the American Experience* (Princeton, 1962)
Perry Miller, *Jonathan Edwards* (New York, 1949)
George A. Billias, *Elbridge Gerry: Founding Father and Republican Statesman* (New York, 1976)
————, *General John Glover and His Marblehead Mariners* (New York, 1948)
Herbert S. Allan, *John Hancock: Patriot in Purple* (New York, 1948)
William T. Baxter, *The House of Hancock, Business in Boston, 1724–1774* (Cambridge, Mass., 1945)
Helen Augur, *An American Jezebel: The Life of Anne Hutchinson* (New York, 1930)
James K. Hosmer, *Life of Thomas Hutchinson* (Boston, 1896)
Bernard Bailyn, *The Ordeal of Thomas Hutchinson* (Boston, 1972)
Ralph and Louise Boas, *Cotton Mather: Keeping of the Puritan Conscience* (New York, 1928)
Kenneth B. Murdock, *Increase Mather: The Foremost American Puritan* (Cambridge, Mass., 1925)

Robert Middlekauff, *The Mathers: Three Generations of Puritan Intellectuals, 1596–1728* (New York, 1971)

John J. Waters, *The Otis Family in Provincial and Revolutionary Massachusetts* (Chapel Hill, N.C., 1968)

John A. Schutz, *Thomas Pownall, British Defender of American Liberty* (Glendale, Calif., 1951)

Esther Forbes, *Paul Revere and the World He Lived In* (Boston, 1942)

Ola E. Winslow, *Samuel Sewall of Boston* (New York, 1964)

Robert F. Moody, ed., *The Saltonstall Papers, 1607–1815*, 2 vols. (Boston, 1974)

M. Halsey Thomas, ed., *The Diary of Samuel Sewall*, 2 vols. (New York, 1973)

John A. Schutz, *William Shirley: King's Governor of Massachusetts* (Chapel Hill, N.C., 1961)

John Cary, *Joseph Warren: Physician, Politician, Patriot* (Urbana, Ill., 1961)

Samuel H. Brockunier, *The Irrepressible Democrat: Roger Williams* (New York, 1940)

Perry Miller, *Roger Williams: His Contribution to the American Tradition* (Indianapolis, 1953)

Edmund S. Morgan, *Roger Williams: The Church and the State* (New York, 1967)

————, *The Puritan Dilemma; The Story of John Winthrop* (Boston, 1958)

Robert C. Winthrop, *Life and Letters of John Winthrop*, 2 vols. (Boston, 1864–1867)

Richard S. Dunn, *Puritans and Yankees: The Winthrop Dynasty of New England, 1630–1717* (Princeton, 1962)

James K. Hosmer, ed., *Winthrop Papers*, 5 vols. (Boston, 1929–1947)

George A. Cook, *John Wise, Early American Democrat* (New York, 1952)

In addition to these individual works, readers should consult John L. Sibley and Clifford K. Shipton, *Biographical Sketches of Those Who Attended Harvard College* (Boston, 1873–) and Samuel E. Morison, *Builders of the Bay Colony* (Boston, 1930).

III. LOCAL HISTORY

There are probably more good local histories of Massachusetts towns and counties than of any other colony or state. Space does not permit a definitive listing here but among the most useful are the following volumes, including both primary sources and secondary works, arranged alphabetically by community.

Philip J. Greven, *Four Generations: Population, Land and Family in Colonial Andover, Massachusetts* (Ithaca, N.Y., 1970)

Richard D. Birdsall, *Berkshire County* (New Haven, 1959)

Edward M. Stone, *History of Beverly, 1630–1842* (Boston, 1843)

Darrett B. Rutman, *Winthrop's Boston: Portrait of a Puritan Town, 1630–1649* (Chapel Hill, N.C., 1965)

Reports of the Record Commissioners of the City of Boston, 39 vols. (Boston, 1876–1909)

Gerald B. Warden, *Boston, 1689–1776* (Boston, 1970)

Walter M. Whitehill, *Boston: A Topographical History* (Cambridge, Mass., 1959, 1968)

Justin Winsor, *Memorial History of Boston, 1630–1880*, 4 vols. (Boston, 1880–1881)

S. A. Bates, ed., *Records of the Town of Braintree, 1640–1793* (Randolph, Mass., 1886)

Muddy River and Brookline Records, 1634–1838 ([Boston], 1875)

John W. Curtis, *History of the Town of Brookline, Massachusetts* (Boston, 1933)

L. R. Paige, *History of Cambridge, 1630–1887* (Boston, 1887)

Townshend Scudder, *Concord, American Town* (Boston, 1947)

D. G. Hill, ed., *The Early Records of the Town of Dedham*, 5 vols. (Dedham, Mass., 1886–1889)

Edward M. Cook, "Social Behavior and Changing Values in Dedham, Massachusetts, 1700 to 1775," *William & Mary Quarterly*, XXVII (1970), 546–580

Kenneth A. Lockridge, *A New England Town, The First Hundred Years: Dedham, Massachusetts, 1636–1736* (New York, 1970)

George Sheldon, *History of Deerfield*, 2 vols. (Deerfield, Mass., 1895–1896)

Francis M. Thompson, *History of Greenfield*, 3 vols. (Greenfield, Mass., 1904)

History of the Town of Hingham, Plymouth County, Massachusetts (Hingham, Mass., 1827)

Joseph B. Felt, *History of Ipswich, Essex, and Hamilton* (Cambridge, Mass., 1834)

Thomas F. Waters, *Ipswich in the Massachusetts Bay Colony*, 2 vols. (Ipswich, Mass., 1905–1917)

C. E. Banks, *The History of Martha's Vineyard*, 3 vols. (Boston, 1911–1925)

Alexander Starbuck, *The History of Nantucket* (Rutland, Vt., 1969)

J. J. Currier, *History of Newbury, Massachusetts* (Newburyport, Mass., 1902)

———, *History of Newburyport, Massachusetts*, 2 vols. (Newburyport, Mass., 1909)

Benjamin W. Labaree, *Patriots and Partisans: Merchants of Newburyport, 1764–1815* (Cambridge, Mass., 1962)

Henry K. Rowe, *Tercentenary History of Newton, 1630–1930* (Newton, Mass., 1930)

Herbert C. Parsons, *A Puritan Outpost* [Northfield] (New York, 1937)

Records of the Town of Plymouth [1636–1783], 3 vols. (Plymouth, Mass., 1889–1903)

Sidney Perley, *The History of Salem,* 2 vols. (Salem, Mass., 1924–1926)

James. D. Phillips, *Salem in the Seventeenth Century* (Boston, 1933)

————, *Salem in the Eighteenth Century* (Boston, 1937)

Richard P. Gildrie, *Salem, Massachusetts, 1626–1683: A Covenant Community* (Charlottesville, Va., 1975)

Mason A. Green, *Springfield, 1636–1886* (Springfield, Mass., 1888)

Sumner C. Powell, *Puritan Village: The Formation of a New England Town* [Sudbury] (Middletown, Conn., 1963)

Watertown Historical Society, *Watertown Records* [1634–1829], 8 vols. (Watertown, Mass., 1894–1939)

F. P. Rice, ed., *Worcester Town Records* . . . [1722–1848], 7 vols. (Worcester, Mass., 1879–1895)

John H. Lockwood, *Westfield*, 2 vols. (Springfield, Mass., 1922)

IV. ENGLISH BACKGROUND

The European background to the age of discovery and exploration is well covered in two works by J. H. Parry, *Europe and a Wider World, 1415–1715* (London, 1949) and *The Age of Reconnaissance, 1450–1650* (New York, 1963), and by Boies Penrose, *Travel and Discovery in the Renaissance, 1420–1620* (Cambridge, Mass., 1952). Works emphasizing the English background to exploration include J. A. Williamson, *Maritime Enterprise, 1485–1558* (Oxford, 1913) and David B. Quinn, *England and the Discovery of America, 1481–1620* (New York, 1974).

The basic study of the first English voyages to America is J. A. Williamson, *Cabot Voyages and Bristol Discoveries under Henry VII* (Cambridge, 1962). Richard Hakluyt, *Principal Navigations, Voyages, Traffiques, and Discoveries of the English Nation* (1582) is the standard source for the voyagers' own accounts, the most important of which are conveniently collected with additional reports in H. S. Burrage, ed., *Early English and French Voyages (Chiefly from Hakluyt) 1534–1608* (New York, 1906) (*Original Narratives Series*). These works should be accompanied by Samuel E. Morison's thoroughly delightful *The European Discovery of America: The Northern Voyages* (Boston, 1971), which focuses on the American conditions encountered by voyagers from the Norsemen to the end of the sixteenth century. Warner F. Gookin and Philip L. Barbour, *Captain Bartholomew Gosnold* (Hamden, Conn., 1963) describes the short-lived colony in the Elizabeth Islands, while in *The Three Worlds of Captain John Smith* (Boston, 1964), Barbour puts Smith's New England explorations in a broader context.

For a view of English life on the eve of colonization Wallace Notestein, *The English People on the Eve of Colonization* (New York, 1954) and Carl Bridenbaugh,

Vexed and Troubled Englishmen, 1590–1642 (New York, 1968) offer somewhat different coverage and interpretation and both should be consulted. Lawrence Stone, *The Crisis of the Aristocracy, 1588–1641* (Oxford, 1965) has still another emphasis, as his title suggests. The early chapters of both Edmund S. Morgan, *The Puritan Dilemma: The Story of John Winthrop* (Boston, 1958) and Sumner C. Powell, *Puritan Village: The Formation of a New England Town* (Middletown, Conn., 1963) give particular accounts of how English conditions affected some of the people who migrated to Massachusetts Bay. Two works, W. E. Minchinton, *The Growth of English Overseas Trade in the Seventeenth and Eighteenth Centuries* (London, 1969) and Ralph Davis, *The Rise of the Atlantic Economies* (London, 1973), treat English overseas expansion in the broader context of European economic development, while A. L. Rowse, *The Expansion of Elizabethan England* (New York, 1955) offers a more general overview.

V. AMERICAN BACKGROUND AND SETTLEMENT

For a general natural history of North America see Peter Farb, *Face of North America* (New York, 1963). Betty F. Thomson, *The Changing Face of New England* (New York, 1958), is a particularly well written account of how New England came to look as it does.

New England's Indians are well covered in several general studies, including William T. Hagan, *American Indians* (Chicago, 1960), Harold E. Driver, *Indians of North America* (Chicago, 1961), Ruth M. Underhill, *Red Man's America* (Chicago, 1953), and George E. Hyde, *Indians of the Woodlands* (Norman, Okla., 1962). More particular focus on the tribes of Massachusetts can be found in Charles C. Willoughby, *Antiquities of the New England Indians* (Cambridge, Mass., 1935), Alvin G. Weeks, *Massasoit of the Wampanoags* (Fall River, Mass., 1919), Albert B. Hart, *Commonwealth History of Massachusetts* (Vol. I, New York, 1927), and Neal Salisbury, "Red Puritans: The 'Praying Indians' of Massachusetts Bay and John Eliot," *William and Mary Quarterly*, XXXI (1974) 27–54.

The relationship between native Indians and European settlers in America is the subject of several recent studies, including William N. Fenton, et al., *American Indian and White Relations to 1830: Needs and Opportunities for Study* (Chapel Hill, N.C., 1957), Nancy O. Lurie, "Indian Cultural Adjustment to European Civilization" and Wilcomb E. Washburn, "The Moral and Legal Justification for Dispossessing the Indians," both in James Morton Smith, ed., *Seventeenth-Century America: Essays On Colonial History* (Chapel Hill, N.C., 1959), and Calvin Martin, "The European Impact on the Culture of a Northeastern Algonquin Tribe: An Ecological Interpretation," *William and Mary Quarterly* XXXI (1974), 3–26. See also Wilcomb E. Washburn, *The Indian in America* (New York, 1975). Roy Harvey Pearce, *The Savages of America* (Baltimore, 1953), offers an interesting interpretation of white attitudes toward the Indian. The most recent and most provocative general study of the topic is Francis Jennings, *The Invasion of America: Indians, Colonialism, and the Cant of Conquest* (New York, 1975).

Works more specifically focused on colonial New England are Douglas Leach, *Flintlock and Tomahawk: New England in King Philip's War* (New York, 1958) and his *The Northern Colonial Frontier, 1607–1763* (New York, 1966), Alden T. Vaughan, *New England Frontier: Puritans and Indians, 1620–1675* (Boston, 1965), Peter N. Carroll, *Puritanism and the Wilderness . . . 1629–1700* (New York, 1969), and David Bushnell, "The Treatment of Indians in Plymouth Colony," *New England Quarterly*, XXVI (1953), 193–218.

For the early settlement of Plymouth, William Bradford, *Of Plymouth Plantation, 1620–1647*, ed. S. E. Morison (Boston, 1952), is the basic source, along with Nathaniel B. Shurtleff, ed., *Records of the Colony of New Plymouth* [1620–1692], 12 vols. (Boston, 1855–1861). George D. Langdon, *Pilgrim Colony: A History of New Plymouth, 1620–1691* (New Haven, 1966) and John Demos, *A Little Commonwealth: Family Life in Plymouth Colony* (New York, 1970) provide two excellent secondary accounts. Two articles by Samuel E. Morison, "New Light Wanted on the Old Colony," *William and Mary Quarterly*, XV (1958), 359–364, and "The Pilgrim Fathers: Their Significance in History," *Colonial Society of Massachusetts Publications*, XXXVIII (*Transactions*, 1947–1951), 364–379, make for provocative reading. The process of peopling both Massachusetts and Plymouth is the subject of T. H. Breen and Stephen Foster, "Moving to the New World: The Character of Early Massachusetts Immigration" *William and Mary Quarterly*, XXX (1973), 189–222. Other general studies of the first years of settlement include Robert E. Wall, *Massachusetts Bay: The Crucial Decade, 1640–1650* (New Haven, 1972) and Everett Emerson, ed., *Letters from New England: The Massachusetts Bay Colony, 1629–1638* (Amherst, Mass., 1976).

The basic sources for the settlement of Massachusetts Bay are conveniently collected and edited in Edmund S. Morgan, *The Founding of Massachusetts: Historians and the Sources* (Indianapolis, 1964).

VI. POLITICAL LIFE

Providing a necessary context for understanding the politics of colonial Massachusetts are Leonard W. Labaree, *Royal Government in America: A Study of the British Colonial System before 1783* (New Haven, 1930), Edmund S. Morgan, ed., *Puritan Political Ideas, 1558–1794* (Indianapolis, 1965), Timothy H. Breen, *The Character of the Good Ruler: Puritan Political Ideas in New England 1630–1730* (New Haven, 1970), and Michael Zuckerman, *Peaceable Kingdoms: New England Towns in the Eighteenth Century* (New York, 1970). Despite its obvious bias,

Thomas Hutchinson, *The History of the Colony and Province of Massachusetts Bay*, ed. Lawrence S. Mayo, 3 vols. (Cambridge, Mass., 1936) remains an invaluable source of political commentary by an eighteenth-century master of the profession. Among other general accounts relevant to Bay colony politics are Clifford K. Shipton, "The Shaping of Revolutionary New England, 1680–1740," *Political Science Quarterly*, L (1935) 584–597, George L. Haskins, *Law and Authority in Early Massachusetts* (New York, 1960), Dirk Hoerder, *Society and Government 1760–1780: The Power Structure in Massachusetts Townships* (Berlin, 1972), and William E. Nelson, *Americanization of the Common Law: The Impact of Legal Change on Massachusetts Society, 1760–1830* (Cambridge, Mass., 1975).

For specific political institutions see Roy H. Akagi, *The Town Proprietors of the New England Colonies . . . 1620–1770* (Philadelphia, 1924), Kenneth A. Lockridge and Alan Kreider, "The Evolution of Massachusetts Town Government, 1640 to 1740," *William and Mary Quarterly*, XXIII (1966), 549–574, John F. Sly, *Town Government in Massachusetts, 1620–1930* (Cambridge, Mass., 1930), G. B. Warden, "The Caucus and Democracy in Colonial Boston," *New England Quarterly*, XLIII, (1970), 19–45, and William Pynchon, *Colonial Justice in Western Massachusetts (1639–1702) . . .*, ed. Joseph H. Smith (Cambridge, Mass., 1961). Many of the local histories listed in section III explain how these institutions actually worked. In addition to the biographical studies in section II, there are several good studies of Massachusetts political leaders, including Richard S. Dunn, *Puritans and Yankees: The Winthrop Dynasty of New England, 1630–1717* (Princeton, 1962), Francis G. Walett, "Sir William Phips: The First Royal Governor of Massachusetts," *Bostonian Society Proceedings*, (1954) 23–36, Edward M. Cook, Jr., *The Fathers of the Towns: Leadership and Community Structure in Eighteenth-Century New England* (Baltimore, 1976), Robert M. Zemsky, "Power, Influence, and Status: Leadership Patterns in the Massachusetts Assembly," *William and Mary Quarterly* XXVI (1969), 502–520, and his *Merchants, Farmers, and River Gods: An Essay on Eighteenth-Century American Politics* (Boston, 1971). George A. Billias, *The Massachusetts Land Bankers of 1740* (Orono, Me., 1959) and John A. Schutz, "Succession Politics in Massachusetts, 1730–1741," *William and Mary Quarterly*, XV (1958), 508–520 focus on two major political controversies in the Bay colony.

Ever since the publication of Robert E. Brown's provocative *Middle-Class Democracy and the Revolution in Massachusetts 1691–1780* (Ithaca, N.Y., 1955) Massachusetts has been a testing ground for historians interested in the question of colonial democracy. The earlier, standard work, Albert E. McKinley, *The Suffrage Franchise in the Thirteen Colonies of America* (Philadelphia, 1905), is still useful. Among the more recent contributions to the debate are J. R. Pole, "Suffrage and Representation in Massachusetts: A Statistical Note," *William and Mary Quarterly*, XIV (1957), 560–592, Richard C. Simmons, "Freemanship in Early Massachusetts: Some Suggestions and a Case Study," *William and Mary Quarterly*, XIX (1962), 422–428, and his later "Godliness, Property and the Franchise in Puritan Massachusetts: An Interpretation," *Journal of American History*, LV (1968), 495–511, Chilton Williamson, *American Suffrage from Property to Democracy, 1760–1860* (Princeton, 1960), George D. Langdon, "The Franchise and Political Democracy in Plymouth Colony," *William and Mary Quarterly*, XX (1963), 513–526, B. Katherine Brown, "Freemanship in Puritan Massachusetts," *American Historical Review*, L (1963), 377–396, Stephen Foster, "The Massachusetts Franchise in the 17th Century," *William and Mary Quarterly*, XXIV (1967), 613–623, Michael Zuckerman, "The Social Context of Democracy in Massachusetts," *William and Mary Quarterly*, XXV (1968), 523–544, David Grayson Allen, "The Zuckerman Thesis and the Process of Legal Rationalization in Provincial Massachusetts," *William and Mary Quarterly*, XXIX (1972), 443–468, Timothy H. Breen, "Who Governs: The Town Franchise in Seventeenth-Century Massachusetts," *William and Mary Quarterly*, XXVII (1970), 460–474, and Alan I. Ginsburg and Robert E. Wall, "The Franchise in Seventeenth-Century Massachusetts: Two Comments on the Brown Thesis," "Ipswich," and "Dedham and Cambridge," *William and Mary Quarterly*, XXXIV (1977) 446–458. B. Katherine Brown, "The Controversy over the Franchise in Puritan Massachusetts 1954 to 1974," *William and Mary Quarterly*, XXXIII (1976), 212–241 is a recent restatement of the debate from the viewpoint of one of the contestants, while in *Voting in Provincial America: A Study of Elections in the Thirteen Colonies, 1689–1776* (Westport, Conn., 1977) Robert J. Dinkin surveys all of the colonies.

VII. SOCIAL AND ECONOMIC LIFE

Still a valuable introduction to the society of Massachusetts Bay is William B. Weeden, *Economic and Social History of New England, 1620–1789*, 2 vols. (Boston, 1890). George F. Dow, *Everyday Life in the Massachusetts Bay Colony* (Boston, 1935) is another venerable work, and Carl Bridenbaugh, "The New England Town: A Way of Life," *Proceedings* of the American Antiquarian Society, LVI (1946), 19–48, also remains helpful. Although primarily a political study Robert E. Brown, *Middle-Class Democracy and the Revolution in Massachusetts 1691–1780* (Ithaca, N.Y., 1955) includes much material relevant to the nature of early Massachusetts society. Among more recent studies the most useful are Kenneth Lockridge, "Land, Population and the Evolution of New England Society, 1630–1790," *Past & Present* 39 (1968), 62–80, Stephen Foster, *Their Solitary Way: The Puritan Social Ethic in the First Century of Settlement in New England* (New Haven, 1971), Michael Zuckerman, *Peaceable Kingdoms: New England Towns in the Eighteenth Century* (New York, 1970), Timothy H. Breen and Stephen Foster, "The Puritans' Greatest Achievement: A Study of Social Cohesion in Seventeenth-Century Massachusetts," *Journal of American History,* LX (1973), 5–22, Bruce C. Daniels, "Defining Economic Classes in Colonial Massachusetts, 1700–1776," *Proceedings* of the American Antiquarian Society, LXXXIII (1973) 251–259, and Richard D. Brown, "The Emergence of Urban Society in Rural Massachusetts, 1760–1820," *Journal of American History,* LXI (1974), 29–51. Kai T. Erikson, *Wayward Puritans: A Study in the Sociology of Deviance* (New York, 1966) is a challenging interpretation of Puritan life. Many of the recent local studies listed in section III, especially those of Lockridge, Labaree, Greven, Demos, and Powell should also be consulted.

Bernard Bailyn, *The New England Merchants in the Seventeenth Century* (Cambridge, Mass., 1955) explains the establishment of the Bay colony's mercantile class, while James A. Henretta, "Economic Development and Social Structure in Colonial Boston," *William and Mary Quarterly,* XXII (1965), 75–92, and Allan Kulikoff, "The Process of Inequality in Revolutionary Boston," *William and Mary Quarterly,* XXVIII (1971), 375–412, focus on social stratification in the colony's largest port. A contrary view of Boston's society is found in G. B. Warden's "Inequality and Instability in Eighteenth Century Boston: A Reappraisal," *Journal of Interdisciplinary History,* VI (1976), 585–620, and in his "The Distribution of Property in Boston, 1692–1775," *Perspectives in American History,* X (1976), 81–128. Additional material concerning the "bottom" of colonial society can be found in Lorenzo J. Greene, *The Negro in Colonial New England, 1620–1776* (New York, 1942), Richard C. Twombly and Robert H. Moore, "Black Puritan: The Negro in Seventeenth-Century Massachusetts," *William and Mary Quarterly,* XXIV (1967), 224–242, Lawrence W. Towner, "A Fondness for Freedom: Servant Protest in Puritan Society," *William and Mary Quarterly,* XIX (1962), 201–219, and Douglas L. Jones, "The Strolling Poor: Transiency in Eighteenth Century Massachusetts," *Journal of Social History,* VIII (1975), 28–54. The influx of new arrivals in the middle period is the subject of Clifford K. Shipton, "Immigration to New England, 1680–1740," *Journal of Political Economy,* XLIV (1936), 225–239. Boston is one of the five colonial cities whose society is exhaustively examined in Carl Bridenbaugh, *Cities in the Wilderness: The First Century of Urban Life in America, 1625–1742* (New York, 1938) and *Cities in Revolt: Urban Life in America, 1743–1776* (New York, 1955).

Edmund S. Morgan, *The Puritan Family: Religion and Domestic Relations in Seventeenth-Century New England* (New York, 1961), Nacy F. Cott, "Divorce and the Changing Status of Women in Eighteenth-Century Massachusetts," *William and Mary Quarterly,* XXXIII (1976), 586–614, Alexander Keyssar, "Widowhood in Eighteenth Century Massachusetts . . .," *Perspectives in American History,* VII (1974), 83–149, and David E. Stannard, *The Puritan Way of Death* (New York, 1977) focus on aspects of family life, while in "The Puritans and

Sex," *New England Quarterly,* XV (1942), 591–607, Morgan considers a perennially interesting topic. Dealing with demography generally is Robert Higgs and H. Louis Stettler, "Colonial New England Demography. . .," *William and Mary Quarterly,* XXVII (1970), 282–294, while Maris A. Vinoskis, "Mortality Rates and Trends in Massachusetts before 1860," *Journal of Economic History,* XXXII (1972), 184–213, concentrates on one aspect of the subject.

Education is the subject of several works, including Robert Middlekauff, *Ancients and Axioms: Secondary Education in Eighteenth-Century New England* (New Haven, 1963) and James Axtell, *The City upon a Hill: Education and Society in Colonial New England* (New Haven, 1974). Other studies include Robert F. Seybolt, *The Public Schools of Colonial Boston, 1635–1775* (Cambridge, Mass., 1935) and his *Private Schools of Colonial Boston* (Cambridge, Mass., 1935), Samuel E. Morison, *Three Centuries of Harvard, 1636–1936* (Cambridge, Mass., 1936), and Clifford K. Shipton, "Secondary Education in the Puritan Colonies," *New England Quarterly,* VII (1934), 646–661.

The best studies of the witchcraft mania are Sanford J. Fox, *Science and Justice: The Massachusetts Witchcraft Trials* (Baltimore, 1968), Chadwick Hansen, *Witchcraft at Salem* (New York, 1969), John Demos, "Underlying Themes in the Witchcraft of Seventeenth-Century New England," *American Historical Review,* LXXXV (1970), 1311–1326, and two works by Paul Boyer and Stephen Nissenbaum, *Salem-Village Witchcraft: A Documentary Record of Local Conflict in Colonial New England* (Belmont, Calif., 1972) and *Salem Possessed: The Social Origins of Witchcraft* (Cambridge, Mass., 1974). For a more dramatic account see Marion L. Starkey, *The Devil in Massachusetts* (New York, 1950).

Many of the foregoing works pertain to economic as well as to social life. The system of land distribution can best be understood through local studies referred to above along with Roy H. Akagi, *The Town Proprietors of the New England Colonies . . . 1620–1770* (Philadelphia, 1924). For agriculture specifically, see R. R. Wolcott, "Husbandry in Colonial New England," *New England Quarterly,* IX (1936), 218–252, Darrett B. Rutman, "Governor Winthrop's Garden Crop. . .," *William and Mary Quarterly,* XX (1963), 395–415, and his *Husbandmen of Plymouth: Farms and Villages in the Old Colony 1620–1692* (Boston, 1967). A part of Howard S. Russell, *A Long Deep Furrow: Three Centuries of Farming in New England* (Hanover, N. H., 1976) deals with the colonial period. A good general introduction to Massachusetts commerce can be found in R. G. Albion, et al., *New England and the Sea* (Mystic and Middletown, Conn., 1972), which should be supplemented by the following more specialized studies: Raymond McPartland, *A History of the New England Fisheries* (New York, 1911), William H. Bowden, "The Commerce of Marblehead, 1665–1775," *Essex Institute Historical Collections,* LXVIII (1932), 117–146, Bernard and Lotte Bailyn, *Massachusetts Shipping, 1697–1714: A Statistical Study* (Cambridge,

Mass., 1959), John J. McElroy, "Seafaring in Seventeenth Century New England," *New England Quarterly,* VIII (1935), 331–364, Murray G. Lawson, "The Boston Merchant Fleet of 1753," *American Neptune,* IX (1949), 207–215, Samuel E. Morison, "The Commerce of Boston on the Eve of the American Revolution," *Proceedings* of the American Antiquarian Society, XXXII (1922), 24–51, and the first three chapters of his *Maritime History of Massachusetts, 1783–1860* (Boston, 1921), William T. Baxter, *The House of Hancock, Business in Boston, 1724–1775* (Cambridge, Mass., 1945), James D. Phillips, *The Life and Times of Richard Derby, Merchant of Salem 1712 to 1783* (Cambridge, Mass., 1929), Charles F. Carroll, *The Timber Economy of Puritan New England* (Providence, R.I., 1973), and William Davisson and Dennis J. Dugan, "Commerce in Seventeenth-Century Essex County, Massachusetts," *Essex Institute Historical Collections,* CVII (1971), 113–142. On business regulations see E. G. Baird, "Business Regulation in Colonial Massachusetts (1620–1780)," *Dak Law Review,* III (1931), 227–256, and Richard B. Morris and Jonathan Grossman, "The Regulation of Wages in Early Massachusetts," *New England Quarterly,* XI (1938), 470–500. Two studies concerning currency controversies are George A. Billias, *The Massachusetts Land Bankers of 1740* (Orono, Me., 1959) and Malcolm Frieberg, "Thomas Hutchinson and the Province Currency," *New England Quarterly,* XXX (1957), 190–208. For early manufactures see E. N. Hartley, *Ironworks on the Saugus* (Norman, Okla., 1957) and the relevant parts of Carl Bridenbaugh, *The Colonial Craftsman* (New York, 1950).

VII. RELIGION AND CULTURE

The religious history of Massachusetts Bay, like its politics and society, has been the subject of voluminous scholarship, much of it focused on the nature of Puritanism. The best collection of Puritan writings is Perry Miller and Thomas Johnson, eds., *The Puritans: A Sourcebook of Their Writings,* 2 vols. (New York, 1963), although Alden T. Vaughan, ed., *The Puritan Tradition in America* (New York, 1972) is also a useful volume. The European background is well covered by Alan Simpson, *Puritanism in Old and New England* (Chicago, 1955), Edmund S. Morgan, *Visible Saints: The History of a Puritan Idea* (New York, 1963), and Michael Walzer, *The Revolution of the Saints* (Cambridge, Mass., 1965). Among the best of several excellent introductory works is Darrett Rutman, *American Puritanism: Faith and Practice* (Philadelphia, 1970).

With the publication of Kenneth Murdock, *Increase Mather: The Foremost American Puritan* (Cambridge, Mass., 1925) Harvard's "three M's" began a revival of writing on Puritanism which continues to this day. Perry Miller's *Orthodoxy in Massachusetts, 1630–1650* (Cambridge, Mass., 1933), *The New England Mind: The Seventeenth Century* (New York, 1939,), *The New England*

Mind: From Colony to Province (Cambridge, Mass., 1953), and *Errand into the Wilderness* (Cambridge, Mass., 1965) are must reading, while Samuel E. Morison, *The Intellectual Life of Colonial New England* (2nd ed., New York, 1956) and Peter Gay, *A Loss of Mastery: Puritan Historians in Colonial America* (Berkeley, Calif., 1966) put the Puritans into an historical context. Larzar Ziff, *Puritanism in America: New Culture in a New World* (New York, 1973) is an important recent interpretation. For two histories of local churches, see Kenneth A. Lockridge, "The History of a Puritan Church, 1637–1736," *New England Quarterly*, XL (1967), 339–424, and J. M. Bumsted, "Orthodoxy in Massachusetts: The Ecclesiastical History of Freetown, 1683–1776," *New England Quarterly*, (1970), 274–284. Emery Battis, *Saints and Sectaries: Anne Hutchinson and the Antinomian Controversy in the Massachusetts Bay Colony* (Chapel Hill, N.C., 1962) deals with an early crisis in the colony's religious life with documentation provided by David D. Hall, *The Antinomian Controversy, 1636–1638: A Documentary History* (Middletown, Conn., 1968). Perry Miller, "The Half-Way Covenant," *New England Quarterly*, VI (1933), 676–715, Robert G. Pope, *The Half-Way Covenant: Church Membership in Puritan New England* (Princeton, 1969), and Ross W. Beales, Jr., "The Half-Way Covenant and Religious Scrupulosity: The First Church of Dorchester, Massachusetts, as a Test Case," *William and Mary Quarterly*, XXXI (1974), 465–480, focus on a later doctrinal problem.

The definitive work on the great revival of the eighteenth century is Edwin S. Gaustad, *The Great Awakening in New England* (New York, 1957), but it should be supplemented by the more recent Alan Heimert and Perry Miller, *The Great Awakening: Documents Illustrating the Crisis and Its Consequences* (Indianapolis, 1967), C. C. Goen, *Revivalism and Separatism in New England, 1740–1800 . . .* (New Haven, 1962), and J. M. Bumsted, "Religion, Finance, and Democracy in Massachusetts: The Town of Dedham as a Case Study," *Journal of American History*, LVII (1971), 817–832. Perry Miller's *Jonathan Edwards* (New York, 1949) is also helpful. Studies of the clergy include David D. Hall, *The Faithful Shepherd: A History of the New England Ministry in the Seventeenth Century* (Chapel Hill, N.C., 1972), Robert F. Scholz, "Clerical Consociation in Massachusetts," *William and Mary Quarterly*, XXIX (1972), 391–414, and Emory Elliot, *Power and Pulpit in Colonial New England* (Princeton, 1975).

A provocative introduction to colonial American culture is Howard Mumford Jones, *O Strange New World, American Culture: The Formative Years* (New York, 1964), while Louis B. Wright, *The Cultural Life of Colonial America* (New York, 1957) is a more conventional survey. More specific aspects of New England cultural achievements are examined in Thomas G. Wright, *Literary Culture in Early New England, 1620–1730* (New Haven, 1920), Harold S. Jantz, *The First Century of New England Verse* (Worcester, Mass., 1944), and Kenneth B. Murdock, *Literature and Theology in Colonial New England* (Cambridge, Mass., 1949).

For studies of the writings of particular Massachusetts authors see F. O. Matthiesen, "Michael Wigglesworth, a Puritan Artist," *New England Quarterly,* I (1928), 491–504, and Richard Crowder, *No Featherbed to Heaven: A Biography of Michael Wigglesworth, 1631–1705* (East Lansing, Mich., 1962); two full-length biographies, Norman Grabo, *Edward Taylor* (New York, 1961) and Donald Stanford, *Edward Taylor* (Minneapolis, 1965) should be supplemented by critical studies of his works by Peter Thorpe, "Edward Taylor as Poet," *New England Quarterly,* XXXIX (1966), 356–372, and Karl Keller, *The Example of Edward Taylor* (Amherst, Mass., 1975); Jeannine Hensely, ed., *The Works of Anne Bradstreet* (Cambridge, Mass., 1967), Elizabeth H. White, *Anne Bradstreet, "The Tenth Muse"* (New York, 1971), and Ann Stanford, *Anne Bradstreet: The Worldly Puritan, an Introduction to Her Poetry* (New York, 1974) are all important studies. For publishing in general see George E. Littlefield, *The Early Massachusetts Press,* 2 vols. (Boston, 1907), Worthington C. Ford, *The Boston Book Market, 1679–1700* (Boston, 1917), and Clarence S. Brigham, *History and Bibliography of Early American Newspapers, 1690–1820,* 2 vols. (Worcester, Mass., 1947).

Other aspects of Bay colony culture are found in Harold R. Shurtleff, *The Log Cabin Myth: A Study of the Early Dwellings of the English Colonists in North America* (Cambridge, Mass., 1939), Frank Cousins and Philip M. Riley, *The Colonial Architecture of Salem* (Boston, 1919), and Marion C. Donnelly, *The New England Meeting Houses of the Seventeenth Century* (Middletown, Conn., 1968). Two other cultural aspects, music and the theatre, are examined in Percy A. Scholes, *The Puritan and Music in England and New England* (London, 1934), Henry W. Foote, *Musical Life in Boston in the Eighteenth Century* (Boston, 1940), Edmund S. Morgan, "Puritan Hostility to the Theatre," *Proceedings* of the American Philosophical Society, CX (1966), 340–347, Otho T. Beall, Jr., and Richard H. Shryock, *Cotton Mather: First Significant Figure in American Medicine* (Baltimore, 1954), and Henry R. Viets, "Some Features of the History of Medicine in Massachusetts during the Colonial Period (1620–1770)," *Isis,* XXIII (1935), 389–405.

IX. EMPIRE, WAR, AND EXPANSION

Much of the history of colonial Massachusetts can be fully understood only in the context of the British Empire. Three works by Charles M. Andrews are still the best on the subject: "The Government of the Empire, 1660–1763," Vol. I of *The Cambridge History of the British Empire* (Cambridge, 1929), *The Colonial Background of the American Revolution* (New Haven, 1931), and his monumental *The Colonial Period in American History* 4 vols. (New Haven, 1934–1940). Another classic, Leonard W. Labaree, *Royal Government in America, A Study of the British Colonial System before 1783* (New Haven, 1930), also remains an invaluable study. A recent interpretation of significance is Michael Kammen, *Empire and Interest:*

The American Colonies and the Politics of Mercantilism (Philadelphia, 1970). For British dependence on New England timber see R. G. Albion, *Forests and Seapower: The Timber Problem of the Royal Navy, 1660–1862* (Cambridge, Mass., 1926), William R. Carleton, "New England Masts and the King's Navy," *New England Quarterly*, XII (1939), 4–18, and Joseph J. Malone, *Pine Tree and Politics: The Naval Stores and Forest Policy in Colonial New England, 1691–1775* (Seattle, 1964).

James J. Burns, *The Colonial Agents of New England* (Washington, 1935) and L. K. Wroth, "The Massachusetts Vice Admiralty Court," in *Law and Authority in Colonial America,* ed. George A. Billias (Barre, Mass., 1965) focus on other particular aspects of imperial relations, as does the very useful work by Thomas C. Barrow, *Trade and Empire: The British Customs Service in Colonial America, 1660–1775* (Cambridge, Mass., 1967). For various aspects of the Glorious Revolution in Massachusetts Bay see Everett Kimball, *The Public Life of Joseph Dudley . . . 1660–1715* (New York, 1911), Viola F. Barnes, *The Dominion of New England: A Study in British Colonial Policy* (New Haven, 1923), Michael G. Hall, *Edward Randolph and the American Colonies, 1676–1703* (Chapel Hill, N.C., 1960), Richard S. Dunn, *Puritans and Yankees: The Winthrop Dynasty of New England, 1630–1717* (Princeton, 1962), and Michael G. Hall, et al., eds., *The Glorious Revolution in America: Documents on the Colonial Crisis of 1689* (New York, 1964.

The Bay colony's attitudes toward the wilderness are discussed in Alan Heimert, "Puritanism, the Wilderness, and the Frontier," *New England Quarterly*, XXVI (1953), 361–382, Peter N. Carroll, *Puritanism and the Wilderness . . . 1629–1700* (New York, 1969) and in parts of Richard Slotkin, *Regeneration through Violence: The Mythology of the Frontier, 1600–1860* (Middletown, Conn., 1973). For involvement in various Indian and other frontier wars see Alden T. Vaughan's "Pequots and Puritans: The Causes of the War of 1637," *William and Mary Quarterly,* XXI (1964), 256–269, and *New England Frontier: Puritans and Indians, 1620–1675* (Boston, 1965), two works by Douglas E. Leach, *Flintlock and Tomahawk: New England in King Philip's War* (New York, 1958) and *The Northern Colonial Frontier, 1607–1763* (New York, 1966), and Howard H. Peckham, *The Colonial Wars, 1689–1762* (Chicago, 1964). Richard Pares, *War and Trade in the West Indies, 1739–1763* (Oxford, 1936), deals with another theatre of war involving Massachusetts. See also Jack S. Radabaugh, "The Militia of Colonial Massachusetts," *Military Affairs,* XXVIII (1954), 1–18. Relationships with other colonies are the subject of Jonathan Smith, "The Massachusetts and New Hampshire Boundary Line Controversy, 1693–1740," *Proceedings* of the Massachusetts Historical Society, XLIII (1909–1910 [1910]), 77–88, Lois K. Matthews, *The Expansion of New England . . . 1620–1865* (Boston, 1909), Harry M. Ward, *The United Colonies of New England, 1643–1690* (New York,

1961), Lawrence H. Gipson, "Massachusetts Bay and American Colonial Union, 1754," *Proceedings* of the American Antiquarian Society, LXXI (1961), 63–92, and George A. Rawlyk, *Nova Scotia's Massachusetts: A Study of Massachusetts-Nova Scotia Relations* (Montreal, 1973).

X. THE REVOLUTION AND CONSTITUTION

Massachusetts Bay naturally plays an important role in the general histories of the American Revolutionary era, but because of the voluminous nature of those writings no attempt can be made here to list them all. There are several valuable accounts written by Massachusetts people during or shortly after the era. They include Thomas Hutchinson, *The History of the Colony and Province of Massachusetts Bay,* vol. III, ed. Lawrence S. Mayo (Cambridge, Mass., 1936), William Gordon, *The History of the Rise, Progress, and Establishment of the Independence of the United States . . .* 4 vols. (London, 1788), Peter Oliver, *Origin and Progress of the American Rebellion: A Tory View,* ed. Douglass Adair and John A. Schutz, (San Marino, Calif., 1961), and Mercy Otis Warren, *History of the Rise, Progress, and Termination of the American Revolution,* 3 vols. (Boston, 1805). There is also much source material available in print. Most useful for the period before independence are L. Kinvin Wroth and Hiller B. Zobel, eds., *The Legal Papers of John Adams,* 3 vols. (Cambridge, Mass., 1965), *The Barrington-Bernard Correspondence and Illustrative Matter, 1760–1770,* ed. Edward Channing and A. C. Coolidge (Cambridge, Mass., 1912), *Bowdoin and Temple Papers, Collections* of the Massachusetts Historical Society, 6th ser. IX (1897), *Letters and Papers of John Singleton Copley and Henry Pelham, 1739–1776,* (Boston, 1914), "John Andrews Correspondence," *Proceedings* of the Massachusetts Historical Society, VII (1864–1865), *Warren-Adams Letters, 1743–1777* (Boston, 1917), "Proceedings of Ye Body Respecting the Tea," ed. L. F. S. Upton, *William and Mary Quarterly,* XXII (1965), 287–300, and *Journals of Each Provincial Congress of Massachusetts in 1774 and 1775* (Boston, 1838). For the John Adams-Daniel Leonard exchanges see Bernard Mason, ed., *The American Colonial Crisis* (New York, 1972). The collections and writings cited in section II should also be consulted.

Four works help provide a sense of Massachusetts Bay's society on the eve of the Revolution: Jackson T. Main, *The Social Structure of Revolutionary America* (Princeton, 1965), James J. Henretta, "Economic Development and Social Structure in Colonial Boston," *William and Mary Quarterly,* XXII (1965), 75–92, Edward M. Cook, "Social Behavior and Changing Values in Dedham, Massachusetts, 1700 to 1775," *William and Mary Quarterly,* XXVII (1970), 546–580, and Robert Gross, *The Minutemen and Their World* (New York, 1976). For political background see Lawrence H. Gipson, "Aspects of the Beginning of the American Revolution in Massachusetts Bay, 1760–1762," *Proceedings* of the

American Antiquarian Society, LXVII (1957), 11–32, Ellen E. Brennan, *Plural Office-Holding in Massachusetts, 1760–1780* . . . (Chapel Hill, N.C., 1945), and Joseph E. King, "Judicial Flotsam in Massachusetts-Bay, 1760–1765," *New England Quarterly*, XXVII (1954), 366–381. See also, John P. Reid, *In A Defiant Stance: The Conditions of Law in Massachusetts Bay, The Irish Comparison, and the Coming of the American Revolution* (University Park, Pa., 1977). The writs of assistance dispute, often considered the beginning of the crisis in Massachusetts, is well handled by John J. Waters and John A. Schutz, "Patterns of Massachusetts Colonial Politics: The Writs of Assistance and the Rivalry between the Otis and Hutchinson Families," *William and Mary Quarterly*, XXIV (1967), 543–567, and the more recent work by M. H. Smith, *The Writs of Assistance Case* (Berkeley, Cal., 1978). Charles M. Andrews, "The Boston Merchants and the Non-Importation Movement," *Publications* of the Colonial Society of Massachusetts, XIX (1916–1917), 159–259, provides an excellent overview of the period 1763–1770.

For particular issues during these years consult R. S. Longley, "Mob Activities in Revolutionary Massachusetts," *New England Quarterly*, VI (1933), 98–130, Oliver M. Dickerson, *Boston Under Military Rule, 1768–1769: As Revealed in a "Journal of the Times"* (Boston, 1936), George G. Wolkins, "The Seizure of John Hancock's Sloop *Liberty*," *Proceedings* of the Massachusetts Historical Society, LV (1921–1922), 239–284, Oliver M. Dickerson, "John Hancock; Notorious Smuggler or Near Victim of Customs Racketeers?" *Mississippi Valley Historical Review*, XXXII (1946), 517–540, Francis G. Walett, "The Massachusetts Council, 1766–1774; The Transformation of a Conservative Institution," *William and Mary Quarterly*, VI (1949), 605–627, and Hiller B. Zobel, *The Boston Massacre* (New York, 1970). For the events immediately preceding the Revolution see Donald C. Lord and Robert M. Calhoon, "The Removal of the Massachusetts General Court from Boston, 1769–1772," *Journal of American History*, LV (1969), 735–755, and Richard D. Brown, *Revolutionary Politics in Massachusetts: The Boston Committee of Correspondence and the Towns* (Cambridge, Mass., 1970). The Boston Tea Party is thoroughly examined in Benjamin W. Labaree, *The Boston Tea Party* (New York, 1964) with supplementary material available in Samuel A. Drake, ed., *Tea Leaves* . . . (Boston, 1884) and Bernhard Knollenberg, "Did Samuel Adams Provoke the Boston Tea Party and the Clash at Lexington?" *Proceedings* of the American Antiquarian Society, LXX (1960), 493–503. Albert Matthews, "The Solemn League and Covenant, 1774," *Publications* of the Colonial Society of Massachusetts, XVIII (1915–1916), 103–122, and Jack M. Sosin, "The Massachusetts Act of 1774: Coercive or Preventive?" *Huntington Library Quarterly*, XXVI (1962–1963), 232–252, deal with the Coercive Acts crisis.

The most reliable works on the outbreak of hostilities remain Allen French,

Day of Lexington and Concord (Boston, 1925) and *The First Year of the American Revolution* (Boston and New York, 1934), and Bernhard Knollenberg, "Bunker Hill Reviewed: A Study on the Conflict of Historical Evidence," *Proceedings* of the Massachusetts Historical Society, LXXII (1957–1960), 84–100, along with Arthur B. Tourtellot, *William Diamond's Drum* (New York, 1959). See also Bernhard Knollenberg, "Did Samuel Adams Provoke the Boston Tea Party and the Clash at Lexington?" *Proceedings* of the American Antiquarian Society, LXX (1960), 493–503, and John H. Edmonds, "How Massachusetts Received the Declaration of Independence," *Proceedings* of the American Antiquarian Society, XXXV (1926), 227–252. There are numerous good sketches of the minor figures involved in the coming of the Revolution, including Malcolm Frieberg, "William Bollan: Agent of Massachusetts," *More Books,* XXIII (1949), 43–53, 90–100, 135–146, 168–182, 212–220, Francis E. Brown, *Joseph Hawley: Colonial Radical* (New York, 1931), Robert J. Taylor, "Israel Mauduit," *New England Quarterly,* XXIV (1951), 208–230, John E. Alden, "John Mein: Scourge of Patriots," *Publications* of the Colonial Society of Massachusetts, XXXIV (1937–1942), 571–599, and George P. Anderson, "Ebenezer Mackintosh: Stamp Act Rioter and Patriot," *Publications* of the Colonial Society of Massachusetts, XXVI (1924–1926) 15–64 and "A Note" same vol., 348–361.

Robert J. Taylor, *Western Massachusetts in the American Revolution* (Providence, R. I., 1954), and Lee N. Newcomer, *The Embattled Farmers: A Massachusetts Countryside in the American Revolution* (New York, 1953), focus on the interior regions of the province. Wartime conditions are dealt with in Gardner W. Allen, *Massachusetts Privateers of the Revolution, Collections* of the Massachusetts Historical Society, LXXVII (1927), Jonathan Smith, "How Massachusetts Raised Her Troops in the Revolution," *Proceedings* of the Massachusetts Historical Society, LV (1923), 345–370, Ralph V. Harlow, "Economic Conditions in Massachusetts During the American Revolution," with remarks by Samuel E. Morison, *Publications* of the Colonial Society of Massachusetts, XX (1920), 163–192, Oscar and Mary Handlin, "Revolutionary Economic Policy in Massachusetts," *William and Mary Quarterly,* IV (1947), 3–26, William B. Norton, "Paper Currency in Massachusetts During the Revolution," *New England Quarterly,* VII (1934), 43–69, and David Syrett, "Town Meeting Politics in Massachusetts, 1776–1786," *William and Mary Quarterly* XXI (1964), 352–366. For the loyalists see E. Alfred Jones, *The Loyalists of Massachusetts: Their Memorials, Petitions, and Claims* (Boston and London, 1930), James H. Stark, *The Loyalists of Massachusetts and the Other Side of the American Revolution* (Boston, 1910), Bruce G. Merritt, "Loyalism and Social Conflict in Revolutionary Deerfield, Massachusetts," *Journal of American History,* LVII (1970), 277–289, Jonathan Smith, "Toryism in Worcester County during the War for Independence," *Proceedings* of the Massachusetts Historical Society, XLVII (1915), 15–25, and Andrew

Oliver, ed., *The Journal of Samuel Curwen, Loyalist* (Cambridge, Mass., 1972).

A still useful overview of the struggle for a state constitution is found in Harry A. Cushing, *History of the Transition from Provincial to Commonwealth Government in Massachusetts* (New York, 1896), but Samuel E. Morison, "The Struggle over the Adoption of the Constitution in Massachusetts," *Proceedings* of the Massachusetts Historical Society, L (1917), 353–411, is the more definitive account. For a more up-to-date interpretation of the period see the first chapters of Oscar and Mary Handlin, *Commonwealth: A Study of the Role of Government in the American Economy: Massachusetts, 1774–1861* (New York, 1947). Those two authors have also provided, in *The Popular Sources of Political Authority: Documents on the Massachusetts Constitution of 1780* (Cambridge, Mass., 1966), all of the significant documentary materials on the subject. Robert J. Taylor, ed., *Massachusetts: Colony to Commonwealth: Documents on the Formation of Its Constitution, 1775–1780* (Chapel Hill, N. C., 1961) is a smaller collection of the essential items, while L. Kinvin Wroth, et al., *Province in Rebellion: A Documentary History of the Founding of the Commonwealth of Massachusetts* (Cambridge, Mass., 1975) focuses on the earlier years only. Recent studies of the period are Theodore M. Hammett, "Revolutionary Ideology in Massachusetts: Thomas Allen's 'Vindication' of the Berkshire Constitutionalists, 1778," *William and Mary Quarterly,* XXXIII (1976), 514–527, and Stephen E. Patterson, *Political Parties in Revolutionary Massachusetts* (Madison, Wis., 1973).

INDEX